Deadly Thirst

The true story of a
foster child's murder

Donna Goodenough

© Copyright 2003 Donna Goodenough. All rights reserved.

No part of this publication may be reproduced, stored in a retrieval system, or transmitted, in any form or by any means, electronic, mechanical, photocopying, recording, or otherwise, without the written prior permission of the author.

Printed in Victoria, Canada

National Library of Canada Cataloguing in Publication

Goodenough, Donna
    Deadly thirst / Donna Goodenough.
ISBN 1-4120-0552-3
    I. Title.
HV6534.P47G66 2003   364'.9794'97   C2003-903397-X

This book was published *on-demand* **in cooperation with Trafford Publishing.**
On-demand publishing is a unique process and service of making a book available for retail sale to the public taking advantage of on-demand manufacturing and Internet marketing.
On-demand publishing includes promotions, retail sales, manufacturing, order fulfilment, accounting and collecting royalties on behalf of the author.

Suite 6E, 2333 Government St., Victoria, B.C. V8T 4P4, CANADA
Phone   250-383-6864   Toll-free   1-888-232-4444 (Canada & US)
Fax   250-383-6804   E-mail   sales@trafford.com
Web site   www.trafford.com   TRAFFORD PUBLISHING IS A DIVISION OF TRAFFORD HOLDINGS LTD.
Trafford Catalogue #03-0921   www.trafford.com/robots/03-0921.html

10   9   8   7   6   5   4

TABLE OF CONTENTS

CHAPTER 1   Perris, California, August 2, 1999 5

PART 1   THE BIRTH PARENTS

CHAPTER 2   Thomas Dee Setzer 35
AKA "Cowboy"

CHAPTER 3   Laura Leanna Utley 45
Her path of self destruction

CHAPTER 4   Double Trouble 51
Cowboy and Laura ride the fast track together

PART 2   AND BABY MAKES THREE

CHAPTER 5   Andrew Thomas Setzer...55
Born tainted and destined to suffer

CHAPTER 6   Into Foster Care...66
Andy's death sentence

PART 3   ALVIN AND THERESA, THE DEADLY DUO

CHAPTER 7   The Early Years of Alvin Robinson 75
"Mildly retarded"...or just dumb?

CHAPTER 8   Theresa Barroso 83
Her way or no way

CHAPTER 9   The Two Shall Be One 99
Alvin & Theresa tie the knot

PART 4   THE NIGHTMARE BEGINS

CHAPTER 10   "We Want to Share Our Lives With Children"............105
Andy and Justin arrive at 216 E. 6th Street

CHAPTER 11   Problems and Abuse...113
Andy's deadly thirst

PART 5 ARRESTS, OUTRAGE AND THE SEARCH FOR TRUTH

CHAPTER 12 Theresa Barroso's Confession 139
"Why am I becoming such a monster?"

CHAPTER 13 A Catalyst for Change 192
Public outrage demands change in foster
care system

CHAPTER 14 Alvin Robinson's Arrest................................206
He knew the consequences

PART 6 JUSTICE

CHAPTER 15 Trial Strategies 226
The "dumb" defense

CHAPTER 16 Sentencing 330
No remorse

CHAPTER 17 Aftermath 346

INTRODUCTION

I'll never forget how I learned about the murder of Andy Setzer. It was November 9th of 1999. I was at a friend's house and happened to glance at an open newspaper. My eyes saw only one headline: "Second Arrest in Foster Child's Death." While my friend was out of the room, I hovered over the paper, reading about the murder of a four-year-old boy in foster care. I cried as I read how he had suffered long-term abuse because of potty training problems and was killed for getting a drink of water. In the few minutes it took me to finish reading the article, my life was changed forever.

I cannot explain what happened next, other than to say I was suddenly obsessed with a heartfelt duty to tell the story of Andy Setzer; the victim in this case. There was no way I could argue with the avalanche of feelings that overcame me that breezy November morning; I didn't even try. I did, however, argue with my own rationale. At the time, I was earning a meager income as a freelance writer of magazine articles and I was afraid to undertake a project of this magnitude. Besides, I didn't like kids, and why was *this* kid so important to me anyway? A kid I didn't even know. In spite of that, I felt totally obligated, *possessed,* as if I had no say in the matter. And so, I began.

I learned that Andy's biological parents were hard-core drug addicts Thomas Dee Setzer and Laura Leanna Utley; both of Hemet. As I began my research for this book, Tom Setzer was serving a prison sentence in Delano, California, so I wrote to him there telling him of my intent to write the story of his son. I thought it only fair to give him the chance to offer his side of a story that was certain to get ugly. I asked him to tell me about Andy and some of the happy times he had experienced as Andy's father. It was an open invitation for him to tell me about himself; an invitation I hoped he'd respond to. I passed along my phone number and asked that he put me in contact with Laura Utley.

I would have been happy to report Tom Setzer's redeeming qualities, if he had told me of any, but my letter was disregarded and I never heard from Laura Utley. Solemnly, I realized that Tom Setzer wasn't interested in helping me piece together the events that had led to the murder of his son. I could only assume that Laura wasn't interested either. Was it because the bloody trail led straight back to them?

1

Deadly Thirst

I began to spend a vast amount of time at the Hemet, Riverside and Indio courthouses pouring over the criminal histories of Andy's biological parents. Within a year, I acquired hundreds of documents that answered most of the questions Tom Setzer had ignored. I contacted the California Department of Corrections [CDC] in Sacramento and asked them to fax me the details of Tom Setzer's prison history. I remember standing in front of my fax machine, watching, as a never-ending stream of pages kept coming and coming!

Although I'm convinced that trouble erupted around Tom Setzer and Laura Utley wherever they went, I chose to confine my research to Riverside County. As I began trying to put Tom Setzer's extensive criminal history in order, it quickly became obvious that he was hell bent on the destruction of his own life. I have never known of anyone who seemed as consistently and intently determined to screw up his chances for success as was Tom Setzer. Throughout my research I could find no evidence whatsoever that Tom Setzer had done anything laudable in his lifetime. He had ample chances to better his life, but each time he chose drugs over everything else. Furthermore, I don't think either Tom or Laura had any concern at all for the welfare of their children, or anyone else for that matter.

Piece by disgusting piece, I began to learn the circumstances that had propelled Andy on his deadly journey into foster care. From the moment of his conception, Andy was a victim of society's most lowly villains and a victim of the drug culture. Soon he became a victim of a floundering, leaderless system that was supposed to protect him.

It immediately became obvious to me that Riverside County Child Protective Services [CPS] did not—and still does not—want the public to know the circumstances surrounding the murder of Andy Setzer or any of the other kids who've died in foster care. I was shocked to learn that deaths of children in foster care have become alarmingly commonplace; the facts surrounding these deaths remain highly guarded secrets that no one at CPS is held criminally liable for.

It is my opinion that as long as CPS is allowed to hide behind their shield of confidentiality, the public will remain unaware and unable to do anything about a dysfunctional, taxpayer-funded system that is arrogantly squandering the lives of children. Without public pressure, more kids will die. Andy Setzer and scores of others like him never had a voice. I am convinced that Riverside County officials would like it to stay that way. I feel Andy's murder is a perfect example—the epitome—of all that's wrong with foster care.

Andy's story is not unusual or unique in any way and that's what's really sad about it. There have been many cases just like Andy's and a horrifying number that were much worse. On any given day, newspapers across America are routinely splattered with foster care horror stories similar to this one and those responsible—hiding behind the almighty shield of confidentiality—do their best to hush it up. Andy was certainly not the first kid to be killed by maniacal foster parents appointed by social workers that were too busy to conduct thorough background checks, and he wasn't the last. In many states there is still statutory immunity on the part of CPS. So, what incentive is there to be careful and prudent when placing innocent children with virtual strangers? Think about it. It seems to me they have appointed themselves to be judge *and* jury. After reading this book, I wonder how many of you will also believe them to be proud executioners of the most vulnerable among us? Yes, *proud!* In the wake of Andy's torture/murder at the hands of his county-appointed killers, callous CPS officials maintained that they had made the *right* and *best* decisions for Andy! This is "child protection"?!

In my opinion, the responsibility for Andy's death should be shouldered equally by three parties; the biological parents, the foster care system and Andy's final foster parents. All three are profiled in this book. You are about to learn the series of deadly blunders that led Riverside County Child Protective Services to herd Andy into a one-way slaughter chute of foster care...and straight into the hands of murderers. After you have finished reading this book, I implore you to take action to bring radical new guidelines and more accountability into the foster care system. Perhaps the system should be dismantled and completely recreated, prohibiting the current deadly, self-governing powers, which have devastated so many innocent lives and sent innumerable children to early graves.

Unfortunately, the American public has become hardened and accustomed to violence, having been force-fed constant doses of it by way of the daily news, in movies, on television, in video games and even in children's cartoons. We have become a society so used to murder we hardly give it a second thought. We have become a culture that is armed to the max and anxious for an excuse to shoot from the hip. Consequently, we have begun to vent our frustrations on the only defenseless people left...children. Just as frightening, no one is speaking out about this alarming trend. Quite frankly, I find the apathy of the American public to be nothing short of nauseating. What will it take to reverse the direction we're headed in?

Throughout the four-year research and writing process of this book, I experienced roller-coaster emotions and many frustrating dead ends. I've been close to giving up, many times, on bringing this story forward. During those troubled times, I looked at the photograph of Andy's grave and saw, chiseled in granite, the reasons why I could not quit. My quest to find a publisher led me straight into a barrage of debilitating insults from literary agents and publishers who sneered at my "morbid fascination" with the torture/murder of a little boy. This subject is practically taboo, I was repeatedly told, something no one would want to touch. The subject matter is "too sensitive," they said. Let me see if I understand this correctly. We're all supposed to look the other way and pretend this isn't happening? In my opinion, it would be "morbid" *not* to try and do something about it, *not* to try to bring exposure to the problem. Another common comment was that

Deadly Thirst

I needed an exposé on foster kids in general, not merely the story of *one* unfortunate child who'd been victimized by the bungling bureaucracy of the foster care system. Apparently, *one* child has no worth. Besides, no one in New York had ever heard of Andy Setzer; he didn't have the "notoriety" of JonBenèt Ramsey or Polly Klaas. They didn't understand that when kids are killed in the foster care system, the system is highly successful at keeping a lid of secrecy on everything, which is exactly why these cases lack the notoriety they deserve. I thought that perhaps bringing exposure to the deadly conditions that foster kids are subjected to might save a few lives. Idealistic? Probably. But it's worth a shot.

I was advised to fictionalize this story, to add a "hero" and give it a happy ending. Andy's story does not end happily and I refuse to pretend it does. We cannot undo his murder, but, with persistent lobbying we *can* change the fate of thousands of other kids still at the mercy of a bureaucracy that is too overburdened and too understaffed to do proper background checks before they sentence kids to live with strangers. Andy's dead, but with your help other foster kids won't have to die. *Please* do whatever you can.

As in any murder case, there are blameless individuals that have been caught in the vortex of a highly intrusive investigation. Therefore, the names of some individuals have been changed. Such names are indicated by an asterisk [*] the first time each name appears in this book. Some scenes and dialogue have been reconstructed based on eyewitness accounts, court documents and published news stories. Much of the quoted conversations have been taken from transcripts, sworn statements and personal tape-recorded interviews conducted by the author.

I wish to express my deepest gratitude to *all* the people who worked Andy's case, whether they are mentioned in this book or not. Special thanks to the people who were kind enough to assist me through the unfamiliar territory of CPS and the criminal justice system. However, due to the subject matter, most preferred to remain nameless. Here, in alphabetical order are a few of the people who did things for me that they didn't have to do: Kevin Bouma, Donna Darin*, Ricardo Duran, Ron & Andra Grove, Pete Harding, Raggi Hollinshead, Vern Horst, Terry Hudson, Chris Montano, John Monterosso, Ven Roldan, Ann Rule, Peter Scalisi, Russell Schooling, and, last but not least, Rhonda L. Strickland.

Andy, this is for you.

CHAPTER 1

Perris, California, August 2, 1999

The 911 call came in at 3:15 A.M. on Monday August 2nd. Child down; difficulty breathing. 216 E. 6th Street in Perris. Five minutes later, a fire engine from Perris station 1 arrived on scene amidst a kaleidoscope of flashing red lights. It was a call firefighter/engineer Manuel Reyes would never forget. Reyes was driving the engine that night; with him were firefighter/EMT Justin Scribner and Clint Blackmon. The first thing they saw was a heavy-set woman standing at the curb holding the limp and seemingly lifeless body of a child, clad in green shorts and a gray T-shirt. The engine crossed over the oncoming lane and came to a hasty stop at an angle to the curb, its headlights illuminating the woman. The beam of an overhead spotlight was also cast in her direction, but the woman shied away from the lights and before Reyes could exit the engine, she carried the child around to the driver's side door. Reyes jumped down from the cab and took the unconscious child into his arms. Almost simultaneously, American Medical Response [AMR] paramedics pulled up. Within seconds, the woman had the undivided attention of nearly half a dozen firefighters and paramedics.

As the men converged on her, she calmly said, "This has happened to him before." And then, like a robot, she said it again, "this has happened to him before." Firefighters and paramedics would later tell police that the whole situation was weird, right from the start. Reyes had been with the Department of Forestry for several years and had responded to hundreds of emergencies, but none had made him feel as uneasy as this one already had.

In emergency situations, things happen too fast to analyze, but something about the woman's first statements struck a raw cord with the crew of station 1. It seemed a strange way to explain what had happened. Usually, the first words they hear upon arrival are a rapid explanation of the symptoms. In cases like this, where a child isn't breathing, they're often met by hysterical parents screaming for help. But not this time. This call was different, right from the get-go. The woman seemed almost too calm, firefighters recalled, too unemotional. Hauntingly vacant.

A yellow backboard was laid on the sidewalk where the engine's headlights were focused. Next to it one of the AMR guys was busy unzipping a nylon trauma bag. Reyes placed the unconscious child on the backboard; the team immediately assessed he was in full cardiac arrest. His skin was pale, moist and cool.

Reyes asked the woman to clarify exactly *what* had happened to the child before; what did she mean? While the team worked frantically, the woman stood back and watched, dry-eyed, as CPR was started. It was 3:25. She calmly explained that the child had gotten out of the house at night on several other occasions. She offered no further explanation and didn't ask a single question. Instead, she just stood there, her hands clasped in front of her as if she were on her way down the aisle to receive communion.

Time was crucial and obviously running out fast for the little blonde-haired boy. Scribner watched the child take two breaths; then he stopped breathing again. AMR paramedic, Matthew Brandt, slid an endotracheal tube down the child's airway and attached a green ambu-bag to it. With the steady squeezing of the bag, breathing was assisted. While Brandt kept up his rhythmical bagging, the backboard was lifted by Scribner and Blackmon, placed on a gurney inside the ambulance and strapped down. Immediately, doses of Narcan, Proventil and Epinephrine were administered. Over his shoulder, Scribner hollered to the woman that they'd be heading to Menifee Valley Hospital. With that, the doors slammed shut and they sped off into the heat of the night, leaving the woman standing on the sidewalk, alone and dry-eyed.

With sirens wailing and lights flashing, the driver radioed Menifee with an estimated arrival time of approximately seven minutes. In route, paramedics tried to detect a pulse at the femoral artery, which passes through the groin. To get a better feel, they pulled down the boy's shorts and were shocked speechless by what they saw. The men recoiled as if they could somehow feel the pain this poor little boy had endured for God-only-knows how long. None of them had *ever* seen a scrotal injury like *this*. His testicles were grotesquely swollen to grapefruit size and discolored to a purplish black. The bruising spread out over his lower abdomen in a ghastly, dark radius. It was a hideous sight.

The scrotum wasn't the only thing that disturbed the paramedics. The boy was literally covered with bruises and he had a large, older abrasion on the inside of his upper right thigh. Scribner took a penlight and shined it straight down into the child's pupils. The right pupil was "blown," a term paramedics use to describe the effects of hemorrhaging and swelling within the brain. Not a good sign. A blown pupil is the most significant indication of major head trauma. They also noted that the child was coated with dirt. In the distance of just a few blocks, all three men inside the ambulance decided this was no ordinary accident. But they couldn't allow themselves to think about that right now; their efforts at resuscitation were beginning to pay off. Little blips were now appearing on the portable cardiac monitor. It looked like they were getting a pulse back and a bit of blood pressure, but the child still couldn't breath on his own.

As the ambulance turned into the hospital parking lot, the driver switched off the siren and pulled up to the emergency entrance. Crimson lights bounced off the glass ER doors where a swarm of hospital personnel stood waiting. They had already been briefed on the incoming situation and began converging upon the back end of the ambulance even before it came to a complete stop. In a blur, the rear doors were flung open and the stretcher was pulled out almost simultaneously. With it came Brandt, totally focused on keeping the ventilation steady. Momentarily, engine 1 pulled up behind the ambulance. Reyes had followed the ambulance to Menifee to retrieve Scribner and Blackmon and take them back to the station. But in the distance of just a few miles, things had developed in an ominously suspicious manner and his men wouldn't be leaving just yet.

Doctor Marlowe Schaffner was in charge of the emergency room during the early morning hours of August 2, 1999. He'd been working emergency rooms and trauma centers for thirty-one years and had seen some of the most horrific injuries imaginable. Sixteen of those years had been spent as a missionary in the dismal operating rooms of central Africa. Still, in spite of more than three decades of blood and guts, the sight of this young child would become something Schaffner would never be able to forget. It was a sight that would remain indelibly etched in his mind for the rest of his life. If there was anything in the child's favor that morning, it was that he had been delivered into the hands of one of the most highly skilled doctors in the entire county. It just so happened that Schaffner's expertise was emergency procedures for critical care neonatal and pediatric patients.

His initial examination quickly revealed that the child was quite literally covered with large bruises in various stages of progression. Some of the bruises were obviously several days old and in such places as the chest, shoulders, back and buttocks. Immediately, he began to suspect child abuse. His revulsion and anger increased with every new discovery. The final bit of doubt about the *real* events that had brought this little boy into his emergency room was forever shattered when he examined the engorged, purplish testicles. The scrotal skin was taut, stretched to the bursting point and the testicles stood high off the body in a shiny, veiny mass. Within three to five minutes of the arrival of the ambulance at Menifee Valley Hospital, Schaffner gave orders to notify the Sheriff that an apparent case of child abuse had come in. Under his breath, he scoffed at his own inadvertent use of the word "apparent." Schaffner continued to become more outraged as each area of the child's body was examined with closer scrutiny. What he saw infuriated him. This was one of the most heart-wrenching sights he'd ever seen; it was absolutely gruesome.

It would be twenty-five minutes before a deputy arrived. During that time, Schaffner's anger would continue to boil as he shouted out the descriptions of several more injuries on the child's frail little body. A nurse stood nearby with an ER chart, frantically scribbling dictation as fast as her hand would move. She'd never heard Schaffner's voice rise to such a crescendo; indeed, no one who'd worked with the otherwise mild-mannered doctor had ever heard him talk this way. Worried glances darted from one face to another as they frantically labored over the unresponsive child.

Deputies Douglas McGrew and Mike Mejia were each at different locations when they received orders to respond immediately to Menifee Valley Hospital: possible child abuse. They both arrived about the same time and walked together toward the emergency entrance of the hospital. One of them punched in a couple of numbers on the security keypad and, when the sliding double doors opened, they walked together into the emergency room at 4:10 A.M.

McGrew remembers walking in and looking into a smaller, curtained-off area to his left. There he saw a naked, black and blue child lying motionless on a gurney surrounded by a frenzied group of emergency room personnel. Even from a distance of fifteen feet, he saw for himself that the child was covered with bruises. But what stood out the most were the swollen, discolored testicles. McGrew took a step closer and stared in disbelief.

Until that moment, Doctor Schaffner hadn't noticed the arrival of the two deputies, although their uniforms clearly made them stand out from the others who were dressed in pale green surgical scrubs. McGrew was patient; he could see the doctor was extremely busy. He and Mejia used the time to stand in different places in the room and observe what was going on. Being inside the ER room was always troubling; it was such a crucible of human suffering and desperate behavior. Whenever the sea of green scrubs would part, they could catch another glimpse of the poor little boy. The floor was strewn with the discarded wrappers from sterilized medical instruments, needles, IVs and snippets of tubing. Bloody, discarded gauze squares and tissues stuck to the soles of the nurses' shoes.

Finally, after about ten minutes, Schaffner was able to break away from the frenzy. Snapping off his gloves and throwing them into a wastebasket, he took the deputies aside, grabbing the ER chart from the nurse as he passed. Flipping through the pages of medical notes, Schaffner wasn't the least bit reserved about telling both deputies exactly what he thought about the injuries this child had sustained. McGrew and Schaffner stood near the curtains, a scant fifteen feet from the gurney and stared at each other. Schaffner's face expressed the hopelessness of the whole situation, a burden that was being quickly absorbed by both deputies. Neither Mejia nor McGrew could keep from looking toward the gurney.

Schaffner's team was exceptional; they were doing everything possible but still the prognosis was grim. McGrew asked Schaffner if he knew the name of the child and Schaffner said the boy had been identified as four-year-old Andrew Thomas Setzer. McGrew agreed with Schaffner that it might be a case of child abuse. He asked about the parents; where were the parents?

"I think that's them in the waiting area," someone said as they passed by, motioning toward the lobby. Schaffner couldn't spend any more time with the deputies, but said he was definitely willing to talk more later. Schaffner handed the chart back to the nurse, snapped on a fresh pair of gloves and dove into the chaos again. Mejia couldn't seem to take his eyes off the little boy. McGrew needed a moment to regain his composure; he had to literally force himself to compartmentalize all that he was seeing, at least for the time being. If he was going to do this little boy any good, he needed to keep his emotions out of the way of his thinking. It wasn't going to be easy.

Life support machines emit an eerie sound as they go about the grim task of keeping a victim alive artificially. The room seemed to resonate with the clicking and wheezing of the ventilator as it pumped air into the boy's lungs. Next to the gurney was the EKG monitor; its steady beeping was about the only good sound inside the emergency room that fateful morning. The boy's vital signs were displayed digitally on another monitor that was mounted on the wall over his head.

Getting one more good look at the little boy was difficult; he'd gone into full cardiac arrest once already and the slew of doctors, nurses and machinery just wouldn't allow McGrew to approach much closer. Whenever there was room for him to step next to the gurney for a better look, his eyes would always go back to the swollen genitals. It was unbelievable. When he looked at them, he felt the pain; it took the wind right out of him. The sight literally sickened him and filled him with disgust. He wondered what on earth had happened to this poor little boy.

Just as the nurse had said, a family had arrived at the hospital and was seated in the waiting area. McGrew could see them through a little square window in the door. They were a racial grab bag. The mother was a heavy-set Hispanic woman accompanied by an African-American man and another child—a Caucasian—who appeared to be around ten years old. Mejia decided to accompany McGrew as a second set of ears to hear what the parents had to say. McGrew would take the lead; Mejia would hang back and observe.

With his own groin aching in sympathy, McGrew pushed open the door. He was glad to be leaving the commotion and heartache of the emergency room behind him to talk with the boy's family and ask them what had happened. He was clinging to the hope that his suspicions were wrong.

McGrew had been a Sheriff's deputy several years and had questioned hundreds of distraught people caught in emotional situations that ran a wild gamut from minor family disputes all the way to murder. He knew he was treading on the fragile ground of a potential homicide. Schaffner had already assessed the boy's condition as extremely grave and his chances for survival were next to nothing. McGrew silently rehearsed some key questions to ask and tried to put his repulsion and suspicions aside. It took some effort, but he tried to consciously erase all signs of anger and accusation from his face. He silently coached himself to act like this was simply routine.

McGrew noted that the adults watched his approach in a calm, yet guarded sort of way. The room had a definite aura of apprehension; he noticed it as soon as he walked through the door. Both parents stayed seated and neither extended their hand in an appreciative greeting. Neither

Deadly Thirst

thanked him for his concern. He introduced himself in a friendly, sympathetic way and pulled up a chair across from the woman. Mejia stood about six feet away, watching and listening.

The emergency waiting area was decorated in a pleasant, light shade of green. There were six comfortable chairs along the wall and a couch, everything matching in décor. In the corner, a lamp shone brightly over a floral centerpiece. In the middle of the room was an oak coffee table strewn with reading material and off to the side, a box of Kleenex. The covers of Parent's magazine, McCall's, People, Highlights and Ladies Home Journal all featured smiling children and happy parents. Those were the only smiles inside the waiting area during the early morning hours of August 2nd, 1999. Oddly, there were no tears either. To both deputies, the absence of tears was yet another disturbing clue that something was amiss. The woman's demeanor and the chirpy, almost robotic way she asked how the child was doing seemed totally out of place. McGrew noted that she seemed detached and unconcerned with the severity of the situation. He had to remind himself that maybe, just maybe, the woman didn't know how serious the situation was. Her attention strayed periodically to a muted overhead television, which was running a late night movie of some sort. The man beside her was solemn and quiet. The kid looked bewildered and sleepy.

McGrew began questioning the three of them together, but the woman did all the talking. McGrew assumed the man with her was her husband even though he was African-American and she was Hispanic. Mixed couples weren't that rare anymore. For a second, he wondered if these were the parents of both the little blonde-haired boy in there on the gurney fighting for his life, and the fair-skinned kid seated next to them. It was a strange and puzzling mix.

McGrew conducted himself in a gracious sort of way and ascertained rather quickly that the two adults were the *foster* parents of the little boy on life support. The woman identified herself as twenty-two-year-old Theresa DeJesus Barroso and she introduced the man seated next to her as her husband, Alvin Lee Robinson, twenty-six. The boy with them was identified as eleven year old Jacob Marquist*, also their foster child.

In response to McGrew's questions about what had happened, Theresa merely stated that the little boy, whom she called "Andy," had somehow gotten outside in the middle of the night and they'd found him lying in the dirt, not breathing. He'd been fine up until that point. And that's all she said about it. But it was the monotone way she said it that made McGrew's flesh crawl. Something was already too strange about this case. McGrew took particular note of the fact that neither foster parent asked when they could see Andy. He noticed that Theresa was very composed as she spelled out Andy's full name, yet she seemed to be a little nervous about something. McGrew couldn't quite put his finger on it, but something was weird. Alvin Robinson hardly said a word and when he did give answers, they practically had to be extracted from him and were always in total agreement with whatever Theresa had just said. Most of the time he repeated her words exactly, like an echo. He offered no additional information at all and he didn't ask any questions about Andy. Theresa seemed to rule the conversation with an iron fist and Alvin seemed totally submissive to her authority. "Yeah, that's how it happened..." or "Right..." was all Alvin would say. He seemed reluctant to talk, or, McGrew reminded himself, maybe he was just too distraught. In situations like this, a person's emotional state often makes them appear to be shy, aloof, giddy or withdrawn because they're just too traumatized to speak or even to think straight. McGrew was a bit emotional too. His feelings raced every which way: anger, pity, suspicion. Still, as suspicious as the situation was, he had to withhold judgment and give these people the benefit of the doubt. After all, who could act normally under these circumstances? And what was "normal" anyway? How would *he* react if he were in their situation? He knew that traumatic events could make people react in strange ways sometimes. McGrew didn't want to jump to any conclusions.

Mejia had stayed in the background, leaning against the wall, listening while McGrew questioned the foster parents for about ten minutes. Then McGrew wanted Theresa to go over all of it again, telling everything she could remember. Theresa stated that Andy could unlock the front door of the apartment and had gotten out of the house at night on several other occasions. She said that she had awaken around 3 A.M. to use the bathroom and decided to check on the kids. She noticed Andy was missing and noticed the front door was ajar. She went outside and found him lying in the dirt, not breathing. McGrew asked both foster parents if they had noticed any unusual bruising or swelling on Andy. No, Theresa said in a tiny, high-pitched voice, neither of them had noticed any bruising or swelling. McGrew asked if they'd notice the swollen genitals. No, but Theresa did say Andy had been walking funny and had complained the previous day about "being sore from sitting."

McGrew was very suspicious of the fact that neither foster parent expressed concern or seemed anxious to see Andy, not even after he mentioned that Andy had bruises and swollen genitals. Strange too was the fact that neither foster parent launched an indignant barrage of their own questions concerning Andy's swollen genitalia and the ominous presence of two uniformed Sheriff's deputies. Surely, if the foster parents had been unaware of the groin injures, they would have demanded to know what the hell was going on, insisting on some sort of further description of what the doctors had found. Or, at the very least, they would have been indignant that a deputy, not a doctor, was questioning them.

McGrew asked them about the last time they'd given Andy a bath. Were they absolutely sure they hadn't noticed his bruises and swollen genitals? Again, Theresa shook her head. No, they hadn't noticed anything unusual. Besides, Theresa offered, they never actually bathed Andy; they just ran his

Deadly Thirst

bathwater for him and let him undress and bathe himself. So no, they hadn't seen any swelling or bruising.

To McGrew it seemed impossible that they hadn't noticed Andy's injuries. And what sort of parent would leave a four-year-old completely unsupervised in the tub? He had kids; he knew an injury like that would absolutely be accompanied by a lot of crying which would draw immediate concern from a parent—foster or biological—even a damned babysitter for that matter. And he was a man; he knew the intense pain a groin injury like that must have caused the poor little kid. Just thinking about it made him cringe. There was no way this little boy wouldn't have cried about it. No way. The demeanor of these two adults and the answers they were giving just didn't fit.

Meanwhile, behind the swinging doors of the emergency room, little Andy slipped from bad to worse and went into cardiac arrest again.

By then, Sergeant Joel Lewis* had arrived and was inside the room with Andy. In a few minutes the place would be crawling with cops. Mejia joined Lewis at Andy's bedside and was assigned to stand watch over Andy until further notice. In the ensuing hours, Mejia would be one of many uniformed and plain-clothed law enforcement officials that would be deeply touched by the tragic circumstances of Andy Setzer.

"He was beautiful," Mejia said years later. "I keep remembering his hair. He had blonde, curly hair. He was a really beautiful baby." Watching Andy struggle through his last remaining moments of life was particularly hard for Mejia. He was a father, with a son close to Andy's age. Even hospital personnel were deeply saddened as they watched Andy slip away. "You could see the concern in everybody's face," Mejia said. "I remember some of the nurses were crying. In fact, I even cried a few times. It was pretty upsetting for me to watch this little boy suffering." As a deputy for Riverside County Sheriff's Department for three and a half years, Mejia had seen other cases of child abuse. He'd seen kids burned and scalded. He'd seen kids die. He knew that becoming emotionally involved with the victim would be begging for trouble. Still, he couldn't help but look at Andy from a father's point of view. "His vital signs were on the screen right above his head and they stopped several times while I was there. His pulse would go down very low and the nurses would gather around him. Then, it would come back up. It was *really* hard to watch."

Meanwhile, in the waiting area, McGrew had heard more than enough for him to form a firm opinion about what had really happened to Andy. Closing his notepad, he politely thanked the couple and wished them luck. Then he stepped outside. As soon as he was out of earshot, McGrew notified his supervisor.

Sergeant Don Farrar arrived shortly thereafter and was briefed on the suspicious nature of Andy Setzer's injuries. Doctor Schaffner made it exceedingly clear to Sergeant Farrar that Andy probably wouldn't live very long. Farrar thought it best to notify Homicide and immediately contacted two of his best investigators, Bob Peebles and Vern Horst from the Riverside County Sheriff's Department.

The ringing sound of a telephone rattled Vern Horst awake just before 5:00A.M. It wasn't a homicide *yet,* but it sure looked like it was going to become one. As a homicide investigator, Horst didn't wear a uniform. He hurriedly threw on a white, long sleeved shirt, a tie and slacks and went to his car. He brought the engine to life with a twist of the key and headed straight to Menifee Valley Hospital's emergency room. It was almost 6:30 when he arrived. Bob Peebles, the other investigator, was already there.

Horst was met head-on by McGrew, Mejia, Lewis, Peebles and Sergeant Farrar. Doctor Schaffner soon joined them. The men huddled together for a few minutes just inside the emergency room doors while each explained what he had learned about the situation as well as their suspicions of child abuse. At Schaffner's prompting, Horst braced for the worst and went over to see Andy for himself.

As he approached the bed, the world seemed to stop. Tunnel vision set in and the area around Andy's bed became a swirling blur of surgical scrubs, gloved hands and tubing. People were talking, but for the first few seconds he heard nothing but the thumping of his own heart. And the wheezing of the respirator.

Standing there, he felt the color drain from his face.

From somewhere, McGrew was filling in the details. "Andrew Setzer... age four...foster child..."

It was an unimaginable sight, one that would remain vivid in his mind forever. Doctors were doing everything they could possibly do for Andy and yet as each minute passed, he slipped closer to death. Mejia was clearly upset as he told Horst that Andy had been pronounced dead at 4:36 but his vital signs returned within a few seconds and doctors resumed working on him.

Although Horst had seen an enormous amount of devastation during his career, *this* case would plague him with more anger and more heartache than any other case he'd ever worked on. Andy Setzer was about to become a person of great importance to him, not just while he worked on the case, but for many, many years. A homicide investigator really gets good at putting up a shield when stuff like this happens, but sooner or later it catches up. As soon as he'd caught sight of Andy's small, battered body lying on the gurney, he was too emotionally involved to shield himself. It had caught him off guard. For several minutes, Horst was completely derailed by the cyclone of emotions that Andy had instantaneously set off inside him. Like McGrew and Mejia, Horst struggled to keep a tight reign on his emotions, but he could scarcely contain the anger that was churning inside him. The sight of the frail little body splayed out on the gurney literally made him sick with grief. The kid was covered with bruises and the testicles...*God, the testicles!*

Deadly Thirst

Doctor Schaffner stood face to face with Horst; gloom shrouded both of their faces. He spared no words in telling Horst exactly what he thought had transpired in the hours...even days...perhaps weeks before Andy had finally been brought in, in *this* condition. They wedged themselves in between doctors and nurses so that Schaffner could point out especially troubling areas of Andy's body.

Horst announced that Polaroid photos had to be taken right away. As flashes of light bounced off every aluminum surface in the ER, Andy's bruised and distended tummy, with his little outie belly button, would rise and fall with the rhythmic pumping of the ventilator. During moments like that, a sense of kinship develops between the victim and the detectives working the case. A sense of kinship is productive; emotional involvement is not.

The scene was especially troubling for Horst because Andy was only four and reminded Horst so much of his youngest son. Horst had three sons, seven, nine and eleven, that were the absolute core of his universe. As a father of three active boys, he was well aware of the way kids bump and injure themselves during ordinary play. They fall, they trip, they cut themselves. They get pretty banged up sometimes. Some of them bruise easily; some are as tough as nails. They bleed...*but this?!*

Doctor Schaffner pointed out that Andy had a large handprint on his back and that one of his pupils had hemorrhaged. This usually was caused by blunt force injury to the head and swelling in the brain, Schaffner explained. There was also a large burn or abrasion-type injury to the inner thigh of Andy's right leg. It was highly unlikely, he said, that the child had simply fallen in the dirt and sustained all these injuries. As he pulled off his gloves, Schaffner said, in his opinion, it simply wasn't possible. Not just that, but many of the bruises were old...perhaps a week or even older. Schaffner was staring at Horst now, face to face with him in a confrontational stance. They stepped away from the gurney for a minute and huddled over the pages of scribbled notes Schaffner was flipping through on his ER chart. Disgusted, Schaffner couldn't help but speak frankly about his own opinion of what had really happened to Andy. There was no doubt about it; Andy had been beaten into this condition. Still, he said, presuming the foster mother's story was true—that they had merely found him lying in the dirt, not breathing—it seemed an unlikely coincidence that they had managed to find him within a minute or two of when he apparently stopped breathing. Was it a stroke of luck? Both men thought the probability of that was nil. And how was he knocked unconscious? A fall? But it was the bruises and swollen genitals that kept coming back into the conversation. According to what McGrew had told Horst, the foster parents said they were completely unaware of any discoloration or swelling in the genital area. Impossible, Schaffner spat. He excused himself and went back to the gurney.

Horst had gotten a good look at the bruises and the scrapes on Andy's body. He noticed the smearing of fecal matter between Andy's legs and agreed with Schaffner that it looked unnatural. As a father, he'd changed enough diapers to know what ordinary feces looked like, but this was different...undigested...as though it hadn't had a chance to stay in the colon long enough before it was violently expelled. Horst couldn't shake the knot festering in his stomach.

To Vern Horst, it felt like the full weight of the world had suddenly fallen on his shoulders. Surely Andy had "real" parents somewhere...but where? Who were they? He agonized for them; they were about to receive word that their son was on life support and was not expected to live. For a second he imagined himself receiving the horrible news about one of his sons and was so thankful that his three kids were at home with their mom, blissfully sleeping. He was reeling in a million different directions, too many of them emotional.

It was almost impossible to pull himself out of the quicksand of emotion, but it was part of a homicide investigator's job to deal with atrocities like this. In order to get to the facts, he would need to stay cool, keep the conversation friendly and keep his emotions out of it. At least for the time being. It would prove to be one of the hardest things Vern Horst had ever done. He ached for Andy's biological parents and wondered if anyone had notified them yet. With a heavy heart, he pushed open the door and approached the only people sitting in the small waiting area.

Horst identified himself as being with the Riverside County Sheriff's office and sat down with Alvin and Theresa. He noticed that both of them viewed his approach with trepidation, but neither questioned the sudden flood of law enforcement that had surged into the ER room since Andy's arrival. The questions Horst began asking quickly honed in on the swollen genitals and the extensive bruising on Andy's body, especially his back, buttocks and groin area. As Theresa talked, Horst concentrated on her demeanor. She definitely had a forced aura of calm about her. From his many years of experience, he knew that sometimes it's not what a person says; it's how they say it.

Both parents, again, calmly denied that they were aware of any bruising and Horst noted that neither of them asked to see the injuries. That was suspicious. Theresa said she knew about the bruises on Andy's shoulders but those were caused by Jacob giving him "frogs." Theresa explained that "frog" was a game the kids played. One would sneak up behind the other and hit him on the shoulders with a fistful of knuckles. But Theresa shrugged it off; all the kids were doing it. She had no explanation for the bruising and swelling of Andy's genitalia, but what was most troubling was the fact that she didn't seem at all concerned about it.

It was Horst's nature to view any homicide—or in this case a *potential* homicide—through eyes looking for evidence of criminal behavior. Surely, Horst thought, any innocent parent would be alarmed; demanding a fuller accounting of injuries like that. But not these parents. With just a few key questions, coupled with his keen ability to judge a person's truthfulness,

Deadly Thirst

it didn't take Horst long to come to the conclusion of child abuse. It was tangible enough to taste. He was sure of it. If this kid dies, he thought, it'll be a homicide.

Jacob, the eleven-year-old boy who'd sat still and quiet throughout the questioning, would clearly have been in danger if he were permitted to remain in the care of Alvin and Theresa. Horst arranged for a representative from Child Protective Services [CPS] to take custody of Jacob. He assigned a deputy to take Jacob to the Perris police station until Horst could question him a little bit later. Then CPS could take him. Horst thought it was suspicious that neither parent asked why they should relinquish custody of Jacob. In fact, they weren't even mildly resistant to the fact that Jacob was being taken away from them. Horst also noted that neither parent ask to see Andy which, in his experience, was an ominous sign. Trying to keep hysterical parents out of the emergency room at times like this was a big problem for hospitals. The doors connecting the waiting area with the emergency room only swung one way—into the waiting area. No one from the waiting area could enter through those doors and they couldn't go around to another door either; they were all opened by numbered keypads. It was a necessity; otherwise, parents would burst in and push past doctors to be near their child. But not these parents. They clearly didn't want to be anywhere near those swinging doors and the heartbreaking scene that was unfolding beyond. By then, Andy had gone into cardiac arrest again.

As the minutes ticked by and Andy's chances for survival became almost non-existent, arrangements were made to transport him to a pediatric trauma center in San Bernardino County with a much more specialized intensive care unit. Loma Linda University Medical Center, a huge, world-renowned facility, was slightly more than an hour away by ground transport, but with the imminent onset of rush hour traffic, they couldn't risk getting stuck. There wasn't time for a cross-country ambulance trip—Andy was fighting a losing battle. Schaffner opted instead for Mercy Air to fly in and airlift Andy as soon as possible. Mercy Air was better equipped than AMR and, if anything happened in route, Mercy would be the better choice. All Schaffner could do now was keep Andy on life support until the helicopter arrived. At 6:48 A.M., Mercy Air 1 touched down on the helipad at Menifee Valley Hospital and Andy was rushed onboard. Minutes later, in a cloud of dust, they lifted off toward Loma Linda.

Mejia's long, sad vigil was over. Exhausted, he returned to the Perris station. His shift was finally drawing to a close. Vern Horst's had only just begun.

There was definitely more to this situation than either parent was admitting and Vern Horst was determined to get to the bottom of it. Horst asked both Alvin and Theresa to return to their apartment with him so he could look around and perhaps they could answer a few more questions for him. Alvin and Theresa were allowed to drive together to their small duplex style apartment. Horst followed behind them in his own vehicle. That put them right in the middle of morning traffic and streets crowded with folks heading off to work. People bustled here and there, smiling and laughing, proceeding with their lives as though it were just another ordinary morning. Maybe for them it was.

On the way, Vern Horst couldn't help but glance into the cars around him and wonder what those people had done with their kids last night. Had they kissed their kids goodnight and cherished the sight of them as they scampered off to bed? Had they tucked their kids under clean blankets with the tender loving care parents are supposed to show their children? Even as he drove, he could still hear the clicking and wheezing of the respirator. And he couldn't erase the sight of Andy Setzer from his mind. His mind was so detached from his hands that the car seemed to drive itself. The image of Andy on life support preoccupied his thoughts. Just thinking about it disrupted his mind so much he couldn't focus on the questions he needed to be forming for the interview that lay ahead.

He thought about his own life's circumstances and all the things that had brought him to this point in time. He thought about what he had done with his own kids the day before. Yesterday. If only he could turn back the clock. Yesterday...suddenly it seemed so far in the past. Right then, to Vern Horst, yesterday seemed like a million light-years ago.

* * *

There's a saying that the best cops come from troubled teens who walked a fine line between right and wrong and could have easily fallen on either side of the law. Arthur "Vern" Horst was one of those frustrated and rebellious teenagers. His parents had divorced when he was very young and Vern had lived with his dad. He'd gotten a rather humbling introduction to "law enforcement" at the age of sixteen in the small, isolated town of Biscuit Flats, Arizona. He'd gotten drunk with his buddies and was blasted beyond repair, something his father didn't approve of. Young Vern was given some choices: he could go live with his mom, he could live on his own somewhere, or he could join the military. In any event, he had to get out. His dad made it clear: there were no other choices.

His dad hated the Marines and Vern wanted to enlist just for spite. In fact, three weeks prior, he'd taken the test for the Marine Corps just to piss off his dad. His scheme backfired when he failed the test.

But Dad meant business. Vern woke up the next morning, hung over, and found his bags had been packed for him and were piled by the front door. Dad gave him ten bucks and sent him on his way.

Having nowhere else to go, he bunked with a friend who was considerably older but not a smidgen wiser. The guy took Vern's ten bucks, went down to the local Circle K, and returned with a couple of loaves of Wonder Bread, some cheese, mayonnaise and two six packs of beer. The cheese didn't last very long; the beer disappeared even quicker. For the next two weeks, all they ate was Wonder Bread and mayonnaise.

Deadly Thirst

It was a turning point for Vern Horst. Seems we all have to get to the bottom of our own barrel one way or another and for Vern Horst, the mayonnaise and Wonder Bread diet was the clincher. There was no way to go but up and no time to waste getting there. He looked at his deadbeat buddy and promised himself a better life. His options were few and none of them glamorous. No matter which way he turned, it would be a tough row to hoe. But there was one thing for certain; young Vern certainly didn't want to end up like his dead-beat buddy.

Too proud to come crawling back to his dad, he called his mom, who was then living in Las Vegas. But she couldn't help him. So, he decided to go back to the recruiter and do a little pleading to retake the test. But it was no use. He was told he'd have to wait six months before he could take the test again...unless, the recruiter confided, he was willing to go to another state and take it.

Vern hitchhiked as far as Wickenburg, Arizona, where his mom sent him bus fare to get the rest of the way into Las Vegas, Nevada. Making a beeline for the nearest recruiting office, he took the test again and passed it—barely. But, as luck would have it, he still couldn't get into the Marines because he'd have to return to Arizona (where he'd flunked the first test) to get his medical exam. It looked hopeless until his recruiter remembered a place in Victorville, California, that just might be able to help him out. So, young Vern headed off to Victorville.

His new recruiter in Victorville was "different" from the others. He saw redeeming qualities in Vern Horst that apparently his dad hadn't seen. The poor kid was homeless, hungry and he *needed* to join up. And he'd come a long way to do it. The kid was desperate and determined. Maybe the recruiter was an old softie or maybe he could tell that Vern would make a good Marine. Whichever, the recruiter let Vern sleep on a tattered old couch in his office for the first week and gave him five dollars a day—of his own money—so he could eat next door at the Taco Bell. That's thirty-five bucks; not exactly pocket change and he sure as hell didn't do that for everyone. Come to think of it, he hadn't done it for anyone. Ever.

Finally, with the help of his fatherly recruiter, Vern succeeded in getting into the Marines. But just as he was being sworn in, the Corporal noticed he was only seventeen and not yet out of high school. That meant he couldn't join. Devastated, Vern was put on a bus headed back to his old recruiter in Vegas when he witnessed a purse-snatching but did nothing to stop it. He was so wrapped up in his own misfortune, the incident didn't warrant any feelings from him at the time. Only problem was, he kept seeing the scene in his mind, over and over, until guilt set in. The guilt was so overwhelming he couldn't get over it. The purse-snatching incident made him all-the-more determined to join the Marines and maybe even get into police work. Perhaps by joining the Marines or becoming a cop it would help make up for not coming to the lady's defense.

His Vegas recruiter quickly arranged for Vern to earn his GED [General Equivalency Diploma] and get into the Marines—seventeen or not. Vern did well in boot camp and graduated at the top of his class.

It wasn't long before he was seduced by a beautiful blond haired, blue-eyed "older" woman. Her name was Abby. He was only seventeen when they met and Abby was twenty-one. A full-grown woman, head to toe and everywhere in between. The "older woman" attraction held tremendous powers over a mere boy of seventeen. They got married. Fast. No sooner were they married than he was transferred to Japan where he got his first look at the Military Police. The MPs struck a cord with Vern and he knew then and there—for certain—that police work was what he wanted to do. The purse-snatching incident was still weighing heavily on his heart. He was a good guy—honest and tenderhearted, almost to a fault.

After a while Vern was sent to El Toro, California, and put himself through the Police Academy at his own expense. The only thing Vern needed was a Smith & Wesson model 19, something he couldn't afford at the time. He was forced to go back to his dad for that. It was humiliating, even though by then they had mended their fences and were on good terms again. By the time he got out of the Marines, he had advanced to the position of Corporal. His dad was proud, even if he did hate the Marines.

It didn't take long for Vern to be picked up as a reserve police officer for the city of Orange, California. Abby was also headed toward a career in law enforcement and had been attending criminal justice classes at Cal State Long Beach. She couldn't help being somewhat chagrined that Vern, with his crappy GED, had upstaged her, but she was eventually hired by Irvine PD.

Eventually, their two careers collided. Vern and Abby ended up divorcing in 1985. Vern Horst was barely twenty-one. Now, more than ever, he wanted to be a full-fledged police officer and went through an additional four months of academy. After what seemed like an eternity, he was behind the wheel of a squad car, patrolling the mean streets of Stanton, California.

While a few areas of Stanton are "rough," the small section known as Crow Village was thought by many to be the absolute worst example of humanity. Crow's horrendous amount of drug dealing and gang violence were legendary. Crow Village rivaled the roughest, toughest, most dangerous ghettos in America. This is where Vern Horst found his niche. He cut his teeth doing patrol in Crow. It was dangerous, but he thrived on the danger. When the chance to get into undercover narcotics presented itself; Vern jumped at it.

Still, being newly single was tough. The guys kidded him in the locker room and tried to hook him up with women. He steered clear of dating female cops though; he'd been down that road once already. Some of the guys told him there was a hot little number working at the dry cleaners in Stanton and suggested that he cruise on over there and have some of his

Deadly Thirst

uniforms cleaned. It would give him the perfect excuse to go in and check out what the guys were calling "a *really* pretty woman."

Days later, with a couple of dirty uniforms slung over his arm, he found himself at the dry cleaning counter trying to look nonchalant. When he first caught sight of her, he couldn't believe his eyes. His buddies had not lied; she *was* beautiful. Every inch of her. Her name was Carmen. Appearance-wise she was the exact opposite of his ex-wife. Abby had been blonde-haired and blue-eyed. Carmen was from Spain; she had olive skin, beautiful dark eyes and a long, luscious mane of thick auburn hair. He asked her out right on the spot. Carmen accepted and the love affair began in earnest.

Working as a "narc" was exactly what Vern Horst enjoyed. In order to look the part, he had to forgo the clean-cut appearance of an ex-Marine-turned-cop and take on the scummy, unkempt look that narcs assume when they work undercover. There's a saying among narcs: if you're gonna run with a pack of dogs, you gotta look like a dog. Horst got shot at a couple of times, but he liked busting heads and kicking down doors. In the beginning, Carmen thought his undercover work was dangerous, but, other than that, it was okay. After all, she reasoned, it was for the betterment of society. Sure, there were aspects of the job that she didn't like, such as the late night hours and his raunchy-looking appearance, but she could deal with it. It was a "work hard, play hard" kind of thing back then. All in all, it was pretty wild.

Just when Vern Horst really started getting the hang of narc work, he decided to take a transfer to the upscale city of Newport Beach. He'd wanted to get into Newport years ago, but they'd said he was too young. Now they were plenty ready for him. Reporting to work with a shave, a new short haircut and a freshly pressed and starched uniform felt odd, yet refreshing to "Officer Horst." But it didn't feel like police work. It was nothing more than a walking desk job. With the exception of the cheeky babes in thong bikinis, it was down right boring. He'd gone from bullets to bikinis and now spent most of his time writing parking tickets.

His private life, on the other hand, had suddenly been thrown into overdrive. He was in love and Carmen was pregnant. They quickly got engaged and were married in October of '87. In March, their first son was born.

About a year later, Horst got hired by Riverside County Sheriff's Department and took a transfer to Moreno Valley, doing patrol work. Moreno Valley was a challenge; some parts were downright scary, which reminded him a lot of his Crow days. Crow seemed like a million light years ago, until he went into gang enforcement. Soon, Horst found himself sucked back into undercover narcs again. It was here that he witnessed his first autopsy.

In spite of a burgeoning feeling of deja vu, he grew his hair long and straggly again to look the part. He let his beard grow and wore filthy clothes. He looked just like the rest of the street vermin that sold drugs. This aspect of his job was somewhat embarrassing for Carmen. All but a select few, who knew his secret, thought she was married to a worthless, scumbag drug dealer. Horst kept his private life and his undercover work completely separated. He had to. Undercover narcs don't wear wedding rings. When he walked out the door, he left his family behind. Far behind. He had to concentrate on the job, not the wife and kids.

A second baby came along around this time and Vern and Carmen bought a bigger house in Riverside.

Working undercover narcotics in Moreno Valley was definitely more interesting, more exciting, than anything he'd done in Newport Beach. He *really* enjoyed his undercover work. But the job required him to be out all night—every night—drinking and dealing with his scumbag dope addict "friends."

Narc jobs are notorious marriage-wreckers and Carmen Horst's marriage was no exception. Her husband's all-day all-night carousing began to eat away at the foundation of their marriage and she had put up with just about all she was willing to put up with. Somehow, when she envisioned being married to a police officer, this wasn't exactly what she had pictured. Carmen didn't know it, but things were going to get a lot worse before they got any better.

It was somewhere around this time that Vern became the national president for a motorcycle club called "The Choir Boys." It was a police-officers-only club, which required every member to have a Harley. He met an actor named Gary Murdock* and began spending most of his days off with Gary in his huge house in Studio City. Gary was filming a movie called "Glass Shield" in which Vern got a small part. He did several screen tests and then got another part a few months later in a film called "Victim of Desire." Before long, he was totally caught up in the movie-star lifestyle. All his free time was spent with Gary and his socialite buddies while Carmen was stuck at home with two kids.

Horst was the cop, but it was Carmen who finally laid down the law. Hell hath no fury like the wrath of a woman and Vern Horst was about to experience Carmen's unique version of hell. He'd seen her mad before, but this was really scary. Once more, Vern Horst was given a couple of choices. Carmen told him it was time to choose what he wanted to keep, his marriage or his social life.

As his second marriage teetered on the verge of disintegration, Horst made the right choice. He gave Hollywood the boot and took a promotion to the Riverside station, which gave him regular, decent, working hours again. And finally, he shaved off the last vestiges of narc work. Once more he was the clean-shaven, Marine-haircut guy. The promotion was an absolute godsend for Carmen. Their third child, another son, had arrived by then and things between him and Carmen were better than ever.

Reflecting on how he had treated Carmen during their early years together, Vern Horst knew he hadn't been—and still wasn't—an easy person
to be married to. "If I was her, I'd have left me a long time ago," he said in
retrospect. But Carmen knew he loved his work and that he loved her and
the kids with all his heart. She was totally devoted to him and the children.
A common case of "love conquers all."

It wasn't long until Horst got his first taste of homicide. As much as he
had loved his undercover work, working Homicide was even better. The
investigative aspect of his job was immensely challenging and he found that
he was particularly good at peeling back the layers of deceit. A good homicide detective comes to know the victim and the killer better than almost
anyone else had known them.

For Vern Horst, nothing felt as rewarding as working Homicide. If a
man really wanted to make a difference, this was the place to do it. There
was no additional pay for his so-called promotion, but it gave him a lot of
overtime. Being an investigator for Riverside County was pretty prestigious;
although the tremendous amount of overtime, by his own admission, was
still pretty taxing on the marriage. But nothing like when he worked undercover. He rolled his eyes just thinking about those early days. However, too
often he was awakened in the middle of the night, or in the pre-dawn hours
as he had been on this particular morning....

Suddenly, he was jolted back into reality. Up ahead Alvin and Theresa
were parking their car. They had arrived at the 6th Street apartment. As his
car came to a stop at the curb, he found himself once more overwhelmed
with pity for Andy. In ways it seemed as though he was parked at the intersection of past and present and for just a fleeting moment he couldn't
remember how he'd gotten from where he'd been to where he was at that
instant. For a fraction of a second, he didn't know where he was or why
he was there.

He'd been in homicide for more than four years now. The last year and
a half he'd been working, ironically, out of the Perris station, about two
blocks away. As the lead investigator in more than fifty cases and the secondary investigator in over a hundred others, he thought he'd seen it all. Up
until now, he'd doubted that anything could shock him anymore. He was
about to be proven wrong. This case was about to turn his life inside out.

As a homicide investigator, Horst worked under circumstances that
most people could never imagine, even in their wildest, most sordid dreams.
Countless holidays had been forfeited so he could go to the murder scene,
pick through the blood and guts of the victim and intrude on the lives of
the family, friends and business associates who knew the victim and/or the
suspect. It had not been easy for Horst to learn to cope with the devastation
that violence can do to a human body, especially a child's body.

Even though his eyes were focused on the situation ahead, the image of
the bruised and battered body of Andy was fixed before him—branded into
his mind's eye. Still sitting behind the steering wheel, he rubbed his eyes,

trying to blink it away, but it was forever seared into his memory. The clicking and wheezing sounds of the ventilator still rang in his ears. Glancing at his watch, he surmised that Andy was probably arriving at Loma Linda about now. The day had started with a rude awakening. He couldn't recall a case that had upset him more than this one had and the case was only a few hours old.

As Horst got out of his car he made a mental note that when he got home from work that evening—no matter what time it was—he would give his three boys the biggest bear-hug he could without squeezing them to death. Maybe he would bring them something…a little surprise that would make them happy. Yes, yes, he would think of something…he would definitely think of something.

Located in one of the worst crime areas of the city, the duplex-style apartment was cramped and dark. There was no grassy yard for the kids to play in, he noted, just dirt and concrete surrounded by a four-foot-high chain link fence. It reminded him of a prison yard.

He explained to Alvin and Theresa that they would have to stay outside while he looked around. Giving him permission to do so, Theresa unlocked the front door for Horst and let him in. He did a quick, superficial check to make sure no one was in the residence and, aside from some dirt on the coffee table, he found nothing suspicious or out of place. Except, of course, the demeanor of the two foster parents. No doubt, he'd be back with a search warrant.

Then he began to do a thorough walk-through, starting with the front door. He took careful note of the screen door and the way it could be locked with a small lever. He clicked the lever back and forth several times and noted that it required considerable effort to maneuver it out of the locked position. He wondered if a little boy Andy's age and size could have mastered it. The front door was wooden and had two locks: one a deadbolt and the other a common twist-type lock in the center of the knob. Both locks were in working order.

The apartment was very small: four rooms and a bath. The entrance was in the kitchen/living room, which was one area, un-partitioned. Straight ahead was the bathroom and to each side of it, a bedroom. There was no rear door. The apartment was decorated in dark tones of green and blue. As he stood with his back to the front door, to his left was the kitchen. It was pleasant enough, a small table for four located on the wall to the left of the sink and directly across from a two door, white refrigerator. Between the table and the sink was a water cooler with a Playmate cooler on top of it. The sink was cluttered with various utensils, cups, dishes and a gallon jug that was half full of water.

To his right was the living room. Several throw rugs covered most of the carpet and a large oscillating fan was standing near the front door. Between the door and one end of a blue corner-couch was a black metal filing cabinet that was apparently being used as an end table. In the middle of the room was a coffee table with a glass top. Horst noticed dirt on the coffee table. Directly in front of the coffee table was a large television. It didn't look like the couple was poor or deprived in any way. Although they didn't live extravagantly, the home had extras that many struggling families couldn't afford, such as an expensive television and decent furniture.

Horst walked straight ahead into the bathroom. A dark green shower curtain was pulled across the tub/shower area and the toilet had a matching green cover. He pulled the shower curtain aside and saw washcloths, shampoo and soap. The apartment looked clean enough, but there was something faintly creepy about it. He could feel it.

Next, he exited the bathroom and turned left toward the master bedroom. The large bed took up most of the room. He noted a small, blue plastic chair sitting in the middle of the floor between the adult bed and a white baby crib. An orange towel was draped across the top of the bedroom door and clothing was draped across the railing of the crib. Directly in front of the door was a white, two-drawer nightstand. On the nightstand was a small lamp, a bottle of lotion laying on its side and a large can of Raid ant and roach killer. A tablecloth with hand-embroidered designs was draped across the top of the nightstand. Nothing seemed unusual, a little messy perhaps, but nothing out of the ordinary. The bed was unmade, as he expected it to be, with mismatched sheets and pillows tossed toward the foot of the bed. The sliding closet doors were pushed to one side revealing a jumbled cluttered mess. There was an unrolled sleeping bag and a freestanding oscillating fan at the foot of the adults' bed. To the right of the closet stood a cheap-looking dresser with an iron, an alarm clock and a television with a stack of clothes piled on top of it.

Horst turned and went into the other bedroom, obviously the kids' room. There were two twin beds, one without linens. On the doorknob hung a plastic Wal-Mart shopping bag. The children's closet doors were also pushed to one side, revealing another area that had been crammed with a little bit of everything. Blankets and pillows were stacked from top to bottom at the left end of the closet with a laundry basket full of clothes in the center. The door of the children's room was about six feet from the adults' bedroom door. Each bedroom had one large window. The bathroom had a small window over the tub.

Alvin and Theresa appeared to lead a normal existence. Horst went back and looked at the lock on the door again. He'd been working Homicide long enough to know not to take anything for granted. He looked at everything, but he did it quickly. The few minutes Horst spent inside the small apartment gave him a more complete and personal insight into the lives of Alvin and Theresa. There's a certain feeling an investigator gleans from walking the premises and Horst was like a sponge, absorbing every possible detail. There was something wrong with this scene; he was sure of it. Other than the dirt on the coffee table, he didn't see anything amiss on his first visit to the apartment, but he certainly felt it. While there's a fine edge of tension that stalks any homicide investigator, always, this place was downright spooky. He'd be back, for sure. Right now, it was just a cursory check, nothing final.

Horst kept coming back to the strange feeling he had about the foster parents. He could feel it creeping up on him. Alvin and Theresa were still standing outside, talking quietly to each other. He invited them to come in and told Alvin to have a seat on the couch.

Theresa was taken into the master bedroom and questioned first. Horst asked her to tell him once more what had happened. Again, Theresa explained that Andy had a habit of sneaking outside in the middle of the night. She'd gotten up around 3:00 to use the bathroom and when she'd checked on Andy, he wasn't in his sleeping bag. She noticed the door of the apartment was ajar and she went outside to look for him. Horst asked Theresa to show him exactly where she had found Andy. Theresa led him outside and pointed to an area in the dirt between the apartment and the carport, near a jungle gym.

It did seem remarkable—and unbelievable—that she had managed to find Andy within a few minutes of when he stopped breathing, but Horst kept this thought to himself. He was convinced that an adult had abused Andy, but which adult? He didn't suspect Jacob at all, but he didn't rule anything out at this point. Anything was possible.

Theresa led Horst back into the adults' bedroom and showed him the sleeping bag at the foot of her bed. She said that Andy had been sleeping in the bag lately because he kept waking Jacob in the middle of the night, complaining about having to go to the bathroom. According to Theresa, Jacob didn't appreciate being awakened every night. It sounded like Theresa was trying to insinuate that Andy had been sleeping in her room to protect him from Jacob and that possibly Jacob had inflicted the injuries on Andy. She was quick to tell Horst that Jacob had some problems of his own. Her words were nothing but small, cryptic stabs of evasiveness and deceit. He knew it and, he wanted her to know he knew it.

Sergeant Don Farrar showed up about that time and took Horst aside to tell him that a team of forensic technicians were on the way to photograph and process the house. The case was already in homicide mode though Andy was still technically alive. Everything would need to be photographed exactly as it was. Nothing was to be disturbed. In crime scene investigation, there is never a second chance to see the evidence as it is. Absolutely nothing is taken for granted or thought to be unimportant.

The questioning was getting no solid answers out of either parent. Since the apartment was so small, it was certain that one parent could overhear what the other was saying. Horst asked Alvin and Theresa to come on down to the police station and answer a few more questions. Before they headed out Horst had Theresa sign a consent form so the apartment could be searched. He took note of the fact that she didn't ask why.

Alvin and Theresa didn't know it, but they would be separated at the police station and their interviews would be tape-recorded. The tapes would prove to be very helpful to investigators later on. One of the deputies was told to remain at the entrance of the duplex until further notice. Aside from the forensic team, Horst told him, no one was to enter the house. All the comings and goings were beginning to attract a crowd of gawkers.

Jacob Marquist was waiting at the Perris station and was the first person to be questioned by Horst. Horst's oldest son was the same age as Jacob, so there was a good rapport between them. The fact that Horst wasn't wearing an intimidating uniform seemed to work in his favor that morning and Jacob was anxious to finally get to tell someone about everything he'd witnessed at the apartment over the past month. Jacob had been an eyewitness to some of the abuse Andy had suffered. He gave Horst a vivid and detailed statement, which provided crucial information for the investigation. Horst was careful to ask Jacob, up front, whether or not he knew the difference in telling the truth versus telling a lie. Jacob understood. Jacob seemed glad that he could finally confide in someone who might be able to help Andy. He had no idea that Andy was not expected to live. In fact, Jacob didn't even know why Andy was in the hospital. The only thing Alvin and Theresa had told him was that Andy was hurt and that the neighbor's dog, Tiger, probably had knocked him down. But now, here was a "detective" asking him questions about whether or not he'd seen Andy being mistreated or hurt. Bravely, Jacob took full advantage of the opportunity to unload all the horrific details of what he'd seen. Horst would later say that Jacob had been "very articulate" and had been a tremendous help in the investigation.

"I asked him what he thought of living with Alvin and Theresa and Jacob said living with them was hard." Horst also asked Jacob about his relationship with young Andy, to which Jacob replied that he didn't often play with him because Andy was a "whiner." He recalled that just the night before Andy had kept everyone awake all night because he was thirsty and had gotten into the refrigerator for a drink.

After Horst was satisfied with all that Jacob had to say, he let CPS take him. Then, Horst took Theresa into a small room where he sat at a table opposite her, a tape recorder and video camera catching every word she said. She still didn't know that Andy wasn't expected to live.

She was wearing a black T-shirt, shorts and dirty tennis shoes and had her hair pulled back off her face in a ponytail that reached halfway down her back. Horst told her she was free to leave at any time and Theresa said, "No, that's fine." He thanked her for coming in and Theresa smiled and said she was glad to do it. "No problem," she chirped in a tiny high-pitched voice. "Anything I can do to help, you know." Horst noted that Theresa seemed perfectly happy and not the least bit concerned about anything that had happened to Andy. Certainly, Horst thought, if Andy had merely wandered outside in the middle of the night and hurt himself while playing, Theresa would have asked why she was being questioned at the police station. But, she didn't ask. Wouldn't an innocent parent or guardian be indignant to have been separated from their child at a time like this? Wouldn't they be anxious to get the interview over with so they could hurry back to the hospital? They might even refuse an interview at such a time. But not Theresa.

Horst wanted a little history of exactly how they had obtained custody of Andy. Theresa said that Andy had come from "a tough situation." She and Alvin both loved kids very much, she said, but they were unable to have any of their own. For such a large and masculine-looking woman, one might expect her voice to be deep and strong, but it wasn't. She spoke in a soft, almost child-like voice. The voice seemed artificial and, after what he'd seen, it made Horst's flesh crawl just listening to it.

Early into the taped conversation, Theresa admitted that Andy had a slight bedwetting problem, but she said it didn't bother her. She said it was normal for a little four-year-old to pee the bed. She considered his potty-training problems to be merely a symptom of being moved so often. She also attributed his bedwetting to the fact that he liked to drink a lot of fluids but was a finicky and light eater.

From all his experience, Horst immediately thought Theresa was being evasive and untruthful in her answers. He wondered if perhaps she was covering up for something her husband had done. She didn't seem concerned that Andy was in such critical condition that Mercy Air had airlifted him to Loma Linda Medical Center. Looking at her, he couldn't help but notice that she didn't seem anxious to get to Loma Linda where she could be at Andy's side during this time when he needed her most.

During the interview Theresa frequently laughed. She insisted that she considered it normal that Andy had a habit of peeing on himself and it didn't bother her in the slightest. Sure, she disciplined the kids, she said, but always in a gentle and kind way. Never physically. Andy had a "time-out chair" that was used as punishment but she laughed and said he actually enjoyed sitting in it. Because of that, she usually made him stand on it when he was being punished. She admitted that he got time-out for potty accidents. Sometimes she would also give him cold showers as punishment, but insisted the water was only "a little cold."

"So, what I did was I made the water less than lukewarm...it wasn't completely cold, it was more on the colder side than the hot side," she said very sweetly. "I haven't done the cold bath thing in a while." Horst asked if there were any other ways they disciplined Andy. Theresa thought about it and mumbled that she sometimes sent Andy to his room.

"Anything else?" Horst asked in a dead-on stare. His eyes had turned hard enough to cut diamonds.

"No." She claimed that she and her husband never actually bathed Andy because they didn't want to be accused of child molestation. Ridiculous, but Horst nodded as if in total agreement. Horst wanted to know about the two days leading up to August 2nd. She didn't know that Jacob had already told Horst all the details of the abuse he'd witnessed in the last few weeks and Horst was careful not to divulge the fact that he'd already spoken with Jacob. He wanted to hear what Theresa had to say.

While he listened to her version of the events, the knot in Horst's stomach twisted even tighter as he imagined the agony Andy must have suffered. Trying to mask his suspicion took all the self-control he could muster. Maybe his gut feelings were wrong, he kept telling himself. After what Jacob had told him, Horst believed that Andy had definitely been abused in the past weeks; but, he reasoned, maybe the kid *did* hurt himself playing outside. Still, it seemed only reasonable that Theresa would have become insistent on that by now. Surely, she would have questioned why she had to leave the hospital and come down to the police station to answer a bunch of stupid questions. But here she was, laughing as though she hadn't a care in the world.

He talked to her in an easy-going kind of way, saying he just needed to know a few routine facts and then they could all go home. He wanted her to know he thought the situation was serious, but at the same time he tried to put her at ease. Hopefully, she would open up a little. He wanted her to feel like he was someone she could talk to, that he was willing to listen to whatever she had to say and he wouldn't stand in judgment of her. He began to ask questions based upon the things Jacob had told him.

In a singsong voice, Theresa recalled the events that had transpired over the weekend. Laughing, she remembered something that happened on Saturday at her place of employment. The two kids had come to work with her that day and Andy had messed his pants. In spite of the extreme temperatures, she admitted wrapping Andy in a large plastic trash bag so he wouldn't dirty the car seats on the ride home. She laughed as she recalled it all. "So then, you know, we like, get home and stuff and it was a hot summer day, so what I did was I rinsed him off with the hose outside." It all seemed so gentle and fun-loving the way she explained it. As he listened, Horst thought about Jacob's chilling version of the hosing-off incident.

At first, Theresa merely stated that she had rinsed Andy off quickly and then immediately wrapped him in a towel and brought him inside. Horst noticed that she was careful to omit the things that Jacob had seen her do to Andy, but he wanted to back up a little.

"Okay, so when you had him outside, he was naked. Is that correct?"

"No..." she stammered. "At first he had his clothes on and then I rinsed him off and brought him inside." Again, she skipped over the abuse Jacob had witnessed. But Horst didn't dwell on it right then. There was a method to his interrogations. Let the person talk. Skip around from one time sequence to another and then back up. This was his most effective snare.

"Okay. At any time, did you tell him to clean himself?" Yes, she said. She'd told Andy to clean his face and, much to her dismay, he'd picked up his soiled underpants and began wiping feces all over his face. Horst didn't believe it, but kept a blank face. Saying that Andy had picked up his *under-*

wear was an unwitting admission that Andy was indeed naked, at least from the waist down, although she had just stated that he wasn't.

"Andy used his soiled underwear to wipe his face?" Horst asked, his pen poised over a yellow note pad.

"Yes, he did," she said. But, she added, she had quickly scolded him—in a very gentle way of course—and told him he was being a nasty boy. That's why she'd called Jacob over to look. "So then, I was like, 'no, no, no Andy...' you know. Then I rinsed him off and I, like, put the hose to his face and I rinsed him off," she said. She made it sound as though she had gently splashed Andy's cheeks with a dash of water. She accentuated the comment with a gentle pat to her own cheek.

Surely then, Horst pressed, since Andy had removed his underwear she must have noticed his swollen scrotum when she hosed him off.

"No," she insisted. But, on second thought, she *did* recall the doctor had warned her about Andy's "large pee-pee" when they first got custody of him on June 3rd. "I've always noticed he had a large pee-pee," she said. Odd, Horst thought, that a foster mother would be sizing up a child's penis. Theresa claimed that she had questioned the doctor about Andy's "big pee-pee" during Andy's physical and the doctor had told her that some boys are just bigger down there than others.

Horst told Theresa that's not what he meant when he'd asked her about Andy's swollen genitals. He wasn't talking about penis size, he was talking about *swelling*. There was a long, blistering moment of silence. Then he told Theresa that he'd already spoken at length with Jacob and Jacob had told him the whole story. Horst leaned back in his chair and let that fact sink in for a few seconds as he gauged her reaction. Finally, he told her that Jacob had said Andy's genitals were bruised and swollen. Horst waited for her explanation. It was a long wait.

"No..." she finally said as sweetly as she could.

"Those are Jacob's words. He named it. He goes, 'his *penis* was all purple and it was big.'" He sat looking at her for an extended minute and then said, "You didn't notice that?"

"No, I didn't," she said. But Horst didn't buy it; he just kept looking at her. A prolonged silence is often enough to make the subject add a few more details and, sure enough, Theresa added something else. Come to think of it, she *did* remember him walking funny for a few days last week.

It was becoming obvious to Horst that Theresa was starting to feel the pressure now and she'd realized that she'd worked herself into a corner. She stammered as she tried to talk her way out of it. She explained, with a smile and a shrug, that Andy had walked funny for a couple of days a week or two ago, but then he stopped doing it.

"So then, he wasn't walking funny yesterday?" Horst asked.

"No...yes, no...yes. That's right," she finally stammered. "Yes he was. Because you know, he was pooping and stuff a lot and he was, like, walk-

Deadly Thirst

ing funny because he had a diaper on. He only did it when he was wearing the diaper."

Horst took note of the diaper comment. He would get back to the diaper thing in a few minutes. His best method of questioning was to mix up the questions and not let the suspect control the conversation. He asked about the day prior, vague in his reference that Jacob had mentioned something about a walk to Stater Bros. market.

Settling back into her chair and smiling as if she were recalling a funny incident, Theresa said yes, they'd walked to the market and on the way home she had noticed they had a lot of bags to carry and that Andy was walking funny. She told Horst that Andy was whining and she'd gently warned him to stop whining or she'd make him carry the heavy stuff. When Andy hadn't stopped whining, she'd made him carry a gallon of milk in one hand and a large bucket of ice cream in the other. Recalling the scene brought a smile to her face. Horst asked her why she made a little four-year-old kid carry two heavy items on such a hot day.

"I did it to teach him a lesson," she answered in a noble sort of way. But she also insisted she had only made him carry the heavy stuff for a minute or two and that Andy was allowed to set the items down whenever he got tired. As she described the walk home from Stater Bros, her version made it sound as if it had been nothing but a joyous adventure for the three of them. Jacob's version of the event had been shockingly different.

"Well," Horst said, "was he wearing a diaper yesterday?"

"Yesterday? He...didn't have a diaper yesterday."

"Well, you told me he only walks funny when he's wearing a diaper," Horst said. "You told me he *was* walking funny yesterday and now you say he wasn't wearing a diaper."

"Right, right," she said softly. Horst stared hard at Theresa. As the video camera continued to tape silently, Horst changed the subject again and got her to admit that she had also "taught Andy lessons" by forcing him to chew hot chili peppers. Horst showed no reaction to any of her decisions about discipline even though it sickened him to hear about it. He needed to get on Theresa's good side in order to uncover the truth about what had happened. However, Theresa adamantly denied ever hitting or kicking Andy.

Switching back to the hosing-off incident, Horst asked her if she'd rinsed Andy off well enough so there wasn't any more feces on him. Theresa agreed that she had hosed him off very thoroughly.

"But what I'm saying is, that if you're washing him, now you say you didn't get a good look at his genitals, but at this point, when he's lying down and you're rinsing him off..."

"No..." Theresa interrupted, "I didn't see nothing..."

"Well, did you see his genitals at that time?"

"Pretty sure I did if he was naked."

"And so you're saying now that you rinsed him off well enough so that you would notice there weren't any feces on him?"

"Right, right."

"Did you notice any discoloration in his…"

"No, I didn't."

"Did you notice any type of swelling at all?"

"No, I didn't."

"Um," Horst took a deep breath and sighed. He reached into his shirt pocket and retrieved a few of the Polaroids of Andy that were taken at Menifee. Selecting one and showing it to Theresa, he said, "You know, he has a little bit of a burn right in here on the inside of his leg." She leaned forward to look at where Horst was pointing. The photo showed the full extent of Andy's swollen, purple scrotum and a dark red abrasion on the inside of his right thigh. She looked at the photo without even so much as a hint of emotion or alarm. If she had not noticed any swelling or bruising on Andy, as she claimed, surely this photo would have elicited shock and a flood of questions about how Andy could have possibly gotten into *that* condition. But there was nothing. No emotion, no questions. No shocked reaction when she saw the photo of the engorged testicles. Nothing. "Do you have any idea what that might be from?" His eyes were locked in a dead-on stare with hers.

"No…"

"No idea what that might be from, huh?"

"No…"

"Well, let me ask you, did it look normal to you…his penis?"

"Yeah. I mean, you know, I would have most definitely noticed if it wasn't normal. From the beginning, you know, I asked the doctor and she's like, 'oh yeah, some kids have them basically larger than others…but…"

"No," Horst blurted, putting a stop to her evasiveness. "I'm not talking about the size of his penis, I'm talking about a bruise," he said tapping the picture, "…swelling…"

"I didn't see any of that stuff," she said. And then she laughed as she recalled how Andy had urinated on her bed during the weekend. Horst was sick of the laughing. He leaned back in his chair again and informed Theresa that Jacob had already told him about some of the abuse he'd seen.

"You know," he said, "Jacob is very articulate and he has no reason to lie to me. He's an eleven-year-old and I'm telling you, I believe the kid. He has no reason to lie to me." He asked Theresa if she'd ever punched Andy in the stomach.

"No, I would never do that," she said.

"Well, Jacob said you did it to him, like 'does this hurt' and 'see, that's all I did to him' and when you jabbed him in the stomach it kinda doubled him over a little bit. Did you, at any time, punch Andy in the stomach like that?"

"No, no," Theresa said, shaking her head.

"Even joking around like that?"

"No."

Oftentimes, cops will ask a suspect to take a polygraph test just to see how they'll react to the suggestion. It was worth a shot, he thought. So, Horst asked Theresa if she'd be willing to take a polygraph test. With a shrug, she said sure. She asked no questions as to why she should take a lie detector test and she showed no fear, no remorse, no concern.

After nearly forty frustrating minutes, the interview ended. He met briefly with several other investigators who'd been watching Theresa's interview on closed-circuit TV. Then, Horst went into an adjacent room where Alvin had been waiting and began questioning him about the events leading up to Andy's hospitalization.

Horst was well aware that the national statistics for child homicides showed a large percentage of deaths were caused by fathers. It would be interesting to hear what Alvin had to say for himself. As Horst had done with Theresa, he told Alvin he was not under arrest and that he could leave at any time. Like Theresa, Alvin was in no hurry to return to the hospital.

During Theresa's questioning, she had mysteriously omitted the fact that she and Alvin were on the verge of a bitter divorce. Alvin however, was more than eager to talk about the troubles he was having with his wife. Yes, they'd had a very turbulent and brief marriage. Matter of fact, they'd just signed divorce papers a few days ago.

"Me and Theresa ain't really living together right now," Alvin said. "So I been gone 'bout a week. The biggest problem was, she was running my money." He said he'd finally gotten fed up with having to fork over all his money to her and having her dole out a measly pittance for him to get by on. "Hey, I had, like, twenty or thirty dollars a month and I pay all the bills. I wasn't having this, so I called my dad and told my dad the situation. About what was happening, you know." On and on he ranted about the money troubles he'd had with his wife and how he was quick to consult his dad about it. According to Alvin, Theresa was stubborn and bossy. "It was either her way or no way, you know? I'm trying to be the responsible one," Alvin revealed. He seemed agitated and volatile one minute, frustrated and resigned the next.

Horst wanted to know if Alvin and Theresa had any set plans for disciplining the kids, if they had set any behavioral boundaries for them. Alvin complained that he didn't have any say in what happened to the kids and freely admitted that he witnessed Andy receive, on several occasions, punishments that were much too severe for a four-year-old child. He'd told Theresa it wasn't right to treat Andy that way. Horst pressed Alvin for details, but, all of a sudden, Alvin seemed to balk at saying anything more. His face was a war zone of anxiety; he seemed close to tears. Horst decided to use a scattershot technique with Alvin. If Alvin balked at one particular subject, Horst wouldn't dwell on it, he'd casually move on to something different. Out of the blue, Horst asked, "How did you get that cut on your arm?"

"Oh, I cut that putting an engine in my car," Alvin said, obviously glad to be talking about something else. Horst took note of Alvin's demeanor. He asked Alvin if he wanted something to eat and Alvin said no; he couldn't eat when he was nervous. Horst wanted to know why Alvin was nervous, but Alvin didn't answer. Was there something Alvin wanted to say? Whatever he knew, Alvin had suddenly decided to zip his lips. Perhaps he was afraid he'd said too much already.

"Are you sure, man, that there's something you're not telling me about this?" Horst asked. A long silence followed and Horst used it to his advantage. "Is there something I should know, man? Seriously. Cause there's a chance the kid may not make it through the night..."

"Right...right..." was all Alvin had to say as he pondered his options. Alvin seemed to be a little dim-witted and Horst wondered if perhaps he had beaten Andy, but hadn't realized how badly he'd hurt him. Horst felt he was nearing the breaking point with Alvin and that some sort of a confession, or at least a satisfactory explanation, was just on the horizon. He had to keep the pressure on.

"Now I'm asking you, man, straight up...what happened?" Horst was leaning forward now, coaxing Alvin. "Getting over that hill is the hardest part," Horst said, "but once you're there, it's okay. I'm telling you, man, getting over that hill is going to be harder for her than it is for you." Still, Alvin kept silent, although his chin had begun to quiver. As tears filled his eyes, Horst turned up the heat. "If something happened that you need to tell me about, now's the time, man. Now's the time..."

Alvin hesitated. "I won't go to jail, will I?" he asked. Tears spilled from his eyes and streamed down his face.

"He came to your house to get away from that kind of shit, man. What happened...Alvin, what happened?" An eternity passed in the silence that followed. The silence bounced off the walls and reverberated in the room like the blast from a cannon as Alvin continued to agonize about the possibility of going to jail. Horst kept the pressure on. "I'm telling you, I'm going to get to the bottom of this one way or another, man...now what happened?" Horst took the Polaroid out of his pocket and slapped it down on the table in front of Alvin. Tapping the picture and inching it closer to Alvin, he noticed that Alvin cringed when he looked at it. "The kid didn't get in that kind of shape without something happening to him. Now tell me...Alvin...what happened?"

"Look, I'll tell you..." he sniffed, "I just don't want to go to jail." Horst was sure Alvin was about to confess.

Then with a deep sigh, it all came gushing out.

PART 1
THE BIRTH PARENTS

CHAPTER 2

THOMAS DEE SETZER
AKA "Cowboy"

As the afternoon wore on and Andy teetered on the brink of death, the investigators prepared to go into homicide mode. Horst's job of solving Andy's murder wouldn't be proving merely *how* he was killed and who did it; he'd have to prove *why* he was killed. It was the only way to form a solid case. Andy had obviously come from a horrible set of circumstances, which at the onset of the investigation were jumbled like a box of jigsaw puzzle pieces. It would be Homicide's job to take each one of the pieces and fit them together so that a complete and detailed picture of Andy's life emerged. Luckily, Horst and his team were good at that.

Retracing the events that led Andy to be placed in the custody of Alvin and Theresa was profoundly frustrating and saddening for everybody working the case. Not only would they have to delve into the private lives of everyone who'd had custody of Andy, they would have to deal with the self-governing, highly secretive forces of Riverside County Child Protective Services, a task no one on the team particularly relished.

The image of Andy splayed out on the hospital gurney was still fixed in Horst's mind as he began his investigation into Andy's pitiful background. It didn't take him long to learn that Andy's biological father was well known at the Riverside County Sheriff's Department and the Hemet PD. Thirty-four-year-old Thomas Dee Setzer, AKA [also known as] "Cowboy," was a Hemet drug addict with an extensive criminal history, dating all the way back to 1983 when he'd turned 18. Cowboy had at least ten aliases, three California driver's licenses and at least two social security numbers. His life was a string of back to back incarcerations and thirteen prison commitments. Not surprisingly, his most constant addresses were those of jails and prisons. Throughout the years countless warrants had been issued for his arrest.

As if that wasn't bad enough, Horst learned that Andy's mother, twenty-eight-year-old Laura Leanna Utley, was also a Hemet drug addict with several aliases and a criminal history involving drugs and weapons. She was currently imprisoned at California Institution for Women in Frontera.

Deadly Thirst

It was apparent to Horst that, right from the start, the odds had not been in Andy's favor. He couldn't imagine a more miserable situation to bring a child into.

* * *

Going back in time and talking about the chaotic years of her early adulthood was about the last thing Donna Darin wanted to do. Tearing open the cauterized wounds Tom Setzer had left behind would not be a pleasant ordeal. She preferred to let bygones be bygones. No sense in poking through the ashes. If she'd not been asked to explain it all, she would have never volunteered the information.

Forced to the farthest recesses of her mind, the passage of time had dimmed her recollections of him, but not the pain he'd caused her and the children. She'd hoped that Tom's problems would never again sully her reputation like they did years ago. Trying to explain how it all began—and why she tolerated it for as long as she did—would be like walking across a bed of hot coals; she'd traverse it as fast as she could, hoping to minimize the pain. She'd never understood why she'd let her life become so blighted and entangled with a type of guy she had always chosen to steer clear of. The best she could do now was chalk it up to inexperience and learn a lesson from it. Still, just being asked about those early years brought back a flood of horrible memories and emotions that soon began to manifest themselves in a torrent of words.

She'd met Tom Setzer when they were both students at Hemet Junior High School. They were both fifteen. According to Donna, Tom had a rough start in life and it was straight downhill from there.

The way she remembered it, Tom was heavily into drugs by the time she'd met him and had already gotten into so much trouble that, soon after they met, his parents sent him to live with his grandparents in Montana or someplace. Someplace far away, she wasn't sure where. His parents figured the hard work of a farmhand would settle him right down. Teach him some value and some respect. A little hard work might do the boy some good.

But it didn't happen quite the way it was supposed to. Big Sky country only served to harden him even more. It soon became obvious to the grandparents that they couldn't handle Tom any better than his parents had and Tom wasn't their responsibility anyway. They were disgusted with his attitude, the drinking and the drugs and became so exasperated they sent him away also, to some sort of reform school or something.

Getting an education wasn't on Tom's agenda and neither was reform. He'd gotten himself thrown out of school on several occasions and that suited him just fine. He didn't like school anyway and made no attempt to graduate from high school. Tom had taken a liking to horses, as Donna recalled, and considered himself to be quite a cowboy. He earned a little money training horses in Big Sky country and felt empowered by his riding abilities. He had a knack for cracking the whip.

He turned eighteen in Montana and could legally do as he pleased, to a certain extent anyway. So he headed back to Hemet, proudly brandishing the nickname of "Cowboy." It would prove to be just the first of many such nicknames and aliases that Tom Setzer would hide behind.

Those who knew Cowboy and his wild ways wondered why in the world he would come back to a small town like Hemet and what it was that made him stay. Hemet seemed to have been caught in a time warp during the previous forty years. Businesses and establishments that had lined its main thoroughfares in the early sixties were still in business, changed only by a fresh application of paint every decade or so and perhaps a new owner or two along the way. Neighborhoods had remained much the same for nearly fifty years. Charming streets lined with whitewashed cottages, some built in the early 1900's, spread out from the center of town near the train depot. Enormous ficus and walnut trees, planted by early settlers, had long since outgrown their small plots of soil in many a front yard. Massive, silent sentinels to a century of life in a small town. Nothing changed much around Hemet, except the attitudes of the newer generation.

A drive along State Street crossed the railroad tracks that officially put Hemet on the map around 1888. By the time Cowboy came back to town in 1983—nearly one hundred years later—its antiquated Santa Fe train depot had long since been abandoned but still stood, dilapidated and forgotten, at the intersection of State Street and Florida Avenue. Only occasionally did the train roll through Hemet anymore, usually just a couple of cars hauling spuds. In the latter part of its early years, Hemet had been an important farming town, citrus and potatoes mostly, and home to the yearly Ramona Pageant, which began in 1923. Agriculture eventually gave way to a moderate attempt at development. In 1965 a small community college was built at the north end of State Street in the adjoining town of San Jacinto. Set against a glorious backdrop of the San Jacinto Mountains, the collage was named to reflect its position; Mount San Jacinto College. Around the same time, a modest shopping mall sprang up along the western section of Florida Avenue. Its main department stores were J.C. Penney and Harris'.

Even so, Hemet seemed to maintain an aura of being old, boring and out of style. It was extremely quiet, which suited the elderly residents just fine, except that it was viciously hot and dry in the summer months. Consequently, the onset of summer beckoned many to pack up and head for cooler climates, which left Hemet even quieter than it normally was. For decades it remained the same, year in and year out, having little with which to draw visitors or revenue. One couldn't help but wonder what it was that drew Cowboy back. After all, in those days Hemet was considered by many to be nothing more than a quiet retirement community for snowbirds. Nothing seemed geared toward young folks.

Fresh off the farm, eighteen-year-old Cowboy was itchin' to stir up some excitement. In spite of his long absence, Donna's attraction to Cowboy was still strong and although she can't remember exactly how it happened, they

Deadly Thirst

quickly rekindled the old flame. As soon as Cowboy got back into town, his drug use and brazen, confrontational behavior went from bad to worse. Employment was sporadic—at best—attempted only when he felt like it, and Cowboy rarely felt like working, at least not in a punch-the-clock type job. Construction, horse training mostly, that sort of thing. Still, there was stuff he wanted in life, stuff he needed like cigarettes, booze and drugs. With no paycheck coming in most of the time, the only way to get what he wanted was to steal. No big deal to Cowboy; he thought society owed him a few freebies. Stuff was way overpriced anyway.

Problem was, his talent for lifting the goods wasn't sharply honed back then and he was arrested on shoplifting charges. In a move that was to become his trademark and the attitude of a million other drug abusers like him, Cowboy took it all in stride and didn't bother to show up for his court date. A warrant was issued for his arrest, but he'd vanished into thin air. Having a warrant out for his arrest gave him a brand of twisted prestige among his drug-addict friends, which he seemed right proud of. The "heat" wanted him, they were looking for him and Cowboy took great delight in shucking off the heat. Cops were patient though; they knew they'd be crossing paths with Cowboy again soon enough. Until then, they'd just wait it out. Guys like him didn't stay out of the system long. Hemet was a small town back then, where everybody knew everybody else's business and lucky for them, Cowboy stayed local. They'd find him soon enough.

But it wasn't just law enforcement riding Cowboy's back during his first year as an adult. Paternity had also reared its ugly head, early on. In hindsight, Donna admitted that all the warning signs were there and she should have known better than to get mixed up with someone like Cowboy. But young love and raging hormones can be daunting obstacles for anyone to overcome, especially two teenagers. When the shoplifting arrest happened in February of 1984, Donna was two months pregnant and more than a little apprehensive about how to tell Cowboy. When she finally told him, news of impending parenthood didn't faze Cowboy in the slightest. He wasn't about to let it become a deterrent to his penchant for drugs. In fact, other than being slightly miffed, he showed no concern whatsoever about "Donna's problem." But Donna had stars in her eyes. She was certain Cowboy would change his attitude when he saw her advancing stages of pregnancy. She was carrying his baby, his love child. She was sure that when the baby was born, Cowboy would be so beguiled by the tiny face staring back at him that the infant would miraculously reconstruct their lives for the better. If it happened that way in the romance novels she read and on TV, then surely it would be that way in real life. For all of his shortcomings she could forgive him because, in her heart, she was sure Cowboy would eventually make a good father. She tended to be confident usually, but there was a nagging voice in her head that told her she was headed straight for disaster. She was only eighteen, still naive and gullible. And she was pregnant. There was nothing she could do about it now; she had already bonded with the fetus inside her. Better just to let the pregnancy continue and be patient with Cowboy. He'd come around when the time got near. She was sure. Or at least she hoped.

As her pregnancy proceeded, her image of Cowboy became somewhat clouded and tarnished. For one thing, he had a serious aversion for work. To support his ever-increasing need for drugs, Cowboy had ways to turn a buck, few of them laudable. In August—five weeks before his first child was born—the authorities finally caught up with him. This time, Cowboy was arrested for false imprisonment and battery and, since he hadn't appeared on the shoplifting charge, he ended up doing some jail time. As far as Donna was concerned, the timing couldn't have been worse. She was frantic that he might not be out in time for the birth of their baby, but Cowboy didn't seem concerned. He knew that the best cons earned their stripes by time spent on the inside and he seemed determined to become the biggest, baddest con of all. Father or not.

Donna gave birth to a daughter named Sherri* on September 12th, 1984, just as Cowboy was finishing up his jail time. Both parents were barely nineteen and Cowboy—the new father—was well on his way to becoming one of Hemet's most notorious criminals.

"I was young," Donna admitted, "and I wanted to be cool too. But I didn't get involved in drugs like Cowboy did. Being pregnant and then nursing gave me a way to say no to drugs and still be cool. That's the only thing that saved me."

Cowboy offered no visible means of support for Donna and Sherri; all his efforts went to satisfy his need for drugs. In the early days of their relationship, speed had been his drug of choice. By the time Sherri was born, Cowboy was a borderline addict, although he hadn't admitted it yet.

Now a welfare mom, Donna took the role of motherhood seriously and tried to keep a decent home for her baby. But she wanted a *real* family, one that included the father of her child. Now that Cowboy was out of jail, they lived a stark existence together in a tiny apartment on the east side of Hemet. Having a happy home wasn't easy with a drug addict in the house. Donna liked country music and always fancied being married to a cowboy. Somehow, her present situation wasn't quite what she'd dreamed of back when she was an idealistic girl of fifteen.

"Back then, I thought he was a real cowboy. That's what he seemed like to me," she said with a tinge of embarrassment.

Donna and Cowboy got married when Sherri was nearly a year old. That was no small feat, as Donna recalled. And it wasn't done completely out of love, certainly not as far as Cowboy was concerned. Cowboy had some charges pending against him and he knew he was headed back to jail. The chaplain told Donna that Cowboy would probably get a lighter sentence if he were married. He'd be viewed as a family man, with a wife and infant daughter needing him at home. It was worth a shot. So, they got married and Cowboy turned himself in a few days later. Donna wasn't en-

39

tirely happy about her new marriage; she knew in her heart that she'd just hitched her wagon to a stationary mule. Cowboy's weeks of incarceration dragged by for her, but she had to admit that when Cowboy wasn't around, life was easier and a heck of a lot smoother.

After his time was up and he was turned loose on the streets, the same old habits took up where they had left off. Married life, fatherhood and all the responsibilities that came with it didn't settle Cowboy down one bit. The situation seemed only to stir up a greater restlessness within him. Coming home to a nagging wife and crying baby sure as hell wasn't his idea of a good time. He smoked marijuana like it was regular tobacco and, by then, was so addicted to speed that he'd spend all the money on drugs while Donna and the baby went without the basic necessities. She was barely able to scrape by; Cowboy undid all her best efforts. The apartment was always full of twitching, zombie-like strangers who came around at all hours of the day and night, stealing her blind.

Donna had an annoying streak of decency to her that irked Cowboy. She began to hide anything of value from him and his gang. Soon she was hiding everything she wanted to keep, whether it had monetary value or not; but, by then, she had few possessions left for him to hock. The apartment was almost bare. Even the baby had almost nothing left by then.

Cowboy turned twenty-one in July of 1986 and unbeknownst to either of them, Donna was pregnant again. About two weeks before Christmas, Cowboy found himself handcuffed in the backseat of a patrol car, arrested on charges of possessing methamphetamines and hypodermic needles. By then, Cowboy was a full-blown addict; shooting-up had become routine. His spindly arms were riddled with poke holes, scabs and speed bumps, which he tried to hide with tattoos. But it was a wasted effort. At a mere glance, it was painfully obvious that Cowboy was an addict.

The situation was particularly discouraging for Donna because Cowboy wouldn't listen to anyone's advice or their pleas for him to quit drugs. Even with another baby soon to arrive, he continued to speed through life with no apparent concern for tomorrow and no thought for the consequences to be paid for breaking the law. Like a million other drug addicts, Cowboy's only concern was scrounging up the money—by whatever means necessary—to obtain his next buy, even if it meant stealing from his own family. No sooner would he shoot up than the cycle would start all over again. He didn't even take time to enjoy the dwindling high. He was so touchy about the situation, Donna tried to stay clear of him; she didn't want to push his buttons. Still, Donna couldn't understand why he didn't get help. Whatever fun or glamour he'd seen in the beginning of his dance with drugs had surely worn off by now. A life centered on drug abuse could never be a happy one, she told him. She pleaded with him to quit and to get into rehab, but Cowboy only saw her as a nagging piece of baggage.

On the horizon, a new year—1987—was about to dawn, a time for resolutions and fresh starts. Almost everyone, at some point in life, used the beginning of the New Year as a fresh start, she told him. She wanted Cowboy to make a commitment to quit drugs. But Cowboy seemed to greet the New Year with a pledge to continue his corrupt lifestyle and his out-of-control drug use. He seemed defiant and proud of what he'd become. Donna was ashamed and desperate for change. By her reasoning, if Cowboy had been half the rough-tough cowboy dude he professed to be, he would have come to the realization that having one small daughter and another on the way was ample reason to turn his life around and get into rehab. Instead, Cowboy chose to gallop headlong down another path, a destructive path of drugs and violence that would eventually pave the way for the murder of one of his own children.

Soon after he got out of jail from the December ordeal, Cowboy was arrested again, on February 16th, for being under the influence of drugs and in possession of a controlled substance, which boomeranged him right back into the slammer. He was twenty-one now and his second baby would be born in a few more months. If this had any affect whatsoever on Cowboy, he didn't let on. To Donna, it was embarrassing standing in line at the jail for visiting hours, feeling the scrutiny of a hundred eyeballs ogling her big belly. In spite of her proud posture, her situation worried and shamed her immensely. Here she was, a young girl in her prime, pregnant and mixed-up with a drug addict jailbird. But she was in the thick of it now, with another baby on the way.

Cowboy did his time and seemed proud of it. Each time he was released from jail he was a little more hardened than before. After the last incarceration, Donna had become scared of him; he was always on edge and irritable. And he was never there when she needed him.

Within a few weeks of his release, Donna was at home when her water broke. The apartment was full of Cowboy's friends, but no one knew where Cowboy was. Scared and apprehensive, she tried to relax throughout the day as her labor increased in intensity. Timing the contractions, Donna was hopeful that he'd show up in time to go with her to the hospital, but it didn't look like she was going to be able to hang on that long. With every contraction, she cursed him.

Cowboy's friends ended up driving Donna to Hemet Valley Hospital. It was a cramped, roundabout ride, as she remembered. There were six people in the car...and Donna. And Donna was writhing in labor. By then, it was nighttime. They drove all over Hemet, stopping at all of Cowboy's haunts. Finally, they managed to locate him. He piled into the car, stoned and stinking of marijuana, bringing the headcount to eight—nine counting the unborn baby.

Donna delivered Cowboy another daughter hours later. They named her Angela*. Cowboy saw Angela's birth, but he didn't know anything about coaching and was no help whatsoever in the delivery room. In fact, Donna would have been better off without him. The next day, when he came to visit her in the hospital, he stole her bedside phone. She didn't see him do it or notice it was missing until she reached for it to make a call, but the phone was long gone.

When it came time to go home from the hospital, Cowboy didn't show up to claim his wife and daughter. Nor was he at home babysitting his other daughter. No one knew where he was. When Donna opened the pre-packed overnight case that all expectant mothers pack ahead of time, she found a cruel joke inside. One of Cowboy's girlfriends had stolen all the clothes that Donna had packed. Her things had been replaced with one tiny, sleazy outfit; about a size five, that was way too small for her. Humiliated at having no one to take her home and nothing to wear, Donna called her mom and asked her to come get her—and could she bring something to wear home from the hospital? Something loose and comfortable please. It was so embarrassing. To add insult to injury, she was billed for the stolen telephone.

The evening Donna and little Angela came home, Donna had the cops forcibly remove Cowboy from her house...and her life. She had put up with his problems long enough. If two kids couldn't straighten him out, nothing could. Things had gotten so bad that she'd slept with her purse during the last year of their marriage. It was just as well. He was blazing a fast path straight to prison anyway and she didn't want the children to be exposed to it all.

April of 1987 was a tough time for Cowboy. Not only had another daughter been born to him; he'd been thrown out of his own house and he was in trouble with the law again. Although Donna surmised as much, she'd gotten rid of Cowboy just in time. His life revolved entirely around drugs; mainly speed. There was no time for marriage, children and a wife who blatantly showed her disdain for drugs.

Donna realized as long as she shared his name, his troubles would continue to haunt her. With a feeling of desperation, she made the decision to legally sever him from her life. In September of 1988, Donna filed for dissolution of marriage and reclaimed her maiden name of Darin. She hoped that shunning the Setzer name would give her a new, fresh start and some much-needed peace of mind. Cowboy received written notice of her intentions while he was serving a prison sentence at California Institute for Men, in Chino. Donna had a suspicion that Cowboy's parental visitations would be practically nonexistent and getting child support payments from him would be like trying to get blood from a stone. The years ahead would prove that she had been an accurate judge of Cowboy's character. He would be arrested at least twelve times within the next seven years and serve six prison terms, all due to drugs. In spite of the countless months he spent behind bars at the county jail and the years spent in prison confinement, Cowboy always headed straight back to Hemet and never wasted any time getting right back into trouble. Many of his arrests happened within days of his release; several times he was arrested on his first day of freedom.

Due to statewide overcrowding in jails and prisons, Cowboy was often released after serving only a fraction of his sentence. For most of his offenses, he was merely booked at the Hemet Police Department and released on his own recognizance and his written promise to appear. Much to the dismay of Hemet police he almost never showed up for his court dates. He was a chronic violator of the terms of his probation and parole, but because his crimes of selling drugs, being in the possession of drugs and under the influence of drugs were not seen as crimes that were particularly dangerous to society, he received extraordinary leniency from the courts. The much talked about "three strikes" program looked good on paper and certainly sounded effective during news conferences, but jails and prisons were overcrowded and Cowboy had learned how to wrangle the system.

Like other drug addicts, Cowboy never stayed in one place too long, frequently vanishing just before the rent came due or the law came calling. Eviction notices followed soon after his arrival. Much of what should have gone into the rent coffers was sucked up into a needle and injected into his veins. Donna had learned the hard way that when it came time for Cowboy to choose what was most important to him, he would always choose drugs.

As the years wore on, his methamphetamine addiction escalated and his crimes became increasingly violent. Along with drugs, the crimes of robbery, auto theft and assault brought the law down on him. Hemet police were as discouraged as anyone with their inability to do much with Cowboy, except arrest him. What the judge and the people at the California Department of Corrections [CDC] chose to do with him was completely out of the hands of Hemet PD. Cowboy was very familiar to most Hemet police officers, but some of them passed him off as nothing more than a nuisance to society. To some Hemet police, Cowboy was nothing but an aspiring criminal; a wanna-be gangster. Throughout his life, Cowboy had shown little interest in becoming a valid wage earner. Although several of his prison commitments offered him the opportunity to learn job skills, Cowboy seemed uninterested in the programs or the prospects of bettering himself. During his short stints of freedom, Cowboy remained unemployed and constantly in trouble with the law.

By the summer of 1993, Cowboy had rotted away much of his life in prison. He'd missed the precious first years of his children. He'd also missed the rejuvenation of his community. By the time he was paroled in July of 1993, his youngest daughter was already six and Hemet had changed dramatically. By then the Diamond Valley reservoir project had been gearing up for some time and Hemet had blossomed into a prosperous town that Cowboy scarcely recognized. In spite of the sudden and tremendous surge in the local economy, most of his old haunts continued to be in areas that didn't see one red cent of the lavish improvements bestowed on the majority of Hemet. His territory remained the same, ugly and downtrodden flop houses where drug deals were rampant even in broad daylight. These areas

Deadly Thirst

were considered to be least responsive to improvements and the last to see funding or refurbishing. By January Cowboy was back in prison.

Drugs were his obsession. He cared about little else. "Trouble" became another nickname which was proudly tattooed on the left side of his neck. As the spring of 1994 approached, Cowboy had been a hard-core addict for many years. His whole body bore the unmistakable signs of drug addiction. His skinny arms were scarred with tracks; he was jumpy; his disposition was constantly volatile and agitated. Gaudy, jail-style tattoos that bragged of gang affiliations covered the upper half of his body, including the full length of both his arms.

But it was July of 1994 that marked an important milestone in Cowboy's life. Within ten weeks of being released from his sixth prison commitment, Cowboy managed to sire a new and tragic addition from his gene pool. He accomplished this through the cooperation and carelessness of a young brunette he'd become acquainted with among his circle of drug-addicted friends. Her name was Laura Utley.

CHAPTER 3

LAURA LEANNA UTLEY
Her path of self destruction

Laura Leanna Utley's birth was the result of an unplanned pregnancy. Her mother, Dawn Masterson,* was nineteen at the time she met sixteen-year old Terry Lee Utley. Dawn was working as a carhop at an Indio drive-in theater in California's Coachella Valley when she became pregnant. Terry was still a baby-faced kid in the eleventh grade of high school.

The legal age of sexual consent in California is eighteen, which made Terry Lee Utley a tempting piece of jailbait for nineteen-year old Dawn. Statutory rape charges can be filed against anyone over the age of eighteen who has sex with a minor. It matters not one iota if the minor is male or female, nor does it matter whether or not the minor gives consent to the act.

When Terry learned of Dawn's pregnancy, he quit high school, took a janitorial job and the two lovers moved into a small apartment on South Jackson Street in Indio. A few months later, on November 7th of 1970, they were married in Coachella. Terry was now seventeen and Dawn was twenty. Laura Leanna Utley was born eleven weeks later in Indio. Things were rocky right from the start, especially the marriage.

Dawn had a solid commitment to her daughter and to the integrity of her marriage, but Terry was just a kid and few would hire an unskilled seventeen-year-old. The birth of his daughter had come way too early for him; he just wasn't prepared. Neither was Dawn, maybe more than Terry, but still, with the new baby and all, life was tough. They couldn't get by on a carhop's paycheck and a janitor's income. Their intentions were good, but the marriage didn't last.

Terry Lee Utley abandoned his wife and baby daughter when Laura was thirteen months old. He was eighteen then and aching to experience his freedom. A wife and baby presented a serious hindrance to his independence and his fun. His visitations were sporadic and, if he had his way, nothing more than a quick conjugal opportunity for him. Within a few months he disappeared altogether.

Dawn tried her best to avoid welfare, but, with Terry gone, there were no other options for her. Trying to better herself, she quit her job at the Indio Drive In. Dawn began working as a legal filing clerk for the Riverside County Clerk's office in Indio, hoping to get a better paying position when the opportunity presented itself. Surely a file clerk had more opportunity than a carhop did. Even so, her gross monthly salary was in the mid $700

Deadly Thirst

range. Income taxes took nearly $100 and union dues gobbled up almost $75. After union dues and taxes were taken out, she was left with only about $450 a month.

Dawn was prudent, choosing to stay in the Jackson Street apartment because the rent was cheap at $130. It galled her at times to think that her rent was almost equal to what she paid the babysitter. Sometimes she cried at the injustice of trying to stay off welfare. It would be easier to collect welfare and stay home with Laura than to pay a babysitter, Uncle Sam and the almighty union.

There were a lot of good things that could be said about Dawn Masterson. She had guts and enough gumption to succeed, come hell or high water. She continued living at apartment #15 on Jackson Street because it was close to work and it was cheaper than any other place she knew of.

As a single working mother, Dawn wasn't able to give Laura exactly what she would have intended, but she did her best. Still, they lived a rather hand-to-mouth existence that could only be described as "precarious." It seemed her days were held together by one common thread: determination. Every day was a financial challenge. As it was, she was getting back and forth to work in a rattletrap Volkswagen bug. Dawn worried a lot about how the bills were going to be paid and how she was going to make ends meet.

With time, Dawn's take-home pay increased and she began rewarding herself with a drink now and then. After six years of struggling to raise Laura single-handedly, Dawn had reached the breaking point with Terry's non-existent role in their lives. As the summer of 1978 began, she'd made up her mind to file legal documents severing his parental custody rights, not that he'd ever shown an interest in being a parent. After all, she'd only heard from him twice in the past two years and those were only short phone calls that ended in argument. He had refused to tell Dawn his whereabouts and had refused to send support money.

It was just as well that she dumped Terry Utley when she did. Shortly after his vanishing act he got mixed up with the wrong side of the law. During the summer of 1978, he had several warrants out for his arrest. Dawn tried to find Terry by calling his mom, also a local Indio resident, but she either didn't know where Terry was or she didn't want to tell Dawn.

Dawn was alone in her efforts to raise her daughter, now seven years old. Severing Terry's parental rights wasn't a decision she made in haste, but why should she grant Terry any say in Laura's life when he had been nothing more than a sperm donor? While working at her file clerk job at the Indio Courthouse, she'd learned a few things about divorce, custody rights and no filing fees for people like her who couldn't afford to pay.

On August 30th, she drove her ailing Volkswagen to the Superior Court of Indio and filed papers for Freedom From Parental Custody and Control against Terry Lee Utley. She was so financially strapped that she was entitled to have filing fees waived as an indigent. It was humiliating though, to have to disclose her meager assets, paltry income and expenditures.

At that time, she was making $761.60 a month at her file clerk job. Uncle Sam took $92.36 and her union dues were up to $77.54. After some other deductions from her check, her take-home pay was $467 a month.

Rent on the Jackson Street apartment had risen to $140 and childcare was now costing Dawn $120 a month. Her one and only asset at that time was her fourteen-year-old VW bug. She jacked up the value of the bug and claimed it was worth $400. She had to list all the things she spent money on and that was particularly embarrassing. Dawn managed to eek by at the supermarket and rarely spent more than $110 a month for food, which boiled down to a starvation diet of $27.50 a week. Utilities were kept to the absolute bare essentials and totaled a manageable $20 a month. If she stuck to these expenditures and spent money on nothing else, Dawn had exactly $77 a month left. But she had to spend money on gas and there were always little things she needed for Laura. And every so often she liked to have a drink. For work, she needed a new pair of nylons every once in a while. Little things. A dollar here and a dollar there. The monetary fruits of her labor never lasted very long. There was always too much month left over at the end of the money. Making one pair of nylons last at least a week was mandatory for a young lady on a tight budget. If a pair should run before the week was up, well, there was nothing she could do about it except act like it just happened. In Dawn's tightly budgeted world, money couldn't be spent frivolously. Laura was outgrowing her clothes faster than Dawn could buy them. Where would the money come from? It was enough to give her a nervous breakdown. She sometimes relied on hand-me-downs to clothe herself and Laura, but at least they had clothes. Even in her dire straits, she knew there were people a lot worse off than she was.

Since Terry Utley was nowhere to be found, Dawn couldn't have the papers served directly to him. She was forced to run a public notice in the Indio Daily News proclaiming her intentions to erase him from Laura's life forever. The ad ran in the October 2nd paper. It said, in part: "To Terry Lee Utley, you are required to appear in the Superior Court of the state of California on October 27, 1978 at 8:45 A.M. to show just cause why the above named minor should not be declared free from parental custody and control."

Terry Utley never showed up in court. Dawn was awarded sole custody of Laura on November 3, 1978. Although she didn't know it, she'd given Terry the boot just in the nick of time. A mere six years later, he would be arrested on charges of molesting his friend's ten-year old daughter and for carrying a loaded firearm. At the time of his arrest, Laura was thirteen and in the midst of budding puberty. If the body of his friend's ten-year-old daughter had excited him beyond reason, could he have resisted an incestuous relationship with a pubescent girl sprouting breasts and flaunting the aromas of dusting powder and cologne?

Now, Dawn was officially on her own and Laura would remain safe from Terry. Alone, Dawn was more determined than ever to raise her daughter in the most dignified manner possible. No mother wants to see her child grow up to be anything other than a happy, respectable, productive individual. Dawn was no exception. Laura, on the other hand, was a lot like her father. She was rebellious early on.

As Laura entered her teens, it was apparent that she was not going to be easy to handle. Although Laura and Dawn were close in many aspects, Laura had a wild streak and was growing up way too fast. Since Dawn was at work five days a week, she wasn't always able to oversee what Laura was doing. Laura was a firecracker early in her teen years and Dawn wondered how much worse it would get before Laura was able to move out on her own.

Tough love had just come into vogue in the mid-80's and Dawn tried many times to tough it out with her rebellious daughter. But her love was stronger than her tough stance toward her only child and too frequently Dawn sought an easier way to ease her burdens. For Dawn, relief came with liquor. By then, her drinking problem had worsened, right in the middle of Laura's teen years. As it often happens, Laura started drinking too. They had moved to Hemet where Laura fell in with a rather discouraging group of hoodlums and, somewhere along the way, Laura was introduced to drugs. At first, it was just pot. Laura didn't think anything was wrong with that. Smoking pot was nothing; all the kids were doing it. She couldn't understand why her mother was so freaked out about it.

Once Laura started drinking and smoking pot, everything seemed to go haywire. She became more wild and unruly. Dawn ranted and raved about it and sometimes resorted to threats, but it all amounted to nothing. Dawn knew it was useless to try to tell a headstrong teenager anything. At that age, they know it all. But then, drinking wasn't exactly something that Dawn could condemn her daughter for. That would have been hypocritical.

Dawn fought a hard battle, but wasn't able to remain free from the scourge of alcohol addiction. She sought comfort from a bottle habitually. Dawn worried a lot about her troublesome daughter and what the two of them were going to do just to eek by. Dawn's alcoholic intake had steadily increased over the years and, as 1989 appeared on the horizon, a whole other batch of problems arose, which put Dawn at a crossroads. It was around that time when she admitted to herself that she was, indeed, an alcoholic. The bitter truth was hard to swallow, but who said life would be easy? Dawn knew that addictions could be overcome. With effort and determination she could succeed at putting the bottle behind her for good. Lord knows she'd tried before and failed. But she would try again.

Meanwhile, Laura complained that her mom was an alcoholic *and* an abusive bitch. In return, Dawn complained that Laura was totally out of control, drinking and smoking pot and God only knows what else. At times it felt like war: mother/daughter war. Although neither knew it at the time, Laura's most urgent problem wasn't alcohol or drugs.

Laura may have been only seventeen when she started sharing time between the sheets with twenty-year-old Lauren Gerald Strait. Before long Laura had something to show for it. She'd been eighteen a whole month when she became pregnant.

The news of Laura's pregnancy clobbered Dawn like a full body slam. She was devastated and fearful of how the baby would be raised. Laura was not exactly a stellar member of the community and neither was Lauren Strait. They were into drugs and Laura's pregnancy couldn't possibly be looked upon in a favorable light. But, it was useless to try to talk Laura into giving up her baby, and an abortion...well, that was out of the question.

As Laura's pregnancy became more apparent, the impending role of grandmother left Dawn with mixed emotions. Regardless of Laura's wild ways and the fact that their relationship was extremely splintered, Dawn did have an inner glow of anticipation about her forthcoming grandbaby. Perhaps it would have been more truthful to phrase it as anticipation mixed with high anxiety. Laura's pregnancy forced Dawn to make a turnaround in her life. Laura's baby would undoubtedly need Grandma's help and alcoholism wasn't something Dawn wanted to expose her grandbaby to. She feared the baby would be exposed to enough bad elements in life as it was and she was determined to at least make *her* contributions positive. Her grandchild deserved to have a good grandmother and, by God, she was going to do her best.

In line with the determination and will power she exerted in everything else, Dawn made up her mind to quit drinking. This time she was successful. She knew she'd be helping Laura raise the baby and there was no room for alcoholism; at least not Dawn's alcoholism. Laura had to make her own decisions, but Laura's mindset wasn't as admirable as Dawn's.

Eighteen-year-old Laura delivered a boy in November of 1989 at Hemet Valley Hospital. She named him Jonathan*. Dawn rightly sensed that she would be the most dependable adult in Jonathan's life. She vigorously set about trying to find better work for herself and succeeded in getting hired at the Agricultural Commission Weights and Measurements. True to her premonitions, she looked after Jonathan much of the time.

As Laura turned twenty-one, she was on probation and already neck deep in the criminal element of a drug-abusing lifestyle. Many of the public defenders and judges at the Hemet courthouse were familiar with the name Laura Utley.

During these turbulent years, Dawn and Laura lived near each other in Hemet. Although Dawn was perplexed and, at times, completely exasperated with her daughter's drug problems, the two managed to maintain a mostly amicable relationship—for Jonathan's sake—as long as they didn't spend too much time together. After all, Dawn was caring for Jonathan extensively while Laura professed that she was trying to get her act together.

Some days Laura seemed sincere in her efforts to get clean; other days she regressed to a dangerous degree. There was no predicting where she would go from here.

The way Laura was abusing drugs, there was only one place, for sure, that Laura would eventually go and that was to jail. While there were minor infractions along her path of drug addiction, by the time she turned twenty-one, Laura had taken on an alarming rough edge.

In May of 1993, when Laura was twenty-two and Jonathan was four and a half, Laura was arrested for being in possession of a switchblade knife. The people she was hanging out with were a rough crowd and quite possibly she needed that knife for protection—and probably for intimidation as well, although she didn't admit to that.

Two months later, when it came time for her to appear in court on the switchblade arrest, she was nowhere to be found. A warrant was issued on July 19th, but warrants meant nothing to Laura. It just meant the cops were looking for her and, if they found her with an outstanding warrant, she might go to jail. But she knew the system and, more than likely, she'd merely be booked and released. Another court date was scheduled for November, but Laura blew that off too and generated another warrant. In June her probation was revoked when she failed to show up for yet another hearing. Finally, in April of 1994, Laura was arrested and arraigned and pled not guilty. Pre-trial conferences started piling up and Laura managed to make appearances at several, but in June there were other, more important things going on in her life and Laura just didn't have time for court.

Dawn agonized that Laura was making no obvious resolutions to better herself. She made little, if any, effort to get into rehab or to raise Jonathan. To Dawn, it didn't look like Laura was going to get her act together any time soon. She still hung around the same crowd of drug dealers and abusers and she was still attracted to men that weren't doing her any good. The one that would make a lasting impression on her and those closest to her was the one everybody called "Cowboy."

CHAPTER 4

DOUBLE TROUBLE
Cowboy and Laura ride the fast track together

Cowboy was released from prison on April 21st of 1994. He was twenty-nine. Cowboy and Laura were so much alike it was pitiful. By the time summer rolled around, they were steadily riding the fast track together; that is, they were getting together quite often to shoot speed. Theirs was a hardscrabble existence that revolved entirely around drugs, especially methamphetamines.

Toward the end of June 1994, Laura once again failed to show up for a court hearing and another warrant was issued for her arrest. Laura had been using meth for quite a while by then. Like Cowboy, she was skinny, downtrodden and straggly-looking. During his brief stints of freedom, Cowboy played guitar in a local rock-n-roll band and considered himself to be a talented musician. Laura made sporadic, half-hearted efforts to get herself employed as an honest wage earner, but every now and then she was tempted to sell a little dope to make ends meet. Maybe she'd skim a little off the top of every packet for herself and sell the rest. If there was a gap left after she'd sampled a little dab, she might fill in the void with inert ingredients. Who would have known the difference?

At first, methamphetamines made her feel like the life of the party. It brought on a feeling of power, at least, for a short time. Meth produced the same high as cocaine but the high lasted a little longer and it was cheaper. Soon though, she couldn't lead a normal life without it. Almost without warning the euphoric high, once so enjoyable, had turned into a vicious, stabbing need. The need grew quickly. She learned the hard way that, unlike cocaine, high doses of meth or chronic use of the drug caused highly elevated nervousness, irritability, violence and extreme paranoia. As an addict, she surged with violence on the way down. The cravings were so powerful she would do just about anything to get it. Cowboy had been at that stage in his life for many years; Laura seemed to be right behind him.

Most cops would admit that meth addicts harbored a sour smell all their own. Some thought it rivaled the stench of death, a rancid body rotted from the inside out. They called it "the smell of the defeated living," a smell that spoke more of hopelessness than any words could have ever conveyed. The stench of dope—especially meth—oozed from every pore; putrid breath spewed from a mouthful of neglected, rotten teeth. Cops knew the smell.

51

There was something else going on around that time. Laura hadn't been feeling well lately. She had a sneaky suspicion about what might be ailing her. A pregnancy test confirmed that she was expecting again. She told Cowboy about it as soon as she was certain and he wasn't happy with the situation either. In spite of Laura's pregnancy, they kept right on shooting speed.

Cowboy was arrested on August 6th of 1994 for possession of marijuana and failure to appear, but once again he was booked and released. A few weeks later, he took advantage of the court's leniency and failed to appear again.

The courts had given him every opportunity imaginable to get his life straightened out. With another baby on the way, his probation officer strongly urged Cowboy to show some effort in the support of this child, his third. Cowboy was forced to enroll in a work release program, which could have done wonders for his bleak situation, but he ignored the program and never showed up. He just wasn't interested. As a "crankster" he was busy and easily lost track of time. He was too busy looking for his next buy. He could concentrate on only one thing: drugs.

On the 29th of October, Cowboy was arrested for being under the influence. The cops ran a check on him and noted his FTA history [failure to appear] as well as a failed appearance on the August 6th marijuana arrest. In spite of all that, Cowboy got leniency from the court, once again.

Despite the fact that Laura was now four months pregnant with his baby, it didn't seem as if Cowboy was trying to get clean. Just as shocking, it didn't look as if Laura was either. It was amazing that they didn't see the light, but they didn't. They were always on the run and, by now, Laura was almost as addicted to speed as Cowboy was. Pregnancy didn't seem to matter to either of them.

During the first week of February, at a new address on 7th Street in San Jacinto, Cowboy was arrested after he failed to appear for his work release program. His life was like a house of mirrors; every direction he proceeded in was wrong. No matter which way he turned, he bumped into law enforcement. Cowboy didn't seem to realize that going straight was the only way out of his self-created maze. He was speeding his life away, racking up fines left and right while Laura was becoming pretty big around the middle.

Laura was now only six weeks from delivery and she was still abusing methamphetamines like there was no tomorrow. Prenatal care was practically nonexistent. Because of her drug addiction her general health suffered a great deal, not to mention the health of her fetus. When she did drugs, her baby was forced to do drugs as well. Laura not only abused drugs, she abused her unborn child.

The state of California has something called "presumptive eligibility Medi-Cal." Usually, a drug-dependant, expectant mother may come in and get a pregnancy test. If it's positive she can get emergency Medi-Cal, which is effective immediately, for thirty days. But the woman has to make a formal application for Medi-Cal at the Medi-Cal office within those thirty days. It pays for prenatal services and is a lifeline for thousands of women like Laura. Even so, many women fear being arrested if they're discovered to be using drugs during their pregnancy. In actuality, the law doesn't work against pregnant women.

"The way the laws are written," said a nurse at the OB clinic in Hemet, "we can't do anything for her fetus at this point. If we called Child Protective Services, they wouldn't be able to do anything either, because there's no child born yet. And we couldn't turn her in to the police either, because her medical records are confidential. All we can do is help her get into a drug rehab program, but it's up to her."

Even so, Laura was none too thrilled at the prospect of having to go to a doctor. Mainly because she was broke, uninsured and addicted to drugs. It's uncertain whether Laura understood that in California a non-pregnant woman would have to pay for her own drug rehab, but if that woman was pregnant, she could get free rehab and also free prenatal care. The emphasis was on treatment and healthy families, not punishment.

"The fetus has no rights until it's born," said the OB nurse. "In any event, she will be tested for drugs when she comes in to deliver. A lot of women just show up at the very last second because they know they'll be forced to do blood and urine tests and they're afraid they'll be arrested or their baby will be taken away. Even if a woman waits until she's in labor to apply for Medi-Cal, it will still pay for her delivery."

If there was ever a time for Laura to get help, it was now. As Laura's second child approached its debut into the world, the health of her baby wasn't exactly in the forefront of her mind. Her veins were screaming for more speed. Laura knew she had to make a decision. For the sake of her baby, she needed to quit drugs. And she tried. She stayed clean for a few days and then she gave in again.

On the morning of April 26th, Laura began to feel the pains. They were subtle at first. She was nervous and desperately wanted to shoot some speed just to take the edge off. The thought plagued her relentlessly throughout the day as her pains increased. As her labor grew stronger, her resolve grew weaker. When the pain got so bad and she could fight her craving no more, she gave in to temptation and did some crank. Just to help with the pain and to take the awful craving away. She was in agony. She would only do it this one last time and never again. She promised herself. Never again.

By morning, she was ready to deliver. Full of apprehension, she headed for the hospital. As expected, Laura was screened for drugs upon her admittance to Hemet Valley Hospital. The social worker, as well as the nurses, spoke frankly with Laura about her drug addiction and explained what her options would be. CPS would have to be notified. It didn't necessarily mean that her baby would be taken away from her and, she would not be arrested. CPS would want to investigate her living situation to make sure she had

Deadly Thirst

adequate means of taking care of her baby and herself. Up until now, Laura had not taken care of either herself or Jonathan or her unborn baby. They did warn her though, that it was likely the baby would be taken until she could straighten herself out and go through drug rehab and a mandatory family reunification program. It wouldn't be easy. She wouldn't be arrested, but she'd have to follow the stipulations of the court; and if there was one thing Laura wasn't good at it, was following the court's instructions.

As she lay writhing in the advanced stages of labor, the social worker also warned Laura that if her baby was taken from her, she would have to appear in court after forty-eight hours and the judge would tell her exactly what she'd have to do to get her baby back. Even if she were to deliver a "clean" baby, more than likely she would be closely monitored by CPS to make sure she stayed clean.

Sadly, the reality was, no matter how much preaching and saber rattling was exerted, babies born to mothers like Laura usually got placed into foster care because the mother didn't follow up on the court appointed program. Then, the child would be placed into adoption.

Drug-tainted or addicted babies are considered "special needs babies." Some can't eat, some are cranky, some shake with violent tremors and suffer through convulsive withdrawals. For nurses, watching a newborn baby pay for the mistakes of its mother is heartbreaking. Some feel it should be mandatory that all pregnant drug addicts be forced to watch the first twenty-four hours of an addicted baby's struggle to live. In spite of all the warnings and the free drug rehab programs the county offers, a large number of drug babies were being born in Hemet. The maternity ward was full of meth babies, especially.

Laura was luckier than she realized. As soon as her baby was born she would be eligible for WIC, [Women, Infant & Children] which would help her with food stamps. She could also get Aid For Dependant Children [AFDC] for three years. AFDC would send her to a program where she could learn job skills. At that moment, Laura had the best chance ever of making a decent life for herself and for her children. Perhaps there was hope after all. It certainly seemed that with the help of these programs, she'd be able to turn her life around.

The hospital social worker warned Laura that if her baby were put into foster care, she wouldn't be able to visit the child until she went to court. At that point, there could be *one* visit with her baby, which would be supervised by a social worker—*if* she went through the rehab program. Laura was told, flat out, that it wouldn't be conducive for the child to keep seeing its mother while in foster care.

"Think about it," they told her, "this child is going to pay the consequences for what you have been doing." With that, they brought out the lights and the stirrups. It was time to push.

PART 2
AND BABY MAKES THREE

CHAPTER 5

ANDREW THOMAS SETZER
Born tainted and destined to suffer

Andrew Thomas Setzer was born on April 27, 1995. Laura was twenty-four. If there's any truth to the theory that newborn babies look into their mother's face to gather some sort of identity, some form of self, it's certain little Andy assembled a stark and dismal vision of reality.

As soon as Andy was born, he was drug tested and diagnosed as tainted with methamphetamines. The social worker was immediately notified and paid Laura an in-hospital visit. She'd been forced to give urine and blood samples when she was admitted and the results came back positive for meth, just as she knew they would. Under pressure, Laura tearfully admitted that she had used meth on the day prior to giving birth, but she was trying to quit.

It was decided that little Andy could stay with Laura, at least for the time being. Social workers noted that Laura's mother seemed to be a positive influence and perhaps the baby's birth would be the moment of awakening for Laura. Social workers always have hope and certainly, Dawn had hope. Dawn was absolutely enthralled with Andy right from the second she laid eyes on him.

After a few days, Laura and Andy went home; that is, they left Hemet Valley Hospital and vanished into thin air. Two attempts were made by the Department of Public Social Services [DPSS] to locate Laura and Andy, once on May 5th and again on May 28th. Surprisingly, even though Laura was a known addict and Andy had been born tainted, since DPSS couldn't find Laura, her case was closed due to the lapse of time.

Several months passed and as autumn approached, Laura seemed to be giving a half-hearted attempt at straightening herself out. The New Year came and went, uneventfully. By then little Andy was eight months old.

On February 20, 1996, Cowboy was sent back to prison. With Cowboy gone, Laura was even more determined to stay out of trouble, but it wasn't easy. Temptation was all around her. Luckily, DPSS had made contact with Laura by then and they were working with her to see that things were maintained in an acceptable way for Andy. On March 6th, a social worker came

Deadly Thirst

to Laura's apartment in Hemet and conducted the first home visit. During this visit, the social worker inspected each room of Laura's apartment. She looked into the kitchen cupboards and refrigerator to see that there was sufficient food and she checked to see that the home had utilities and basic necessities. She was pleasantly surprised and noted on her report that Andy and Laura were doing well. About two weeks later, another social worker, a man, made a second home visit and noted that Laura and Andy were bonded. They were doing well, they had food and everything was fine.

Unbeknownst to DPSS, Laura had begun to slip back into heavy drug use and things were not as fine as they seemed. Cowboy was due for early release from prison soon and when he got out, he and Laura were planning on getting a place together. This was not good news to Dawn. She begged Laura to stay away from Cowboy. At that point, Laura could still have saved herself and little Andy, but Cowboy seemed to be headed straight to hell. Dawn warned Laura that any association with Cowboy would do nothing but drag her down. Dawn begged Laura to turn Cowboy out to pasture.

June 4th Cowboy was let out of prison and, he headed straight back to Hemet. He moved in immediately with Laura and fourteen-month-old Andy. Within a few weeks, the atmosphere inside the little apartment had changed dramatically—for the worse.

On August 25th of 1996, an anonymous complaint was called into CPS concerning Laura and Cowboy. The caller made allegations of abuse toward Andy. The sixteen-month-old toddler was reported to have a handprint across his face. There were also hard drugs being used at the home, namely heroin and speed, the caller alleged. DPSS promised to send a social worker to the apartment as soon as possible. Five days later, on August 30th, a female social worker went to the apartment and conducted an unannounced face-to-face visit with Laura. Things were not going smoothly since Cowboy came back to town. It was apparent that Laura couldn't live with a drug addict and not succumb to using drugs herself. The social worker was appalled at what she saw. Laura didn't look well, the apartment was filthy and there was no electricity. The meeting was worrisome, for both Laura and her caseworker. Shortly thereafter, Laura abruptly moved, taking Andy with her. Cowboy soon joined them.

On September 25th, CPS received a call that said Laura was at Sun Ray Addictions, a rehab facility in Hemet. There, she admitted to counselors that she had an open case with CPS and that they were looking for her. The staff at Sun Ray was worried about Laura and Andy. Laura appeared extremely thin, stressed and very tired. Her overall health had been neglected. But it was Andy, in particular, that upset them. He was such a cute little boy, an innocent victim of his mother's drug addiction. If Laura was hell-bent on destroying her own life, that was her problem. But to drag an innocent child into the dangers of a drug-addicted lifestyle was something most people at Sun Ray just couldn't stomach.

The next day social workers, accompanied by Hemet police, paid a surprise visit to Laura and Cowboy's apartment. What they saw was frightening. The apartment was appallingly filthy and there were used syringes on the floor. Police made Laura roll up her sleeves and show them her arms. More than a dozen needle marks were noted. Cowboy's spindly arms had also been punctured repeatedly. As Laura was arrested for being under the influence of drugs, police discovered that she had three outstanding warrants against her. Cowboy was arrested too and sent back to prison for parole violation. Hemet police removed Andy from the apartment and handed him over to CPS.

The following day, September 27th, Andy was placed in a temporary shelter; he was seventeen-months-old. Laura had asked her mom previously to take Andy and she did for a while. But Dawn was living in an adults-only mobile home park and she had her hands full just trying to hide Jonathan from the supervisor. Dawn wanted very much to have custody of Andy, but she wanted the arrangement to be long-term. She didn't think it was good to bounce kids back and forth. Being a mother is either a full-time commitment or nothing at all. Dawn began looking for somewhere else to live. She decided to sell her mobile home and move someplace where she could keep both of her grandsons.

Laura didn't stay in jail very long and within a few days she had reclaimed Andy. CPS had had a very stern talk with Laura and she'd agreed to take part in a voluntary parental support program. CPS warned her that they were not going to put up with much more. As much as Dawn worried about her daughter and her two adorable grandsons, there was nothing she could do to get Laura pointed in the right direction. Tough love was hard for Dawn to dish out, even though she tried. Looking into the innocent face of Andy, Dawn couldn't help but pledge support. In spite of their differences she loved Laura. Andy had instantly wormed his way into her heart and Jonathan—thanks to major help from his grandmother—had grown into a fine six-year-old boy.

Around the middle of October, almost three weeks after Laura's arrest and while Cowboy was still in prison, another anonymous complaint came in to CPS. The caller alleged that Laura was abusing drugs again. Social workers moved fast to find out what was going on. Two attempts were made to locate mother and child, once on October 24th and again on the 31st. On that last day of October, Dawn again told the case worker that she would like to have custody of Andy and this time CPS thought Dawn's offer was probably a good one. It was obvious that Laura's drug problems were here to stay, at least for a considerable time and CPS was obligated to try to place the children with suitable blood relatives whenever possible. They were relieved that Dawn had offered. During the month of November, they made three more unsuccessful attempts to locate Laura and Andy. By then, another anonymous complaint had been phoned in to CPS. This call centered on child abuse, not drugs.

Deadly Thirst

By then, Cowboy's half-sister, Doris Velmere,* was also expressing an interest in taking Andy. Doris had kids of her own and had been doing her best to help Cowboy and Laura clean up their act. For some reason, although she wasn't licensed for foster care, on November 15th, Doris was chosen instead of Dawn to have custody of Andy. Feeling slighted by CPS, Dawn began making the necessary arrangements in order to qualify as Andy's legal guardian. Ditto for Doris. Dawn had a good job at that time; she'd been employed by the Agricultural Commission Weights and Measurements for several years and she'd been sober all that time as well. Everything seemed to support Dawn getting custody of Andy and yet he was sent to live with Doris. Dawn vowed to keep trying.

Although Andy wasn't quite three yet, he held his own with his older playmates. In fact, he stood his ground with almost everyone who looked after him while his mother was trying to get her act together. The wrangling spirit inherited from his father went hog-wild during Andy's so-called "terrible twos" and Aunt Doris was frequently irritated to find that Andy had taken all her silverware outside to dig in the dirt. Spoons became dump trucks that chugged along, filling plastic buckets with mountains of dirt. She couldn't turn her back on him one minute that he wasn't into something else. He was faster than greased lightening and simply not to be trusted around an open beverage of any kind.

On January 3, 1997, Doris finally got around to signing a foster eligibility form with DPSS and one month later, a social worker paid a visit to Doris' home. Andy was observed to be doing well, although the social worker noted in her report that housekeeping standards were relaxed and that Doris had no phone or car. In spite of this, Doris' home was deemed to be adequate but it was also quite crowded. Still, Andy seemed to be happy there, so that's where he remained.

Shortly thereafter, Andy was officially declared a dependant of the court. If Laura were to regain custody of Andy now, she'd have to go through the rigors of the court-mandated programs and that wasn't likely to happen. In the year 1997, only thirty-five percent of the people referred by social workers to county drug programs successfully completed the course. So, Andy remained with his Aunt Doris.

Laura, now unencumbered by either of her children, continued her collision course with disaster. Cowboy had introduced her to a couple named Clinton and Jennifer Darling. Jennifer was Cowboy's half-sister. If there was one thing that could be said about Laura, it would be in reference to her slick, chameleon-like ability to camouflage herself. Somewhere in her circle of jailbird friends, Laura had learned the power of masquerading behind an alias. And true to the lack of value common among drug addicts, it mattered not at all whose identity she chose to steal, nor how much trouble she caused the individual. Jennifer Darling's past had already been somewhat blighted by various tickets and penny-ante drug possessions. But Jennifer had two kids with Clinton and they were at least making an effort to stay

58

out of trouble. That was not to say they were staying away from drugs, just that they were more careful about what they did than Laura and Cowboy were. According to Clinton's relatives, Cowboy was viewed as a trouble-maker. When he started bringing Laura around they became a bad influence on both Jennifer and Clinton. Pretty soon, Laura started causing problems on her own. Although only one person knows for sure how it happened, Jennifer's wallet was stolen along with all of her identification.

* * *

On March 3, 1997, two caseworkers from the County of Riverside's Department of Social Services conducted an unannounced face-to-face visit with Doris Velmere. They observed Andy with a shaved head, dressed in shorts and a Harley T-shirt, playing outside the house and they noticed he had a black eye. On closer examination, they saw scratches and bruises on his face. From the opposite side of a locked screen door they questioned Doris about this and asked to be allowed inside the home to look around. Doris told them they could not come inside because she was moving fur-niture around. She brushed off the injuries to Andy, saying they'd been caused by horseplay. The caseworkers looked at Andy's back and chest for other bruises or scratches but found none. They didn't check his buttocks. With an uneasy feeling about the whole situation, they took two Polaroids of Andy and included them in his case file. Then they left.

Meanwhile, Cowboy had been serving time in Ironwood State Prison in Blythe, California. Ironwood is well known as perhaps one of the best pris-ons in which to get vocational training, education and job support. Inmates can get a GED [general equivalency of high school diploma], learn valuable job skills and get the chance to better themselves in anticipation of their release. Cowboy had all these favors bestowed upon him and on April 10th he was released back into society. Right away, it was obvious that he was none the better after his latest stint behind bars.

In a disastrous turn of events, on June 15th, Doris was arrested for be-ing under the influence of drugs, which threw a wrench into her plans to keep Andy. It also flushed her already stretched-to-the-max finances straight down the toilet. Social workers moved as fast as they could to revisit Doris' home after her drug arrest. Six weeks later, a meeting took place and Andy was reportedly doing well at that time.

Seven days after Doris was arrested on drug charges, the police arrested Cowboy for selling hypodermic needles without a permit. This time he used the alias of Lauren Gerald Strait, the father of Laura's first child. As usual, he was booked and released on his signed promise to appear. It was a date that would never happen.

It was 10:40 P.M. on July 27, 1997 when Hemet police again made con-tact with Cowboy. Police traveling westbound on Oakland Ave., noticed a car coming toward them with only one headlight illuminated. Making a u-turn and activating the overhead lights, the officer pulled over a gray Honda with a familiar-looking person at the wheel. The driver identified himself as

Thomas Setzer and he admitted that he didn't have a valid driver's license. The police asked him to step out of the car. When he complied, they immediately knew he was under the influence. His speech was very rapid and he couldn't keep still. As they talked to him, they noticed he was grinding his teeth. When the flashlight was shone into his eyes, his pupils didn't react; they remained dilated. It was a sure sign of being under the influence of speed. Police asked Cowboy if he'd done any dope lately and he admitted that he'd eaten some speed about 1:00 P.M. that afternoon. *Click* went the handcuffs. He was booked and released with a hearing date of September 9th. But Cowboy didn't show up and, like all the other hearings and arraignments he sloughed off, another warrant was generated for him.

On August 14th, there was a review hearing concerning Andy's situation at Doris' house. Although Andy was reportedly doing well with Doris, Laura had sunk to an all time low. According to the report, she had no permanent address and was essentially homeless, owning few possessions other than the clothes on her back. There was no indication that either Laura or Cowboy had put any effort toward Andy's well being. In fact, at the time of the review hearing, Cowboy's whereabouts were unknown. Laura was referred to several drug rehab centers such as Our House, House of Hope, La Vista, and Sun Ray Addictions. But she continued to wallow in self destruction.

On September 13th police caught up with Cowboy again. Rumor had it that Cowboy was holed up in a little apartment on Elk Street in Hemet. Officers went there shortly after 8 A.M. on a parole search and, sure enough, there was Cowboy, under the influence—again. Hemet PD hauled him in and the revolving doors of justice allowed him to be booked [using the alias of Lauren Gerald Strait] and released. In spite of the fact that Cowboy's criminal history was ample testimony that the book-and-release method wasn't having any positive effect on him, and in spite of the fact that he was a chronic parole violator and rarely appeared on his written promise, Hemet PD once again decided to book and release him on everything, including the outstanding warrants. He was scheduled to appear before the judge on October 31st.

Four days later, on September 17th, he was arrested again for possessing and selling hypodermic needles without a permit. This time, he was in the company of a female friend. Since his dilapidated Honda had been impounded, Cowboy and his lady-friend were getting around via bicycles. While on routine patrol, Hemet PD had noticed two people riding their bikes on the sidewalk, which was in violation of the law. So, with lights activated, the squad car pulled in front of the two bikers and forced them to stop. Right away, the officer recognized Cowboy from prior contacts. The woman with him was familiar too; she was April Lamb*. The officers first dealt with Cowboy, asking him if he had any weapons on him. Cowboy said yes, there was a syringe in his pocket. He was immediately arrested.

Then the cops dealt with the woman. She was "speeding" so fast she couldn't keep her mouth shut for more than a few seconds. "She kept interrupting me while I was talking to her," the officer said. "I noticed fresh puncture wounds on both of her arms directly over her veins. Both of her arms had fresh scabs on them and on her left arm I saw a wound that was still bleeding slightly." April Lamb admitted to shooting up the day prior, but the officer was fairly certain, due to her still-bleeding arm, that the shoot-up was much more recent. Probably within the past hour or so. Both of them were booked and released. Cowboy, who by now was regularly using the alias of Lauren Gerald Strait, was scheduled to appear on October 29th, two days prior to his last scheduled appearance. Like every arrest before, this one was nothing but a slight inconvenience. Cowboy was audacious and had little, if any, intention of showing up for anything. Eventually though, this arrest would cost Cowboy forty-five days in jail.

Sixteen days later, on October 3rd, he was arrested again for possession of meth. This time, cops had been called about a fight in progress at 127 S. Juanita Street in Hemet. The caller said it sounded physical. Two units were dispatched and two officers followed the noise toward apartments six and seven. As they approached, a woman who had been standing on the front porch ran back into the apartment when she saw the law coming. With a loud bang the door was slammed shut behind her. The officers knocked. From within, a male voice innocently asked, "Who is it?"

"You know it's the police. Open the door!"

About thirty seconds later, the door slowly opened. The officers immediately recognized Cowboy. From behind him came a cloud of smoke and the whole apartment seemed to be burning.

"The apartment was filled with smoke," one officer said, "and I could smell something burning." Apparently, the apartment was without utilities. Cowboy had been burning papers for light! Officers peeked into the apartment and saw a woman wiggling around on the couch. They immediately recognized her; it was Cowboy's bicycle-riding friend from a few weeks prior and they suspected that it was the same woman they'd seen running back into the apartment moments earlier. To be sure, one officer went into the smoke-filled bedroom, but it turned out that April Lamb and Cowboy were the only people in the apartment.

Cowboy said that there were no problems between he and April and seemed surprised that the police would come knocking on his door. The officers could tell Cowboy was under the influence and they could plainly see fresh puncture marks on his arms, some still raised and red. Cowboy exhibited all the symptoms typical of speeders and after flunking the Rhomberg test, he was promptly arrested.

Next, police concentrated on the woman who was wiggling around on the couch. They asked her if she'd been the one involved in the disturbance and she said no. The officers couldn't help but notice she was speeding too. They asked her if she'd been using drugs and she denied it even as she

Deadly Thirst

continued to squirm around on the couch. "Not since yesterday," she spat in a rapid-fire burst. The officers stood there and looked at her, sizing her up. She was—no doubt—under the influence and even though she denied it, she gave off obvious signs. She was extremely agitated, constantly moving and vigorously rubbed her fingers together throughout the conversation. They checked her pulse; it was twice as fast as it should normally be. Her pupils were dilated, her mouth was pasty white. They asked her to show them her arms. Reluctantly, she held out both arms and they saw the fresh, dotted tracks of IV drug use. She was immediately placed under arrest.

The only thing left to settle was who'd run into the apartment just as the police arrived. Since there was no one in the bedroom and no rear exit, it was determined that the woman seen on the front porch was the same woman who had been lying on the couch, trying to appear relaxed when Cowboy casually opened the door.

Cowboy was so well known by then, that almost every officer in Hemet knew his face and his reputation. But still, burning papers for light! They looked at each other and shook their heads in disbelief as they transported Cowboy and April Lamb to the station where they were booked and promptly released. Both were given an appearance date near Thanksgiving, but Cowboy would let the November 26th arraignment date slide by just like the others. He seemed determined to get in at least one more arrest before the end of the year. He exceeded his goal; he was arrested *two* more times. By the end of 1997 his criminal history would include seven new arrests. His next arrest was, of course, for being under the influence and for failing to appear. It happened right after Thanksgiving, on November 30th. In spite of the fact that he almost never appeared on his signed promise, he was once again booked and released on his own recognizance.

It was December 12th. While San Jacinto police were on routine patrol they did a traffic stop on a car full of folks who, at first glance, looked awfully familiar. Before it was all over, there would be so many people involved in this arrest it would take eight pages of statements for police to explain it all. This time children were involved. And so were guns.

A guy named Ron Fisk* was driving. With him, were two females, Dana Rust* and Denita Benner*. Officers immediately recognized Fisk from prior dealings and knew Rust was a drug rehab registrant who was currently out on parole. Ms Rust was asked to exit the vehicle and as she complied, officers found a plastic-wrap bindle that contained an off-white powder. Officers assumed it was speed. In a field test, it proved to be 1.6 grams of pure speed. In her purse was a glass smoking pipe and a glass snort tube. *Click* went the handcuffs.

Ron Fisk was asked to step out of the car. He admitted that he didn't have a valid driver's license, but he did have a knife. Yes indeed he did. Officers pulled a huge double-edged dagger from his right boot. *Click* went the handcuffs.

Donna Goodenough

When officers searched the car, a 22-caliber revolver was found under the driver's seat and nine bullets were found on the dashboard. Fisk and Rust were booked at San Jacinto PD and were determined to be under the influence of drugs. Ms Benner was not arrested or cited.

Ron Fisk had stated that the three were on their way home and gave his address as 1013 Seventh Street in San Jacinto. The officers thought it would be wise to go to the residence to see if Dana Rust had been adhering to her parole terms. Upon arrival, they found a whole slew of people living in the tiny house. Two of those people were infants belonging to Dana Rust.

A young woman who'd been living at that address for two years did most of the talking as police looked around. She said that Fisk and Denita Benner were a "couple" and had been living there, sharing a bedroom, for only two weeks. Since Dana Rust was on parole, her bedroom was thoroughly searched and the officers found a machete, another double-edged dagger, half an ounce of meth and additional drug paraphernalia. In the garage, a triple-beam scale was found and booked into evidence along with all the other stuff. Throughout the search, Dana Rust's infants lay nearby. It was definitely cramped quarters; a total of eight people were living there. Ten counting the infants. Officers were amazed at the size of the machete and the double-edged daggers. They were deadly weapons alright; one good swing and you could almost cut someone in half.

In a roundup of other occupants, two of them happened to be none other than Cowboy and his girlfriend, April Lamb. Not surprising, both were found to be under the influence. The young woman who had answered the door seemed sincere in her efforts to be honest with police and she admitted that she too had had some problems with drugs in the past. And, she admitted, drugs were being sold from the house. She seemed ashamed in her plea for leniency and said she had tried to get the others to quit selling drugs from the house. In all, four people were arrested. Cowboy was one of them.

For Cowboy, the year of 1997 was a banner year for arrests. Seven in Riverside County alone. April 27th, June 22nd, September 13th, September 17th, October 3rd, November 30th and December 12th. Finally, Cowboy had pushed the judge far enough and prison commitment was ordered. But it would be a short stint. For reasons that, officially, remain unexplained to this day, Cowboy served only eight days in prison, although his early release might have been due to overcrowding. He was shipped back to Hemet, to thumb his nose at the cops who'd arrested him only days prior.

In January of 1998, social workers met with Laura and told her that the time allotted for her to get clean and sober was almost up. They told Laura they knew she loved Andy, but it was time to ask herself if she loved him enough to stop the drugs and alcohol and start a safe and healthy lifestyle. If so, Andy could eventually be returned to her. As the New Year unfolded, it seemed that trouble loomed ahead for almost everyone involved in Andy's life.

Deadly Thirst

By February 2nd 1998, an unfortunate set of circumstances had developed at Doris' home. She phoned her caseworker and reported that she could not keep Andy as she had hoped. She'd been having financial problems since her arrest and she'd decided to move up to Humboldt County. She also complained that Laura had been visiting Andy lately and Doris didn't like it. Even though Doris reluctantly had to give up Andy, she still made it clear to CPS that she wanted to be notified if anything went wrong with his new placement. She'd take him back in a flash. But it would all be wasted breath because three days later Doris was arrested again on drug charges. That was the end of Doris Velmere's presence in Andy's life. Laura was nowhere to be found and couldn't be contacted about her son's dilemma. Once more, Andy was uprooted and sent to another unlicensed caretaker. Once more, Dawn Masterson was passed over as Andy's legal guardian.

Cowboy, true to his nature, was arrested again for drugs on February 12th. He was released on probation almost immediately, but he never appeared on the charges.

February 12th would also mark the beginning of a very confusing odyssey that would forever merge the identities of Jennifer Lyn Darling and Laura Utley, at least as far as the CDC was concerned. On the same day Cowboy was arrested, someone claiming to be Jennifer Lyn Darling was arrested on drug charges involving meth. Court documents show that she was booked under the name of Jennifer Lyn Darling with the alias of Laura Utley. She was charged with being under the influence, possession of methamphetamines for sale and possessing hypodermic syringes. The forty-year-old male friend she was with was arrested for selling meth, being under the influence of a controlled substance and having a .22 caliber revolver in his possession.

Some theorized that Jennifer had always assumed Laura had been the one who'd stolen her wallet in order to use her identity and that Jennifer had retaliated by using Laura's identity. Others theorized that it was actually Laura Utley who had been arrested on February 12th and identified herself as Jennifer Lynn Darling. No one knew for sure, except Jennifer and Laura and they weren't giving up any secrets. The situation wouldn't get scrutinized until eighteen months later when the public finally got wind of a possible mix up and began demanding answers. Meanwhile, the mysterious woman booked in as Jennifer Lyn Darling, AKA Laura Utley, was in serious trouble with the law and quite possibly headed for a hefty prison term.

Almost simultaneously, another review hearing was being held to see if Cowboy and Laura were making any progress whatsoever in the family reunification program. The mere fact that county officials even considered this notion was preposterous; yet they held a hearing to discuss this remote possibility. In spite of the fact that Laura had been given more than ample opportunities to get clean—at the county's expense—and regain custody of Andy, she remained a bloody-armed crankster. She had not complied with the orders to submit to drug testing, but how could she with both arms

64

Donna Goodenough

sporting more poke holes than a voodoo doll? And Cowboy? What had he contributed toward the welfare of his son?

CHAPTER 6

INTO FOSTER CARE
Andy's death sentence

This time, Andy would be moved to what some might consider the lap of luxury. After Aunt Doris was arrested, he was sent to the home of Mary Broughton* in the new upscale community of Menifee, about thirty miles south-west of Hemet and just outside the beautiful, gated community of Canyon Lake. Perhaps this would be the move that proved permanent for Andy; although, like all the others, his newest foster mother was unlicensed.

Despite the problems his biological parents were having, Andy was thriving and growing like a flower in sunshine. Mary Broughton enrolled Andy in a fine preschool and he seemed to be adjusting to his new environment quite well. Undoubtedly, it was the best care that Andy had ever received in his lifetime. However, within a couple of weeks things began to change. At first, it was subtle. Then after a few more days, Andy's teachers began to notice that he was displaying aggressive behavior with the other children. He wasn't minding and he had become a bully to some of the smaller kids. This upset Mary and she mentioned it to her caseworker the next time they spoke on the phone.

Perhaps Andy had inherited his aggressive behavior from his father. Cowboy, using the alias of Lauren Gerald Strait, had been arrested on a warrant and was incarcerated in Banning, a town near Hemet. While he was cooling his heels in the Banning jail, he assaulted another inmate on March 3rd. According to the jail's correctional deputy sheriff, a bloody-faced inmate approached him and reported that Cowboy had ordered the inmate to get out of the barracks or be "socked up." The inmate, who was equal to Cowboy's height and weight, refused, so Cowboy let him have it. The inmate was transported to the hospital with a broken nose and a bruised ego.

Laura was doing no better. On March 8th, she was arrested again for being under the influence of drugs and for failure to appear on her last arrest. Courthouse records show that at the time of her arrest she was using the alias of Cowboy's first wife, Donna Setzer. Laura was slick and the *real* Donna Setzer, who by that time, had reassumed her maiden name of Darin, remained unaware that her ex-husband's girlfriend was soiling her name.

After that, Laura managed to stay out of trouble for almost an entire month until she was arrested again—this time with the alias of Donna *Lynn* Setzer—on April 7th for being under the influence. While Andy's parents were falling farther into the abyss, Andy was doing an about-face. Of the three, Andy was the only one who was getting his act together.

After Andy had lived with Mary Broughton for two months, he learned how to behave himself and in the process, managed to charm the pants off the entire neighborhood. Everyone loved Andy, especially a young couple that had been friends with Mary for many years.

Mike and Lynn Herman* had thoroughly enjoyed every encounter they'd had with Andy. There was just something about that little blonde-haired, blue-eyed, grinning-faced boy that set their hearts on fire. By the time April rolled around, Mike and Lynn had lain awake many nights talking earnestly about the seven good years they'd been together and the little blond-haired mischief-maker that had stirred some yearnings within them. Always convinced that children would happen when the time was right, they suddenly felt anxious. Too anxious to wait. Seeing the joy that Andy brought to Mary made the Hermans consider getting into the foster care program themselves. There were so many kids who needed loving homes and so few homes available. On April 21, just six days before Andy's third birthday, Mike and Lynn Herman submitted their foster home application to the state. They were thrilled. They found it almost impossible to think that life could get any better than this.

Andy's grandmother, Dawn Masterson, was still expressing a strong desire to take custody of Andy and had recently been in contact with Andy's social worker. Dawn was told that Andy was in a new foster home and that he was doing very well there. Across town though, things took a dramatic plunge a few weeks later when Mary became seriously ill. She became so sick that she couldn't care for Andy on her own. In fact, she could hardly care for herself. Since Lynn had known Mary from the time she was eleven years old, Mike and Lynn invited Mary and Andy to move in with them.

Andy was astounded to find himself in such lavish surroundings. The house was enormous from Andy's point of view; a blue two-story with a tile roof, a big, round-top picture window in the front and a white garage door that would open, like magic, when he pressed a button. He even had a room of his own. Compared to the first two and a half years of his life, the Herman's home seemed like a royal palace to Andy. It was sparkling clean and spacious beyond anything he'd ever known. The lawn was healthy and green, manicured to perfection. Along the sidewalk leading to the front door were thick blankets of gaily-colored flowers.

* * *

While Andy was reveling in his new home, Cowboy was sent back to prison for a few months as a result of his face-bashing antics while in the Banning jail. He served some of that time at Folsom.

* * *

Oblivious to the problems his parents were having, Andy bonded almost instantly with the Hermans. When it didn't look like Mary was going to be regaining her health anytime soon, Mike and Lynn asked that custody of Andy be transferred to them. Mary had complete confidence in Mike and Lynn and the transfer seemed like destiny for everyone involved. During the first week of June the state made a "pre-license" visit to the Herman's house and noted that they seemed to be perfectly suited for Andy and vise-versa. Five days later, the state approved their foster home license and by the end of the week, Andy was officially their foster child. They began calling him Andrew John Herman, but mostly just "Andy."

Right off the bat, Andy flourished. If there was one thing all of Andy's county-appointed guardians could agree on, it was that he was quite a talker. Now that he had adults who would listen to him and interact with him, he had all kinds of things to say. He would count aloud, recite his colors, and he carried on long-winded conversations with anyone and everyone. He could talk the hind leg off a mule. Some swore he'd been vaccinated with a phonograph needle. And laugh, laugh, laugh. The slightest thing would launch him into gales of laughter.

Eventually, Mary reclaimed her health and resumed life on her own. From the beginning, Mike and Lynn were adamant about telling Andy the truth concerning where he came from and why he had come to live with them. They told him his real mother and father loved him very much but they couldn't keep him. By the end of the conversation, Andy understood that his real parents were very sad to lose him, but Mike and Lynn were very happy that Andy had come to live with them. Andy thought it was cool to have so many grandmothers.

Mike and Lynn were glad to let Dawn be a part of Andy's life. They understood that Dawn was not responsible for the mistakes her daughter had made; they knew Dawn was a decent woman and she loved Andy with all her heart. She sincerely wanted what was best for Andy.

Since Lynn was an elementary school teacher and Mike a computer salesman, it wasn't long before Andy was enrolled in a Montessori preschool and could mouse his way across the computer screen. His room soon filled with toys and games, enough to keep him—and ten other kids—happily occupied. Andy was thriving like never before and the Hermans felt that their sudden good fortune was somehow a dream. A dream that neither wanted to ever wake up from. Everything was perfect.

Andy was a quick learner. Lynn taught him some sign language and Andy would work it into his conversations without prompting. They bought him roller-blades that appeared huge on his little feet. They bought a helmet and enough pads to make sure his elbows and knees would never get scuffed. They taught him to skate in the kitchen and then they turned him loose on the neighborhood sidewalks. He seemed destined for Roller Derby. They bought him a swing set and Mike spent hours putting it together in the backyard. As the swing set was taking shape, Lynn looked out the window to see Andy giving Mike close supervision, pelting him with a never-ending barrage of questions.

Donna Goodenough

His preschool teacher labeled Andy a leader and marveled at the way he could organize games with the other kids. He was a take-charge kid, not shy in the least. He seemed far advanced for his age and within a few months he was saying "hello" in Japanese, Spanish, French and German. As far as Mike, Lynn and Andy were concerned, things couldn't have been better.

* * *

Cowboy, on the other hand, had been released from prison on August 31st and had come straight back to Hemet. He was arrested again on drug charges in mid September and was eventually sentenced to a year in county jail for it.

* * *

Dawn was having some problems too. She had recently married a man she hadn't known that much about and the marriage was already on the skids. Along with all the other nerve-wracking things that were happening concerning Laura, she filed for an annulment on the grounds of fraud. The split was businesslike; each party got to keep whatever they'd brought into the marriage and neither got any property that had belonged to the other. The annulment was a relief. Dawn was too wrapped up with Andy to cloud her mind with marital problems. After all those years of being single, why had she jumped into marriage at this time in her life? Dawn felt she needed no one else to accomplish the goals she had set for herself. She was a strong, independent woman. She didn't need a husband hanging around her neck. She chided herself for being so gullible.

* * *

Meanwhile, the long hot summer was finally coming to a yawning end and a cold autumn wind began to blow. It's unclear exactly what happened in the Herman's Menifee neighborhood in mid-September of 1998, but it would mark the beginning of a long and painful ordeal for many people. According to a county report, after Mike and Lynn had returned from an evening at a neighbor's house shooting pool and drinking with friends, Lynn had walked into the garage and caught Mike in an embrace with a woman who lived nearby. Heated words were exchanged and Mike left. A short time later, he returned home, calmed down and ready to talk rationally. Lynn and Mike were open and honest enough to discuss the incident, the ensuing argument and their resolution of the problem with their social worker soon after it happened. They stressed that Andy had definitely not seen or heard the fight because he'd been asleep. Mike admitted to an inappropriate relationship with the other woman and said he'd been extremely upset in his flight, but they had worked it out and things were fine again.

Still, child protection officials went on the defensive and claimed that Andy had probably heard some shouting. They concluded that due to Mike's inappropriate behavior Andy had more than likely overheard some verbal abuse between his foster parents. Yelling in front of the children, the social worker said with a blanched look of disdain, was against the rules.

69

Nothing more was said or done about it and the Hermans assumed it was settled...until three months later. The woman that had been involved in the embrace incident called police and accused Mike of attacking her in his garage that September evening. A report was filed but the woman said she didn't want Mike arrested. Nonetheless, Mike was vulnerable to some serious criminal charges. While Mike and Lynn were still grappling with the ramifications of the charges, their social worker received a strange phone call from someone claiming to be Andy's aunt. She said her name was Jennifer Darling and she wanted to adopt Andy.

By December of 1998, the time CPS had allotted Laura to get clean had run out. Mike and Lynn wanted to formally adopt Andy and since Laura had not complied with the terms of the family reunification program, Andy was cleared for adoption. At last it looked as if Andy was about to become "theirs." But first, CPS needed to get in touch with Laura and tell her. But where was she? She'd always been hard to track.

They finally located her in The California Institution for Women in Frontera. State prison. She'd been booked under the alias of Jennifer Lynn Darling and was serving a sixteen-month sentence for drug charges stemming from the February 12th arrest. Since Cowboy was in prison too, the parent reunification efforts were terminated once and for all on December 18th. The Hermans could now adopt Andy. They applied immediately.

To celebrate, they took Andy to Sea World where he had the time of his life. He came home completely tuckered out and smothered in the back seat by stuffed animals, trinkets, Shamu memorabilia and fish books. He'd seen fish swimming around in tanks so big he could scarcely believe his eyes. It had been a day to remember, for everyone. When they finally arrived home and pulled the car up to the garage, Andy was fast asleep, still clutching his stuffed Shamu. Mike picked Andy up and carried him inside. Lynn pulled back the covers on his bed and watched her husband lovingly tuck Andy and Shamu away for the night. They would unload the car in the morning. Life was good after all.

Still, all was not going exactly on course for Andy. He had some potty-training problems that once in a while got the better of him. He wet his pants and messed in them from time to time, but Mike and Lynn took it all in stride. After all, Andy had been shuffled around an awful lot in his short lifetime so a little mishap here and there was no big deal. It was to be expected of a "special needs" child, which Andy was. If there was anyone who could have raised Andy to become a conscientious adult, it was Mike and Lynn.

Not long after the excursion to Sea World, they took Andy to the San Diego Zoo. They were amazed at how much fun they had watching Andy's reaction to all the animals. They couldn't help but think that if Andy were still with his birth mother, he would probably never have gotten the chance to see the wonders of nature. Lynn and Mike were thankful they could bring some sunshine to Andy's life and they were grateful that he had brought so much happiness into theirs. They truly loved Andy and had begun to actually count the days until the adoption would be final.

1999 started with Cowboy being pulled out of Folsom for his final child custody hearing. Andy was up for adoption and the Hermans had applied. But Andy's grandmother, Dawn Masterson, was again asking for custody. She had recently begun working, coincidentally, for the Department of Social Services' Hemet office as an eligibility assessor. She'd made the move because she felt she could get better advancement and better pay. Her life was good and solid and she was still caring for Laura's first child, Jonathan. She wanted to raise both of her grandsons together.

The caseworker mentioned something to Dawn about some allegations against Mike and Lynn Herman and said that if the allegations proved to be true, Andy would have to be removed from the home. Dawn made it clear she was ready and *very* willing to accept Andy anytime. The caseworker told Dawn to have her ducks in a row and, if Andy were indeed pulled from the Herman's home, that she would be getting custody. Dawn was tickled pink.

Cowboy was released from Folsom prison on March 21st, but he didn't seem too disturbed about the prospect of losing Andy to adoption. Andy's birthday, April 27th, was right around the corner and would have been the perfect time for Cowboy to arrange to see him one last time, but he didn't.

On April 8th, just nineteen days prior to Andy's fourth birthday, DPSS made their annual visit to the Herman's home and disparagingly noted unlocked wine, beer and knives. DPSS also paid a visit to Dawn's home in Hemet and gave her a favorable review but warned her that Andy had relapsed a bit in his toilet training. This news didn't phase Dawn in the slightest; she assured the caseworker that she could deal with Andy's potty problems and any other problems he might have.

Andy's fourth birthday was a joyous occasion. And it couldn't have come at a better time for the Hermans. They needed a little giddy detour from the turmoil they had recently been experiencing, courtesy of their friend Mary Broughton. Lynn suspected that Mary had committed fraud in Lynn's name. Lynn confronted Mary, demanding repayment for the debt. According to Lynn, Mary countered by threatening to do whatever she could to get Andy taken away from them. When Mary wouldn't pay off the debt, Lynn called the police to see what could be done. Supposedly, this infuriated Mary and that's when all the trouble started.

On May 9th and 10th, two people made anonymous complaints to CPS alleging physical, sexual and emotional abuse of Andy by Mike Herman. The callers also alleged that Lynn had made Andy go without clothing and had told Andy he'd have to wear a diaper for defecating in his pants. The caller reported that Mike was heard screaming at Andy and had slapped him across the face. Within ten days, the Department of Public Social Services was banging at the Herman's front door wanting to discuss the allegations and have a look around. They also wanted to inspect Andy. Horrified, Mike and Lynn insisted the allegations were untrue, but their words fell on deaf ears. During the search of the premises, social workers found a loaded gun in the garage, which wasn't locked away safely. They were aghast to learn that Andy had been left in the care of "unlicensed people" namely, Mike and Lynn's very capable and loving parents.

To Mike and Lynn, the accusations were enough to shatter their world; but when social workers stood in their living room, looking down their noses at them and lecturing them about leaving Andy with "unlicensed people" they were too shocked to respond. How in the hell could CPS find it perfectly acceptable to shuffle Andy around from one unlicensed home to another and then punish the Hermans for supposedly doing the same thing for extremely brief periods of time? It angered them beyond their ability to think straight. By the time the social workers left, Mike and Lynn were so mad they were shaking. How could good intentions get so screwed up so fast? It was an appalling injustice to even *think* that Mike and Lynn would ever abuse Andy. CPS was always complaining about the shortage of good foster parents, yet they failed to see the shortage was, in part, due to the way the system treats the "good" parents.

The Hermans felt fairly certain they knew who'd made the anonymous complaints. To their way of thinking, it had to have been Mary Broughton. Who else would do such a thing? And there was something else that Mary Broughton had done that irked the Hermans. She'd contacted CPS and said she was interested in regaining custody of Andy.

At the same time, from prison, Laura had supposedly turned over a new leaf and had suddenly become a concerned parent. She wrote her social worker a long letter, vowing once again to turn her life around and expressed her fears for Andy's safety. *"As long as he is safe and is taken care of, and not hurt, that's all I care about right now. I think about him and pray for him every day. I am hoping and asking you to PLEASE make sure Andy is all right and taken care of, PLEASE!! Sometimes I have dreams…more than I should, so please go see him and make sure!! Thank you."*

Although Mike and Lynn didn't know it, on May 26, 1999, the state of California completed its investigation of the allegations against them. Allegations of physical abuse [spanking and hitting Andy because of toilet training problems] and emotional abuse due to the diaper threats were sustained. They also concluded that the Hermans had tried to change Andy's identity by calling him a different name. Furthermore, they felt that Andy had been subjected to general neglect when he witnessed fighting between Lynn and Mike over Mike's inappropriate relationship with the neighbor woman. In conclusion, they decided that Lynn had failed to protect Andy from Mike's abuse. Social workers wrote in their report that Mike was impulsive and unpredictable. Unbeknownst to Mike and Lynn, spanking was one of CPS's most frequently cited reasons for intervention. But, they remained oblivious to the department's findings. No one at CPS said a thing to them about it. Mike and Lynn had no idea what was in store for them.

Also unbeknownst to either Mike or Lynn, an unsubstantiated, anonymous tip is all it takes to become listed as a child abuser and/or molester on the Child Abuse Central Index, or simply CACI. Once a person's name is added to this list, that person becomes listed for life. There's no way to get off the list once you're on, not even if the allegations are proven to be false.

"That's just the way the Child Abuse Index works," snipped a Child Protection spokesman in Sacramento California.

Teachers and physicians are required to report even *suspected* child abuse or molestation, but allegations can just as easily come from disgruntled neighbors or anyone vindictive enough to want to stir up mega trouble for someone else. California takes a vicious stance against sexual predators of children. Almost all businesses, organizations and clubs that employ people to work with children cross check a person's name to see if they are listed with CACI. Based on the whim of one person, careers can be cut short, families divided, reputations irreversibly slandered, employment denied and innocent people thrown into financial ruin. Being registered on CACI can easily ruin an innocent person's life. No matter how secure a foster family may be, they are never more than one accusation away from catastrophe.

Just as frightening is the fact that the person who makes such an anonymous allegation—even if it is made maliciously—is guaranteed complete anonymity and immunity. In fact, accusations of child abuse and molestation are some of the most effective weapons used in divorces. It is also a devastating weapon for anyone with any reason, political or personal, to destroy the career and good reputation of someone else. The Hermans were poised to find out how much damage an unsubstantiated complaint can do.

CACI works completely opposite to the principle that a person is to be presumed innocent until proven guilty. What boils down to an outright violation of constitutional rights is a common and much respected practice for the child protectors. The United States Constitution provides that an accused person is entitled to due process and a fair trial. CPS and those in charge of maintaining the CACI registry seem not to be familiar with any of these elements of due process and fairness. Apparently, CPS doesn't always operate inside the bounds of the Constitution.

Mike and Lynn were oblivious to the fact that an immediate removal of Andy from their home was ordered. CPS notified Dawn Masterson and told her to get ready. Get her ducks in a row.

On June 3rd, while Mike and Lynn were at work and unaware of all the arrangements that were being made, social workers paid an unannounced visit to Andy's Montessori preschool and seized him. Mike and Lynn would never see Andy again.

According to CPS, Andy would be better off somewhere else. Dawn waited and waited but Andy never arrived. When several days had passed,

Deadly Thirst

she learned that Andy had been sent somewhere else. That's all CPS would tell her.

PART 3
ALVIN & THERESA, THE DEADLY DUO

CHAPTER 7

THE EARLY YEARS OF ALVIN ROBINSON
"Mildly retarded"...or just dumb?

The Webster's New World Dictionary describes a retarded person as some-one who is slowed or delayed in development, especially mentally. Alvin Lee Robinson fit that description.

He was raised in Alabama. It didn't take long for his parents, Leroy and Susie, to notice that something wasn't quite right with Alvin. Although they couldn't say exactly what they thought was wrong with him, compared to other kids his age, he just seemed slow. His slowness became apparent when Alvin started school; he had problems understanding even the sim-plest things. His teacher became concerned when Alvin failed to keep pace with the other kids in his class; in fact, he lagged so far behind his school-mates that his teacher became alarmed. She decided to speak with Susie and Leroy about the trouble Alvin was having and ever-so-gently suggested psychological screening to see exactly where Alvin placed on the scale of intelligence. If he has a mental disability, she told them, it's better to find out about it now. It was a bitter pill to swallow, but Susie and Leroy had had their suspicions about Alvin's slowness right from the start. Still, they couldn't help but feel offended to have his teacher suggest such a thing, even though they knew she meant well.

Even back in the late 70's, it was quite common for schools to provide special no-cost tutoring or study teams for children struggling to keep up with the others. These teams usually consisted of parents, other teachers and sometimes the principal. One or two days a week, after school, the teams would get together and work one-on-one with lagging students. This important intervention and extra help was often all that was required to bring the child up to speed, but in Alvin's case it didn't help.

After a while, Susie and Leroy decided to go along with the idea to have Alvin evaluated by a psychologist. During the exam, his academic function-ing, perceptual development and IQ would be tested and scored. There were ten individual assessment tests for parents to choose from. Conferring with the teacher, parents could chose to have their child tested in all areas of development or just one. Broad testing was always more conclusive and

Deadly Thirst

at the time, it made good sense to have Alvin thoroughly evaluated. Back then, each state had its own requirements for scoring these psychological evaluations and if a child met certain requirements, the school would provide special learning assistance at no cost. This assistance often comes in the form of "Special Day Classes" or SDC.

A few weeks later, Alvin spent an entire day with a psychologist. He was too young to understand that he was being evaluated. This would be only the first of several such evaluations Alvin would receive over his lifetime.

First, his general learning aptitude and his stage of intellectual maturation were carefully measured by subjecting him to a variety of verbal, numerical and visual-spatial tasks. His coordination in body movements came under scrutiny as well as his ability to use and understand English. His current adjustment in social, emotional and behavioral areas as well as his health status were carefully screened and scored. Lastly, and without Alvin's knowledge, he was sent back to his classroom to be monitored by a "planted" psychologist who was introduced to his class as a teacher in training. From her position at the back of the classroom she observed Alvin's every movement and comment. She strolled up and down the aisles of the classroom looking at the assignment each student was working on. As the other children scribbled away, Alvin's paper remained as blank as the look on his face. She followed him outside into the schoolyard and watched him during lunch and recess. Always appearing to be looking the other way when Alvin looked at her, she successfully carried off her observations and was able to give an honest and well-rounded assessment of Alvin's social and intellectual level.

He did not score well. Not only did he score low enough to qualify for SDC, his score landed him squarely in the classification of "mildly retarded." Susie and Leroy were shocked and somewhat indignant at the diagnosis. They knew he was slow…but *retarded?* Surely there must be some mistake. Doctors and educational authorities tried to ease their anxiety by stressing that it was only *mild* retardation. With proper training Alvin could succeed, certainly not to the same degree as other youngsters, but he was what they classified as TMR [trainable mentally retarded].

Alvin's younger sister however, was not so fortunate. Her retardation from Down's syndrome left her completely unable to care for herself in any way. She suffered seizures and would be totally dependant on her parents for the rest of her life. Even in his late teens, Alvin was only allowed to look after his sister once in a while, for no more than an hour at a time, partly because of her seizures and partly because Leroy and Susie felt he couldn't even take care of himself, let alone a person with a severe handicap. In many ways, Alvin suffered the same fate as his sister; he was socially isolated and never developed an independent lifestyle. Instead of teaching him how to succeed, Susie and Leroy let him slack off and withdraw when things got tough.

Donna Goodenough

There's a saying that children learn what they live and there's no better proof of this than Alvin. Although Leroy and Susie didn't realize the damage they were doing with their persistent use of negative reinforcement, Alvin was extremely sensitive to the fact that he was somehow different and wasn't as smart as other kids. He felt like an oddball. After all, he'd heard his parents refer to him as "slow" and if Momma and Daddy said it, it must be true. After hearing this constantly during his developing years, Alvin began to believe this about himself. Feelings of inadequacy plagued him throughout his early school years. Alvin had more than his fair share of developmental and social problems, but then again, a lot of kids do. Although he attended public schools where he was mixed in with normal kids, he continued to be enrolled in SDC classes. During his elementary years he was frequently discriminated against and ridiculed by kids who'd seen him entering and leaving what they referred to as "the retard room." He was teased about being the class dork, which gave Alvin an inferiority complex of a completely different sort. His self-esteem was pulverized long before he was able to form any sense of self-worth, and his parents were partly to blame, albeit unwittingly. From his early school days onward, he always carried a sense of being inferior in everything and, apparently Susie and Leroy kept on reinforcing this with unintentional negativity. They always gave him an easy way out instead of showing him how to cope on his own.

Things had improved slightly by the time junior high rolled around. Even though he was still struggling to learn his alphabet and read, he enjoyed sports as any other boy would and was anxious to participate. A few medical problems kept Alvin off the teams intermittently, such as an operation to repair a hernia when he was fourteen and an appendectomy at eighteen. Even in his adult years, Alvin would look back on his school sports activities remembering the hurt and embarrassment he'd felt at being the last person to be chosen for a team. He was a "leftover" and it hurt his feelings. He'd try to reason with his memories and tell himself that it was because he was asthmatic and needed to use an inhaler, that's probably why the kids had passed him over. But deep inside he knew the real reason was because he was "retarded." When situations got Alvin down, his parents were always there for him, encouraging him to just walk away from the kids that were harassing him. But when the harassment came from within the family, Alvin discovered it wasn't so easy to walk away. What made matters worse, was that the problems Alvin began having around that time concerned his older stepbrother from Leroy's prior marriage. These "problems" were of such a nature that he was sure it wasn't something he could talk to his parents about, especially his dad. And how could he explain what was going on anyway? According to Alvin, the older stepbrother frequently spent the night and began to sexually molest him. There was no way in hell he could talk to his dad about *that*. Not in a million years.

Deadly Thirst

Molestation is often subtle at first, a touch here and there, nothing too obvious. And so it was with Alvin. With each touch, the boy gauged Alvin's reaction. Because Alvin didn't protest the touching at first, the boy's advances got bolder until Alvin finally realized what was going on. Indignantly, Alvin insisted he wasn't a "queer," but his stepbrother was older and wiser; he was someone Alvin had always looked up to. Alvin was still completely green around the gills at that time, but he was curious about oral sex and besides, the touching did spark some arousal in him.

Alvin claimed his stepbrother "forcibly" orally copulated him, many times, and even tried to sodomize him. The fear that this type of behavior might rank him as a homosexual didn't sit well in Alvin's mind. He began to feel guilty and consequently, when this stepbrother would visit overnight, Alvin would sleep in the living room to avoid being subjected to him. The stepbrother was persistent though and Alvin was too weak to resist the gratification of being pleasured. In spite of the thrill he got from it, he still felt it was "wrong" and wrestled with it in his conscience. Nonetheless, Alvin allowed the behavior to continue throughout the next couple of years.

In 1991, when Alvin was eighteen, his family moved from Alabama and settled in California. In spite of the fact that Alvin never did learn to read and write well, he somehow managed to graduate from Valley View High School in Moreno Valley in 1992.

In 1992, Moreno Valley had become embroiled in racial problems. Violent crime was on the upswing and some areas of the city had become gang turf; literally patrolled and ruled by thugs. Walking in these areas, even in broad daylight, was dangerous. Schools were racially mixed, with a high percentage of Latinos and African-Americans. In the years following Alvin's graduation, drive-by shootings became popular. However, a wide portion of Moreno Valley was upscale and considered safe.

It was common for young men and women to go to work right after high school and begin a new life on their own. Most were anxious to get out from under the rule of their parents. But Alvin couldn't seem to swing the dreary task of finding employment and showing up for work every day. For starters, he couldn't even fill out an employment application because he was illiterate.

Alvin had been introduced into the adult world with an IQ of 66, the equivalent of an eight to ten-year old. He finally managed to acquire a driver's license through the help of family and friends. Because he couldn't read or write and still had a problem understanding even simple things, he flunked his written driver's test several times before he was allowed to take an oral exam. He could understand the concept of driving, but the reading and writing part of the test were way beyond him.

As for life in general, there were other obstacles that Alvin needed to deal with. As an adult, he needed to become independent, to get a job and become a responsible citizen. But Alvin was timid and easily confused. He felt inferior to the other people his age.

On the upside, Alvin was a comic, an easy-going kind of guy who made friends fast. He certainly knew how to have a good time, even though he needed a little help sometimes. Alvin's friends knew he had problems coping with the simplest, most trivial things and that he had trouble, sometimes, understanding his obligations, such as reporting to work every day whether he felt like it or not. He didn't comprehend very well so, to hide his ignorance, he took on an attitude of silence and general agreement when he was around other people. Alvin didn't make waves. He didn't want to draw attention to himself, so when problems arose, Alvin's way of dealing with it was simple: he'd keep his mouth shut or he'd leave. That seemed to solve all his problems. Just leave and the problems would go away like magic. Alvin was definitely non-confrontational.

Alvin continued to live with his parents and depended heavily on them for almost everything. His momma did all his laundry and cooking for him. His dad did what he could to help Alvin become independent; often calling upon people he knew to hire Alvin. Whenever Alvin applied for work, he always brought along a handwritten "cue card" that had routine information on it such as his address, phone number, social security number and so on. He also brought along, what he called, his "mini diploma" from high school so that people would know he'd graduated. Even so, a friend or parent always accompanied Alvin when he sought employment and helped him fill out the forms. Several friends, including Chas White*, recalled having to fill out entire applications for him.

"He didn't understand where to put certain information on the application," Chas said. "He had to use the cue card his mother had written up for him, but he still couldn't seem to put the right information in the right blanks. He could sign his name and that was about it."

On several occasions written tests were required, which Alvin sometimes took home and had his friends or family complete for him. A day or two later, Alvin returned to the business and submitted his application and falsified test. Other times, Chas said, he'd just go with Alvin and fill out the application and take the test for him right there. When Alvin finally did land a job, someone had to take him to each new place of employment at least once before he actually started the job because Alvin couldn't read the street signs and had an uncanny knack for getting lost. After learning the route by landmarks, he was able to make his own way into work from then on.

Chas managed to get Alvin a job at Air Force Village West, near March Air Force Base and for a short time they worked together. Alvin's job was cleaning the kitchen. While he worked there, Alvin frequently spent the night with Chas and at the homes of other friends as well. He didn't have a strong personality and resented the fact that the other employees at Air Force Village teased him about being stupid. When feelings of inferiority and embarrassment set in, he quit that job.

Deadly Thirst

A couple of years after the Robinson family moved to Moreno Valley they struck up a friendship with John Davenport*. Davenport developed a strong affection for Alvin and took him under his wing, so to speak. In 1994, Davenport was a supervisor at a Perris mail order company called Star Crest Products. There were plenty of jobs at Star Crest that someone with a mental deficiency could handle and Davenport sought to get Alvin employed as a stocker. Davenport recalled that Alvin had a lot of trouble filling out his work application and that he was much slower than other applicants. Still, Alvin was hired as a stocker, but it proved to be too difficult a task for him so, Davenport got Alvin placed somewhere else within the company. He became a runner for Star Crest, delivering items to different areas of the warehouse. Before long, that job also became too difficult for Alvin. Friends said that he was easily embarrassed about his mental slowness and due to his fear of failure and his low self-esteem, he'd often quit projects before they were complete. Often, he wouldn't produce his best efforts, because he felt that even his best efforts were inferior. Alvin had no confidence in himself and he hated the fact that others were making fun of him. Consequently, he shied away from all but a few people.

When it came to making friends, Alvin made good choices because the few he chose would stay with him throughout his life. John Davenport was one such friend. Davenport sincerely liked Alvin and knew there must be something his young friend could do. Alvin required close supervision all the time and because two people had to be paid to do the job of one, he was hired at a loss to the company. After several positions failed to pan out for Alvin, Davenport sought other work for him. As a last resort, Davenport succeeded in keeping Alvin employed at Star Crest by letting him do janitorial work. But even that position didn't last long. As usual, people began teasing him and Alvin became frustrated and ashamed, quitting soon thereafter.

Davenport had always been a religious man and had become a minister for the United Pentecostal Church about this time. Susie and Leroy frequently called on Reverend Davenport for consultation and guidance and through the years he remained a close family friend.

There were a few other brief employment stints in Alvin's adult life, but none amounted to much. The Cadillac Bowl hired him as a janitor and Alvin was determined to keep the fact that he couldn't read or write a secret. But something like that is hard to hide. It eventually got out and people started making his workplace a place he didn't want to be, so he left. Repeatedly, Alvin was hired to do unskilled jobs with low pay. He'd work for a short time and then he'd quit. He worked at the Green River Country Club in Corona doing kitchen work and as a warehouseman at a place called Texas Wheel. As always, he didn't stay at these jobs for long and continued to live with his parents. He didn't understand the concept of sticking with it. No one told him that when the going gets tough, the tough get going. Alvin's solution to his problems was to leave—walk off the job.

80

Donna Goodenough

Alvin's best and longest-lasting friend was Richard Crane*, a handsome young African-American man who'd befriended Alvin as soon as the Robinson family put down roots in California. Richard also tried to get Alvin jobs. "I knew he was slow," Richard said of his friend. He spoke of how Alvin did an average job at things that didn't require much skill and how Alvin didn't have the perseverance to succeed at anything. It was Richard who got Alvin the job at Cadillac Bowl. They worked together there, Alvin doing janitorial stuff and occasionally helping Richard set up his DJ equipment in the lounge. Alvin thought it was totally cool that Richard owned a DJ service, so Richard decided to hire Alvin part-time to haul and set up the equipment for gigs at other places. Alvin drove a black Chevy S-10 truck that came in handy for hauling all the equipment around. Alvin liked that job more than all the others because he could hang out with friends, meet women and be cool. It didn't really seem like work. Alvin and Richard would be best buds for more than fifteen years.

By then, Alvin was in his twenties and still living at home. Much to the horror of Leroy and Susie, Alvin had taken up the sinfulness of liquor. Susie and Leroy didn't drink and they sternly admonished Alvin for doing so. Still, Alvin made up his own mind about certain things and drinking was what he wanted to do.

Eric Varholms* became a friend of Alvin's during 1996 and recalled that Alvin could get quite belligerent when he'd had a few too many beers. In April of that year, Eric threw a birthday party for himself and invited a bunch of friends over to celebrate. Alvin was one of many attending that night who had agreed to forfeit his car keys and ride home with a designated driver if he had too much to drink. Around 2:00 A.M., Alvin decided he'd had enough noise and he wanted to go home. He walked into the kitchen and demanded his car keys. Eric refused to turn the keys over to Alvin, reminding him that he was drunk and friends don't let friends drive drunk. This infuriated Alvin so much that he grabbed a steak knife from the counter and, again, demanded his keys.

Eric didn't want a scene, so he reluctantly gave Alvin his car keys and watched him storm toward the door. Just as he was about to leave, Alvin turned and punched his fist through the wall. After proudly surveying his handiwork, he jumped into his black Chevy S-10 and recklessly peeled out. Well aware of his own liability if Alvin were to get into a wreck, Eric thought he'd better call the Sheriff and report what had happened. A check was run on the license number Eric Varholms had given and it revealed that a vehicle matching that description belonged to Alvin Lee Robinson of Moreno Valley. Just as Alvin was backing his truck into the driveway of his parents' house, a deputy drove up. When the deputy activated his overhead lights, the truck suddenly lurched backward and struck the front of the house. The driver quickly jumped out and ran toward a fence separating the houses. The deputy yelled for Alvin to stop, but Alvin jumped over the fence and disappeared into the night.

Deadly Thirst

It was about 2:30 A.M. when a knock at the front door of the residence awoke Leroy and Susie Robinson. They appeared fearful as they answered the door. Two deputies banging on the door in the middle of the night wasn't a good sign. Oh God, what now, Susie thought as Leroy cinched up his robe. Yes, she said, her son did own a black pickup and yes he'd been driving it that night. Was he all right? The deputy asked if they'd like to come have a look at the damage their son had just caused to the front of the house. A few minutes later, Susie and Leroy were standing at the corner of their garage staring in disbelief at what Alvin had done. Yes, she said, Alvin did have a drinking problem and the reason he'd run away was because he was scared of the police. She didn't know why he was scared of the police; Alvin was a good boy. Slow as heck, but a good boy. Susie and Leroy tried to cover for Alvin as best they could and told the deputy they didn't want to press charges against their own son. Eric Varholms didn't press charges either, but he did ask Alvin to pay for the damage he'd caused to the wall the night of his birthday party.

Around Susie and Leroy's neighborhood though, friends and family had already reluctantly resigned themselves to the fact that Alvin just couldn't make it independently and he obviously would never be able to. Thanks in part to the negative reinforcement of his well-meaning parents; at twenty-four years old, he still didn't seem to have the mental ability or the confidence to care for himself. He rarely made sound decisions when the going got rough. Even when things were going smoothly, Alvin's actions were sometimes irrational, immature and dangerous.

According to Alvin's own admissions and those of several close friends, he had a nagging lust for women and he sure liked to drink and party. One of Alvin's favorite hangouts was a nudie bar called Temptations. Alvin could never get enough flesh. On more than one occasion, Chas had to drive him home after a night of heavy drinking in the bars. It was in the dimly lit scene of a local sports bar that Alvin met a rotund young lady who set his heart aflutter. Her name was Theresa.

CHAPTER 8

THERESA BARROSO
Her way or no way

Theresa Barroso was a tad on the plump side. When she met Alvin Robinson, she weighed around two hundred and fifty pounds.

Right away, Alvin took an urgent liking to Theresa. As for Theresa, there hadn't been an abundance of romance in her life thus far, so Alvin's attention was quite flattering to her. He made her feel pretty and special, something she hadn't felt in quite some time.

* * *

Theresa's family was a typical, close-knit Hispanic family. She was born in Los Angeles, California, and shared the love and attention of her parents with two older brothers and three sisters. During her formative years, her family was in constant contact with other relatives that lived in the area, as well as some that lived south of the border in Mexico. They picnicked together, attended church together and they stuck together when the going got rough. They were friends; they were there for each other, no matter what happened. Theresa would later say the thing she liked best about growing up was living in a big, happy family filled with the laughter and commotion of little children. On traditional holidays such as Thanksgiving and Christmas, the Barroso's had relatives that flocked from far and wide to attend family get-togethers. When problems arose, the Barroso's worked it out together.

Theresa was already overweight as she entered her teens. Her family moved to northeastern California and settled in the foothills of the Sierra Nevada Mountains, not far from the Nevada state line. The scenery was far more beautiful than anywhere else she'd ever lived, but the altitude took some getting used to. Before long she became somewhat asthmatic and began to take a small inhaler with her wherever she went. Most of the time she never needed it, but she kept it with her just in case.

In 1995, Theresa completed high school at Sierra Nevada High, in the small town of Susanville, north-east of Sacramento. It was beautiful there; close to the tranquil setting of Honey Lake. Unlike other young adults who relished the thought of independence the second they turned eighteen, Theresa still basked in the close relationship she maintained with her parents and continued living with them. By that time, she had begun to develop other health problems. Along with the asthma, she began to get blinding migraine headaches. She had to have her gallbladder removed and

Deadly Thirst

she suffered backaches, which could have been caused by her excessive weight.

Theresa wasn't a difficult daughter to bring up; she never got into any serious trouble and always maintained a very open and honest relationship with her parents. There was only one small episode of misbehavior that warranted any dealings with the police and that was when she was eighteen. She was at a hotel partying with some of her under-aged girlfriends and the party got a little out of hand. Someone in an adjacent room complained about the noise and the police showed up. Since Theresa was the only person who was over eighteen, she was given a citation for contributing to the delinquency of a minor, which she ended up doing some community service for. Looking back on it, she actually enjoyed doing the community service. It gave her a better insight into the lives of other people and some of the problems that plagued the disadvantaged. It made her realize how good she had it.

Soon after graduation she enrolled at Lassen Community College where she took a one-year course to become a certified medical assistant. When the M/A course ended in 1996, her brand new certificate, coupled with her love of children, suddenly filled her life with direction and purpose. She knew that helping others was what she wanted to do.

Throughout her life she had been especially close to her grandmother, Antonia, who suffered from diabetes. Antonia had been sickly for quite some time and had to pay strict attention to her diet and medication. Living in a big Hispanic family, food was a big focal point of family get-togethers, so Antonia didn't have an easy way to deal with the restrictions of a diet. Still, she did her best to stay within the guidelines her doctor had set for her. When Antonia was stricken with cancer, Theresa could hardly deal with it. In no time, the cancer spread throughout Antonia's body and seemed to center, with a vengeance, in her leg. The leg withered, causing Antonia horrific pain, but she refused to have the leg amputated, as was recommended. Consequently, she died a slow, agonizing death, which the whole family endured. When her demise finally came, it left Theresa in a fit of despair. It would be a long time before she came to grips with it. So strong and lingering were her feelings of loss that, a few years later, Theresa paid a tribute to her favorite grandmother by having Antonia's name and tombstone tattooed on her back.

According to Theresa, her fondest memory of home was the kids who were always running around. When Theresa's parents decided to move back to southern California, she went with them, but by then she was getting antsy to be on her own. Her parents dreaded having an empty nest and talked Theresa into attending foster parenting classes with them. "At that time I was still living at home," Theresa recalled. "We started checking into foster care and we went to the classes, but we never actually became foster parents then. We just went to the classes. I've always been interested, like, in children."

Donna Goodenough

By the time she turned twenty, Theresa had become a bit too self-reliant and overtly dominant in her ways. Though she was still as close as bread and butter with her parents, she wanted her own space. The Barroso family had settled in Riverside County, which borders San Diego County and, in mid-1997, Theresa moved into her own apartment in Perris. Her parents owned some properties there and it seemed like a good place to start out on her own. "I moved out," Theresa said, "and my parents basically felt lonely. You know, they have a big house and they wanted me to fill it up with kids. They love grandchildren. You know, we love kids. So then, they decided they wanted to get back into foster parenting."

Before long, Theresa's parents operated a legitimate, licensed foster care home and at times had as many as six foster kids at once. Theresa noticed that foster parenting brought her folks a lot of happiness and she admired them for it. It seemed to be a very laudable thing to do. Lord knows there were way too many kids and not nearly enough suitable homes for all of them. Helping others seemed to be a natural inclination for Theresa, although she wasn't sure she wanted to tie herself down with a bunch of kids right away. One or two maybe, in a few years. "By now I was already living out on my own. So, at the time I was like 'no, I'm not going to do it.' So *they* went ahead and did it. I had my fingerprints [on file] and my first aid [training] and everything, so they just added me to their license. I was the one there in case of emergency, things like that." When her parents got their first few foster kids, Theresa seemed envious. "Sure enough, you know, me loving children just like my parents, you know, I was always there with them, taking them out to the movies, camping, you know."

Intent on bettering her chances for having a successful future, Theresa figured additional schooling wouldn't hurt so she began attending Riverside Community College at night. The classes she took were general and enhanced her training as a medical assistant. For income, she babysat her parents' foster children and her relatives' kids. Juggling the daytime babysitting job and the burden of studying for her classes was exhausting, but she persevered. She certainly didn't lack determination and direction. When she wanted something, she set about getting it, no matter what.

In the summer of 1997, Theresa was, in a manner of speaking, foster parenting her five-year-old half-brother Jessie* whom she liked to think of as her own child. Jessie went to live with Theresa in the new apartment and called Theresa "Mom." To Theresa, "Mom" became a word with a happy ring to it.

Like Moreno Valley, parts of Perris were dirt poor and unsafe, even in the daytime. Certain areas of the city seemed to attract a high percentage of unemployed residents, wine-o's, hookers and vagrants. In the vicinity of Theresa's apartment in 1997 and all of her apartments thereafter, it seemed that welfare recipients far exceeded the number of residents who were gainfully employed.

Within five miles of Theresa's Perris apartment there was a small, yet world-renowned airport which was famous as a primo skydiving locale among thrill seekers. This wild group of free-fallers probably poured more money into the Perris economy via bars and restaurants than all the residents of Perris combined. Some of the neighborhoods in Perris were old, run-down and dominated by low-cost housing that had fallen into a sorry state of dilapidation. In some sections of town gang graffiti was scrawled on almost every available surface. Boarded up windows marred houses and businesses alike. Although the Perris police station was within two miles of Theresa's apartment, crime raged on as if there wasn't a cop in the whole state of California. Drug dealing was rampant in alleyways, yards and on the streets. Drunks and beggars were a common sight shuffling along nearby streets such as 4th, D Street and Perris Blvd. At least one street within close proximity of the police station had to be barricaded to through traffic to discourage drive-thru drug dealing and drive-by shootings.

Air conditioning was a luxury that low-cost housing didn't have. In the oppressive summer heat, tenement dwellers would cool off by sitting on the front porch stoop or in lawn chairs, smoking cigarettes and drinking beer while the kids frolicked in the spray of a garden hose. Abandoned shopping carts were left to rust in yards overgrown with weeds. For the yards that lacked a shopping cart, there were sometimes the picked-apart remnants of an old lawn mower that was left stuck exactly where it had given up the ghost, or an abandoned shell of an automobile. Tattered laundry, which spoke volumes about the people who'd worn it, hung from droopy clotheslines within full view of the street and, it seemed, the entire world. Filthy mops propped up against front doors were standard, as were bowling trophies in the living room windows and garbage cans that never seemed to remain upright due to hungry, marauding dogs. Some parts of Perris were down right dismal, but that was where Theresa chose to live.

Not all parts of Perris were like that. Far from it. Many sections of town were elite and very showy. However, there was a fair amount of space in between with mediocre housing separating the haves and the have-nots.

It was around this time when Theresa met Alvin Robinson. Although she didn't do much dancing, she enjoyed hanging out at nightclubs, sports bars and other places where she could groove to the tunes, try to meet men and have a good time. Smiling and trying to pad an almost non-existent self esteem, she approached the bar one night during the summer of 1997 and planted herself next to a guy whose weight was also a little on the hefty side. His name was Alvin. The two had a powerful, feral attraction to each other right from the start.

It was immediately obvious to Theresa that Alvin was slow, but that didn't matter. He took a liking to her, which was something few other men had done. And so it began. They exchanged phone numbers and a romance soon developed. Alvin was twenty-four and still living at home with his parents; he thought it was cool that Theresa had her own apartment. Before long, she and Alvin were steadily dating; that is, sleeping together at her place. Within a month or two, he was there all the time.

From the beginning, Alvin expressed his love for Theresa and, she said she loved him too. The relationship they were about to embark on, however, would have more ups and downs than an elevator. As soon as it began, their relationship was a volatile one. Most of their arguments were about money and work, or rather, Alvin's lack of both. It irked her to the bone that Alvin was still firmly attached to his momma. Alvin would get odd jobs here and there, but was more often than not unemployed—living off his parents. His dad had tried to keep him somewhat employed over the last eight years as a partner in "A & L Mobile Auto Service", a small car repair business Leroy owned and operated. Even when Alvin was working, Theresa complained that it was *her* money that paid for everything and Alvin's biggest gripe was that Theresa was "running his money." And, he said, she was a serious battleaxe to boot. Her moods were hard to chart. She could be sweet one minute and toxic the next. Over trivial things, mostly. Always bitching about something. Alvin viewed himself as the calming factor, the levelheaded one. Between the two of them, he considered himself to be the responsible one. Even so, when the going got tough, he'd bail. When they quarreled, Alvin would leave; he'd just take off. He spent many a night estranged from Theresa, either sleeping in his car or with friends or with his folks. In spite of the fact that by now he had all but officially moved in with Theresa and Jessie, he'd still go home at least two or three times a month and spend a few nights with his mom and dad. Usually, he just wanted to be near them.

It was about this time that Alvin managed to convince Theresa to quit school. Theresa was ready for a change anyway and at the end of the semester she gave up her schooling to get a full-time job.

A few months later, she was hired as a caregiver at Walkers Board and Care Facility* in Canyon Lake. Her job was to care for elderly patients with dementia and Alzheimer's disease. Being able to put some of her medical training to good use finally, Theresa was glad to get the job. She didn't object to the tasks of cleaning up puke, emptying bedpans and changing the dirty diapers of adults. In fact, she insisted that she liked to help others. She fed her feeble, infirmed patients and gave them water when they were thirsty. But Theresa wasn't well liked at Walker's, at least not by the residents. According to them, Theresa was no Miss Manners. Employee Jan Wilkes* got a peek at the draconian side of Theresa when they worked together at Walker's. "She didn't treat the residents very well," Ms Wilkes said. "She would sometimes yell at them and be very gruff with them. She seemed to have no patience whatsoever with the elderly." Apparently, Theresa wrongfully assumed that her patients were too senile to fink on her. But it didn't take long before the residents of Walker's started complaining...loudly. They took their gripe to the administrative staff and demanded that something be done about the way Theresa was treating them. The

Deadly Thirst

owner of the establishment called Theresa into her office and had a stern talk with her. Embarrassed to realize that her elderly patients were more mentally intact than she'd assumed, her attitude toward the residents of the facility changed dramatically and immediately.

The personal relationship between Jan Wilkes and Theresa also improved after Theresa was reprimanded. In fact, they developed a friendship outside of work and Jan had the opportunity to visit Theresa's apartment one afternoon. What she saw shocked her. Theresa often spoke about her son, Jessie. But Jan noticed Theresa had very little patience with Jessie. "She'd say, 'Okay I've had enough! You're going back to your grandmother!'" Jan recalled. It was confusing and made her think perhaps Theresa's mother was raising Jessie. According to Jan, Theresa also was short tempered with Alvin and really gave him hell on a regular basis. It seemed that Theresa was always venting on someone, usually someone who was disadvantaged in one way or another.

In September of 1997, Theresa and Jessie moved again, to a small apartment on C Street and soon Alvin was living there too. The new place was no better than the apartment she had just moved from but it was upstairs, which she thought made it safer, and it had an enclosed garage. It was good to have a real garage instead of a carport. Apartment "A" faced C Street and was directly across from a large, vacant field. It was within walking distance to a small, Mexican market and the fire department was only a block away. Theresa's only complaint was the wail of sirens that woke her up almost every night. But it was a small price to pay for the comfort of knowing help, should she ever need it, was close by.

According to Theresa, Alvin was mule-headed and there were certain things you couldn't change his mind about. Her Pontiac, old and ugly as it was, was still in good running condition, or so she thought. Alvin insisted it was a piece of crap that was on the verge of needing major repair. He advised her to get rid of the Pontiac before it was too late. Better to sell it while it's still running than to try and sell it after it crapped out, he warned. Theresa didn't agree that the Pontiac had one foot in the grave, so to speak, but relented and sold the car several weeks later. With the Pontiac gone, she was now car-less and dependent on Alvin to take her back and forth to work, which bothered her. She was fiercely independent and resented the fact that, for the next couple of weeks she was going to have to coordinate her schedule with Alvin whenever she wanted to go anywhere. It pissed her off even more that Alvin would just take off and not tell her where he was going or when he'd be back. Sometimes he'd stay gone all day and late into the night, leaving her stuck with no way to get around.

Soon after the Pontiac was gone, she began to get suspicious about why Alvin had wanted her to sell it. All too late, she began to suspect that Alvin intended to use her lack of a car as a way to control her and Theresa didn't like it one bit. She wasn't about to jump to the crack of Alvin's whip, or anyone else's. She was the alpha-female.

Not only that, but they were constantly fighting about Alvin's unemployment, his drinking and his laziness. She thought he was immature and totally lacking in any sense of authority or responsibility. She said he drank while she was at work and she claimed he got drunk almost every day. Alvin didn't deny it. "I just wanted to sit around and watch TV," he said. To top it all off, he was frequently late to pick her up from work. Often, he completely forgot about her and she had to catch a bus home. And then they fought about it for hours after she got home. She was fed up with the situation, but she was also stuck between a rock and a hard place because the Pontiac money had already been blown on something else. So, Theresa did without a car of her own for several more weeks. The transportation woes did nothing to enhance their already corroded relationship, which most of the time was nothing but a source of frustration for both of them. According to Alvin, Theresa called him names but he just laughed it off. She hated being mocked. On more than one occasion, his laughter stopped abruptly when Theresa gave him a swift kick in the balls. With that, Alvin's bravado vanished and he left, totally humiliated and in pain. Again and again throughout their relationship, Alvin learned firsthand how it felt to get kicked in a man's most sensitive spot.

At 8:30 P.M. on October 5th of 1997, violence erupted at 114 C Street apartment "A." Alvin and Theresa had another one of their colossal arguments; but this one quickly escalated into a physical altercation. Arrest records show Theresa was the reporting victim and witness.

As dispatchers were trying to get the facts, the phone line suddenly went dead. According to Theresa, as she was dialing 911, Alvin pulled a knife and threatened to kill her with it. Then, while dispatchers were on the phone with her, he used the knife to cut the telephone cord and then stomped into the bedroom, pulled the second phone from the wall and proceeded to go on a kicking rampage. According to Theresa, he kicked the glass door on the stove and shattered it, tried to rip the refrigerator door off its hinges and kicked his stereo into the wall, breaking the cassette deck. Reveling in the euphoria of power, he continued to vent his anger on objects inside the living room. The stereo speakers were kicked into the wall, leaving a twelve-inch crack in the plaster. After his rage was expended to his satisfaction, he hightailed it out of there, tearing away for his parents' house. By the time deputies arrived, Alvin was long gone.

"The place was pretty trashed," said responding deputy Michael McClanahan. Theresa told deputies that Alvin was headed to his parents' home in Moreno Valley and gave them the address. McClanahan dispatched another deputy to go to that address and sure enough, there was Alvin. Each accused the other of being the one who had started the fight and causing all the damage. Theresa had told McClanahan she wanted Alvin prosecuted for what he had done to her apartment.

Deputy McClanahan decided to drive to Moreno Valley himself and ask Alvin what had happened. Alvin said Theresa was pissed off because he

Deadly Thirst

wanted to go out with his buddies. She was jealous, that's all there was to it. According to him, Theresa threw a lamp and a VCR at him, but he hadn't thrown anything at her. Furthermore, Alvin insisted he hadn't cut the phone line or broken the stove door or kicked the stereo. He didn't do nothing', he insisted, but in hindsight he was livid about the whole incident. As Alvin explained it, Theresa just had her garters up her crack, that's all. When Theresa went around the bend, she went all the way, man.

When McClanahan had heard enough, he read Alvin his rights and asked him if he understood. He said yes. Alvin was arrested and charged with vandalism, trying to prevent and dissuade a witness, and damaging a telephone & power line. He was booked into the Robert Presley Detention Center in Riverside.

It would be almost two years before anyone in charge realized that a very important procedure had accidentally slipped past the person in charge of fingerprinting all incoming arrestees. Alvin was booked and served two days in jail for that offense but was never fingerprinted. It was a serious error that would come back to haunt the Riverside County Sheriff's Department.

Arrest records show that Alvin listed the address of his parent's home in Moreno Valley as his residence, instead of 114 C Street where he actually lived with Theresa. Whether it was due to the fact that he couldn't remember his real address because it wasn't written on his cue card, or whether it was because he felt like his home was with his parents, remains a mystery. Maybe he simply felt a determination to end the relationship and distance himself from Theresa.

Alvin's parents were furious that their son had been locked up in jail. Theresa indignantly recalled how Leroy had called her and accused her of ruining Alvin's life. Leroy and Susie didn't like Theresa and did their best to dissuade Alvin from getting back together with her, but their words of advice went unheeded. As always, they reminded Alvin that he was slow and unable to take care of himself. They told him he should get away from Theresa and move back home with them. Alvin could never make up his mind about anything. He was torn between living with Momma and Daddy and living with Theresa. There was no doubt that he loved his parents more than anyone else in the world, but Theresa's lure was far stronger than anything Momma and Daddy could use to bring Alvin back. That lure, which Theresa strategically dangled in Alvin's face when it suited her, was sex.

The next day, Alvin brushed off his parent's advice and called Theresa from jail to apologize, saying the booze had made him do it. He begged her to drop the charges. She was somewhat softened by his vows of repentance and called Deputy McClanahan saying she'd changed her mind and didn't want Alvin prosecuted after all. She said the phone cord had been accidentally broken during a playful scuffle between the two of them and that Alvin hadn't cut it. The case was then turned over to the Riverside District Attorney's office for review.

"I believed he was going to change," Theresa said. By her own admission, she had already fallen hopelessly in love with him. They were an incendiary combination and their relationship seemed to thrive on conflict. Their "love" transcended bizarre. Leroy and Susie were appalled that Alvin ran straight back to Theresa as soon as he got out of jail.

At his November 5th hearing, Alvin was given a twenty-four month term of probation which was to expire on Oct 7, 1999. He was also required to repair the damage he'd caused and specifically ordered not to have any contact with the victim. He didn't dare tell the judge they had already gotten back together as soon as he walked out of jail. Alvin knew when to keep his mouth shut.

In the end, only the vandalism charge stuck but Theresa refused to testify against him. Alvin now had a documented criminal record involving domestic violence, something that isn't taken lightly in the state of California.

On Christmas Eve, eighty days after Alvin allegedly threatened to kill Theresa with a knife, he bought her an engagement ring with part of a $7,000 car insurance settlement he'd received earlier that month. Alvin even got down on his knees to propose to her, but Theresa said no.

"But by the end of the night I said yes," she recalled.

With another portion of his insurance pay-off, Alvin bought them both Motorola pagers, which had a printed read out where he could not only send and receive messages, but get other information too, like weather and sports. Pages were soon flying back and forth between the two lovebirds and if pages went unanswered, accusations and a fight ensued.

As a new year got underway, Theresa started working at a retirement home in Sun City. The shift was seventy-two hours on, seventy-two hours off which meant that if Alvin and Theresa wanted to see each other, Alvin had to come to the retirement home. Mrs. Volt*, the owner of the home, was lenient about letting Alvin visit during non-peak times, but it irritated Mrs. Volt that Theresa was on the phone with him a lot, even during the busiest hours of the day. At night, after everyone had eaten supper and were pretty much settled down and drowsy, Alvin usually showed up. They sat in the kitchen and talked for hours or watched TV. None of the residents at the Sun City home complained about Theresa, but Mrs. Volt noticed that she was pretty set in her ways.

Her grand exit from the job in Sun City came rather suddenly. It was nearing 7:00 P.M. and Theresa's shift was almost over. The problem was, her relief had called in to say she was having car problems and she would be late. But, Theresa needed to leave precisely at the stroke of seven—just like Cinderella had to leave the ball precisely at midnight.

Mrs. Volt vividly remembered the angry phone call from Theresa. "She said my husband needed to get there right now and relieve her and that she'd give him thirty minutes to do it," Mrs. Volt said. "And if he was not there at that time, she was going to leave without any care provider present."

Mr. Volt took off like a bat out of hell and headed, as fast as he could, over to the retirement home. As he pulled up to the residence, Theresa was backing her car out of the driveway. She didn't even slow down. The Volts were horrified that Theresa had left the elderly residents without anyone to care for them. Needless to say, that was the end of Theresa.

By March, Theresa had made arrangements for Jessie and her to move into another apartment, a few blocks from where they currently lived. The new place was a blue stucco duplex that her parents owned, located at 216 E. 6th Street in Perris. Theresa and Jessie moved into apartment "B" and a few weeks later Alvin officially moved in too, although he would always consider his parent's house to be his real home.

Soon after that, she and Alvin and Jessie spent a rainy afternoon at the mall. The outing was pleasant until Alvin picked a fight with her on the way home. Suddenly, Alvin stopped the truck and forced Theresa and Jessie to get out. Next thing she knew, he sped off without them. Shocked at being left stranded in a downpour, Theresa managed to get to a phone and called Alvin's mom. Though Susie was disgusted with the relationship, she agreed to come and get them.

That wasn't the only time Alvin left Theresa and Jessie stranded. A few weeks later, they were at an auto parts store with some of Alvin's friends and one of the guys got caught shoplifting. In true Alvin fashion, he jumped into his Chevy S-10 and laid rubber out of there, abandoning Theresa and Jessie. Theresa was furious. Where in the hell was he? When he finally came back for them, Theresa had grown horns. She was mad enough to tear him in half! On the way home, a huge fight erupted.

Theresa insisted on doing the driving and her stubbornness only served to further infuriate Alvin. Nonetheless, he relinquished the driver's seat to her but ordered her to take him "home." In a huff, she headed in the direction of Susie and Leroy's house. That was Alvin's place of refuge whenever he needed security and, right then, that's where he was demanding she take him. All the way home he raged about how his parents offered him love and security and Theresa was nothing but a vile piece of ass. Onward they sped toward Moreno Valley, screaming at each other, mile after mile. Poor little Jessie was in the back seat of the king cab, terrified and crying.

As Theresa remembered it, when they pulled up to Leroy and Susie's house, Alvin got out, went around to the driver's side, reached in and clicked off the ignition. "He was yelling, 'get the fuck out of my car!' and he started smacking me," she said. Alvin reached in and pulled the lever that popped the hood open. Theresa said she tried to drive away, "But Alvin jumped in and punched the windows out. Glass was flying everywhere. He broke out the windshield and the passenger window. He was hollering for his mom and trying to drag me out of the truck." Finally, Susie came out and separated the two, telling Theresa to go into the house. After a while,

Susie drove Theresa and Jessie home. "We talked all the way home about Alvin's behavior," Theresa said.

That event was enough to make Theresa break her brand new lease on the 6th Street apartment and ditch Alvin. For the next three weeks, she stayed with her parents. During her hiatus, Alvin vacillated between staying with his parents and keeping drunken company with friends. But that arrangement was only a temporary cooling off period for the couple. She and Alvin eventually moved back into the apartment on 6th Street. Not surprisingly, Jessie was no longer in Theresa's care, except to spend the night occasionally. Theresa's parents had become uneasy with the couple's volatile relationship and had reclaimed Jessie. Putting Alvin and Theresa together was like pouring gasoline on a fire; it was downright explosive.

By the summer of 1998, Alvin's drinking had increased to the point that it was causing further damage to their already splintered relationship. But according to Alvin, Theresa had no one to blame but herself. She was the one who did all the grocery shopping and she always bought him the big bottles of booze. Theresa had a smoldering resentment that Alvin's life consisted of him lollygagging around the house all day drinking up all her liquor and watching TV. Even so, they still planned on getting married eventually.

Alvin finally got a job driving a forklift at Rim Warehouse Manufacturing and took great pride in describing his position as a "certified" forklift operator. Forklifts are considered heavy machinery, dangerous—even deadly—if used in a reckless manor. Since every warehouse is stocked with thousands—and sometimes millions—of dollars worth of merchandise, it's imperative that a forklift operator demonstrate he has the ability to understand how the machine handles as well as what its limits and capabilities are. There are certain ways to move pallets of stock from one area to another in a safe yet speedy fashion, so it takes a skilled person to safely operate a forklift. The inventory inside a warehouse is very systematically arranged and stock needs to be kept in a precise order. Oftentimes, stock needs to be rotated to ensure the product is moved out before it expires. The position of forklift operator required an ability to read, at least to a certain extent. Shipping and receiving forms can be somewhat puzzling, even for intelligent people. Reading work orders, releases and inventory placements are just a few of a forklift operator's duties. Filling out the wide variety of forms that go along with the job also required the applicant to have some ability to read and write. Apparently, Alvin demonstrated that he understood all the complexities of operating the forklift to the satisfaction of his supervisor and at least described the limitations of his reading and writing abilities. Evidently, his supervisor felt confident enough to hire him. As a forklift operator Alvin made very important decisions all day at work, decisions that were binding for the company that employed him. Rim was responsible for Alvin's actions whenever he was behind the wheel of that

Deadly Thirst

forklift and during his employment at Rim there was never a mention of Alvin driving haphazardly.

In August, Theresa's left knee was severely injured during yet another argument with Alvin. According to her, they had been at a party and Alvin had gotten into a ruckus with a couple of street-hardened girls. When Alvin threw a beer bottle at one of the girls, Theresa nailed him for it and decided they should leave. As usual, fighting then broke out between Alvin and Theresa and continued all the way home. They were still arguing at the curb in front of the 6th street apartment when she fell between the curb and the truck, twisting her knee. The pain was horrendous; she thought she had broken her leg. It pissed her off that Alvin was only a little remorseful about her injuries and kept right on drinking. Forty-ounce malt liquors were his weakness. The way Theresa told it, his frequent imbibing got worse, to the point where his friend Chas White became concerned. According to Theresa, Alvin got mean and mad when he drank. "He'd go on binges," she said. "He'd call me a fat bitch." Compounding Alvin's excessive drinking was the fact that he had recently injured his hand at work and was perfectly content to sit around the house and draw a disability check from it. Theresa viewed it as pure laziness.

For the last few months, Theresa had been working at yet another elder care center in Sun City, not far from the residents that she had abandoned precisely at the stroke of seven. The owners of Ellis* Daycare Center would remember Theresa very well. The program director, Mrs. Gaines* said that Theresa had only been employed four weeks when she injured her left knee at work. With a doctor's note, she was off work for approximately seven weeks. Within three or four days after her return, she claimed that she'd re-injured her knee, *at work*, and took an additional thirty days off. Soon after that, Theresa filed a workers' compensation claim and never came back to Ellis Daycare.

Despite all their ups and downs, they still professed a love for one another. Alvin proved his love for Theresa by getting her name tattooed on his chest. Soon after that, she responded with her own statement of adoration and paid a visit to the tattoo artist. Along with Grandmother Antonia's tombstone on her back, her right breast was now emblazoned with "Alvin."

Feeling rejuvenated after their tattooing sessions, they secretly began rekindling the marriage plan and even discussed having a baby together. Alvin thought they'd make cute babies because they were a mixed couple; he was African-American and she was Hispanic. Skipping over the marriage process entirely, they began an earnest attempt to make a baby. After a couple of months without success, they decided to go to a clinic and get checked out. Something must be wrong with one of them, or else they'd surely have a baby on the way by now, they both thought.

Theresa always said that having kids was something they both wanted, but they also realized that children would make any plans for full time employment rather difficult. "We'd been talking about having kids," Theresa said, laughing. "But neither one of us basically wanted to stop working."

They soon learned that the problem rested with Alvin and were disappointed to learn they could never have kids of their own. Leroy and Susie were oblivious to the fact that Theresa had railroaded their son into thinking he could even begin to fill the position of father. Had they been privy to any of this, they would have blown a major fuse. Apparently, Alvin knew better than to confide certain things to them and Theresa certainly didn't think it was any of their business.

"First she went and got checked out," Alvin said. "Come to find out, it wasn't nothin' wrong with her. So I went to the same doctor she went to and they referred me to a place in Riverside where they check your sperm out, you know. They said I had a low sperm count and that I couldn't have kids." In truth, Alvin really wasn't sure what his problem was. He was confused about the definitions of sterile and low sperm count. "Actually, I really don't know what the problem was," he admitted.

That news led them to briefly consider the adoption option. But since Theresa's family had always been in the foster parenting network, fostering was something she was already accustomed to. It had worked well for her family and brought her parents a lot of satisfaction and joy, something that her current situation was completely lacking. She told Alvin that foster parenting was a better alternative than adoption. For one thing, it was faster. They could have a kid of their own within six months through foster care, as opposed to a year or more through adoption.

It didn't matter what Alvin thought of the whole idea, she'd already made up her mind and that's all there was to it. Immediately she began looking into the possibility of becoming foster parents. At that time, her parents had four foster kids in their home: one age 12, one about 9, one 2 and an infant. To Theresa, it seemed her parents' house was such a happy place because of all the kids. To her, it was a natural assumption that having kids in the house would make it a happier place. She completely over looked the fact that kids could cause an enormous amount of anxiety and frustration; nor did she seem to realize that kids could make a bad relationship even worse.

They began to allow themselves the luxury of thinking that perhaps their relationship was improving. After all, a month or so had passed without any major blowups and they'd been trying lately to resurrect their marriage plans. This brief lull in the fighting would prove only to be the calm before the storm.

Though their relationship was still undeniably volatile and unstable and Alvin didn't have a good feeling about the foster parenting idea, Theresa went ahead and signed them up for parenting classes in early November of 1998. It would be Theresa's second go-round at foster parenting classes. "Alvin was, you know, new at it," she recalled.

She knew that Alvin still had one more year of probation left, but the only thing that concerned Theresa was their unmarried status. She was afraid that fact might hinder the application and her quest for a foster child.

By the end of November, things went haywire again and they were involved in the most violent altercation yet. Because she was on crutches and her leg was still in a brace from the fall she suffered in August, Theresa asked Alvin to drive her to her doctor's appointment. But Alvin didn't want to. He said he was sick and tired of her nagging and nitpicking about everything and she could damn well drive herself.

Theresa later told the police that they hadn't been getting along and were in the midst of a separation. Alvin was gathering his stuff so he could move out when an argument flared. She said when Alvin locked her out of the house she threatened to call the police. As she was walking toward the carport, Alvin called her a fat bitch and a "ho." Theresa's handwritten narrative about what happened next is perhaps the best evidence of what their relationship was really like.

He pushed me to the ground and as I tried to get up he punched me in the face and threw me on the hood of the CRX [his car]. He held me up there just slapping me and when he bent over to pick up a wood block, I kicked him in the face as I tried to get off the car. He then threw the wood block at me and told me I drove him to do this. I was just constantly bitching and nagging and that was why he was doing this. He said, "You ain't shit!" and I told him the cops were on the way. Then he picked up a pipe and busted the windows on the car and called me a stupid bitch. "I'm gonna fuck you up, get in my face again and I swear I'll put your head through that windshield! I hope you rot in hell!!"

Then I asked him to please let me leave because I was running very late to my doctor's appointment. Then I saw the mailman come so I went to check the mail. He called his parents and said Terry is putting me out, please come get me. So I yelled tell them why I'm putting you out because you beat my ass.

On and on she wrote, scribbling more than two full pages of abuse she'd suffered at the hands of her fiancé. She continued to vent her hostility onto the paper until it sounded almost too long-winded and ridiculous. Certainly not a harmonious relationship.

Alvin's story was just the opposite. Yeah, they were splitting up. He was in the process of moving his stuff out when she started shootin' her mouth off, big time. "It's her way or no way," he said. Yeah, he locked her ass out of the apartment because he couldn't take any more of her bitching. But it was Theresa who picked up a four-foot section of chain link fence post and brandished it at him, threatening to bust the windshield out of his car. She stomped over to his car and proceeded to bash the hell out of the passenger's side rear window and the windshield. Then she went around to the front of the car and bashed in the fender. Upon seeing his car being battered, Alvin didn't hesitate to dial 911. Theresa saw Alvin make the call and immediately left the scene. The cops came looking for her two separate times, but Theresa was nowhere to be found.

Alvin was the reporting victim in this latest fiasco and said he was willing to make a private person's arrest but Theresa was long gone. Alvin was seething. Nobody was gonna beat up on his car and get away with it. No sir. The case was forwarded to the District Attorney's office with a declaration in support of arrest for Theresa. Alvin said he was willing to testify against her in court. It looked like the relationship at last had come to a disastrous end.

From Theresa's point of view, that was Alvin's final straw. That incident angered and frightened her enough to make her file for a restraining order. She filled out the paperwork right there at the Temecula courthouse and turned everything in at the same time. Court documents show that a "petition for injunction prohibiting harassment" was written on November 24th and was accompanied by two handwritten pages describing the violence and abuse she'd suffered at the hands of her fiancé, Alvin.

At that point in time, Theresa swore that she absolutely hated Alvin and didn't want anything whatsoever to do with him, ever again. The acrimony between them had reached the flash point, but somehow, she never saw to it that the restraining order was ever formally served on him. Amazingly, Alvin continued living with her, stating that he would never leave her. The restrainer clearly ordered Alvin to stay at least one hundred yards away from Theresa, but it only seemed to weld them tighter together. They seemed to feed on violence.

By the next day, Theresa said, Alvin was back, promising to make things better and to change his ways. He pleaded with her not to send him back to jail. The restraining order made not one iota of difference to either of them. They picked up where they had left off. According to Theresa, they began attending church together about that time and, by the grace of God, were working to straighten out their problems. Forgiveness is a big part of Christianity and the Bible says, "Let ye who is without sin cast the first stone." Although she claimed the marriage idea was entirely Alvin's, she did want to get married so they wouldn't be living in sin anymore.

Alvin remembered the situation differently. "I depended on her to take care of me," he said. "I didn't know what a restraining order was; no one explained it to me." Moreover, he insisted that the whole marriage thing was *her* idea and he went along with it "because she wanted to." As for the foster parenting commitment he was about to plunge into, "I didn't even know how to take care of myself. I told her I didn't want to do it and she start fussin' with me, so I say 'okay, whatever you want'. I was scared of her because of the way she do me." Alvin never wanted to rock the boat. He insisted that the only reason he got back together with her was for sex. Theresa definitely had her own climate. She was either sub zero or boiling; there was no in between for her. When Alvin couldn't take Theresa's frozen shoulder anymore, he'd leave and go back to Momma and Daddy.

The judge signed the restraining order on December 1, but it altered nothing. Incredibly, seven days after the restraining order was signed, they were back in foster parenting class as usual, as if all was rosy between them. Come hell or high water Theresa was determined to get a child. Neither of them mentioned to the Department of Social Services the fact that Theresa had just filed a restraining order against Alvin, or that he was still on probation from the October 1997 vandalism arrest.

Alvin admitted that he seldom paid attention during class nor did he ever study the manual. After all, he couldn't read. Sometimes he got so bored that he would leave. In any event, he never really considered himself to be an active participant. "Theresa take care of everything," he said. "I had no idea what being a foster parent meant. I didn't know what I was supposed to do with kids." Theresa had told him to butt out and let her handle everything. *She* would be the one taking care of the kids, not him. By then, Theresa had bulked up to a whopping three hundred pounds and, coincidentally, had begun working full time at a weight loss clinic in Lake Elsinore.

There did seem to be, however, one small, insignificant factor that concerned Theresa. Something that just might throw a glitch into the whole child custody arrangement. The trivial issue of marriage.

CHAPTER 9

THE TWO SHALL BE ONE
Alvin and Theresa tie the knot

Slightly more than one month later and a few days before Valentine's Day, Alvin and Theresa hastily decided to tie the knot around their toxic relationship. The news of an impending marriage sent a virtual shockwave through friends and family.

"It was an all-of-a-sudden thing," Alvin's mom recalled. "We were dumbfounded and had no idea at all he was even thinking about marrying her." Apparently, Alvin delayed telling his friends and family about his marriage plans because he knew no one would agree with his decision. But then, according to Alvin, he really didn't have much of a choice. Instead, he chose to tag along on someone else's dream.

"I got married because she wanted to," he lamented. Theresa played him like a fish. As to why he'd allowed himself to be roped into marrying Theresa, Alvin would always be at a loss to explain his actions. "You know what? That's the same question I keep asking myself, over and over again. I thought I loved her."

Chas White, Alvin's best friend for fifteen years, was shell-shocked when he learned about the marriage. "I found out about the marriage on the day of the wedding!" he exclaimed. What astounded Chas even more was that he had never even met this woman that Alvin, his best pal, was planning to spend the rest of his life with! As it turned out, Chas would only meet his best friend's wife four times during their marriage. It seemed like Alvin was trying to hide something and Chas didn't like it. In Chas' opinion, best friends should be closer than that. It was obvious to everyone that things were still not going well between Alvin and Theresa. Alvin deliberately chose not to give Chas or anyone else advance notice about his impending nuptials because he didn't want to argue about it.

Aside from the soon-to-be happy couple, the Reverend Davenport was the only one who knew about the wedding plans and the only reason the Reverend knew about it was because Alvin asked him to perform the ceremony. But Reverend Davenport declined. He was close friends with Leroy and knew all about the rocky relationship Alvin had with Theresa and he knew all about Alvin's frequent desertions. The Reverend knew that if he went ahead and married Alvin and Theresa, Leroy would never forgive him. The Reverend clearly wanted no part in this. He felt the two should undergo counseling first, but Theresa didn't want to be bothered with that.

Deadly Thirst

Undaunted, Theresa managed to lasso a minister at the very last second and they stormed ahead with their impromptu plans. In front of a small and bewildered audience, they were married in Gateway Park in Moreno Valley on February 13th, 1999. The marriage application showed Alvin was employed as a forklift operator with Rim Warehouse Manufacturing and Theresa listed her occupation as medical assistant.

Alvin's buddy, Richard Crane, his close friend for ten years, didn't get wind of Alvin's marriage until *after* it was too late. He was shell-shocked, to say the least. "She had an aggressive attitude and it seemed like she had control over him," Richard said. He knew things would probably never work out because Alvin had spent many a night at Richard's house, just trying to get away from Theresa. And now he had gone and married her!

By Alvin's own admission, his marriage vows never stood in the way of his extramarital sampling of forbidden fruits. "I had a lot of 'em out there too, you know. More than one. I was a very popular guy in Moreno Valley. One day, she'd caught me cheating on her, you know. And she took me up on this mountain in Moreno Valley and told me if I ever cheated on her again, she'd kill me. I thought she was just playing, you know...but when I saw the gun..."

Still, Alvin continued to noodle around behind Theresa's back. He still liked to hang out at Temptations nightclub, a local strip joint adjacent to the 91 Freeway in Riverside. Alvin and his buddies liked to spend their nights huddled at the edge of the runway, gawking and gazing at the ladies.

Alvin knew it was wrong to cheat on his wife and he was careful to hide his extra curricular shenanigans, frequently enlisting his parents to cover for him. "I was clever with it. You know, when she'd call I'd always have my mom and dad say I was asleep, you know?" They didn't think much of the fact that their son had gone and married a Mexican woman. Leroy and Susie had been married for more than two decades by then and they knew what it took to make a union last, yet they didn't seem to want their son to have the same success. They apparently knew about their son's secret episodes of horizontal activity with other women, but said nothing about it.

Nine weeks after the restraining order was filed, and just twenty days after they plunged into marital mayhem, Alvin and Theresa officially applied to open a foster home at the tiny 6th Street apartment. On their application Theresa wrote, "We want to share our love and our lives with children."

Alvin did admit, on the application, that he'd been convicted for vandalism, but when he explained it to the social worker he downplayed it so much that it sounded rather trivial. Neither Alvin nor Theresa alluded to the *true* condition of their relationship or to the restraining order or to the fact that the vandalism charge was much more serious than they were leading their social worker to believe. Theresa filled out Alvin's criminal record statement for him because Alvin's handwriting wasn't all that great and his spelling was even worse. On the back of the page Theresa wrote:

Donna Goodenough

February 23, 1999
I destroyed a stereo that I owned in an apartment that we were rent-
ing at 114 S. C Street, apartment "A". A neighbor heard the wracket [her
misspelling] and called police. They thought the stereo wasn't mine so they
charged me with vandalism. When I went to court and presented receipts
they said it wasn't my apartment and because I did it at the property I didn't
own [apartment] it was considered vandalism. Even though it was my own
stereo. This was a long time ago about 2 years on 11/97. I thank you for your
time for reading this.
Sincerely, 2/23/99 Alvin Robinson

Alvin took the pen from Theresa and signed his name.

It was the agency's responsibility to find out if the statements on the licensing application were true and accurate. Had CPS verified Alvin's version of events, they would have easily discovered the police report in which Theresa said Alvin kicked the stereo into a wall, smashed the stove window, cut the telephone line with a knife, threatened to kill her and tried to tear off the refrigerator door—all in a fit of rage.

The bloody path of domestic violence that had occurred between Alvin and Theresa was right there, like an open book, waiting to be read. But no one bothered. CPS could have easily discovered the restraining order that had been filed five short months prior. They could have read for themselves Theresa's gruesome, handwritten description of all the things that had led up to it. CPS chose to ignore, rather than explore, Alvin's criminal record statement seemingly because they were too busy to check. Besides, CPS considered Theresa's parents to be good foster care providers.

The facts behind the vandalism arrest were enough to bar Theresa and Alvin from becoming foster parents, but for some reason, it didn't seem important to CPS at the time. CPS had the freedom to overlook whatever they felt was too trivial to investigate. Besides, CPS had its own way of checking people out. Apparently they thought it was perfectly safe to judge Theresa based on the track record of her parents.

Had CPS done their obligatory homework correctly, they would have easily learned the overwhelmingly violent truth about Alvin and Theresa. That was precisely why the background checks were of paramount importance. To pass over this important step—for whatever reason—was to virtually pave the way for murder. But CPS was too overburdened and too understaffed and they didn't have time to check things out the way they should have.

As if all were well between them, the newlyweds wasted no time getting right back into their foster parenting classes. They learned the rights of the child and their responsibilities as foster parents. They learned the right and wrong ways to discipline a child and they learned about the cycle of domestic violence and child abuse. Due to the nature of their work, CPS was fully aware of the insidious way domestic violence evolves in a cycli-

Deadly Thirst

cal, chain-reaction way, filtering down from one generation to another. Children who witness domestic violence between adults often grow up to become batterers themselves (although there is no evidence that Theresa was abused or witnessed abuse as a child). Furthermore, CPS was aware that statistics have documented that child abuse is much more likely to occur in households where adult domestic violence is present. Studies show that women who have been beaten by their partner or spouses are twice as likely to abuse a child. Studies also show that women can be a formidable violent force in many relationships, as was Theresa, and that many of these women also vent their anger on children.

Furthermore, studies also point to the ominous link between stress and child abuse. Number one on the list of stress factors is the relationship between the parents, married or not. Conflicts and tensions between the parents are negatively associated with the quality of parenting. Social isolation is number two on the list of stress sources. Theresa's obesity and Alvin's slowness were more than likely problems that caused at least some feelings of isolation in each of their lives. Thirdly, unemployment and the stress that accompanies it are all too often sources of conflict between parents. Alvin and Theresa definitely fit the profile for potential child abusers. Unfortunately, CPS remained blind to all that was wrong with Alvin and Theresa's bid to acquire a child. Their history of domestic violence was completely overlooked when social workers ran a quick, superficial background check through the state of California. The state check came up with nothing and they didn't bother to pursue it locally.

The reason the state had no criminal record of Alvin's conviction was because he'd never been fingerprinted when he was arrested for vandalism in October of 1997. The paperwork had been sent to the Department of Justice in Sacramento but the information could not be released because it lacked the crucial identifier: fingerprints.

In California, if Alvin had been applying to buy a gun, authorities would have checked to see if he had had any restraining orders issued against him. But since Alvin was only asking to become a foster parent, those in authority did no search for such records. CPS was poised to hand over a child to two people who were nothing more than strangers to them.

As the parenting classes drew to a close, Alvin and Theresa were taught gentle and understanding remedies for bedwetting. They learned how to praise the child and to encourage him. Many of these classes were already familiar to Theresa, as she had attended them with her mom in 1996. Theresa's name was listed as a backup on her mom's foster license and Theresa planned to list her mom as a backup on hers.

Because the classes were taught orally, Alvin's illiteracy wasn't a factor that kept him from learning everything he should know about becoming a foster parent. The class concerning responsibilities was especially important and both Alvin and Theresa attended that class. It was verbally drilled into their heads, over and over, that it was absolutely mandatory to report even *suspected* child abuse. That particular aspect of the class was extremely important and the instructors made sure that all the attendees understood their obligations.

Theresa even attended the enriched team class that taught specific ways to deal with kids that had been through multiple placements. Those "special needs" kids were usually tougher to handle than a kid who'd only been through one or two foster homes. After taking the enriched class, a prospective foster parent should be soundly qualified to deal with problem children.

Luckily for Alvin, written tests weren't mandatory and were given only for make-up of missed classes. Even though attendance at all eight classes was required before a license could be issued, Alvin had missed the third class concerning discipline. But boredom was something Alvin couldn't deal with and, to him, all this foster parenting stuff was boring. Theresa told him to just shut up and sit there; she would handle everything. But Alvin was restless and admitted to spending much of his class time hanging out in the bathroom. Sometimes, after the teacher took a head count, he'd take off and go visit a friend. Apparently, their instructor never did a roll call or took a head count after the break. Young, innocent lives were at stake here, but CPS seemed oblivious to the deadly games that were being played—blatantly—right under their noses.

In spite of this, at the orientation class, Alvin and Theresa received their booklet of licensing rules and regulations. Alvin had absolutely no use for the booklet since he couldn't read and besides, Theresa told him that she would be the one taking care of everything. As Alvin remembered it, Theresa told him the foster parenting thing "didn't concern him."

"I told her I didn't want to do it, but she started fussing with me, so I just say, 'okay, whatever you want.'" He wasn't brave enough to argue with her. His way was to get along by going along. Whatever she said, he'd just snap off a mental salute and make a hasty retreat. At that point in time, Alvin only looked at Theresa in two ways: she was either an easy piece of ass or she was a prickly iron-maiden bitch. The mother of all bitches. According to Alvin, Theresa had told him to just stay out of it and that was fine with him.

Relentlessly, Theresa began pouring cement into the footings of her plan to acquire a foster child. It appeared that things were falling into place nicely even though their application hadn't been approved yet and they didn't yet have the proper license to legally operate a foster home. In California, the law allows social workers to place children in homes that have almost completed the process of acquiring their license if social workers determine the home meets minimum standards and the applicants have no criminal history and no other alternative for the child is available. In such cases, social workers are supposed to visit the home routinely to ensure the safety of the child.

Theresa always saw to it that Alvin was never around when the social worker came by, but at the very end she had to allow him to be present, apparently for no other reason than to prove that Alvin did indeed exist. In their final interview, Theresa played the part of Ms Congeniality and did all the talking while Alvin just sat there, smiling like a paragon of virtue. The only thing missing from the scene that afternoon was the soft, melodious crooning of Perry Como in the background and dainty paper doilies under their teacups. In statements that sounded like they had been gleaned from a slave's diary, Theresa described Alvin as a "hard worker." Alvin meekly returned her compliment.

"She's a strong woman and she treats me well."

According to her own admission, Theresa painted a rosy picture for their social worker who was so impressed and in such a hurry that he was eager to sign off right then and there. He saw no need to let formalities such as licensing or thorough background checks stand in the way. Thanks to his shortsightedness and the shortsightedness of many others, plans were hurried along to accommodate Theresa's greedy quest for a foster child. According to their social worker, the paperwork for Alvin and Theresa looked okay and the apartment met minimal standards, therefore, Alvin and Theresa were deemed to be suitable foster parents.

The days got hotter and the sickness that was their marriage went from a summer cold into full-blown pneumonia. In the four months since their wedding in the park on February 13th, much had transpired that should have red-flagged Alvin and Theresa as unsuitable foster parents. At least it should have discouraged them from proceeding any further with it. Alvin's drinking was at an all-time high and, except for the times he solicited Theresa for his own sexual gratification, he sought to put as much distance between himself and his wife as he possibly could. To send an innocent child into the custody of two adults who were as violent and hell-bent on destruction as Alvin and Theresa were, would seem to be the last thing a child protection agency would permit, yet plans proceeded blindly, at full throttle.

During the first week of June, CPS officials assigned two little boys to embark on a journey that only one of them would survive. One was eleven-year-old Jacob Marquist* and the other was four-year-old Andy Setzer.

PART 4
THE NIGHTMARE BEGINS

CHAPTER 10

"WE WANT TO SHARE OUR LIVES WITH CHILDREN"
Andy and Jacob arrive at 216 E. 6th Street

Not all females are meant to be mothers. Studies show that the mothering instinct is completely absent in a small percentage of females in both the human and animal population. Only a tiny percentage of women recognize this in themselves. Yet, many others are persuaded to go along with what society expects of them and each year thousands of kids pay the price.

Theresa may have thought she was fit material for foster parenting simply because her family had sheltered many children in the foster care system and she had participated in their care over the years. But when the full responsibility of two young children befell her in one day's time, Theresa's dark side began to prevail like ominous black clouds on the horizon.

Who could have known that she was about to reveal her sinister side; a side so violent and maniacal it would horrify the entire County of Riverside and sadden thousands of people.

It was blistering hot on June 3rd, a Thursday afternoon, when social worker Angela Reynolds* from CPS phoned Theresa at home asking if she was ready to receive a child. Theresa said she was and, within a couple of hours, Jacob Marquist was dropped off at the 6th Street apartment along with his possessions. Jacob scarcely had time to settle in and put his clothes away when the phone rang again.

This time it was Mary Holms*, the social worker for a four-year-old boy named Andy Setzer. Theresa explained to Mary that she had just received an eleven-year-old a couple of hours before. But, after hearing all the attributes and needs of little Andy, she told Mary that she was willing and able to take another child. Andy could share a room with Jacob. Relieved that Theresa was so accommodating, Mary told her to come right away and get Andy at the Perris office on North A Street.

The office was just a few blocks away and the drive took about five minutes. When Theresa was introduced to Andy, she was greeted by a mischievous grin. Theresa spent about an hour filling out the forms and talking with Mary Holms about Andy's grandmother, Dawn Masterson. Theresa was told that Dawn wanted custody of Andy but CPS thought he would be too much for a woman Dawn's age. Apparently, social workers thought forty-nine-year-old Dawn was antiquated, too old to be chasing around after a high-strung kid like Andy...but they thought an obese woman *could*? Mary asked if Theresa could arrange for Andy to visit his grandmother from time to time and let them get reacquainted at a more gradual pace. Theresa seemed agreeable to this arrangement. And so, as she swirled her flamboyant signature across the dotted line, Andy and Jacob were unceremoniously plunged into the fiery abyss of Theresa Barroso's protective custody.

There were concerns red-flagging Dawn Masterson as Andy's potential custodian. CPS was certain that a youngster as rambunctious as Andy might overwhelm Dawn, even though she was in excellent health both mentally and physically. It seemed not to matter that she was begging for custody or that she was finishing her foster care training or that she was in the process of moving to a more appropriate, child-friendly location. CPS seemed only to focus on the age factor and the pesky problem of Andy's biological mother trying to worm her way back into Andy's life if Dawn got custody.

No one suspected the dangers regarding Theresa and Alvin. But then how could they? Theresa had done an excellent job of masking all their problems and shortcomings. Alvin had even admitted on his application that he'd been convicted on the vandalism charge, but made light of it and everyone concerned seemed to think it was no big deal. Since nothing is permanent with foster care, everyone concerned decided to give it a shot. After all, if Theresa realized it wasn't working out, she could call her social worker and send Andy back. People did that with problem children all the time.

Within two months, Theresa would show her social worker and everyone else at CPS just how permanent Andy's placement really was.

Andy, looking totally bewildered, arrived at 216 E. 6th Street wearing his only possessions. Being uprooted again and being moved to a strange home was especially troubling for four-year-old Andy; he was far too young to understand why he couldn't remain with Mike and Lynn Herman.

Alvin recalled how Andy walked up to him and asked if Alvin was his new daddy and then asked for a kiss and a hug. "It made me feel good, you know? I couldn't say no."

It's doubtful that Andy could comprehend the stark differences between the beautiful, spacious home he'd been living in with the Hermans to the dreary, cramped duplex he would now be forced to call home for the rest of his life.

Jacob Marquist, at eleven years of age, had a little better understanding of his circumstances. Jacob had been forced to shoulder adult burdens early in his life, but his newest placement bewildered him nonetheless. Jacob was a smart young man and got excellent grades in school. Having come from a shelter, he was used to sharing and getting along with other children. For Jacob, Andy was a good little buddy. Although the two boys had seven years difference in their ages and had never met before June 3rd, they quickly hit it off. Andy's mischievous giggles and pranks were contagious and within a few hours the two of them were fast friends.

While Jacob had arrived at Alvin and Theresa's house with all his stuff, Andy came with nothing but the clothes on his back. Andy had loads of toys during his stay with Mike and Lynn Herman, but at the new home in Perris, he had next to nothing. Even his medical records were incomplete, forcing him to go through a physical and the full series of shots all over again. Seven shots in one day was a pretty frightening experience for a four-year-old. From a youngster's point of view, the needles were huge horse needles and they hurt. Theresa took note of Andy's fear of needles. She also took special note of the size of Andy's penis. To her, Andy's penis seemed abnormally large.

"At first," Theresa recalled, "we didn't have, you know, almost nothing for him 'cause we weren't, you know, ready for a *little* kid. I started getting him toys. I got him, like, little Hot Wheels and a map. I wasn't really told much about Andy," she said. "They just said he was a really sweet kid and everything, you know."

While Andy was sweet, he was also a mischievous prankster, "a brat," as his Aunt Doris would later describe him. Andy was a lot like his father. Anyone that knew Andy's dad could definitely see a resemblance. Jacob played big brother with pride and taught Andy how to play Nintendo, or at least he tried. Both kids were assigned chores and Theresa told Andy that one of his chores was to make his bed. Andy had a different take on the situation. He told her in no uncertain terms that he was only four and he didn't have to make his bed.

Andy and Jacob were assigned to share a bedroom across the hall from Alvin and Theresa. A small bathroom separated the two rooms. Jacob's bed was nearest the door and within listening distance of the adult's bedroom. He was too young to know much about sex—or to even care for that mat-ter—but he knew what fighting and arguing were all about.

In the days that followed, Jacob would overhear many quarrels and arguments, but seemed to be able to block it out pretty well by closing him-self off and playing Nintendo...and playing and playing and playing until he couldn't see straight. Jacob was an exceptionally good kid, smart and respectful toward adults. He was blonde, blue-eyed and as cute as could be. It was obvious that Jacob would grow into a tall, good-looking teen. He was polite and very well mannered.

If friends and family had been shocked to learn about the marriage of Alvin and Theresa, they were absolutely appalled when they found out about the foster kids. One day early in June, Alvin showed up at Chas White's home with two little kids in tow. Right away, Chas asked who the kids belonged to and was hit head-on with the joyful news that Alvin was now a foster parent!

Deadly Thirst

"That was the first I knew of the foster parenting plan," Chas said, "when Alvin showed up at my house with two kids. He was kinda acting like a big brother to them, you know? He didn't seem to know what his duties were." Chas had a son of his own and considered himself a good parent. He knew that the responsibility of being a father—whether biological or foster—was a serious, long-term commitment, often filled with frustration. He was absolutely baffled as to why Alvin would want to tie himself down with not just one kid, but two! Chas had never understood Alvin's reason for marrying Theresa either, but that was between Alvin and Theresa. Chas had enough problems of his own and wasn't going to bog himself down in Alvin's problems. Still, knowing the details of several violent encounters between Alvin and Theresa, Chas would not be able to shake the uneasy feeling he had after learning of the arrival of two little kids at their home.

While Alvin and the boys were at Chas' house, Andy had to use the potty. Chas recalled how Alvin seemed almost grossed-out by the prospect of having to wipe Andy's bottom.

"He asked me to go in and wipe Andy's butt," Chas said, shaking his head. Seeing the predicament that was unfolding before his eyes, he asked Alvin what in the hell was going on. Why was he doing this? Why was he letting Theresa rope him into something that he was totally unprepared for? And who, for crying out loud, would put two kids into the care of people as unstable—both emotionally and mentally—as Alvin and Theresa? What in the hell was going on?! Alvin shrugged him off and mumbled that it was all Theresa's idea. Chas was dumbstruck.

Susie Robinson tells a similar story. "I first learned about the foster parenting thing when he brought the two kids over to visit," she said. "We didn't know he was even considering being a foster parent." She was so stunned she could barely gather her wits about her enough to stammer out a few questions. When did all this happen and whose idea was it? Of course, she knew whose idea it was. She and Leroy had scarcely recovered from their shock at the marriage that had taken place just four short, stormy months ago. Now this! Good grief!

Every time they turned around Alvin was back home, bemoaning his married life. What next? The marriage had seemed to make not one iota of difference in the way Alvin and Theresa interacted with each other, so why would the addition of two kids help? Oftentimes, kids only make a bad marriage worse.

Alvin's parents were absolutely horrified, but never assumed—in their wildest dreams—that the placement would be anything more than temporary. What in the world was going on, they wondered. Although Susie was certainly distraught, Leroy showed his emotions more outwardly. They questioned Alvin's motives and tried to reason with him, but they knew Theresa, not Alvin, was master of the household and there wasn't any point in trying to talk to *her*. Might as well go talk to a brick wall.

"It was done her way or not at all," Susie said. There wasn't much anyone could do about it now. Leroy and Susie considered calling CPS and telling them they'd made an awful mistake, but decided to censor their inner voices and stay out of it. Let CPS come to that conclusion on their own. Besides, they were sure the whole thing would fall through one way or another. Surely, anyone could see that Alvin was retarded. While Susie and Leroy decided to stay out of it and let things work themselves out, they certainly didn't feel comfortable with the situation.

Though the Reverend Davenport was a close family friend, everyone thought it was best not to mention these two newest developments to him. Like Alvin's parents, the Reverend Davenport was still upset over the marriage. So, until early August, the Reverend remained unaware of what had transpired. But, by then it would be too late.

Meanwhile, Theresa's job at the weight clinic was giving her steady hours and before long she was working ten-hour days, Monday through Friday 9 A.M. to 7 P.M. She usually let Alvin, who was still drawing disability, or her mom look after the kids. On Saturdays she'd work four hours, from 9 A.M. to 1 P.M. Her only day off was Sunday. But it didn't seem like a day off because there was always a long list of chores that she needed to do around the house. There was laundry, cooking, cleaning and grocery shopping and minding the kids. Suddenly her life was chock full. She was tired and stressed out. When Alvin was babysitting he'd spend his days leisurely, with friends or at his parents, dragging Jacob and Andy along with him. Sometimes he'd take the kids to the park. Stuff like laundry, cleaning and grocery shopping never got done when Alvin was in charge.

Alvin and Theresa began looking around for a house to buy. The 6th Street duplex was tiny even for two adults, but when four people began inhabiting it, it became downright claustrophobic. At that point, they'd been prudent enough to do a little investing in property. They were part owners of a place called Mount Lakes Resort, up in the San Bernardino Mountains. It was a place where families could go and camp in tents and trailers; do a little fishing and boating. A good family retreat. So, as soon as he could, Alvin took Jacob and Andy to Mount Lakes Resort for a full day of fun. The kids ran around as excited as ants at a picnic. Initially, as Alvin was talking about it with Jacob, he thought the first trip should be just the two of them; but Andy overheard the conversation and wanted to go too.

So, it was settled; Alvin would take both youngsters. The boys loved it and Alvin had a great time with them. It was a lot like Chas White had said, Alvin acted like a big brother to the kids. The trip to Mount Lakes was an all-day event, just Alvin and the kids.

The first week or two of June had gone along smoothly enough, at least as far as the kids were concerned. They seemed to be the least of Theresa's aggravation. Alvin continued to spend many nights away from her and the kids and seemed to come home for only one reason: sex. And Theresa resented it. She was also mightily annoyed that Alvin wasn't pulling his fair share of the load around the house. In her opinion, all he did was sit around watching TV, or he was over at his friend's house or with his parents or tinkering with his car. It seemed Alvin did practically anything to keep from working. He didn't act like a responsible adult. To her, it was like having three kids!

From Alvin's point of view, Theresa had turned into a snarling, dominating, money-grabbing bitch-on-wheels that he just didn't want to be around. He was already sick and tired of watching the kids and asked Theresa to cut her work hours so she could look after them. After all, it had been *her* idea to have kids, not his. It was a constant power struggle, which Theresa always won. It was her way or the highway and for Alvin, it was always so much easier to leave than to stick around and fight about everything. Besides, he felt like she was the master of his money, inasmuch as he'd get his disability check and she would be the one to decide how the money was spent.

"Man, she'd only give me about twenty or thirty dollars a month," he lamented. According to her, Alvin wasn't good with money; he just didn't have the management skills required to run the budget, so Theresa took care of that.

One day a credit card came in the mail with Alvin's name on it. He couldn't seem to understand that an activation fee and a membership fee would be charged to it simultaneously with his first purchase. Theresa had a hard time convincing him of that because Alvin only saw the credit card fiasco as yet another instance where Theresa was trying to control things.

It didn't take long for Alvin to decide that babysitting and playing Mister Mom wasn't his bag. Plus, he was tired of the way Theresa was constantly bitching at him about sitting around the house all day. Alvin applied at three different temporary agencies: Arrow Temps, Intertech Staffing Services and Corestat.

* * *

Meanwhile, Mike and Lynn Herman had feverishly petitioned the grievance board regarding the abrupt removal of Andy. They provided the board with twenty-four letters of glowing recommendations, a letter from each of Andy's preschool teachers and they even had a letter from a witness that had stayed several days at their home. But none of that mattered to CPS. Stone-faced authorities listened to Mike and Lynn's grievance, but were unmoved. Days later DPSS sent a terse letter, which simply stated that the department had acted appropriately and within its power. To Mike and Lynn, the board members had seemed indifferent and uncaring. Until the rejection letter came, they'd kept Andy's room just as it had been, as if he'd be coming back any day. After the letter arrived, Lynn packed up his room, crying the whole time.

Dawn Masterson was also perplexed as to why Andy had not come to stay with her. After all, she'd been told to get ready and to have her ducks in a row. But, according to CPS, Andy would be better off at another home. It didn't make sense, but Dawn wasn't into pushing.

Alvin's mood improved when he started working, but he still stayed away from the wife and kids for days at a time. Whenever he did finally decide to come back to Theresa, a fight would inevitably ensue. In a duplex as small as theirs, a fight between two combative adults was certain to cause distress to the children.

Jacob had already developed ways of dealing with the unpleasantries of 216 E. 6th Street. He was old enough to go over to his friend's house when things got wild. Or, he'd close his bedroom door and play Nintendo for hours until finally, he could block out all the bad things that were going on around him. Or he could simply take off on his bike. But for little Andy, things were different. He wasn't old enough to go visit friends or to take off for a long ride on his bike. He didn't even have a bike. He was stuck at home to endure and listen to whatever was happening between his new parents. When he heard yelling, he'd go investigate. Being only four and very inquisitive, he didn't know enough to leave Alvin and Theresa alone to battle it out between themselves.

Apparently the situation disturbed Andy a great deal, perhaps more than anyone involved could have realized. But, because Alvin chose to walk out when things got difficult and because Theresa was a virtual powder keg looking for a match, Andy's problems went unaddressed—at least in a constructive and helpful way. Because CPS had already decided that they had placed Andy in a home where he was better off, they remained in the dark about all that was occurring inside Alvin and Theresa's house. It's quite possible that no adult bothered to notice just how distraught Andy had become toward the end of June.

There were several things going on that Theresa had already grown impatient with and much of it focused on Andy. He was the smallest member of the household and the one who was most dependent. Andy, little more than a toddler, was totally reliant on Theresa. He was a chatterbox. His continual barrage of chatter seemed only to be interrupted by all too frequent bouts of whining, which Theresa showed a particular disdain for early on.

Like many youngsters his age, Andy was sneaky and had to be watched very closely. He got into things. Much to the dismay of practically everyone who'd been his guardian, Andy would often sneak into the kitchen, open the refrigerator and get into whatever looked yummy to him. He'd gouge his fingers into the dessert, grab a slice or two of cheese or drink milk straight from the carton. If cookies were left at the counter's edge, he'd help himself. If he could reach the bread, he'd get into it. But when it came to a full-fledged meal on a plate, he never seemed to be hungry.

Soon after he'd arrived at Theresa and Alvin's, he'd become such a picky eater that he was hardly eating enough to keep a bird alive. Theresa would ask him if he wanted a hot dog for lunch and Andy would say yes. Then, after she'd prepared it and put it in front of him, he wouldn't eat it. At first, she made Andy sit there until he ate at least a couple of bites. Most of the time, he'd sit and sit and sit until she finally gave up and sent him off to bed without his meal. By the time the next meal rolled around, Andy was good and hungry and would usually eat a little of whatever was offered to him. Unless, of course, it was vegetables.

It was during one of these especially hungry times when Andy saw Theresa and Alvin eating hot chili peppers with their meal. Being an inquisitive child, he asked if he could have one. Theresa selected a nice, big juicy one for him, which Andy popped straight into his mouth and crunched down on as they had done. The smile he'd been wearing quickly vanished, his lips puckered and his eyes welled up with tears. His reaction was comical to Theresa and Alvin. Andy cried and complained that his mouth was burning and hurting. He tried to spit out the chewed up bits of pepper, but the damage had already been done. It was a long time before the burning in his mouth eased and Andy's tears stopped.

The cruel effects of the hot chili pepper didn't go unnoticed by Theresa. She thought peppers would make useful tools to threaten Andy with whenever he wouldn't eat. When the next meal rolled around, she got her first opportunity to try out her new idea.

"He never wanted to eat," Theresa said. "First, you know, I look at myself as a mom. Okay, I say 'this child has to eat', you know what I mean? And I would basically, you know, sit him down like, 'you can't get up until you eat' because I didn't see him eat nothing. And then by the next meal he was real hungry and he would eat."

Many times over the ensuing weeks, Andy would be offered an unpleasant ultimatum: either he'd finish his meal, or Theresa would make him eat a hot pepper.

Although Jessie was no longer a full time resident at Theresa's home, he did visit quite often. According to Jacob, Theresa favored Jessie and whenever Jessie did something bad, Jacob got blamed for it. It also irked Jacob that Theresa didn't treat all the kids the same. One day, Theresa bought water pistols for the kids. Seven-year-old Jessie got a primo model Super Soaker, capable of knocking down a house fire. Eleven-year-old Jacob got a smaller, cheaper, less powerful version and four-year-old Andy got a "hand gun" model that held about three tablespoons of water. Not fair, Jacob thought.

CHAPTER 11

PROBLEMS AND ABUSE
Andy's deadly thirst

When Andy and Jacob had been at the Perris home about two weeks, Andy began having potty accidents. It seemed that Andy waited until the last second before he headed off to the bathroom and frequently he waited until it was too late. When Theresa noticed him fidgeting and holding himself, she asked him if he had to go. As many little kids do, Andy said no and then the accident happened minutes later. This was hardly unusual for a child. Most parents understand that with a little more coaxing and questioning, a child can be helped to the realization that, yes indeed, he does have to potty and he'd better go to the bathroom now, before it's too late. But Theresa wasn't patient enough to do this. She'd ask once and, if Andy said no, she didn't question him. That's when the accidents occurred.

The first few times it happened, Theresa dealt with it in an appropriate way, but as the problem worsened over the next week, she grew frustrated enough to mention it to her social worker. When Alvin and Theresa had gotten custody of Andy, they were unaware of anything in his paperwork that suggested Andy had not successfully completed his potty training.

"The social worker said 'he has a history of it,' and that was the first time they had told me about it," Theresa said later. Apparently, Andy was suffering from something the social worker called *attachment disorder*. "It was 'cause he'd been moved so many times." It was suggested that Andy just needed some time to adjust to his new surroundings and that things would soon settle down. But that's not quite the way things evolved. The situation inside 216 East 6th Street was never going to settle down and there was no way that a four-year-old child could adjust to the horrific things he was hearing and seeing on a daily basis.

As Alvin and Theresa's marital misery reached a crisis level and their fighting escalated to an ear-splitting, all-out verbal assault on each other almost every time they came face to face, Andy began wetting his pants almost daily. Sometimes he'd have several accidents during the course of a single day. Quite often, no sooner would Theresa get Andy into a dry pair of pants, than he'd wet himself again. Because of the turmoil between Alvin and her, Theresa's patience with just about everything had worn mighty thin and she wasn't about to put up with a kid that peed and pooped in his pants several times a day. Unfortunately, she chose to hide her ever-worsening marital problems from her caseworker. Theresa was never honest enough to admit—to her caseworker, her mother or anyone—that the

113

atmosphere inside the home had been consumed with hate, violence and deafening arguments. Arguments that, contrary to foster parenting rules, often took place in front of the children. Theresa never made the connection between the daily turmoil and Andy's potty accidents, but she knew that exposing foster children to parental fighting and arguing was just cause for the kids to be taken away from her. *That* connection she definitely made and went to great lengths to conceal all that was negative in her life, which was almost everything.

Still, things only seemed to get worse. Theresa felt that Alvin was a slacker. In her opinion, she worked her ass off at the weight clinic and then, on her time off, she had to deal with the kids almost single-handedly. It was too much and lately Alvin's laziness and irresponsibility had become the flash point of many arguments. Alvin needed to get off his butt and start participating in the household. Theresa was adamant about it and insisted they come to some sort of agreement to balance out the chores and responsibilities that came along with running a home and taking care of two little kids. They argued about it at every opportunity, often long into the evening. With shouts and arguments ringing in his ears as he fell asleep, it's little wonder why Andy began wetting his bed at night.

By the time July rolled around, Andy's potty problems were aggravating Theresa, big time. It was miserably hot outside and the urine smell emanating from Andy's bed and the clothes hamper made the whole house reek. But it wasn't just that. She was angry about Alvin; her brief marriage was obviously on the rocks and she wanted a divorce. She was at her wits end with Andy... and with everything else. Something had to give!

Over the past two weeks, she'd noticed that Andy was seldom hungry; instead he always wanted something to drink. Soda, water, juice...he'd drink anything. His thirst seemed unquenchable. If anyone left an opened can of soda unattended, Andy would guzzle it down in a flash. Ditto for beer, wine, juice, water or anything drinkable. He was a drink rustler and would often sneak into the refrigerator and drink whatever he could get his hands on.

"He would always say 'no' to food, always, but he would always say 'yes' to a drink," Theresa recalled. She began to suspect that perhaps Andy's potty problems stemmed from the fact that he was always loading up on fluids and hardly eating enough to keep a sparrow alive. So, she decided to limit his intake of liquids and laid down a rule that Andy couldn't have anything to drink until he finished all his food. But that didn't always work. Even when she knew he hadn't had very much to drink, he'd still wet his pants and that really grated on Theresa's already frayed nerves.

Many times, contrary to what she had learned in foster parenting class, Theresa ridiculed Andy and called him a baby for wetting his pants. She taunted him with the threat of having to wear a diaper if he didn't stop. Andy knew a diaper was something only babies wore and he felt like he, at four, was a "big boy." The idea of wearing a diaper certainly didn't appeal to Andy, but try as he did to control his bladder, he kept right on having accidents. Consequently, Andy frequently had his bottom swaddled in a diaper and he didn't like it one bit.

With children, praise goes a long way. Reinforcing good behavior can do more good than punishing the bad. Surely, Theresa had learned this in her third parenting class which discussed discipline, or her sixth class on behavior modification, or the seventh class that covered child development. If all those failed to ring a bell with her, surely, during the class on self-esteem she had learned that praise is so much more effective than criticism. More than likely, she was told about the power of praise during every class, whether or not it was the main topic. Foster kids had enough negative situations in their lives, why add to it?

Instead of praising Andy when he successfully used the toilet like a big boy, she chose to verbally assault him and demean him when he regressed, inflicting even more emotional anguish upon his already broken spirit.

One evening Theresa asked Andy why he insisted on using his bed for a toilet. Apparently, four-year-old Andy failed to grasp the seriousness of the situation. In a silly streak, Andy giggled and said his bed was for pee-peeing and the toilet was for sleeping. He was being silly, but Theresa didn't think it was funny.

"Okay," Theresa said, taking him by the hand. She led him into the bathroom, pointed to the toilet and told him to get on his "bed." There he sat, in the dark, until Theresa decided he'd learned his lesson—again by the use of negative reinforcement. When she finally came in to get him, Andy was slumped on the toilet, asleep.

If Theresa had consulted her mother, whom she claimed to be so closely bonded to, she might have been able to better understand Andy's predicament. Her mom had been in the foster parenting network for several years and had dealt with many children who had been bounced from place to place. Some apparently suffered from the same attachment disorder as Andy did. What had she done in situations like this? Could she have possibly aided in Andy's potty training? Could she have intervened in the trouble that was brewing? Was Theresa's mom aware that Andy was signing his own death sentence every time he wet his pants? Obviously not.

Theresa had a lot to hide. She knew that if she were honest enough with her social worker to confess that her marriage was on the skids and that there was a lot of fighting going on in front of the children, she'd loose custody of them. She knew CPS might decide that Andy and Jacob would, once more, be better off somewhere else. That would have been the end of it, right then and there. Had she admitted that one simple fact, things might have developed differently for everyone involved—especially Andy. But Theresa didn't want to be branded a failure and she certainly wasn't about to be humiliated by loosing the children, so she kept her mouth shut. Unfortunately, so did Alvin and everyone else even remotely aware of the horrific situation that was unfolding.

Alvin and Theresa were too busy working on the demise of their marriage to realize how much their problems had also affected the children, mainly Andy. Considering the close relationship Theresa had with her mom and that her mom had had years of experience with foster kids, it was baffling that Theresa didn't confide her ever-burgeoning dilemma with Andy's potty problems. Throughout the ensuing weeks, the issue with Andy seemed to have been left to fester and to further infect Theresa's already vile and poisonous personality.

It seemed the sordid events going on inside their apartment were kept under tight wraps. So secret were the actions and problems of Alvin and Theresa that not even Alvin's best friends or his parents knew about many of them. Sure, Richard and Chas knew that Alvin and Theresa didn't have a good marriage and that Alvin was screwing around on her, but they had no idea how awful the situation really was. Only four people knew the real magnitude of the anger and hatefulness that was raging inside the small, blue duplex at 216 E. 6th Street—and one of them would carry this dirty little secret to his grave.

Alvin continued to spend night after night away from Theresa and freely admitted he only went over there for sex. Alvin talked to his friends about some of his marital woes and his parents were encouraging him to move back home where he belonged. Leroy and Susie would have been thrilled to pieces if Alvin had left Theresa. As for the kids, well, Alvin just didn't have much to do with them.

"I didn't know what to do with the kids," Alvin said later. Even though Alvin had known Richard for ten years, Richard still did not know Alvin had acquired two foster children. Like the Reverend Davenport, Richard would not learn about Andy or Jacob until early August. By then it would be too late.

The second week of July wore on. Dawn Masterson had been beseeching CPS to let her visit Andy under the supervision of Theresa. CPS was agreeable to this arrangement. They wanted to re-introduce Dawn and Andy slowly.

On July 16th, Dawn met with Andy in a public park in Hemet. At first, Andy seemed withdrawn and hesitant to be friendly with her; he would only address her as "excuse me." But Dawn managed to loosen him up. She drew him into a game of Frisbee and they had a good time. However, she noticed that Andy was dressed in long pants and a long sleeved shirt. She thought this was very strange, it being the middle of July and all. Still, she thought that Alvin and Theresa seemed like open, honest and caring people. At the end of the get-together, Andy said he'd call her. She tried to tickle his belly, but Andy quickly pulled away from her. Apparently he didn't like having the lower part of his belly touched, so she gave him a light hug instead.

Dawn had just finished her foster parent training with Social Services on June 30th and she was still anticipating that Andy would soon be coming to live with her. Although she had enjoyed the meeting in the park, it left her feeling rather slighted to have to turn her grandson back over to Theresa. The three adults talked about possibly taking Andy, Jacob and her other grandson, Jonathan, to Disneyland someday soon. Andy's eyebrows jumped into his hairline at the prospect of getting to meet Mickey Mouse in person. Dawn wanted Andy so much!

Mike and Lynn Herman had called Dawn a couple of times in mid-July, wanting to talk to her about why Andy had been taken from them, but Dawn was leery. She told Mike she would only correspond with them via E-mail. Then, abruptly, Mike received an E-mail from Dawn that said not to contact her any more. Dawn advised them that any further attempts to contact her would be viewed as harassment. Mike and Lynn were shocked. What on Earth was going on?

Because Dawn was employed by The Department of Public Social Services, she knew she was not supposed to be in contact with Andy's other guardians. She didn't want anything to become problematic in her efforts to obtain custody, so, in an effort to be upfront and honest with her social worker, Dawn printed copies of all the E-mails and turned them over to her case worker.

Soon after the meeting in the park, Theresa got fed up with Andy's potty problems. Theresa decided to restrict him from having anything to drink after dinner. She figured that if he didn't drink before bedtime, he wouldn't wet his bed. That idea may have worked well with other children, but in this particular case, it had no effect whatsoever on Andy's bedwetting dilemma. The problem continued unabated. No matter what Andy did—or what Theresa did—the potty problems only got worse, as did the marital problems. At that point in time, Theresa was nothing but a raging, snarling maniac. Life, in general, was pretty wretched for everyone at 216 East 6th Street. It was like walking on flypaper. Each step only worsened the situation. Theresa was totally disgusted; she was surging with anger and felt desperate to find a way to break Andy's bad habit.

Perhaps a little "time-out" would do the trick. Yes, that was it, the magic solution to at least one of her problems. Domination and wicked thoughts of possible punishments slithered through her mind. There was nothing she could do about that son-of-a-bitch Alvin, but there was damn sure something that could be done about Andy. Yes, Andy would get time-out when he wet his pants. That would teach him!

Andy had a small, blue chair that was designed especially for pint-sized tykes like him. Up until now, the chair had been his to sit in and watch TV. Little did he realize his favorite chair was about to become a platform for murder.

Theresa began calling it the "time-out chair" and made Andy sit on it, sometimes facing a wall, when he misbehaved or had potty accidents. But Andy, being the rascal that he was, rather enjoyed sitting on the time-out chair. He liked being the center of attention and sat there with a big grin on his face, which infuriated Theresa even further. There was no way Andy could have understood that the chair had taken on a new purpose. His goofy clowning quickly got under Theresa's skin and she groped to find something else that would seem like more of a punishment to him. Pretty soon she was making him stand on the chair.

In ways, it seemed Theresa had a sparring partner with Andy; after all, there was rebel in his bloodline. The infamous Cowboy Setzer was his father and Cowboy sure knew how to spur the bull into action. Andy was only a fraction of Theresa's size—weighing just forty-four pounds—and only four years old, but the fact that Andy challenged her only made a bad situation worse. It must have annoyed her greatly that her opponent was only a helpless little kid. To Theresa, it seemed that Andy wasn't trying to get his potty problems under control; he wasn't viewing the situation with the seriousness it merited. She had no patience with his silly antics and she didn't appreciate the fact that Andy thought standing on the chair was funny.

It wasn't funny for very long though; it soon became downright terrifying whenever he was ordered to stand on the little blue chair. That's when the chair that had once been his plaything became a "bad" thing. He stopped sitting in it unless he was told to do so and he gave it a wide detour and a cautious glance whenever he passed by it. The chair seemed to have a force all its own, lurking in the corner, anxious for another chance to become part of his discipline. The little blue chair seemed to taunt Andy whenever he looked at it. Just the sight of it soon became something that upset him.

The days wore on and got even hotter. And, the potty problems persisted. As the temperatures increased, so did Theresa's obsession with castigating Andy. Much of her anger stemmed from the trouble she was having with Alvin. She was powerless in her marriage, unable to keep her man at home. It infuriated her to think that the only power she had was over a four-year-old kid; a little kid who was about as helpless as a kitten on a freeway.

To intensify Andy's punishment, she made him stand on the chair and hold his arms straight out. When he began to complain about his arms being tired, Theresa seemed glad that she'd finally found a form of punishment that got a serious reaction from Andy. When his arms drooped, he got a vicious onslaught of threats spewed in his face. Alvin remembered another form of punishment Theresa began inflicting on Andy about that same time.

"We had a little brown stool and she'd make him lay on it with his stomach right here and stretch his arms out. And his feet would be stretched out too." Alvin claimed to have tried to intercede on Andy's behalf, but as soon as Alvin told Andy to get off the stool, Theresa would order Andy to stay on it. There was Andy, spread-eagle on the stool, caught between two massive, combative adults who were ordering him to do opposite things. Andy was confused about which parent to obey. Fatigue tempted him to obey Alvin, but fear warned him that he should obey Theresa. So, on the stool he remained, crying in agony. Even in Alvin's deficient mind, he surmised the way Andy was being treated amounted to nothing less than torture. Each day Andy seemed to get a little more traumatized by the constant barrage of punishments that came his way no matter what he did. It was little wonder that his potty problems got worse.

To anyone with enough interest to find out some of the many reasons why children wet their pants, printed research clearly indicates that stress is a major factor. With bed wetting, deep-sleep patterns and heredity are also important factors. There is no set age limit as to when a child should become potty trained. Indeed, many thousands of teenagers—much to their distress—continue to wet the bed at night, sometimes until they're on the verge of adulthood. In 1999 there were hundreds of books on the subject of potty training and bedwetting and an endless number of magazine articles were printed in a wide variety of publications. All of this was right at Theresa's fingertips...if only she had cared enough to seek a solution.

In her opinion, Andy's problem was his attitude. When she asked him why he wet his pants, he came back at her with smart-aleck answers. Theresa didn't like his sassy mouth or his cavalier attitude about something that was driving her nuts.

There was a white baby crib in Alvin and Theresa's bedroom that was used when Theresa took care of her mom's infant foster child. This crib soon became yet another device which Theresa used to threaten and humiliate Andy. She told him she'd make him sleep in the baby bed if he continued to wet his pants and bed. Andy didn't like being called a baby and the prospect of having to sleep in the baby bed was very unsettling to him. Wearing diapers was bad enough, but Andy had no way of communicating to Theresa or Alvin that he wanted very much to get his potty problems under control. He simply couldn't. It wasn't that he did it on purpose; it just seemed to happen. He didn't know why. He didn't enjoy it any more than she did and he was doing his best to be a big boy.

Theresa was resourceful at finding new threats and punishments that could be used to intimidate Andy. Theresa vividly remembered the first time she told Andy-she'd give him a cold shower if he wet his pants.

"And then one day, it was like real hot outside and I told him, 'you know what, if you pee-pee on yourself, I'll give you a cold shower.'" And she kept her promise. The cold shower proved to be quite a deterrent for little Andy; after just one cold shower he stopped wetting his pants for almost a week. Of course she was diligent in keeping his punishment foremost in his mind at all times. Over and over throughout the day Theresa would glare at Andy and remind him of the cold shower that awaited him if an accident happened. That would scare Andy and he would plead with Theresa not to subject him to a cold shower again.

Deadly Thirst

Cold showers weren't the only things that Andy had grown fearful of. Theresa had begun using Andy as a target whenever she needed to vent about something. Her rage was overflowing into almost every aspect of her life and Andy, being totally defenseless, was a sitting duck...the perfect victim...the ultimate match that would set off her powder keg of violence.

At eleven years old, Jacob was a sixth grader at A Street Elementary school. If Theresa had treated Jacob the same way she treated Andy, Jacob would have been able to report her to someone in authority at school—a school nurse, or a favorite teacher, or even the principal. But school was out of session at that time, so Jacob had no one to talk to about the way Andy was being treated. Jacob was a smart kid and Theresa knew it. Even though Jacob was always respectful, he intimidated Theresa more than Alvin did. She could bully Alvin and get away with it, but Jacob just might tell someone. Like Alvin, when she did things she knew were wrong, she was clever with it. She only abused Andy physically when Jacob wasn't around. She began pushing Andy and treating him roughly. It was around this time that Alvin happened to see her push Andy off the bed backwards. Andy landed on the floor—hard—on his butt and he cried about it. In his own meek way, Alvin tried to reason with Theresa.

"Why you do that?" But whenever Alvin opposed Theresa, she'd turn her viciousness in *his* direction. He was careful not to set her off. Much of the time Alvin was perplexed at Theresa's behavior; there was no rhyme or reason for the hateful things she said and did. Alvin always hated it when she'd trip-out on him.

"Man, she's trippin' again..." he'd mumble as he headed for the door. Leaving worked well for Alvin, but the kids, especially Andy, paid a heavy price during Alvin's absence. One of them was about to pay the ultimate price.

It wasn't long before Jacob came to Alvin and told him that things were tough at home when he was gone. Alvin could clearly see that Jacob was upset about something, but Alvin felt powerless and was afraid to intercede. Jacob said Theresa was mean to Andy.

One day not long after that, both Andy and Jacob were with Theresa at the weight clinic. Theresa had ordered a fast food breakfast for the boys, an Egg McMuffin for Jacob and some French toast strips for Andy. Within a few minutes, Theresa became impatient because Andy wasn't eating fast enough. "Eat!" she yelled. Andy tried to comply and took a few more bites without swallowing. But every time she yelled, he got more upset until he finally lost his appetite altogether and began to whine. "Eat!" she said, glowering over him. Exasperated, she stuffed several strips of French toast into his mouth and ordered him to hurry up and eat it. With his mouth packed to the extent that he couldn't even swallow or close his mouth, he couldn't immediately comply with the order. Theresa went berserk and began pricking Andy in the lips with a hypodermic needle. Jacob could hardly believe his eyes. Poor little Andy couldn't cry out because his mouth was full, so he only moaned.

Later, Theresa would insist that the safety cap had been on the needle and that it was unused, but that's not how Jacob remembered it. By her own admission, Theresa said she used needles to scare Andy when he wouldn't eat. She didn't think anything was wrong with that. "I scared him with a needle to make him eat," she said rather matter-of-factly as she swiveled demurely back and forth in her chair.

The kids often had to go with Theresa to the weight clinic because Alvin wouldn't or couldn't baby sit. At the clinic, finding ways to amuse themselves quietly as the hours dragged by wasn't easy, especially for Andy. He quickly grew impatient and bored. It wasn't fun. He couldn't run around and blow off the enormous amount of energy which is typical of a four-year-old kid. He had to be still and quiet. Consequently, he did a lot of coloring. Boring, boring, boring. One day he was whining and making a fuss that was disturbing the one and only patient in the clinic at that time. Jacob heard Theresa tell Andy to knock it off. When he looked around he was shocked to see Theresa slap Andy across his face. Of course, that did nothing to help quiet him.

There were other abusive acts; some that Jacob didn't actually see, but he heard them and he witnessed the aftermath of them. One such instance occurred behind the closed door of Theresa's bedroom, which was directly across the hall from the boys' room.

One day while Jacob was watching television, he thought he heard Andy being strangled. He turned down the volume on the TV and listened more closely. Sure enough, it was a choking, strangling sound and it was definitely Andy's voice. Before he could respond, the bedroom door swung open and out came Theresa holding Andy up by his arm. Jacob was horrified by what he saw. Jacob said that Andy's face was red and he couldn't stand up. It looked as if Andy was on the verge of passing out. To Jacob, it appeared that Theresa had strangled Andy, but he couldn't really be sure of it. He wanted to think that maybe Andy had just choked by himself, but Jacob doubted that. Surely, if Andy had been choking, Theresa would have said so. But she didn't. She just said, "Look at how he drops," insinuating that Andy had thrown another one of his falling-down tantrums. With Andy, she could go from civility to savagery—and back again—in seconds. Jacob was suspicious about what had happened that day behind the closed door of Theresa's bedroom and he continued to suspect that Theresa had done something bad to Andy. While he didn't know exactly what had happened, he didn't think Andy had thrown a tantrum because he would have been able to hear it. When Andy threw a tantrum, everybody heard it. The choking sounds would come back to haunt Jacob for a long time.

Around the middle of July, Theresa became infuriated yet again when Andy wet his pants. Alvin had just returned from one of his "away" times and he and Theresa were fighting about it. Alvin was coming out of the bathroom when he saw Theresa kick Andy in the groin.

"I kinda glimpsed and I seen her kick him," he said. "She kicked him in the nuts. I pulled his pants down and his testicles had swelled up. So I told her, I say, 'you gotta take him to the doctor.' And she say, 'fuck you! Blah, blah, blah...' So I gets on the phone and I was like, man, what should I do? And she goes, 'well you do anything and my family's gonna fuck you up.' And so I'm like...man..." his voice trembled when he recalled the scene. "She was sitting on the bed and he was standing on that little chair, and she kicked him in the nuts, like that..." Alvin said Theresa had kicked Andy in the groin repeatedly, about five times. Alvin recalled that Andy had dropped like a puppet with the strings cut—screaming, his face contorted with pain. "I seen him go down. He goes down off the chair and hits the floor. But she's still fussing at him, you know. I kept telling her, 'you can't do this' but she'd kicked him 'cause he'd peed on himself."

Later that same day, Theresa drew a tepid bath for Andy and as he was getting into the water she too noticed his genitals were very swollen and angry-looking but she didn't offer any apologies. Just before bedtime, Alvin noticed Andy was limping and had become very sullen, so Alvin thought he'd have a little man-to-man talk with him. Alvin picked Andy up and sat him on his lap, but Andy cried out in pain, insisting his wee-wee hurt. Alvin peeked inside Andy's pajama bottoms and saw that Andy's testicles and penis were still very swollen and red. Alvin knew it was painful for Andy, especially since Alvin had many times been the subject of Theresa's violence toward male genitalia. It was a sight no man could have easily ignored. It worried Alvin enough to call his mom, who was a nurse, and ask her what she'd do for someone who had "swollen nuts." Susie, completely unaware of *who* was suffering from swollen nuts, advised the person to put ice on it. So that's what Alvin and Theresa did. They crushed some ice, wrapped it in a towel and made their four-year-old foster child hold it on his swollen genitals. Susie's medical advice helped; the swelling went down somewhat so nothing further was done about the situation. Theresa figured that if he wasn't bleeding, he'd be okay. And that was that.

The swelling had eased a little, at least temporarily, but the pain still coursed through Andy's body with agonizing jolts of misery. He continued to suffer excruciating pain, the likes of which Alvin, a grown man, easily understood. Perhaps Alvin had some sympathy for Andy, but he certainly didn't tell anyone about the abuse because, in his own words, he knew the consequences of it. "I didn't want nothin' to happen to *me*, man." He didn't want to make any waves with the almighty Theresa. Alvin always sought the easy way out of every confrontational situation. "She'd tell Andy to 'come here' and then when Andy would come to her, she'd kick him."

The kicking seemed to be a phenomenal release for Theresa's maniacal temper and it most definitely made Andy very sorry about what he'd done. It was a way to blow off steam, vent some anger and some hatred and to punish by means of pain. Poor little Andy was traumatized, confused, afraid and in constant, excruciating pain as a result of his testicles being repeatedly kicked with three hundred pounds of brute force. He knew wetting his pants was a bad thing to do, but he couldn't help it. Over and over, he promised to be a good boy.

Soon after that he began having trouble controlling his bowels.

One evening after Andy had defecated in his pants, Theresa sent him into the bathroom to sit on the toilet. Exactly what this was supposed to accomplish after the fact is unclear, but as Andy was getting off the toilet, he smeared the seat with fecal matter. Seething, Theresa wiped the feces on Andy's face and made him clean up the mess.

It was nearing the end of July and temperatures were soaring close to one hundred degrees every day. One afternoon, Alvin was home watching the kids and, in Alvin's words, Andy had "pooped himself." Alvin hadn't done anything about it because he'd been so absorbed with the TV. Or maybe he was just too lazy. After all, taking charge was not Alvin's thing. Around noon, Theresa came home from work for her lunch break and immediately noticed Andy had a stinky problem. When she looked into the back of his pants and saw what he'd done, she went holy-hell ballistic.

Enraged, she grabbed Andy and dragged him into the bathroom. There, she did the unthinkable...she forced him to eat his own feces. Alvin heard the commotion and went into the bathroom to see what the hell was going on. Apparently, Theresa had reached into Andy's pants, grabbed a handful of poop and had crammed it into Andy's mouth. By the time Alvin got to the bathroom, it was too late. There stood Andy, gagging, his face and mouth smeared with excrement. Andy had been horribly degraded and violated by the person he was most dependent on. He was defiled in one of the most inhumane and dangerous methods of abuse one human being could possibly inflict on another. It was inconceivable that an adult—entrusted to protect the child—had resorted to such hideous means of discipline.

"She literally put it in his mouth," Alvin said. "So I says, 'Man, you go sit down! You don't do that!' But then she threatened *me* and said she was gonna call the police on *me*. So I says 'go ahead, I got an earful to tell 'em too!'" Unfortunately, Alvin never said another word about it. Not to anyone.

Alvin claimed to have no say in anything that happened around the house, especially anything that had to do with the kids. Theresa had told him to stay out of it, the kids were *her* concern, not his. According to Alvin, it was Theresa's way or no way. And Theresa's way was becoming dangerously sadistic.

"I had no say over nothing; I was just there," he said. But most of the time, Alvin *wasn't* there. His marriage was already in its death throes and he continued to spend many nights at his parents' home and with his friends. It seemed that anyplace was better than 216 East 6th Street. Sleeping in his car was better than sleeping with the venomous snake that Theresa had become. By then, she was regularly taking out her frustrations on Andy and she hadn't been caught by anyone other than Alvin. The abuse became addictive for Theresa. She tried it, she liked it and as long as Andy could take it, she would do it again and again. She was torn between the fear of getting caught and the overwhelming release she got from it. By then she harbored a virulent hatred for her husband and was taking out all her frustrations on Andy.

It was right around this time that Theresa began to jab Andy in the stomach. She pretended it was all in play, but every once in a while her jabs caused Andy to double over in pain. On one occasion, Jacob witnessed a particularly hard jab to Andy's stomach and voiced his concern to Theresa. Angered at being challenged by an eleven year old kid, Theresa quickly gave Jacob a jab in the stomach to show him that it didn't hurt. But it *did* hurt and Jacob let Theresa know it, in no uncertain terms. Later, Theresa would look back on the stomach-jabbing game and claim it had all been harmless fun. She likened it to a game called "frog" that involved whacking each other on the shoulders. So why all the fuss about a harmless jab in the tummy?

At the end of July, Alvin had been gone nearly a week. As far as she was concerned, he had just hammered the last nail into the coffin their marriage had become. During his absence, she'd been taking the kids to work with her and had made up her mind once and for all that she wanted a divorce. Theresa promptly got divorce papers drawn up. She garnished them with her flamboyant signature on Thursday, July 29th and felt gratified that the decision had finally been made. She planned to officially file for divorce on Monday morning, August 2nd. When she got home that night, she set the divorce papers in a prominent place on the black metal filing cabinet next to the front door.

The following day Alvin showed up at the weight clinic. When Theresa gleefully announced that she had divorce papers for him to sign, Alvin was absolutely shocked. He made it clear that he had no intention whatsoever of signing any goddamned divorce papers. Theresa wasn't going to argue with him about it, at least not at work. Her mind was made up and that's all there was to it. Her way or no way.

Alvin took off and stewed about it for the rest of the afternoon. He ended up going over to the apartment that evening to discuss the divorce issue. That's when Theresa triumphantly blasted him with the news that she was moving out…without him. She'd already arranged to rent a better apartment in a safer part of town and this time Alvin was *not* invited to join them. It would be just Theresa and the kids. Period.

As usual, an argument erupted and went straight to the bone when Theresa insisted the apartment would be in her name only. Alvin was not only incensed that Theresa was leaving him; he had suddenly begun to feel abandoned. His parents had taken care of him his whole life until he married Theresa, at which time she took over the duty. But now, with Theresa leaving him, Alvin was beginning to feel like he'd have to go crawling back to Momma and Daddy again.

By the next day however, Alvin had changed his tune. He was eager to sign; ranting and raving about how Theresa should have made an extra copy for him so that, if she didn't file, *he* could do it.

That evening Theresa was still reveling in her sense of power. While she and Jacob were in the living room watching TV, Andy was misbehaving. It irked her that Andy was interrupting the movie, so she decided to punish him with the stool again. Pulling the stool to the center of the living room, Theresa told Andy to lie on his back on the stool and hold his arms and legs straight out. With his testicles still swollen and extremely sore, just trying to get into this position sent jolts of pain shooting throughout every inch of his body. Andy immediately began to cry and beg for leniency. Andy looked over at Jacob and cried for help, but Jacob remained frozen in terror. He wanted very much to defend Andy, but he knew better than to go against Theresa.

It was impossible for Andy to stay in the commanded position for more than a few seconds. He defiantly got off the stool without getting permission. Wailing in protest, he limped off to his bedroom and slammed the door. Theresa grabbed a snack, heaved herself onto the couch and resumed her movie. Minutes later, Jacob excused himself for bed. Early.

On the morning of Saturday July 31st, Alvin hadn't planned on being anywhere near Theresa and the kids, but somehow things worked out that way.

The day dawned bright and hot. Temperatures were already pushing one hundred degrees by 10 A.M. Theresa still worked at the weight clinic half a day on Saturdays, from 9 to 1. On this particular morning, Alvin was accommodating enough to drive Theresa to the clinic because her car wasn't running. They brought Andy and Jacob along. He and the two boys decided to spend a fun day at nearby Lake Elsinore while Theresa put in her four hours of work. Then he would drive her back home. Apparently, Theresa felt confident enough about Alvin's mental abilities to trust that he wouldn't let Andy or Jacob wander dangerously close to the water or out into traffic. She knew that Alvin had enough sense to be able to take care of himself and two little kids. He knew enough to make sure Andy was safely strapped into his car seat and that he and Jacob wore a seatbelt.

Alvin had no trouble navigating around town that day. Driving in Lake Elsinore could be a taxing experience, especially in the summer months when lakeside traffic was bumper to bumper. For drivers anxious to park their car and go for a swim, the tow-away zones and no parking signs that flank Lakeshore Drive could be daunting obstacles to get around. More importantly, the shores of Lake Elsinore are buffered with one-way streets, which were frustrating even to smart drivers. All those rules and regulations would have confused most retarded people, but apparently, Alvin had no trouble at all that afternoon. Well, perhaps there was one problem... the

Deadly Thirst

divorce issue was still eating away at him. In fact, he was damn pissed-off about it.

After he and the boys visited the lake and stopped by an auto parts store, he took the kids to Carl's Jr. around 10:30. There he ordered everyone hamburgers, fries and drinks. Carl's was in the same parking lot as the weight clinic and Theresa joined up with them for an early lunch. A pall seemed to fall over the group as soon as she arrived. As usual, Andy had gulped down all of his drink before he had done much damage to his hamburger and then began whining about being full. Right away, Theresa started in on Andy with another one of her loud, stern reprimands. "What did I tell you about doing this…" Before long, Andy was crying and had become too upset to finish his hamburger. Several customers in the restaurant had become annoyed by all the yelling and crying and were now glaring in her direction, but Theresa didn't care.

That wasn't the first instance when Andy had been brought to tears at mealtime. Practically every meal had become something that only filled him with grief. No wonder he was never hungry. With the temperatures hovering at the one hundred degree mark almost every day, it was also easy to understand why he was constantly thirsty. As a medical assistant, Theresa knew full well how important it was to keep the body hydrated during the hot weather, but she only saw Andy's thirst as the cause of his potty problems—which she intended to put a stop to one way or another!

The landlord of the building had mentioned to Theresa that he was looking for someone to do some clean-up work around the grounds and told her he'd pay forty dollars to get the job done. Theresa had told him Alvin would probably be willing to do it. So while they were still at Carl's she talked about it with Alvin and he said okay. It would be easy money and a good way to pass the time until Theresa got off work at one o'clock. Since Andy was irritable and whining, they went back to the office and Theresa put him down for a nap on a cot in the back room.

Outside, Alvin offered to split half the forty bucks with Jacob if Jacob would help pick up the debris. Jacob thought that was cool and off they went to pick up trash, each toting a plastic trash bag.

After a while, Theresa poked her head into the room where Andy was sacked out and immediately noticed a bad smell. She went over and peeked into the back of Andy's shorts and discovered that he did indeed have a problem. It wasn't long before the whole office started to stink, so Theresa banished Andy from the office and sent him outside to ferment in the oppressive heat.

Once outside, the combination of the stifling heat and the uncomfortable, smelly problem that was now seeping through his shorts, made Andy quite miserable. He followed Alvin and Jacob around, whining and crying until Alvin told Andy to either sit down and shut up or go back inside.

According to Alvin, Andy went back inside and was getting a drink from the water fountain when Theresa caught him red-handed in the act of getting a forbidden drink. Already mad that Andy had soiled his pants and had come back into the clinic after she'd told him to get out, she stomped over to him and stabbed him in the arm with a hypodermic needle.

"Yeah," Alvin would later recall, "she stuck it all the way in him...for drinking water! I saw her stick him!" But Alvin kept his mouth shut and, as usual, didn't come to Andy's defense. Once more Andy was banished from the office. Out by the car, he stood alone and crying while everyone else went inside to cool off and relax.

One o'clock finally rolled around. By this time, the seat of Andy's pants was an awful mess. Theresa didn't want him getting into the car like that and proceeded to wrap Andy in a plastic trash bag. It was over one hundred degrees outside and poor little Andy was being wrapped in a plastic bag for the half hour ride home in a sweltering car.

Maybe Alvin was unaware of the true extent of Theresa's anger at Andy for having soiled his pants. Rage and resentment—and Theresa had plenty of both—hidden behind a bland façade can explode in ways never imagined. It was entirely possible that Alvin didn't know Theresa was at the end of her rope, with not only the marriage, but with Andy as well.

When they arrived at the apartment, Alvin went inside for a minute, then continued on his way to visit his mom and some friends. Jacob ran around to the side of the apartment and started playing basketball. Theresa was fuming mad that Andy had messed his pants and hauled him over to where a garden hose was connected to the faucet. There, in the side yard of the small apartment building, Theresa hosed Andy off as if he were some kind of mongrel dog. She was sick and tired of working half a day on Saturdays only to come home to more work and a four-year-old kid that messed his pants every day. Furthermore, she was sick and tired of Alvin's invisible role in his share of the responsibilities. She was clearly in a rage.

As Andy stood—humiliated—in the mud, she told him to take off all his clothes. Shivering and still in tremendous agony from his swollen scrotum, Andy did his best to obediently step out of his shorts. The ground had quickly become a slippery, muddy mess, which made his assignment even more difficult. Andy no sooner managed to get all of his clothes off than Theresa began whipping him with the garden hose.

Jacob heard the screams. From where he was standing, he was only able to catch glimpses of what was happening; but he could see Theresa wielding the hose over and over and could plainly hear Andy's blood-curdling screams. Jacob was riveted with terror, but he didn't dare try to intervene.

After she'd whipped the living daylights out of him, Theresa retrieved Andy's soiled underpants from the mud. Seconds later, she called Jacob over to "see what Andy had done to himself." Jacob came from around the corner of the apartment and saw Andy—his face smeared with excrement—sprawled on his back in the mud with his legs wide open. Theresa began squirting Andy directly in the face while Andy screamed. Jacob could clearly see that Andy's scrotum and penis were swollen and had turned an ugly, deep shade of purple. He got a real good look. It was awful. He knew something was terribly wrong, but he was afraid to confront Theresa. He'd seen the treatment Alvin got whenever he opposed her and Jacob knew better than to bring that wrath on himself. With his heart pounding in his throat, he turned and began angrily bouncing the basketball.

Andy's abuse scared Jacob half to death, but he felt like he could do nothing about it. He wanted to run and get help for Andy. He desperately wanted to tell someone…tell them that his little foster brother was being beaten. Perhaps he could tell a neighbor…or maybe the police. Please, someone, help us! But Theresa had a tight reign on Jacob that particular day and didn't let him wander. The sight of Andy lying there in the mud would remain vivid in Jacob's mind for many years.

Finally, Andy was deemed to be clean enough to enter the house. As he stood there naked and shivering, Theresa went into the apartment and brought him a towel. Herding both boys inside, she drew a tepid bath for Andy and told him to get in. That proved to be almost impossible for Andy. Merely lifting his legs high enough to put one foot in front of the other and walk was almost too painful to endure. Now he was being forced to swing one leg up and over the side of the tub, which was almost half his height, and climb in. Hurry up, she barked.

Somehow, Andy got in and slowly lowered himself into the chilly water, his teeth chattering. She told him to wash himself—she wasn't about to have anyone accuse *her* of child molestation. After his bath, Andy again had to straddle the side of the tub; his tender scrotum brushed precariously close to the rim as he climbed out of the slippery bath. As further punishment, she made him wear a diaper. He winced as the diaper was pulled up snuggly between his legs. Then he went into his room, put on some clean, dry clothes and hobbled into the kitchen. It was around three as Theresa recalled. "I asked him, 'are you hungry?' and he said 'no,' so I said, 'ok, that's fine. Do you want to take a nap?'" Andy said he did and turned toward the bedroom. He'd been lying down for about an hour when Theresa called him and Jacob back into the kitchen for some hot dogs. Andy managed to eat one plain hot dog and then complained of being sleepy. Because his bed was still wet from an earlier accident, Theresa agreed to let Andy lay down on her bed.

A short while later, she peeked in to check on him and was outraged to see him standing on her bed urinating. He had taken his diaper off and had tossed it aside. She threw open the door and stomped toward him. Grabbing him by his penis and scrotum, she yanked him forward, giving his swollen scrotum a deliberate, hard squeeze. Andy screamed in agony as his sore scrotum was squeezed to the bursting point. Blood dripped from the tip of his penis.

"Didn't I tell you not to be peeing!" she hollered, yanking him off the bed. Then she noticed blood on her hand and on Andy's penis. Fearing she had done some *real* damage this time, damage that might warrant outside help, she marched him into the bathroom, stood him in front of the toilet and commanded him to go pee. Immediately. She figured that as long as there was no blood in his urine, he'd be all right.

How terrified he must have been. He didn't have to relieve himself; he'd just done so on Theresa's bed. But to disobey her would surely have been the wrong thing to do. So there he stood in front of the toilet, trying his best to pee. The swelling in his penis had caused his urethra to almost completely close off and it took some effort for Andy to comply with the mandatory urine sample. Just to touch his penis caused him unimaginable pain.

No matter what he did it was wrong and painful. There was a fierce stinging sensation as the first few drops of urine trickled from the end of his penis and seeped into the cut on his shaft. Finally, Andy was able to release just enough urine to satisfy Theresa, who stood there glowering down at him. She was relieved to see there was no blood in his urine, but was still furious that he'd peed on her bed. Remembering the blood on her hand, she quickly turned on the faucet and rinsed it off. Snatching a paper towel from the rack, she wiped the last traces of abuse from her hands as Andy finished up.

Then she noticed there was blood on Andy's hands. With a yank, she hoisted him up and sandwiched him in between her massive body and the hardness of the bathroom sink so he could wash his hands. With one arm she held Andy around the lower part of his abdomen while she turned on the water with her other hand. Andy screamed in agony as his inflamed and horribly swollen genitals were crushed against the sink.

The scream was so shrill and bloodcurdling it was a wonder the neighbors didn't call 911. Andy was plunked down on the floor and handed a paper towel to dry his trembling hands. Theresa then handed him a washcloth to hold against his bleeding penis and told him to go to bed. Slowly, he made his way into his room and crawled onto the bare mattress that was his bed.

Alvin had been out with his buddies when he got a page from Theresa around 8:00 P.M. When he called her, she asked him to come home right away. She needed to talk to him about something, but she wouldn't discuss it on the phone.

Alvin was a little embarrassed to admit to his friends that he was going to have to call it a night and go home to the wife and kids. He joked about it though because, in his mind, he figured he was gonna score himself a piece of ass. Shit, she was practically begging for it.

"I was already thinking, hell...I'm gonna get me some..." But when Alvin arrived back home a whole other scene awaited him. Theresa was upset. She hadn't called him back home for a romp in the sack. "I went over there and she said, 'I don't know what I'm gonna do,' and I was like, 'what do you mean?' and she was, like, 'I just got mad and I pulled his dick.'"

Deadly Thirst

Theresa claimed to be at the end of her rope with the marriage and with Andy and with everything else. She bawled and told Alvin she just couldn't deal with it anymore. She said Andy had wet her bed and she'd gotten mad about it and yanked on his penis— "dick," as she called it.

It's hard to imagine a medical assistant being bashful about the proper terminology for a child's penis. But Alvin knew what a dick was and went into Andy's bedroom to have a look. There was Andy, lying on the bare mattress, his cries coming in little hiccups. He was trembling, his face streaked with tears. He looked terrified, almost cowering. And he was holding a bloody washcloth around his penis. Alvin pulled the washcloth aside and got a good look at the damage his wife had done. He could see that Andy's foreskin had been ripped and was obviously causing him a lot of pain. Alvin also noticed the hideous scrotal swelling was still there, worse than ever, but he didn't try to comfort Andy in any way. In fact, Alvin didn't say a word to Andy; he just left him lying there, whimpering in pain.

When Alvin emerged from the kids' bedroom, Theresa was frantic. Again she tried to explain that she was under a lot of stress because of the divorce and she just couldn't take it anymore. According to her description of what happened, she just "snapped."

It finally dawned on her that motherhood was something she wasn't ready for after all. She hated to think that she was a failure. A failure at marriage, a failure at motherhood! Alvin and Theresa sat down and talked about it and decided not to seek medical assistance for Andy...none of any sort. They both knew that to do so could get them into serious trouble. Even Alvin knew the consequences of child abuse. This time, Andy's injuries didn't even warrant a phone call to Alvin's mom. Later, Alvin would remember thinking, Man...this ain't happening...

One can only wonder, with great pity, what Andy must have been thinking.

Alvin had some supportive words for his soon-to-be ex-wife though, as she readied herself for bed. "It'll be okay babe," he told her as the idea of a sexual encounter still lingered in the back of his mind. "If it's not hurting and it's not bleeding, then he'll be okay. If he starts saying it's hurting, we'll take him to the hospital."

How much louder did Andy need to scream in order for Theresa to hear that he was hurting? How much more did his genitals need to swell before Alvin could see that Andy was hurting? She felt like she was living on the rim of an active volcano, but Alvin's words were somewhat comforting to her. Theresa sat on the bed, thinking things would be better by morning.

Mercifully, Andy managed to fall asleep on the bare mattress. Sleep is one way the body calms itself after a trauma. Sleep is a tremendous escape for the mind, body and soul. During sleep, pain and the horrors of daily life fade away. On that last night of July 1999 Andy couldn't take any more of either.

However, in the middle of the night, Andy awoke in pain, crying because he'd wet his bed. Theresa threw a sleeping bag on the floor at the foot of her bed and told Andy to sleep there. Once more, he lay down and drifted off to a much needed and very welcomed sleep. Alvin left the house around 11 P.M. for work and to take his car to his dad's house.

The hot August sun broke over the horizon at 5:20 A.M. By breakfast time, the sun was already hot on the kitchen window. Andy and Jacob had been at Theresa's house for only two months. To Andy, those had been the two longest, most frightening and most painful months of his life. During those two months he longed, many times, for the gentle loving arms of Mike and Lynn Herman or his grandmother. But those people were a distant memory for Andy. His life had turned into a nightmare and no adult in his immediate circle had gentle, loving arms. The only person that could have intervened on Andy's behalf was Alvin, but Alvin chose to ignore the atrocities that were occurring in his own home.

As he had done for the last two weeks, Andy awoke to the throbbing pain in his groin. His testicles were a hideous deep shade of purple and by now the ghastly bruising had spread in a radius across his lower abdomen as well. Rubbing the sleep from his eyes, he struggled to ease himself off the sleeping bag. He had to grab on to something and pull himself up. The pain was almost unbearable, causing him to keep his legs together and take tiny baby steps to keep his testicles from jiggling around. Slowly, he limped out to the kitchen where Theresa was making Apples 'n Pancakes and eggs. It was pretty late as she recalled. After brunch, they sat around watching movies all day. It was her only day off. Alvin was still at his mom's house, working on the car. His dad had a car business and all the tools Alvin needed to fix the car.

After a couple of movies and a lunch of potpies, Theresa made Jacob and Andy accompany her on a walk to the supermarket for some groceries. Since Stater Bros. market was less than half a mile away, they walked there, because Alvin had the car. It was very late in the afternoon and the air felt like it was coming from a blast furnace. They went out past the carport and took a shortcut through the alley. Junked cars were lined up along a rusty chain link fence. Garbage dumpsters overflowed and broken glass littered the pavement.

For an average adult, making the short trip to Stater Bros. would take about ten or fifteen minutes. However, because of his crippling pain, Andy could barely walk and lagged a considerable distance behind. Oblivious to Andy's agony, Theresa constantly yelled for him to hurry it up.

They cut through an empty basketball court, its rusty hoops bent and missing their nylon webbing, the backboards scrawled with filthy words. They turned left on F Street, passed the First Baptist Church of Perris, walked two blocks and turned right on 4th. Then they continued down 4th until they were almost in front of the Perris Police station and crossed over.

4th Street was one of several main thoroughfares in Perris that had a fast flow of traffic and few crosswalks for pedestrians. Even for a sprinting adult, crossing 4th Street without the benefit of a traffic signal was dangerous. Crippled with pain as Andy was, it was nothing short of a miracle that he managed to make it to the other side alive. By the time they finally reached the air-conditioned haven of Stater Bros., Theresa was sweating heavily. Andy had slowed them down quite a bit and she was plenty pissed off because of it.

She bought some bread, a 2-liter soda, a large plastic bucket of ice cream, a gallon jug of milk and a couple of other things. As they left the checkout counter, she doled out the milk and a couple of bags to Jacob and assigned Andy to carry the bread. Then, they started the long walk home. Theresa warned Andy that he'd have to walk fast or else the ice cream would melt. In a hurry to get home with her precious cargo of ice cream, Theresa turned around several times and hollered at Andy to hurry up. Her anger was percolating.

"Walk right!" she snapped. But Andy was suffering excruciating pain and the otherwise simple task of walking was almost more than he could manage. He began to cry and whine. Jacob was concerned about Andy, especially after what he'd seen the day before during the hosing-off incident. He came to Andy's defense and tried to encourage him and keep him company. Andy's pain brought no sympathy from Theresa though; she issued him an ultimatum. "Andy, if you don't stop whining, I'm going to make you carry the heavy stuff!" He tried to silence his whimpers, but he couldn't. "Okay, fine!" she bellowed. "Jacob, give him the gallon of milk!"

Jacob didn't want to do it, but it was dangerous to disobey Theresa. Resigned to the fact that he would have to participate in the fiendish torture of his little pal, Jacob walked back to Andy and handed him the nearly nine pound jug of milk. Tears streaked down Andy's chubby cheeks as the full weight of the milk transferred from Jacob's hands. As the pain in his groin intensified with the strain of carrying the heavy milk, Andy began to wail. He sat the milk down on the hot pavement and complained about the pain in his "sore tummy." But Theresa had a cure for that. She snatched the bag of bread away from him and awarded Andy with the bucket of ice cream that weighed almost seven pounds. Then, Andy was ordered to carry the seven pound bucket of ice cream in one hand and the nearly nine pound jug of milk in the other.

"Now walk! Come on! Hurry up!" she screamed like a drill sergeant. Stomping ahead and nudging Jacob along, she turned every so often to hurl more orders at Andy. "Catch up! Keep up, keep up!" But it was no use. Andy couldn't manage another step. He sat both containers down and started bawling. "See? That's heavy, huh?" she clucked as she stood over him.

Yes. It was all that Andy could say in between sobs. But Andy's tears didn't soften her heart. Once more, she nudged Jacob ahead and left Andy behind to carry his burden. Soon, Andy was way behind again.

"Okay, keep whining," Theresa said, mopping sweat from her face. "If it takes us two hours to get home, that's fine."

They came to a point where they had to cross 4th Street again. Theresa looked both ways and then shouted at the boys to run. Jacob ran like lightning and was safely standing on the other side while Theresa was still in the middle of the street hollering over her shoulder at Andy. He had just stepped down from the curb and was trying desperately to catch up. Hurrying as best he could, with the ice cream in one hand and the milk in the other, he stumbled and fell face first in the middle of the street. The gallon jug of milk rolled away, but didn't break. The asphalt was literally sizzling, like a frying pan and Andy scrambled to his feet as fast as he could. Theresa came back to pick up the milk and ice cream and to usher Andy quickly to the other side. There, she reissued him the dirty jug of milk and the bucket of mushy ice cream and told him to hurry up.

Onward they marched. But Andy couldn't walk fast enough to please Theresa. She started walking behind him, kicking the soles of his shoes, badgering him to hustle. Each kick sent jolts of misery straight to his groin, causing him to trip several times. Savaging Andy seemed to fill Theresa with an immense feeling of power. She craved power and sought it in any form she could get.

Struggling to carry a load that equaled almost half his body weight, it was an agonizing eternity until the welcomed sight of the wretched alley-way loomed ahead. They were almost home. He was exhausted and very thirsty.

Suddenly, the plastic handle on the bucket of ice cream broke and the bucket hit the ground with a thud. Then Andy dropped the milk. When she heard the thud, Theresa came unglued.

"Andy don't do that! You're gonna break the milk open!" Even as the ice cream liquefied in the heat, Theresa didn't let up on Andy's punishment. She was going to teach him a lesson about whining! She made Jacob refasten the plastic handle on the ice cream and ordered Andy to pick it up. Ready to faint from the pain, he gripped the handle. With tears spilling from his eyes, he hoisted the bucket an inch or so off the ground. Then he picked up the milk and continued the final phase of the death march. As he stumbled along on the few remaining yards toward home, the bucket scraped along the scorching pavement. His groin was throbbing; the pain was almost paralyzing.

Finally, they were home. Before he could come inside, she made Andy wash the dirt off the milk and then snatched it away from him. He desperately wanted a drink of water, but he would get none. It was about 7:30 P.M. by then and the sun was still high in the sky. Andy repeatedly asked for a drink, but all he got was a stern reminder that he wasn't allowed to drink before bedtime.

A late dinner finally rolled around and Theresa made chili-cheese dogs for her and the kids. It was a fast, easy meal that the kids enjoyed and it didn't require a lot of cooking in the already stifling kitchen. Originally, she was going to make a roast, but at the last minute decided against it and opted for the chili-cheese dogs instead. Too much hassle to get the kids—especially Andy—to eat roast. If it was anything that sounded even remotely like it might be good for him, Andy balked at eating it. Hot dogs and macaroni and cheese never failed.

She called both boys to the table and Jacob noticed Andy could hardly get off the couch. To Jacob, Andy looked like an old man trying to get up. He was clutching the arm of the couch, his face twisted in pain. He walked in a hunched-over position, taking baby steps all the way into the kitchen. For Andy, it was a long walk. Over the distance of about twenty feet, he was ready to collapse. Jacob was worried about Andy, but didn't dare say anything.

Mealtimes around Theresa's house weren't pleasant times. After all that Andy had been through, he wasn't hungry. He was in too much pain to even think about food. His thirst, however, was consuming. Cotton-mouthed, he couldn't eat. In protest, he spit his chili-cheese dog all over the floor. Specks of chili flew onto Theresa. Highly irritated, she tried to force the food into his mouth and got bit in the process. Not until he managed to choke down about half of his chili-cheese dog, was Andy allowed to have a drink. It was just a few sips, barely enough to satisfy him for the time being. He was so thirsty. He wanted more, but Theresa didn't want him to have anything to drink before bedtime.

Shortly after supper, Andy was still sitting at the kitchen table and passed gas loudly enough for Jacob to hear it from the living room. Jacob reminded Theresa that whenever Andy farted, it usually meant that he had to go to the bathroom. Theresa asked Andy if he had to go and, as usual, Andy said no, maybe because he didn't want to walk all the way to the bathroom. In his condition, every step seemed like a mile. But Jacob persisted to tell Theresa that if she didn't hurry up and make Andy get to the toilet, he'd poop in his pants. Realizing Jacob was probably right, Theresa finally sent Andy limping into the bathroom to sit on the potty. Within a few minutes, Andy had defecated. When Theresa went in to see about him, she was angered that Andy had sunk down into the toilet and had allowed his bottom to make contact with the contaminated water in the toilet. For that, Andy was forced to stay in that position for ten minutes. It was his punishment for being a nasty boy.

After his punishment was finished, Andy wanted to go to bed. He was exhausted from the long, painful walk to Stater Bros. and he didn't feel good. The sleeping bag was still in a crumpled pile at the foot of Theresa and Alvin's bed and Andy's bed was still without linens. Instead of hassling with making Andy's bed, Theresa told him to go ahead and camp out again. He hobbled into Theresa's bedroom and eased himself down onto the sleeping bag. He tried to sleep, but the throbbing in his groin was so intense. A short time later he got up, crying that he couldn't sleep, so Theresa punished him by making him stand on a green towel, just in case he peed. Then, she and Jacob began watching "Wrongfully Accused" on TV.

Alvin was at his parents' house when his pager alerted him. It was Theresa. She said the kids needed him and missed him. Theresa wanted him to come back home. To Alvin, it sounded like she finally wanted to get laid; she was just using the kids as an excuse. At that point in their relationship, sex was about the only thing that could have possibly enticed him to go back. He didn't give a hoot about the kids and, since she'd slapped him with divorce papers, he was already considering himself a free man.

Alvin arrived around 10:30. When Andy heard Alvin's voice, he came out of the bedroom again, crying. With his testicles swollen to the bursting point, it's no wonder he couldn't sleep. But Theresa told him to get back on the towel. Alvin showed no sympathy for Andy either. He wasn't there to see the kids; he'd come back to take care of his own needs. In spite of all the horrific things that were happening, Alvin managed to get Theresa to sit on the living room couch and watch some porno movies with him. It had been a long time since he'd had any and he was hoping the x-rated movies would help him score some much-needed relief. He figured that with all the shit that had been happening lately, she needed some visuals to get her in the mood. But it didn't happen quite the way Don Juan hoped it would. He was in overdrive, but she was stuck in neutral.

After Alvin's plans for the evening had been deemed a complete failure, they headed off to bed. Andy was finally asleep on the sleeping bag at the foot of their bed. Alvin asked Theresa to bring him some water; he'd worked up a powerful thirst watching those porno movies. She brought him a whole gallon jug of water and plunked it down on the nightstand beside their bed. Alvin took a long, satisfying drink and sat the jug back down. He set the alarm for 4:00 A. M., turned out the light and called it a night.

The darkness, however, had only just begun...

It was around 3:00 A.M. when Theresa woke up to the sounds of Andy gulping water from the jug. Furious that Andy had violated the "no drinking at night" rule, she leaned over Alvin and slapped the jug out of Andy's hands.

"What did I tell you!" she screamed. "Didn't I tell you not to be drinking water in the middle of the night?"

Alvin had been rousted from his sleep by all the commotion and soon joined in the tirade. "Why are you drinking water?" he yelled. "You know you're gonna pee on yourself!"

Andy cowered in the corner, crying, while Alvin hollered for him to hurry up and find the top to the jug. Andy fearfully set about searching for the cap, finally locating it. By then, he was screaming, terrified of what he knew was coming his way. His screaming threw Theresa further into a fit of rage. The screams also woke up Jacob. From his bed, Jacob could hear Andy screaming and Alvin yelling. He sat up in bed and listened, wondering what Andy had done to upset Theresa this time.

"Shut the fuck up!" she bellowed, hauling herself—completely naked—to a kneeling position with Alvin in between her and Andy. Alvin jumped into the melee and yelled at Andy to shut up, but Andy was too terrified to quiet himself and kept right on wailing at the top of his lungs. "Get your time-out chair!" she screamed.

Knowing full well what the time-out chair meant, Andy fearfully pulled the chair close to the bed and climbed up on it. There he stood, facing Theresa, his face streaked with tears, his mouth wide open in a plaintive wail.

"Didn't I tell you to be quiet," she screamed, right in his face. Then, Theresa took the palm of her hand and smashed it into Andy's face, sending him flying backward off his time-out chair. With a thud, his head hit the nightstand, increasing his panic. His screams grew in volume and intensity, enraging Theresa even more. "Get back on that chair and shut up, right now!" Trembling in a combination of pain and terror, Andy climbed back up on his time-out chair and faced his opponent for the last time. Bringing her right leg into position, she leaned over Alvin and screamed, "I told you to be *quiet!*" accentuating the word "quiet" with a fierce kick to Andy's stomach. Once more, Andy fell backward off his chair and struck his head on the nightstand. But this time Andy became silent.

Andy was unconscious.

The next few minutes whizzed by in a chaotic blur of panic for Alvin and Theresa. Andy was convulsing on the floor with his eyes rolled back into his head. He was silent now, except for the gurgling, gasping noises. Both adults stood over him, watching him gasp and twitch. Then, Alvin and Theresa went through a strange and instant metamorphosis, like reptiles shedding their withered skin. In the space of less than a minute, their attitudes shifted abruptly from abusive anger to concern. But their concern wasn't for the unconscious child that lay sprawled in spasms, gasping for air, on their bedroom floor. Their concern was self-centered. For several weeks Andy had withstood horrendous abuse and Theresa had been able to pull off her vicious attacks in relative secrecy. But now, things had taken an unexpected turn for the worst. In both their minds, it was as if a neon sign had begun flashing its ominous prediction: jail…jail…jail…

Theresa's first thought was that Andy was faking it, so she bent down and shook him and told him to knock it off. Then she flipped on the light. With the light came a shocking dose of reality. It was immediately obvious that Andy was in serious jeopardy. There was no way a four-year-old child could fake something like *this*. Suddenly, Andy's predicament became their focal point, but not for laudable reasons. And not for very long.

"Alvin, something's wrong with him…" she said, her voice filled with apprehension. "What's gonna happen?" Terror engulfed the bedroom as Andy failed to respond to the shaking he'd received from his county-appointed guardians. As usual, Theresa took charge.

"You gotta call 911!" she barked. But Alvin didn't think he should be the one to make the call.

"Hey, I didn't do nothin'!" Alvin retorted, already trying to distance himself from what had happened. As Theresa stood there wringing her hands, Alvin looked down at Andy. "Oh shit..." he mumbled. He pointed his finger at Theresa and said, "*You're* in trouble. *You* did it and don't put me in the middle of all this 'cause I didn't do nothin'. Matter of fact, I'm gonna leave."

Grabbing his arm, Theresa was insistent. "You gotta call 911! I don't know what I did Alvin!" While precious seconds ticked away, they kept squabbling about who should do what. Finally, Alvin lunged at the phone and punched the numbers for help. As Alvin waited for the connection, Theresa picked Andy up off the floor. "Tell them we found him outside," she said, carrying her cargo toward the door.

Dispatchers received the call at 3:15A.M. While Alvin talked with the dispatchers, Theresa took Andy outside and around to the side yard of the apartment. There, she laid him in the dirt. Her mind was racing, trying desperately to think of some way to make what she had done look like an accident.

Thinking only of herself, instead of doing CPR, Theresa methodically rolled the unconscious, non-breathing child back and forth in the dirt so that it would look like he'd been outside playing when they'd "found" him. For extra effect, she grabbed a handful of dirt and smeared it around on his face. There—that should look convincing.

Less than forty-eight hours before, Andy had stood right there, in that same dirt, while Theresa beat him with the garden hose. Now, that same dirt was being used to coat his body—front and back—like a piece of chicken on its way to the frying pan.

Then, she picked him up and brought him back inside. When she reentered the apartment, Alvin had just ended his conversation with the dispatcher. As he clicked off the phone, she dumped Andy into Alvin's arms and rushed to put on some clothes. Alvin later said, "I could feel his heart beating, next to mine, so I put him on the coffee table and then she start doing CPR. I was just stuck. I didn't know what to do."

Alvin stood there watching as Theresa first got dressed and *then* checked Andy's pulse. She was able to detect an ever-so-feeble pulse at his carotid artery. She started smacking Andy in the face and telling him to wake up but that failed to revive him. Clearing the phlegm from Andy's mouth, she covered his mouth with hers and gave him a couple of quick breaths, but only got a glimmer of response. Twice she tried to give him mouth-to-mouth, but Andy was growing more unresponsive as the minutes ticked by. Fearing the worst, she tried to make a pact with Alvin. Leaving Andy lying on the coffee table unconscious and unable to breathe, she turned toward Alvin and grabbed his arm. "I love you no matter what," she said. "Don't say nothing; we're in this together." But Alvin wasn't about to get mixed up in her shit.

"No!" he said jerking away from her deadly clutch. "*You* fucked up, not me! I ain't going to jail for what *you* did. I *can't* go to jail, I got too much to lose!" As Andy lay dying on the coffee table, Alvin and Theresa stood over him and argued about who did what and what kind of a story they could concoct that would get them out of this mess. Her biggest fear was that Alvin, stupid doofus that he was, might be a loose cannon. They had to stick together! Theresa scooped Andy up and they both hurried outside to await the paramedics.

As the faint sound of sirens approached, Theresa suddenly remembered that she'd left the divorce papers lying right in plain view on the file cabinet by the front door. Once again she dumped Andy into Alvin's reluctant arms and ran back inside to hide the papers. After they were safely hidden from sight, she took one quick look around the bedroom, but failed to notice a slightly wet spot on the carpet by the nightstand. With her heart pounding in her throat, Theresa returned to Alvin and repossessed their unconscious foster child. By then, Andy had turned blue from lack of oxygen; his skin felt cold and clammy. More than ten minutes had gone by.

Alvin clearly wanted no part in this and was more than happy to turn Andy back over to Theresa. His instincts told him to run and get the hell out of there, but Theresa grabbed his arm again and admonished him not to say anything. "Remember," she said, "we're in this together." As the sirens got closer and the flashing red lights came around the corner, Theresa tried to erase all traces of guilt from her face and rushed to the curb holding Andy in her arms. Alvin disappeared into the background. Once again, Alvin strove to put as much distance between himself and Theresa as he possibly could. By the time help arrived, Alvin was nowhere in sight.

PART 5
ARRESTS, OUTRAGE AND THE SEARCH FOR TRUTH

CHAPTER 12

THERESA BARROSO'S CONFESSION
"Why am I becoming such a monster?"

The Mercy Air helicopter landed at Loma Linda University Medical Center in San Bernardino with Andy in full arrest at 7:25 A.M. He was admitted to the pediatric intensive care unit in grave condition. He underwent x-rays, a urology screening, an abdominal ultrasound and a battery of other tests. Andy's grandmother, Dawn Masterson, was notified of his condition and rushed to Loma Linda to be near him. With compassion in their voices, the doctors told Dawn that Andy was not expected to survive and graciously allowed her to spend a few precious moments alone with him.

Approaching his hospital bed, everything felt surreal, as if she were walking through a dream—a very bad dream. Andy was covered with a white "warming blanket" and from his mouth ran a long, clear tube connected to a ventilator. All she could do was hold his little hand and cry. Dawn could hardly believe her eyes when she saw the awful state that Andy was in. Just a few short weeks ago, when she had played Frisbee with him in the park, Andy had been so full of vitality and giggles. And now, he was splayed out on his deathbed, being kept alive by life support machines. Over and over she silently begged for an answer to the one question that loomed like a thick fog in her mind: Why didn't they give him to me?

By 10 A.M. Andy had coded four times. He was on high frequency ventilation for severe respiratory distress and doctors concluded that his condition was consistent with brain death. Hospital procedure would require a second examination in six hours to corroborate this finding. If things had not improved by then, Andy would receive a final brain death declaration. If he became more stable, he would probably require exploratory brain surgery to determine the extent of his brain injuries.

* * *

Back at the Perris police station, it was 12:36 P.M. when homicide investigator Vern Horst concluded his initial interview with Theresa. It was frustrating that he hadn't gotten more out of her; he was sure she knew more than she was letting on. After assuring her that he would have some-

139

Deadly Thirst

one bring her something to eat, he went into another room where several investigators were waiting. They'd been watching Theresa's interview on closed circuit TV and immediately began offering opinions about her statements. The overwhelming consensus was that her demeanor was highly suspicious. No one liked what they'd seen; all the laughing and smiling was getting on everybody's nerves. They felt sure that Theresa wasn't being honest about the circumstances that had landed Andy in the hospital, but was she covering up for something her husband had done? It was certainly possible. Maybe Alvin had been abusing both her and Andy and maybe she was just too embarrassed to admit it. Maybe she was afraid of Alvin. Or perhaps *both* adults had been abusing Andy. All these ideas were considered. In Horst's opinion, it wasn't even a remote possibility that Andy had wandered outside and hurt himself while playing, like Theresa had said. Horst was absolutely certain that an adult had beaten him unconscious; *he knew it!* But which adult? Everyone was anxious to hear what Alvin had to say about it.

It was past lunchtime and Horst was starving, but he didn't want to interrupt the interviews with a lunch break. While Alvin's interview wouldn't take very long, Horst thought he'd better get Alvin and Theresa something to eat right away. As far as he knew, they hadn't eaten anything all day.

After a brief conference, Horst left his investigators, walked down the hall and entered a room where Alvin was sitting next to a desk. He told Alvin that lunch was on they way and tried to assume an easygoing style of questioning, hoping to loosen things up a little. Horst eased into the interview by asking routine questions like address, phone number and occupation. Alvin took out his wallet, trying to find the phone number for his employer. Horst commented that Alvin's wallet was too thick, "It's bad for your back," he told him. Alvin gave the comment little notice. He looked exhausted.

"How is he?" Alvin asked in a flat voice.

"You know, he's pluggin' along. I mean, that's all I know. They're going to call me if there's any change. But, it's taking a little bit of effort to keep up with him."

Alvin sighed and let his gaze fall into his lap. "Right."

Once all the trivial information was given, Horst asked Alvin to tell him everything that had happened with Andy. In Alvin's opinion, the biggest problem was Theresa's greedy quest for power. He complained that Theresa was in total control of his money and he was sick and tired of it. They'd split up recently and he'd been living with his folks again. Alvin said she'd gotten divorce papers drawn up and he berated her for not getting an extra copy for him. Horst asked Alvin to talk specifically about the kids.

His relationship with the kids, Alvin said, was much better than the relationship he had with his wife. Especially Jacob; he was eleven and Alvin enjoyed playing Nintendo with him. Then, he complained again that Theresa's parents were always poking their noses into his business. "It just

140

seems to me that, when I make the money she'll take it all. And then it's not just me and her talking, it's her family talking too. Getting in my business all the time." Horst nodded in agreement, but tried again to steer the conversation back to the kids.

"And now you've got a couple of kids in addition to all this."

"Right," Alvin said sorrowfully. He said his mom and dad didn't like Theresa and they especially didn't like her as a daughter-in-law. Alvin didn't want to upset his parents with all his marital troubles, but he didn't have anyone else he could go to. His mom and dad had always been there for him, he said. It irked him that Theresa had the support of a large, tightly-knit family and Alvin only had his mentally handicapped sister and his parents. Finally, in the throes of divorce and needing an escape, he'd called his friend, Chas, and asked him if he wanted to go bar hopping. "He likes going to those nudie bars," Alvin said with a grin.

To Horst, it seemed that Alvin's most urgent problem wasn't Andy's condition; it was the condition of his relationship with Theresa that bothered him most. Once more, Horst tried to turn the conversation in a direction that would get Alvin to talk about what had happened to Andy. According to Alvin, the kids had gone to work with Theresa on Saturday and before long, Andy had dirtied his pants. This had presented quite a problem when it came time to go home.

"We put Andy in a bag 'cause he had poop on his pants." Alvin said he'd tried to tell Theresa that it would work just as well to spread the plastic bag over the seat and let Andy sit on top of it, but Theresa was adamant. "She said, 'No, I'm doing this and you don't live at home with me no more.' I say, 'Okay, that's that.' But I'm very upset. I'm trying to tell her, this is not right Terry, putting him in a trash bag. That ain't right, man. I told her I said, 'you can't do that, Terry.' She's like, 'This is my car and I can do whatever I want to do.' I can't say nothing in edgewise because if I do, I'm already the bad one anyway." Alvin was about to let the conversation wander again.

Still vivid in Horst's mind was the conversation he'd had with Jacob and how Jacob had told him about several incidents of abuse he'd witnessed. Horst tried to get Alvin to talk about any abuse he may have witnessed, especially after they arrived home with Andy dressed in the trash bag. "Well, at some point doesn't she have the hose out...washing little Andy?"

"I didn't see that," Alvin said.

"Did you get out of your car and go inside the house that afternoon?"

"I can't remember." It seemed like Alvin didn't want to talk about anything except his marital problems. Horst was beginning to lose patience with Alvin's vagueness. Perhaps they were both guilty of abusing Andy and they were sticking together on it.

"Let me tell you, it would behoove you to be truthful. Right? I mean that's the only way to get through this."

"Right," Alvin mumbled into his lap.

141

Deadly Thirst

"I feel like I'm having to pull all this information out of you," Horst said. "So it'll help me if you tell me before I have to ask you. You see what I'm saying?" Alvin nodded. "That way I'll know you're being truthful with me. Did you ever see her physically discipline him?"

"No."

"Did *you* ever do anything like that?"

"I never did."

"Did you ever smack him on his back or anything like that?"

"Know what? I never even touched neither one of them kids, 'cause I knew the consequences on it."

"Did Andy make any motion like he was hurting or anything like that?"

"No, he didn't," Alvin said. Horst had neared the end of his patience with Alvin. He thought it would be a good time to mention the polygraph.

"You know, one of the things that um, that Theresa is going to do for us, is she's volunteered to go down and take a polygraph. Would you be willing to take a polygraph?"

"I'll take a polygraph," Alvin said in a slightly indignant tone. Horst commented that lunch was on the way, but Alvin said he didn't want anything to eat. He was too nervous. Horst wanted to know why he was so nervous, but Alvin wouldn't talk about it. A look of gloom had suddenly settled over his face.

"Is there something I should know, man? Seriously. Is there something you're not telling me about this?" Alvin remained guarded, saying nothing. "There's a chance that the kid might not make it through the night, man."

"Right."

"It just ain't worth it," Horst said. "I'm asking you right now, man. Something happened and you need to tell me." Still, there was silence, although Alvin's chin had begun to quiver. Tears welled up in his eyes. "Now's the time. Come on, man, what happened?" As tears began to stream down Alvin's cheeks, Horst kept the pressure on. He was sure that Alvin was about to confess. "I'm telling you, man, I know. I've been doing this a long time. The kid didn't get into that kind of shape without something happening to him. What happened?"

"I won't go to jail?" Horst made no promises. "Look it," Alvin sniffed, "I'm just upset. I'll tell you anything you want to know. I just don't want to go to jail."

"I want the truth, man. That's all I want is the truth, okay? What happened with this little boy...tell me what happened to that little boy. He didn't deserve that. What happened, Alvin? What happened?"

"I ain't going to go to jail, man?"

"Alvin, I want to know what happened! I'm telling you I'm going to get to the bottom of it one way or another, man. Now what happened?"

"She did it," Alvin blurted through his tears. "She kicked him in the nuts, about two weeks ago." Horst was shocked. Alvin said he'd seen her

142

kick Andy and push him off his time-out chair. "I'll tell you the truth. I don't want to go to jail. I want to stay at my parents' house." From then on, Alvin was a virtual tidal wave of information. "That's how he got all the bruises and stuff. I couldn't take it no more. I had to leave. 'Cause I knew if I didn't they were going to fall on me [meaning the charges] and I would get messed up."

"Did you see her when she did it?"

"Yes."

"How many times did she kick him there?"

"About five times."

"Did he cry?"

"Yes! He cried." Wiping the tears from his face he went on to tell how Theresa had claimed that she "hadn't touched the kid all week," but whenever Alvin was home, she turned into a monster. Alvin didn't like the way Theresa blamed it all on him. "It ain't my fault," he said, shaking his head. "I didn't do nothing. It ain't my fault."

As the interview began to reveal unbelievable acts of torture, the air inside the room became heavy and stale. Then, the conversation took a new, grim turn. Alvin became despondent again, sobbing, as he told of seeing his wife force Andy to eat his own feces. He said he knew it was the wrong thing for her to do and he tried to tell her to stop, but she wouldn't listen. He also saw her stick a hypodermic needle in Andy's arm. Horst's throat was as dry as cotton, but he had to compartmentalize all this and keep Alvin talking. Keep the pressure on. The best way to do that was to tell Alvin that all he wanted was the truth. Keep the pressure on...

Horst slapped down a Polaroid of Andy, taken while he was at Menifee Hospital. Alvin cringed when he looked at it. It was the same photo that hadn't elicited one smidgeon of surprise or remorse from Theresa. "You see this kid right here?" Horst glared at Alvin from across the table. "Right there man," he said tapping his finger on the picture. "That's who you work for. 'Cause what happened to him ain't right, man. What happened to him ain't right..." He inched the ghastly photo of Andy a little closer to Alvin and watched as Alvin forbade his eyes to acknowledge it. The photo was having a powerful effect on Alvin, whereas it had had no affect whatsoever on Theresa. Even Horst couldn't look at it without getting choked up and he'd seen some horrific stuff in his long career. As he pushed the photo closer to Alvin, Horst had to look *through* it and not let his eyes actually focus on it. It was too horrible.

"What's gonna happen?" Alvin whimpered. Horst told him he wasn't under arrest and to just relax. Then Horst asked Alvin if he'd ever hit Andy.

Hanging his head, Alvin said, "No sir."

"Look at me up here and tell me that."

Alvin looked up at Horst. "No sir." Tears streamed down his face.

"You didn't hit him?"

"No," Alvin said and then began to puke out the *real* events that had brought Andy into the emergency room at Menifee Hospital. Over and over, Alvin insisted that he "didn't do nothin'."

"She's like 'you gotta call 911' but I didn't do nothin'," Alvin pleaded.

"Is that what you said, 'I didn't do nothing?'"

"Right."

"How'd he wind up outside like that, man? What happened? How'd that go down?"

"She took him outside, put some dirt on him," Alvin said, sniffing and wiping tears off his face. Still, Alvin was only concerned about what was going to happen to him. Was he gonna go to jail for it?

"Did you ever see your wife do some disciplining of the children that you thought was inappropriate?" Horst asked. He wondered if Alvin would understand what inappropriate meant.

"Yeah, I didn't agree with all that."

Horst asked Alvin if he'd been trained to do CPR.

"Yeah," he said. "I got trained in CPR." Then, he started hollering about how he told Theresa that he wasn't about to go to jail for something *she* had done to Andy. "I said '*you* fucked up, not me. I ain't going to jail for what *you* did.' I told her straight out, man."

"Was anybody worried about the kid?"

"I told her, I said, 'hey, look at that kid.'" Alvin was like a caged bear all of a sudden. He got out of his chair and angrily paced the floor. Alarmed, Horst tried to settle Alvin down a little.

"All right, all right, all right, okay. All right, man. Relax, okay? Have a seat, man."

With a huff, Alvin slumped back into his chair. After the whole wretched story had been exposed, Alvin asked for a drink of water. But first, Horst wanted to go over a few more things. Alvin clearly had diarrhea of the mouth. Horst was determined to take advantage of it and learn a few more details of exactly what Alvin knew about Andy's abuse. When they were finally finished, Alvin again asked for a drink of water.

"I'll take that glass of water now."

Later, after Alvin had been invited to step outside for a breath of fresh air, Horst met with the other investigators who'd been watching the interview on the closed circuit TV. Everyone seemed to think that Alvin had been pretty informative, but could they believe him? All along, they'd felt certain that Andy had been beaten and, at least for a while, Alvin seemed likely to have been the one who'd done it. But now, he put the blame entirely on Theresa and Horst believed him. Unfortunately, Alvin had incriminated himself when he admitted that he'd witnessed several incidents of abuse, but never came to Andy's defense.

Horst made arrangements for Alvin and Theresa to be transported to the San Bernardino Sheriff's station where they would undergo the polygraph tests. Within a few minutes they were on their way.

Horst made a call to the District Attorney's office and spoke with Danuta Tuszynska who was in charge of the Riverside County SACA unit [sexual assault/child abuse]. It was around 8:45 when he told her the circumstances of four-year-old Andy Setzer and that Andy was not expected to live. Tuszynska then paged another Deputy DA who was on call that particular morning. His name was John Monterosso.

As a Deputy District Attorney and as the person on call for SACA, it was John Monterosso's duty to go to the crime scene as soon as possible. Riverside County was fortunate in the respect that the DA's office and Sheriff's department worked very well together. A Deputy DA goes to a crime scene, not to investigate, but to be there as a resource for legal assistance. He shares his legal advice and expertise on search warrants and gathering evidence that might be needed during trial. There's a saying at the DA's office; "It's better to have it and not need it than to need it and not have it." As soon as Monterosso got the call, he left his sixth floor office and headed straight over to Perris.

* * *

John Monterosso was born in San Francisco. His grandparents, Italian immigrants, had come to America in the 20's and settled in the Bay Area. Monterosso grew up in the small town of Novato, about 30 miles north of San Francisco, graduating from the University of San Francisco in 1987.

"I never actually said to myself, 'I want to be a lawyer.' It just sort of evolved that way over the years," he said. But, as he looked back, it was almost as if it were preordained. Maybe his mom had something to do with it. "My mom always said I was going to be a lawyer." He started college with no thought of becoming a lawyer. His interests were foreign affairs, diplomacy and international relations. Actually, he was more interested in sports than anything else. He thought maybe he could play some baseball, which he did a little during his freshman year, but mostly he sat on the bench. Because of the time commitment with the team—traveling, practicing and so forth, his grades took a dump. Carousing took a chunk of his time too. Carousing and baseball. Not a combination to insure good grades. He lived and breathed for baseball season and his beloved San Francisco Giants.

He didn't make the team in his sophomore year and was totally devastated by the rejection. Still, he noticed that his grades improved when he wasn't spending all his time with the ball team, so he decided to move on to other things. Had he stayed with his love of baseball, he would have never made it into law school.

During his senior year of college, he applied for a job at the Defense Department and the State Department and was in the process of applying for a teaching credential. He wanted to teach history or government at the high school level and possibly coach some baseball. Wisely, he decided not to limit his options and took the entrance exam for law school. In his own words, he "barely got in." Even so, Monterosso had no idea that becoming a lawyer was really what he wanted to do.

Deadly Thirst

"I just wanted to see what law school was like."

USF is a small Jesuit university started by Saint Ignatius several hundred years ago. As a strict Catholic boy, that was where he first studied law. Later, he studied at the University of Santa Clara. It didn't take him long to get hired by a big, prestigious law firm in San Francisco doing civil work. He hated it.

"After just one summer, I knew there was no way I'd ever go into civil law," he said. "So, I thought I'd try to be a district attorney."

By his third year of law school he started applying for jobs, but no one in the Bay Area would hire a newcomer. That year, representatives from two southern California counties came to his campus to recruit prospective applicants. One was from Riverside County and Monterosso sent them his application. In November of '89, with eight more months until graduation, he was offered a job at the Riverside District Attorney's office. All Monterosso knew about southern California was that Palm Springs was somewhere down there. He remembered getting a California tourism brochure in the mail about that time, showing hot air balloons, snow capped mountains, green golf courses, pristine beaches and blue skies. He was about to find out the hard way that southern California's skies are as brown as dried tobacco most of the time.

The week before Thanksgiving he went down to Riverside just to see what it was like. The selling point wasn't the scenery, it was the people. He accepted the job and moved south in August of '90. He didn't see the mountains for months, even though they were just a few miles away. The heat was overpowering and the air quality was horrible. He began to have second thoughts. In any event, he was sure he wouldn't stay in southern California very long.

Within a few months of his arrival, he began dating a beautiful court clerk and in February of 1994 they were married.

As usual, with a demanding job that required a total commitment, his wife had to be accommodating and understanding when his court calendar took precedence. A few years later, as the birth of his first child was imminent, he sat with his wife in the doctor's office, looking through his court calendar for a convenient delivery date.

"I'll go to my grave feeling guilty that I actually had to pull my calendar out and agree to a day that was convenient for *me* to allow my wife to have her labor induced so we could have our baby." Such was the life of the district attorney.

When Monterosso walked by, appraising female eyes admired him. Although he seemed oblivious to it, women, both young and old, gawked at him with a respectful but obvious mixture of fantasy, and sexual attraction. Monterosso had an enticing smile; he was refined, well dressed, polite and extremely handsome. At thirty-four he was one of the youngest Deputy DAs in Riverside. Without question, Monterosso was one of the most respected Deputy District Attorneys in the entire County of Riverside. He had a solid record of convictions. His colleagues trusted him; they admired him. He was affable and easy to work with, unless, of course, you found yourself on the opposing side of the counsel table.

* * *

Loma Linda Medical Center was in San Bernardino County and was just a few blocks away from the Sheriff's station. Andy was not expected to live and his death, when it came, would happen in San Bernardino County, not Riverside County. While Theresa was being transported, Monterosso, Horst and Alvin drove together back to the Perris apartment on 6th Street. There, a crime scene photographer and several other investigators were already hard at work.

Alvin was clearly distraught and was honest enough with detectives to show them exactly how it all happened. He led the group of men into the bedroom. Tearfully at times, he told the detectives that Andy wasn't allowed to drink anything at night because he had a bedwetting problem.

Alvin said he was diabetic and, because he always became thirsty in the middle of the night, he kept a jug of water on the nightstand beside his bed. Wiping tears, Alvin told the men that about three o'clock in the morning Andy had sneaked around to Alvin's side of the bed and had been drinking from the jug of water when Theresa woke up. She flew into a rage and made Andy get on his chair, Alvin said. He demonstrated exactly how Theresa was positioned when she kicked Andy off the chair and where Andy had hit his head on the nightstand. Horst noticed the little blue chair was still sitting upright in the middle of the room. He asked Alvin to role-play. Horst played the part of Andy and knelt on the chair while Alvin sat on the bed and demonstrated how Theresa had kicked Andy in the lower abdomen, causing him to fall backward, hitting his head on the corner of the nightstand, two separate times. While this demonstration was going on, Monterosso noticed a white cotton tablecloth covering the nightstand and quietly suggested to Horst that it should be taken for evidence. If Andy had hit his head on it, there might still be tissue or hair adhering to it that could be used as evidence. Horst agreed and the cloth was carefully folded in an inward fashion and slipped into a brown paper evidence bag.

Horst checked the floor in front of the nightstand to see if it was wet. "Where's the jug of water?" Horst wanted to know. Alvin looked around and stammered that he guessed it was in the kitchen. Knowing glances bounced around between the detectives. Someone stepped into the kitchen and confirmed that a jug of water was, indeed, sitting on the kitchen counter. Either Alvin or Theresa had obviously taken the time to put the water jug in another room before heading off to the hospital. Now why would they do that? Horst wanted to know. Alvin had no idea. Perhaps Alvin realized he'd just stabbed himself in the back.

The apartment was photographed from every angle and then Alvin was asked to go into San Bernardino and take a polygraph test. They told him

Theresa was on her way there to take one. Since he "didn't do nothin'" then he didn't have nothin' to fear, right? Right.

Outside, the crowd of gawkers had grown and reporters were clustered along the fence. Alvin was escorted to a waiting patrol car and quickly ducked past the crowd, shielding his face as best he could.

The apartment was swarming with cops. There were more squad cars in front of 216 E. 6th Street than there were at the police station. They'd come armed with a search warrant. After Alvin left, the search got underway. A search warrant is an intensely personal invasion, granted only when there is sufficient cause to believe that evidence connected to a crime will be found. Such a warrant plunges law enforcement officers into the personal business of someone's daily life. Friends and family of the suspects are all pulled into the invasive vortex of the investigation. The little blue chair was tagged as evidence and taken; so were several other things, including the divorce papers, which Theresa had hidden.

A deputy, fluent in Spanish, was sent out to canvass the immediate neighborhood questioning residents who might have heard something. That time-consuming effort produced no additional leads.

It was early afternoon when Horst and Monterosso headed over to San Bernardino. They had some unfinished business to take care of.

* * *

At the San Bernardino County Sheriff's station, Theresa was just arriving for her polygraph test. It was around 3:30P.M. Horst had already been on duty ten hours. Since Theresa's first round of questioning, her demeanor had changed remarkably. She was visibly nervous now. And she was worn down, just the way Horst wanted her to be. Horst was chomping at the bit to take up where he'd left off with her, but for the time being, he would have to wait and watch. The polygraphs were videotaped and played live on a closed circuit television monitor in an adjacent room. Horst and Monterosso had a ringside seat.

It was arranged that a female polygraph examiner would first spend some friendly time with Theresa. Kathleen Cardwell was going to be the one to administer the polygraph and went into the room to loosen Theresa up a little before she started the testing. Cardwell had a cheerful, understanding tone of voice and a pleasant, caring disposition. She told Theresa that Andy's condition was extremely grave, but the news didn't get so much as a ripple of emotion out of Theresa.

In an adjacent room, Horst was glued to the television monitor. His chance to grill Theresa would come later. For then, he sat there and watched as Theresa underwent a warm-up interview. It was sickening to watch as she tried to erect a distracting wall of giggly chatter. In another room, Alvin was being subjected to the same procedure and investigators watched his videotaped warm-up and subsequent polygraph through another closed circuit TV monitor.

When Theresa was asked to state the name of the company she worked for, she launched into a chirpy, flippant recital of the way in which she answered the phone at work. After reciting the long, mouthful of words, she bellowed a hearty laugh.

Once the basic information was obtained from Theresa, plus a little background information, Cardwell began the serious conversation by asking Theresa to tell, in her own words, why she was taking a polygraph. Cardwell wanted to know if there was anything Theresa was afraid or leery to tell the police. Well, she said, she had been scared to tell them about the trip to Stater Bros. market the day prior and how she'd made Andy stand up on his time-out chair and how she'd made him sit on the toilet as punishment. "I was scared to tell them, because, you know, it's more than licensing will allow." Theresa admitted that she knew it was against foster care rules to use corporal punishment with the children.

Cardwell was shrewd in her method of questioning; she'd been doing polygraphs for a living for many years and was considered an expert by many in her field. She began to throw in questions that were uncomfortably direct regarding what had brought Andy to the emergency room. She told Theresa that the doctors already knew that a person—an adult—had caused Andy's injuries and she asked Theresa, straight out, who did it. Theresa said she didn't know and then launched into a whining, long-winded explanation. The sentences were blurted out, rapid fire, with hardly a breath in between. Her pudgy hands waved around in exaggerated, theatrical gestures. To Cardwell, it was the War and Peace of explanations. Way too long and animated. Not just that, it had a phony ring to it—animated yet hollow.

"I don't know," Theresa began to whine, "I didn't know about most of his injuries. When they told me, it was like a shock to me. They started asking questions about his pee-pee and all that and I'm like, I don't know what you're talking about, because I didn't." She then began explaining how Andy kept getting out of the house at night, so they had him sleeping in a sleeping bag on the floor at the foot of their bed so she could keep an eye on him. She recounted how she'd awaken around 3:00 to use the bathroom and noticed Andy was missing.

"And I'm like, 'Oh my God! He went outside!' So I told my husband, I say, 'Alvin, Alvin, Andy's not in the house! The door is open and I think he went outside!' And he jumped up and started walking behind me and I went outside and I saw him lying on the ground. He's known to get up in the middle of the night and go sleep somewhere else, so I'm thinking he was asleep and I started saying 'Hi honey' you know, 'Here we go, we can't leave you outside...' and as I'm saying this he's like, gasping for air."

In an animated fashion, Theresa demonstrated the gasping sounds Andy had made. "And I was like, whoa, and my husband is right there, like ten feet away. I said 'Andy's not breathing' and he's like, 'What?' And I took him in the house and I laid him on the coffee table and I went to puff in

Deadly Thirst

his mouth and my husband called 911. And I'm like, 'Andy wake up, Andy wake up.' And then he would go [gasping] and then he would stop. And then," she said with a slight shrug, "I took him out to the paramedics."

It sounded contrived. There was some discussion about how Andy could have gotten out of the house and then Theresa began talking about how the Menifee doctors had asked her about some bruises, which she claimed to know nothing about.

"But I found out later that Andy had bruises, I believe they said on his back and they started asking me about those and I told them I didn't know what they were talking about. Then, they later asked me something about his wee-wee and I believe they told me it was, um, swollen or something. And I said no; I'd watched him all day go pee you know, not up close, but from far away and I was just noticing that pee was coming out. And that's when I started, like, whoa what's going on?" She said that initially she thought Andy might have had an asthma attack or something. "But then when they started asking me about all this other stuff, I'm like, whoa, what's going on? And then they asked me about his wee-wee and his back and all that and I said 'no,' you know, 'I don't know nothing.'"

Theresa was beginning to stumble over her own words. Cardwell just listened and let Theresa talk as much as she wanted. Theresa confessed that she'd hosed Andy off in the yard on Saturday, but hadn't noticed any swelling of Andy's genitals.

"And um, like I said, I would have noticed something like that." From the adjacent monitoring room, Horst took special note of that comment. She had already confided to Horst that she'd "always noticed" Andy had a larger than normal pee-pee. She'd sized him up early on.

Cardwell asked Theresa if Alvin could have inflicted Andy's injuries. Theresa was adamant that Alvin would never do something like that. Cardwell questioned her sternly as to whether or not Theresa was trying to cover up for Alvin or protect him. "No," she said. Cardwell asked her if perhaps something happened accidentally that could have caused Andy's injuries. After a moment of reflection, Theresa said that Andy had fallen on the way home from Stater Bros. yesterday. As they were running across the street he had fallen face first and dropped the milk. Smirking, she used her hand to show how Andy had fallen forward. Cardwell wanted to know if the milk jug broke open. "No," Theresa giggled, "but he got it all dirty."

Cardwell asked Theresa if she'd ever seen Jacob hit or kick Andy and Theresa said no, but on second thought, her mom had told her that she'd seen Jacob being mean to Andy. "There's like, a big gap in their ages and Jacob had kinda wanted to be more to himself and he was kinda like, shoving Andy, like, all the time." Cardwell's method was clever. She'd make small talk for a while and then she'd slam Theresa with hard-hitting questions about Andy's injuries.

"If the doctor says that the injuries sustained by Andy were caused by another person…an adult…and Andy and Jacob were with *you* on the weekend, it would have to be either you or Alvin that inflicted the injury that caused Andy's unconsciousness resulting in his hospitalization. Who did it? How'd it happen? Was it accidental or intentional?"

"I...don't know," Theresa whined. "I didn't do anything and my husband was right next to me all night, so…"

After a little more small talk, Cardwell asked Theresa if she was the kind of person who could hurt a kid and then lie about it.

"No," Theresa said. "I always tell my husband, I say 'all I have in this world is my word.'" As Theresa rambled on and on about how her word was worth its weight in gold, she kept her purse clutched tightly on her lap, the strap continually falling off her shoulder. Absent-mindedly she kept putting the strap back over her shoulder only to have it slip off again seconds later. It was a hefty sign of nervousness.

Cardwell played right along with Theresa and began typing out the questions she'd ask during the polygraph. Most of the questions were about lying. Cardwell told Theresa to relax and they would go through the questions in advance. There was no trickery involved in the polygraph. The questions were worked out and agreed on beforehand.

"Have you ever lied to someone you loved and who trusted you?"

"No."

"Have you ever lied to the authorities?"

"No."

"Have you ever lied just to get yourself out of trouble?"

"No."

"Have you ever lied on a job application?"

"No."

"Will your husband tell the police anything different than what you have told me?"

"No."

"During the first 18 years of your life, do you ever remember telling a lie to anyone in authority?"

"No."

"During the first 21 years of your life, did you ever, *ever* tell a lie to anyone in authority?"

"No," Theresa said with a smile, "not even my mom. I always say the truth will set you free. No matter what, whether you're happy or sad, you know, if you got your word, you got everything."

"Did you yourself cause any or all of the injuries that resulted in Andy's hospitalization this morning?"

"No."

"Do you believe me when I tell you I will not ask you any questions other than the ones we discussed?"

"Yes."

"Is your true last name Barroso?"

"Yes. I haven't changed it yet."

Deadly Thirst

Finally, Cardwell announced that she was ready to start the test. She instructed Theresa to sign a form saying she was not forced or coerced into taking the test. She led Theresa over to an orange, vinyl couch and told her to get comfortable. The vinyl cushion whistled and moaned as three hundred pounds of female flesh flattened it.

They were using a Lafayette LX2000 computerized polygraph instrument, which records a person's psycho-physiological responses and evaluates them using the APL scoring algorithm program devised by Johns Hopkins University. The Lafayette is so accurate that it's recommended by the U.S. Department of Defense. Two accordion type tubes were strapped around her rotund midsection, one just under her arm pits and one around her stomach. Metal fingertip attachments were slipped onto the ring and index fingers of her right hand and a cardio cuff was positioned above her left elbow. The cardio cuff is similar to a blood pressure testing cuff insomuch as the cuff is pumped full of air. During blood pressure readings, the cuff is inflated, and then the air is allowed to escape. In polygraphs, the pressure is maintained throughout the entire test. It can get a little uncomfortable, especially if the subject is nervous. Theresa was most definitely nervous. She kept wiping the palms of her hands on her shorts. Apparently, her hands were getting sweaty. In bygone days, the polygraph results were recorded on a horizontal moving chart which resembled an earthquake seismograph. These days, with modern technology, the polygraph results appear on a computer screen and are printed out like any other document. The polygraph reacts to a person's fear that deception will be detected.

And then the questions began. There were nine of them, but only two would be the important ones. The same question was asked two different ways.

"Did you, yourself, cause any or all of the injuries that resulted in Andy's hospitalization this morning?"

"No."

"Regarding Andy's hospitalization this morning, did you, yourself, inflict any or all of his injuries?"

"No."

The examination was conducted three separate times and each time Cardwell noted enough deception to blow ink all over the walls. She let the pressure off the cuff and began to engage Theresa in common banter while she saved the test to floppy disk and printed out the results. Theresa laughed and complained that her arm was completely numb and felt like it was going to fall off. As Cardwell took the apparatus off Theresa, she assured her that she had been "a good responder." She told Theresa that she could get up and stretch her legs if she wanted to and that she was going to step out of the room briefly to score her charts. Theresa grunted as she hauled herself up off the orange couch. The distinct sounds of sweaty skin being peeled off the vinyl seat cushion echoed throughout the room. She left a cavernous impression in the cushion, which let out a monstrous groan

152

as it tried to re-inflate. While Cardwell was out of the room, Theresa spent the next few minutes wolfing down a hamburger someone had brought her from Burger King. It had been sitting in a bag on the desk since the beginning of the interview. She hadn't eaten all day and she was hungry. She wiped her mouth and gulped down a few swigs of soda.

Out in the hallway, Cardwell discussed the results with Horst, and then came back in to give Theresa the bad news. By then, Theresa was finished eating and had resumed her seat at the desk next to the computer screen. Cardwell came in, sat down in front of Theresa and took both of Theresa's hands in hers. That's when Theresa knew she was in trouble. She began to sweat under the hot glare of suspicion.

Theresa's face plainly revealed how horrified she was. The color literally vanished from her face. She turned stark white. In a hushed whisper, Cardwell told Theresa that she hadn't done well on the test. She asked for an explanation, but all she got from Theresa was a ghost-like stare. Over and over, Cardwell asked Theresa what had happened, but Theresa remained mute. Inside she was quaking. The fear and apprehension registering on her face was unmistakable. And the video camera was recording it all.

"Your husband has given us a very different statement. Now I want you to tell me in your own words, what happened last night." In a squeaky little voice Theresa wanted to know what Alvin had said, but Cardwell was firm in her refusal to divulge that information. She wanted to hear it from Theresa. "Please tell me…come on honey…talk to me…" Cardwell reached out and hugged Theresa, giving her a long, comforting embrace.

"I'm scared…" Theresa whined, clinging to Cardwell like a frightened child. "What's gonna happen?" Cardwell pulled away from Theresa, but continued to sit face to face with her, holding both of Theresa's hands in a gesture of support and encouragement. As the women sat knee-to-knee, face-to-face, Theresa's expression reflected overwhelming apprehension and fear. Cardwell continued to reassure Theresa, telling her that being scared was all right and perfectly understandable. If there was anyone who could get Theresa to open up, it was Cardwell.

"Was it accidental or intentional?" A horrible long silence hung over the women as Theresa and Cardwell continued to hold hands and stare into each other's face. "I want to hear it from you, honey. Did you intend to hurt Andy?" Theresa was at the end of her rope. After several moments of silence, she shook her head slightly as her chin began to tremble.

"Was it an accident? Tell me," Cardwell whispered. "If it was an accident, okay. Tell me…what was Andy doing that caused you to lose your temper?" Trying to shift the blame—as though Andy had "provoked" Theresa—was a common way to get subjects to open up. But Theresa remained absolutely mute, paralyzed by fear. The silence between each question was deafening and endless. Theresa was weighing her options before she opened her mouth. "Come on honey," Cardwell gently coaxed, "what did Andy do?" It seemed like forever and still Theresa remained mute. "Did you intend to hurt Andy?"

"I'm scared."

"I know you are honey. Now come on...what was Andy doing that caused you to lose your temper?"

"They're gonna send me to jail..."

Cardwell assured Theresa that if it had been an "accident" the authorities needed to know that.

When Theresa could bear it no more, she shook her head no. Then the whole wretched story began spilling out along with a flood of self-pitying tears. She hadn't meant to hurt Andy. It was an "accident." She'd just been so stressed out because she'd been without a car all week and she and the kids had to take the bus everywhere and she was just so stressed...

From an adjacent room, Horst was still watching and listening as Theresa began her tearful confession to Cardwell. Horst knew the first forty-eight hours after a crime were the most important and he felt relieved that things were beginning to fall in order rather quickly.

"I love Andy so much," she bawled. After about four minutes, however, the tears came to a screeching halt and she continued talking in a totally un-emotional, detached way. It was almost as if Theresa were describing how someone else had abused Andy. During her emotionless explanation of what had really transpired, Cardwell held Theresa's hand and reassured her that it was much better to tell the truth and get everything out in the open. When Theresa had given a brief statement that had unequivocally fingered her as Andy's abuser, Cardwell said she was going to let a detective come in and talk with her some more. She asked Theresa if there was one detective she preferred over the others and Theresa mentioned Horst.

Horst had been licking his chops in anticipation of hauling this vicious bitch off to jail in handcuffs. He got up and went into the room where Cardwell was standing over a teary-eyed Theresa, rubbing her shoulders and comforting her. He didn't let on that he'd been watching. Just as he was about to begin questioning Theresa, he was summoned to take a phone call from Don Farrar. It had been expected—and dreaded. He was pretty sure he knew what the call was about. He left the room momentarily. When he returned, he looked very solemn. Clicking the door shut behind him, he sighed and glanced at his watch. He'd been on duty fourteen hours by then and was dog-tired, but still totally focused on his investigation. It was almost 7:30 P.M. when Horst sat down across from Theresa, within arms distance of her and gently eased his way into the conversation. He assured Theresa that Cardwell had spoken very highly of her and that she had already gotten over the hardest part.

"I'm telling you something," he began. "We all in our lives do things that we'll regret. But here we are right now, when we got to look back and say, does he deserve for me to try to cover up what happened to him?" Theresa couldn't speak; she could only shake her head no. It was with great pleasure that Horst began reading Theresa her Miranda rights. She knew the game had just turned serious. When he'd finished, he asked her if she understood everything he'd just said to her. She nodded yes, her heart pounding in her throat.

"Now, I want you to be thinking about Andy, you know? What does *he* deserve?"

"Can I see my husband in here when all this goes on?" Theresa sniffed.

"Well, I got to tell you, your husband has already told me what happened, Okay? And what I want to do now is confirm what he has told me. This is your opportunity to stand up for what you have done."

"Will I be taken to jail?"

"Huh?" he stammered. He could hardly believe his ears. He was amazed that she was still only concerned about herself. Truly this woman had nothing more than an icicle for a heart. "Why don't you tell me what happened here. What was it, what was it exactly…what happened?"

"It all started about a week ago," she lamented with a heavy sigh. "I was like really stressed out and he had been peeing and pooping…and I was just frustrated one day and um…he had peed and I kicked him right there…" [Indicating the groin area].

"Where?" Horst asked. He wanted the words.

"In his weenie," she said. The tears had been turned off like a faucet and Theresa was speaking in a dry, emotionless monotone.

"Okay, what do you call that? His genitals? His penis?"

"Yes. About a week ago. I did it twice, about a week ago." Horst asked if she had received any special instructions from CPS about how to take care of a child and Theresa complained that she hadn't. "No, they didn't tell me nothing about how to take care of him."

Horst asked her what conversation had transpired between her and Andy right before she kicked him. Theresa said that Andy had sassed her. "Then I just snapped. Then I, I like, kicked him."

"I want you to kick my hand as hard as you kicked Andy." Horst stood up, held his hand out to the side and told Theresa to kick it. "Kick my hand…show me how hard you did it. Come on, I'm a big guy I can take it." With that, Theresa stood up, reared back her right leg and gave Horst's hand a powerful kick. "That hard? Wow, that was a good kick," he said, rubbing his hand. Theresa agreed. Getting a kick like that would put an adult male out of commission. He could only cringe as he considered what it had done to little Andy.

"And then I noticed his wee-wee got swollen," she continued, "so we put ice on it." Horst wanted to know what kind of shoes she'd been wearing when she'd kicked Andy. Tennis shoes, Theresa replied. She said she only owned two other pairs of tennis shoes, besides the ones she was wearing, so it would have had to have been tennis shoes. He pulled the Polaroid photo from his shirt pocket and showed it, once more, to Theresa. Pointing to the large abrasion on Andy's upper right leg, he questioned her about what might have caused it, but again Theresa showed no adverse reaction to the sight of it. Theresa still insisted that she had no idea what might have caused the abrasion.

After her initial outburst of tears, which evaporated in four minutes, Horst was amazed at the dry, unemotional way Theresa talked. Her tears could apparently be turned off and on at will. She described her abuse of Andy as if it were a common, everyday event. In hearing her answers, Horst did not allow his expression to convey his true feelings. Instead, he acted as if he had no opinion regarding Theresa's actions.

"Did you ever kick him more than once?"

"No, the second time I grabbed his wee-wee,' she said. Her voice was sickening; so sweet and high-pitched.

"Well," Horst said, his voice heavy with exhaustion. "I want you to understand the dynamics of what your husband has told me. He says you kicked him in the genitals and that you did it several times. Probably five times." Looking her straight in the face he asked, "Did you kick him more than one time?" Embarrassed, Theresa nodded in agreement. "So how many times was it?"

"Probably five times."

"Did you guys think about taking him to the hospital at all?"

"We were going to take him, but with the ice, the swelling went down tremendously. And then he peed normal."

Horst asked Theresa to go back to Saturday, the day when Andy had been to her workplace and had pooped in his pants. She insisted that everything she'd told him about the hosing off incident was true but Horst wanted her to go back over it again.

"Did Andy wipe the feces on his face or did you?"

"No, *he* wiped it on his face."

"Did you tell him to do that?"

"No I didn't."

Then Horst asked Theresa to tell him about how Andy had gotten a torn penis.

She explained that she had caught Andy standing on her bed, peeing. "And I just kinda like, I snapped again. And what I did, I grabbed his wee-wee and I told him, 'Didn't I tell you not to be peeing?' and I guess I squeezed him hard and he started bleeding."

Horst wanted Theresa to demonstrate how she'd pulled Andy's penis. He used his own hand as a substitute penis.

"Okay, we're going to pretend that this is it, his penis. How did you grab him?" Horst had one finger sticking out with the other four fingers curled into the palm of his hand. Theresa reached out and grabbed his whole hand, demonstrating that she'd grabbed Andy's penis and scrotum too. "Oh, so you grabbed his scrotum and everything?"

"Yes," she said.

"And you squeezed him hard?"

Theresa nodded. Imagining what that must have felt like sent a shiver through Horst. The thought brought back a vivid picture of Andy lying on the hospital gurney. Several moment of silence elapsed while Horst took a good, long look at Theresa's face. The stress she exhibited seemed to be caused, not by remorse for what she'd done to Andy, but by fear of what was about to happen to *her*. The woman had ice water in her veins. "I pulled him toward me. And then I took him into the bathroom and I told him to go pee. Then I put a wash cloth on him and I says, 'Hold it on your wee-wee. And then I called Alvin to come over and I said 'Why am I becoming such a monster?'" The whole wretched story was now spilling out faster than Horst could absorb. He was glad it was all being caught on videotape because he couldn't take written notes that fast. Theresa would cry for a few seconds, and then she'd stop. Mostly, she was so dry and so totally lacking in emotion that listening to her made Horst cringe.

"Was that the word you used?" he asked. "Monster? That's how you depict yourself? Is that how you felt?"

"That's how I felt."

"Like you were a monster?"

"Yes."

"And what did Alvin say?"

"He was like, 'It'll be okay' and, you know, 'we gotta stick together.'"

Now Horst wanted Theresa to tell him about last night.

"Well, my husband asked me for some water, so I just brought him the whole gallon. And then that's when at about three o'clock in the morning I woke up to, like, guzzling." Through her intermittent tears she tried to imitate the sounds of Andy gulping water. "And I snapped, because that's why he's been peeing, you know. And my husband started yelling at him and by now he's like, screaming, you know, crying. And I told him to get his timeout chair and he was screaming and he, like, stood up on it. And that's when I snapped." Her voice had turned into a high-pitched, pleading whine. Tears dripped off her chin. But her tears would soon disappear along with the last bit of emotion. As she continued her story, her tone of voice changed once more to the flat, monotone Horst had heard before. She seemed able to detach herself at will. It was this aspect of Theresa Barroso that Horst found most chilling.

"And then what happened?"

"Then I told him, 'Didn't I tell you to be quiet?' and he kept crying so I like, pushed him in his face." With that, she demonstrated how she'd taken the palm of her hand and slammed it into Andy's face, sending him toppling backward off his chair, striking his head on the nightstand. "He hit the dresser and he started screaming and I told him, 'Get back on your chair and be quiet.' And then he was still crying so I did it again…but when I did it the second time… he just kinda like, passed out."

"No more crying?" Horst asked.

Deadly Thirst

"No more crying. He was just, like, making gasping sounds and I thought he was throwing a tantrum or something. And then we turned on the light and that's when I seen he was like, you know, kinda like, you know, out of it. And I picked him up, and I was like, 'Andy, Andy wake up,' you know. And I like freaked out, you know. So my husband goes, 'Let's call 911.' But we started freakin' out, you know, we got scared. And he goes, 'We'll just tell them we found him outside.' And that's when I took him outside and, at the same time, I'm like talking to him, I'm like, 'Andy, Andy wake up,' and I laid him on the dirt and I kinda moved him and then I brought him back into the house."

"You *rolled* him?" Horst clarified.

"Yeah."

Her dry reenactment of the worried scurryings in the minutes after Andy's fatal attack was nothing short of nauseating.

"But it was *Alvin* that told you to put him outside? *Alvin* says that?"

"Yeah. We were both kinda like freakin' out."

"Did you check his pulse?"

"Yes. He had a pulse, but he wasn't breathing. And he had, like, phlegm coming out so I would remove it and then I puffed in his mouth a couple of times and then he would, like, make gasping sounds and then he would stop again. Then we heard the paramedics come, so I went outside and I handed him to them."

Horst wanted to backtrack again. He went back to when Alvin had walked into the bathroom and had seen Andy standing there with feces smeared all over his face. "Alvin says you were upset and that you took some of the poop and put it on Andy's face."

"No," Theresa said.

"You didn't put any poop on Andy's face?"

"No."

"Nowhere at all?"

"No, no."

"Why do you think Alvin would tell me that?"

"I don't know."

"Okay," Horst said. He reached in his pocket and fished out yet another Polaroid of Andy taken at Menifee Hospital. It showed Andy on the yellow backboard, two gloved hands turning him onto his side. Large bruises were clearly visible on his back. Leaning toward Theresa, he pointed to one of the bruised areas on Andy's back. "There's a handprint here on Andy's back. Was that from you or from Alvin?" Theresa looked at the photo without so much as a glimmer of remorse.

"I have no idea," she said, with little consideration.

"Did you ever smack him on the back like that?" No, she hadn't. But she did say that Alvin had whipped Andy with a belt recently. Horst asked Theresa to tell him about other times she had disciplined Andy and Theresa could only come up with trivial, insignificant examples. Horst narrowed his scope of discipline to spankings. "Were there any other spankings? Other times when you physically hit him?"

"No," she said, "But I like, never went crazy…"

"Now, I gotta ask you about the bite marks on Andy's face. Is that from you biting him?"

"No, I didn't bite him…"

"Right here on the round part of his face and he has another one on his leg. Did you ever bite him?"

"No, he bit me and Jacob seen him."

"Why did he bite you?"

"Because I was trying to put food in his mouth."

Just then, Horst was summoned from the room. Something about him was different when he came back in. He seemed distracted. He reclaimed his position across the table from Theresa and tried to resume the interview, but he'd forgotten where he'd left off. Finally, after grappling with his thoughts for a minute, he decided to move on to something else.

Clearing his throat, he wanted Theresa to show him exactly how much force she had used when she hit Andy in the face with the palm of her hand. His tone of voice had changed; there was a rough edge to it now. Horst held up his hand in front of Theresa, telling her to pretend that his hand was Andy's face. Her demonstration was pretty graphic; a loud "slap" resonated throughout the room as she hit him full force.

"Like that," she said, showing little, if any, embarrassment.

"So, the second time you hit him it had even more force?"

"Yeah," she said.

His palm continued to sting long after its assault. Even to a grown man, it hurt. He couldn't help but wonder how much more it must have hurt and frightened a small child like Andy. He cringed when he thought about how much Andy must have suffered at the hands of his county-appointed caretaker. What aggravated Horst the most were Theresa's monotone voice and her vacant, unemotional state. Once the initial confession had been made, her flow of tears had abruptly stopped. She spoke of her actions toward Andy as if she'd done nothing more than scold him.

Unable to hide his agitation, Horst stammered through several more questions. Then, there was another pause. He seemed upset. His emotions were beginning to creep in and, as much as he tried to remain stoic, his voice betrayed him.

"Why did you want to be a foster parent to begin with?" Horst asked, his voice sounding defeated. "I mean, was your heart really into this?" There was a tinge of sadness to his words. It seemed as if he were speaking confidentially now, that whatever Theresa said would be kept in confidence between the two of them. Poor little Andy had spent almost his entire life in foster care, being shuffled around like a recyclable commodity, never finding stability. Why had he ended up with people like this?

"Yes it was, it really was," Theresa said, sensing Horst's emotion. "Um, I can only speak for myself...my heart was there." She insisted that things had been good in the beginning and then when Andy started peeing and pooping all the time, she "just lost it." As if peeing and pooping and drinking water were some sort of unforgivable crime, some sort of deadly sin, Horst thought.

Finally, with a heavy sigh Horst tried to compose one last question... *why?* He rolled his chair closer to Theresa and positioned himself directly in front of her. They were almost knee-to-knee.

"Why?" He was staring at her now, face-to-face, searching for some sign that she was even a little bit concerned about Andy. The tears he saw came from self-pity. When there was no answer from her, he asked her again. "When you saw yourself turning into this monster why didn't you just call CPS and say, 'come take him away?'" He used his hands a lot as he spoke, gesturing toward Theresa in a persuasive sort of way.

"I tried..." she whined, wringing a tissue in her hands, but Horst was shaking his head in disbelief.

"I just don't understand why you didn't give him back." It seemed that Horst was pleading, trying to unearth a satisfactory explanation as to why a four-year-old child had been beaten unconscious for peeing and pooping and for drinking water. He seemed distraught, emotional. It seemed as though the interrogator within him had vanished, replaced by a father of three small, defenseless boys. The silence hung heavy, but he wanted an answer. "Why didn't you just give him back?"

Something was going on; even Theresa could see it. Horst's demeanor had changed, dramatically, all of a sudden. With a sigh of resignation, he rolled away from her, collected his yellow notepad, stood up and walked toward the door. As he twisted the doorknob, he stopped and turned toward her again. "I'm going to talk to your husband for a minute, okay?" Standing there, he waited, his face reflecting the disgust that was churning in his gut. Mentally, he cursed her; the very sight of her repulsed him.

Turning to look at Horst, Theresa, finally, in a sweet little voice, asked about Andy.

"How is Andy?' Waiting for his answer, the two looked at each other.

"Andy has died."

Horst pulled open the door and left the room. As the door clicked shut behind him, Theresa burst into tears. She cried for exactly forty-five seconds before she regained her composure. Then, she sat with her head in her hands, whispering to herself, "Oh my God, oh my God..." When the full weight of what she'd done sank in, she realized she'd committed murder. The neon sign began flashing again, jail... jail...jail...

Theresa got on her knees and began praying.

* * *

While Theresa was beginning the warm-up interview for her subsequent polygraph test, Alvin was undergoing the same procedure. His questioning came from Dave Williams, a pleasant, easy-going guy who'd been earning his living for twenty-five years testing people on the veracity of their word.

One of the first things Alvin said was that he didn't think he should have to take the test. He thought that Theresa should be the only one taking it. Williams assured him that Theresa was having her own test done at that very same time. Alvin sat in a chair to the right of Williams, who was positioned in front of a computer screen. Williams gave a comforting, no-hassle impression as he began talking with Alvin. He wanted to know if Alvin had ever lied. Alvin said yes. He seemed pretty forthcoming about the lying he'd done throughout his life and admitted that, when he got caught in a lie, it usually resulted in trouble. He admitted that he had lied to the police back in November of '97. He said he'd agreed to take a plea bargain on the vandalism charge because he didn't need the hassle at that time. He admitted that he'd lied to his mother on numerous occasions and, somehow, she was always able to tell.

"How'd she know?" Williams asked. "She could tell just by looking at you. You can walk through the front door of the house and your mother can look at you and she can tell that there's something wrong. Can you do that?"

"No," Alvin said shaking his head. He was at a loss to explain the phenomenon.

"Mothers do that very well." After a pause, Williams asked Alvin who was the most important person in his life. Alvin was quick to tell him that he considered himself to be most important. That's when Williams began telling Alvin how the polygraph machine worked. The body does certain things when we lie. It's something we can't control. Alvin's mother had been able to tell when Alvin was lying and the polygraph machine would be able to tell too. Alvin nodded. Then, Williams encouraged Alvin to tell him about the abuse he'd seen directed toward Andy.

Alvin said that Theresa would sometimes tell Andy to "come here" and when Andy approached, she would kick him in the groin. Alvin said that when Andy tried to tell Jacob about his sore genitals, Theresa cut him off with a stern warning: "Andy, be quiet."

Williams asked Alvin about the hosing-off incident and questioned him about whether or not Andy smeared his own face with his soiled underpants.

"Well, that's what *she* said, but I don't think it really happened that way," Alvin said. "I think *she* rubbed it in his face. Because once on occasion, Andy pooped on his self and she rubbed it in his mouth. What happened was, he'd barely made it to the restroom and he pooped on the toilet seat. And she took it and rubbed it in his mouth. About a month ago."

Williams asked Alvin what he and Theresa had done in the hours preceding going to bed last night. Alvin shifted around in his chair and said he was uncomfortable talking about shit like this. He mumbled something

Deadly Thirst

about a little sexual encounter of some sort that he thought was possibly gonna happen that night. At least he had hoped it would.

"So," Williams said, smiling, "you and Theresa are going to have a little sex. Right?" Alvin thought about it and acted embarrassed. He snickered and covered his mouth.

"Well, that's what I thought," he said, laughing, "but uh, it didn't happen that way." We sat on the couch and we...uh...we...watched adult movies on the TV."

"You're a horny little shit, aren't you?" Williams said, laughing. "Is that all you think about is sex?" It was Williams' way of putting Alvin at ease. Guy talk, man to man. They shared a good laugh when Alvin told him he'd wanted to go to Temptations strip joint with his buddy on Saturday night. Theresa had been paging him all night, but Alvin didn't return her calls. Finally, he spoke with her on Sunday and made up some excuse that his car had broken down and he had been unable to call her.

"I told her my car broke down. She got a '92 Hyundai and I got a '93. Mine's all fixed up and hers is poo-poo." This brought a big laugh from both men. Alvin clearly thought he could relax and shoot the bull with Williams. They talked about cheating on their wives and Williams said he'd never done it physically, only mentally, maybe. Alvin laughed and, in spite of the fact that Williams cautioned him not to go into detail about his cheating, Alvin boasted that he'd cheated on Theresa five times. After that little slip, Williams brought Alvin back to last night.

"So you arrive at the house and then what happens?"

"So I get there and Andy is standing on a green towel. He'd been there a while, cause I heard her go in there and she said, 'I didn't tell you to sit down. I told you to stand up.' But yet, I can't say nothin' or do nothin' because I'm...I can't get a word in edgewise. She says one night Andy got out and that's how he got that bruise on his face. But I think that's a bunch of bullshit. I think *she* did it. She said he got out and opened the padlock and all that, but I don't think he can do that. I don't think he's that smart. So I says, 'Andy you got to go to the bathroom?' and he says, 'no' and I says 'don't lie to me' and he says 'yeah, I gotta go.' See, the thing about Andy is, when I ask Andy to do something, he do it. When she ask him, he don't do it."

"Gee," said Williams with a moan, "I wonder why."

"Me too. She said the reason he's in our bedroom is cause he'd gotten outside. But I think that's bullshit. I think that's to keep him away from Jacob because of his testicles. That's what I think." It was obvious that Alvin knew Andy had been an easy target for Theresa's maniacal temper and that Andy had tried to solicit Jacob's attention about his painful genitals.

Williams wanted to know if Theresa had ever abused Jacob.

"No," Alvin said. The reason was simple. "Because Jacob could tell."

Williams decided they'd had enough small talk and began formatting the questions he'd use for Alvin's polygraph. There were ten easy questions which he went over beforehand with Alvin.

Is your true name Alvin Lee Robinson?

Do you believe me when I promise you I won't ask any questions we haven't reviewed?

Regarding Andy's injuries, are you going to answer all my questions about that truthfully?

Between the ages of twelve and twenty-four, have you told any serious lies in order to protect yourself?

Did you, yourself, cause any or all of Andy's injuries?

Have you ever been so mad that you wished someone were dead?

Did you cause any or all of Andy's injuries that put him in the hospital?

Between high school and the age of twenty-one, have you ever been so mad that you wanted to hurt someone?

Have you told me the whole truth about how Andy got those injuries that put him in the hospital?

Are you afraid I will ask you a question we have not reviewed?

Williams asked Alvin if he could read and Alvin said he had a problem with reading. Williams took a piece of paper out of his notebook and explained to Alvin that it was a form he'd have to sign before they got started on the test. Williams read it aloud and made sure Alvin understood each and every clause. Some of the sentences had to be rephrased and simplified for him. After Alvin signed, he was asked to go sit on an orange couch so they could begin the test.

Theresa was tested in room #2 and Alvin was tested in room #4. Both rooms were furnished identically. The same orange vinyl couch in each room, the same chair beside the desk. The only difference was Alvin's chair was on the right side of the desk and Theresa's was on the left.

Alvin was hooked up and instructed to remain very still while the test was being administered. He stared straight ahead as the series of questions were asked three separate times. When his test was finished, Alvin was quick to disconnect the attachments from his body and get up off the couch. By the time he returned to his seat beside the desk, Williams was printing out the test results. Williams spread the sheets of paper on the desk in front of Alvin and pointed to the areas that represented deception. He told Alvin that the polygraph had concluded he hadn't been "completely honest" with his answers and asked if he'd like to be more truthful about his involvement in the abuse of Andy. After several minutes of prodding, Alvin meekly added a few more details.

He admitted that he'd hit Andy with a thin, cloth belt, but didn't think it had hurt him.

"But it was just, like, a tap and Andy said it didn't hurt." After that, he spanked Andy on his butt, leaving a bruise. *That* probably did hurt him,

Alvin admitted. Most recently he'd "flicked" Andy's ears as punishment. But he insisted that that was *all* he'd ever done to Andy in terms of discipline. Williams was not quite satisfied with Alvin's answers. He would later write in his report to Horst, "It is my opinion that Alvin could feasibly have inflicted other injuries that he is not willing to admit to me at this time."

It was Williams' turn to step aside and let Horst take over. By the time Horst entered the room, Alvin was sitting on the vinyl couch again. Horst pulled up a chair and sat right in front of him. On his lap was a yellow legal notepad. Horst began by telling Alvin that the two stories weren't matching up.

"Now I can't be bullshitting you about this, okay?" Horst began. "She talks about Sunday night and he was peeing on himself. She says *that's* when you hit him with the belt."

"No," Alvin insisted, shaking his head.

Horst was patient and kept his tone of voice gentle. He'd been working this case since 5 A.M. He was dead-tired. It was way past dinnertime; his stomach was growling and his head was throbbing. He placed his note pad on the desk and spent a few seconds in silence, staring at the floor, thinking. Alvin sat there, waiting, while Horst pondered what to do next.

"She says she doesn't *kick* him off the chair but she does this to him..." Horst demonstrated how Theresa said she'd "pushed" Andy in his face, causing him to fall backwards off the chair. "Did you see that, or no?"

"Yes I did."

"Did you see her *kick* him?"

"Yes I did."

Horst gave Alvin's answer a long moment of thought and then asked who's idea was it to put Andy in the dirt. "She also says it was *your* idea to put him outside. She says *you* said, 'Tell them we found him outside.' She said that was *your* idea."

Alvin was adamant. "No. We can do the test over again and you can ask me that question."

"Okay," Horst said. He believed Alvin. "She wants to talk to you. Do you want to talk to her?"

"Yeah, I'll talk to her...unless she's upset..."

"She's crying man. I mean, I just told her Andy died..."

"Andy died?" Alvin asked.

"Yeah. Andy's dead." Horst could hardly believe what he'd just said. Andy was dead. "He's passed on."

As Alvin digested the horrible news, he appeared calm and completely unemotional, nodding his head as if to say, 'Gee, that's too bad...' But, he didn't say anything.

"Now I'm putting her in here, but don't touch her. Don't hit her, ok? I'm gonna be right out here." With that, Horst picked up his note pad and left the room to get Theresa.

Both polygraphs were conducted at the same time and each session had ended about the same time, 8:30P.M. As Theresa waddled into Alvin's room, she started wailing again. She sat on his lap and sobbed. "Andy's dead." With the video camera still recording from its perch in the top right corner of the room, Alvin whispered something in Theresa's ear and gestured toward the camera. Theresa cocked her ear closer to Alvin's mouth and stopped crying long enough to listen and whisper something back. Then, as if on cue, she began to wail once more. After the couple had shared a few minutes together, Horst went into the room and separated them for the last time.

Detective Vern Horst had the extreme satisfaction of placing Theresa Barroso under arrest for the murder of Andy Setzer. Alvin was taken back to the Perris police station and released. He ran straight back to Mama and Daddy in Moreno Valley. Alvin may have thought he was no longer a suspect, but nothing could have been further from the truth.

* * *

As valiant as the doctors' efforts were, Andy never regained consciousness. At 4:21 P.M. four-year-old Andy Setzer was pronounced dead.

Andy's clothing, a gray T-shirt, green shorts and red and white fecal-stained underwear were handed over to a deputy. The soiled pair of underwear was put inside a plastic bio-bag and the three items were taken to the Perris police station.

Dawn Masterson was still at Loma Linda when Andy expired. His death, even though it had been expected, plunged her into a fit of grief. She was so thankful the doctors had let her see Andy briefly while he was still clinging to life, but it was extraordinarily difficult to watch him struggle through his last remaining moments. She held his hand and told him how much everybody loved him. She kissed his cheek and cried. The tears came from the depths of her soul. Then, Andy was finally at peace. The doctors were sympathetic and allowed Dawn to see her grandson one more time, in private, before they took him away to the morgue.

The area around his bed was quiet then. No more noise from the respirator. No more beeping from the cardiac monitor. No more pain and suffering. No more anything.

When a person dies under suspicious circumstances, the case immediately becomes a coroner's case. All the therapeutic appliances that had been in use at the time of Andy's death were kept in place. He had an endotracheal tube down his airway, an orogastric tube in his mouth, a triple bore vascular line in his right clavicular area, ECG pads affixed to the anterior torso and vascular lines in the back of his left hand and the top of his left foot. There was also a plastic cannula inserted into his urethra with some overlying dressing on his penis and the frontal area of his scrotum.

His tiny body was lifted off the hospital bed and transferred, along with his paperwork, to a special stainless steel morgue cart and covered with a sheet. He was wheeled down to the hospital morgue where he was put into a plastic body bag and then into a large refrigerated room. His paperwork lay right next to him. There, Andy's body would have to wait two hours, until California Mortuary Transportation service came to pick him up.

At 6:30 P.M., a non-descript, white van backed into the loading area of Loma Linda's hospital morgue and transported Andy's body a few miles to the San Bernardino County Coroner's office on Lena Road. There, he was issued one last memento of his brief stay with Theresa Barroso: a white coroner's identification tag attached to his right big toe. Andy Setzer was now case #99-4607RK.

When coroner Brian McCormick learned the circumstances leading to Andy's death, he immediately called Horst, but only got his answering machine. It was 10:00 P.M. when Horst finally returned McCormick's phone call. Although he'd been on duty seventeen hours, Horst's day wasn't anywhere near being over. August 2nd was a very long and exhausting day for everyone involved in the case.

Police work is often long, unglamorous days and nights filled with countless hours spent sitting behind a government-gray desk doing paperwork and dialing phone numbers until fingers are worn to nubs. It's interviewing and talking, talking, talking.

It was well past midnight before Horst finally dragged himself home, tired to the bone. By then, his three sons were asleep, just as they had been when he'd left them almost twenty-four long, dreadful hours ago. He'd missed an entire day of their lives, which, after what he'd just been through, saddened him even more. Silently, he crept into their bedrooms and stood over each of his boys, looking at them while they slept. How beautiful they were. How lucky he was to have them. He mumbled to himself that he would certainly have to do something special for them...and his wife...but right then he was just too tired to think. He collapsed into bed, exhausted, both physically and mentally. Carmen knew better than to ask how his day went.

* * *

Bright and early the day after Andy died, Alvin was on his way back to the apartment on 6th street. He wanted to get his $400 TV set and a bunch of other stuff that was his. He wasn't about to leave all his stuff behind for Theresa's family to steal. When he got there, he looked around and noticed he had too much stuff to haul away in his little car. He did not concern himself with the things that Andy had left behind. Leroy loaned Alvin enough money to rent a U-Haul truck. However, when Alvin drove the truck over there the following day, he was shocked and indignant to find that Theresa's family had already changed the locks. Leroy didn't let it ruffle his feathers though; he told Alvin to just hang loose. "Just wait 'til everything blows over," said Leroy.

* * *

Cowboy, Andy's father, had only been out of prison five months when Andy was murdered. Because of his illegal lifestyle, he was somewhat of a drifter and no one could find him right away to tell him that Andy was dead. Andy died on Monday; it was Wednesday afternoon when reporters caught up with Cowboy.

Cowboy told reporters that the last time he'd seen his son was last summer. The last time he'd heard anything about Andy was a long time ago and he assumed Andy had been sent to live with Laura's mom. He said he supported the idea of Andy living with Dawn Masterson, because that way, Laura could visit Andy when she "got out." Perhaps that was part of the reason why Child Protection officials decided to place Andy elsewhere. Maybe they didn't want Laura anywhere near Andy. Laura had nothing positive to contribute to Andy so, the farther she stayed away from him, the better.

Cowboy tried to play the part of grief-stricken parent during his spontaneous interview. He posed for pictures, cigarette in hand. He admitted his corrupted past and that he and Laura didn't always see eye to eye on everything, but insisted that Andy was always well cared for and loved. No, there was never any abuse. They didn't have much, he lamented, but they always had love.

Perhaps a more truthful statement would have been that they didn't have much, but they always had drugs. Obviously, Cowboy had conveniently forgotten the circumstances that led to Andy being confiscated by CPS. He'd forgotten that Andy was born drug-tainted. But all that was water under the bridge. Cowboy was in the limelight now and he relished every second of it. He claimed to be outraged over the death of his only son.

Cowboy's attorney was quick to phone Brian McCormick to solicit the right of control over Andy's remains, although Cowboy didn't have a penny with which to bury his son. McCormick advised the attorney that the coroner's office would require signatures from both parents before Andy's body could be delivered to the mortuary which Dawn Masterson had chosen. However, there was a problem with that. Laura Utley couldn't be contacted right away because, according to Dawn, Laura was in prison on drug charges.

When the story of Andy's murder was splashed across the front page of The Press Enterprise, both Cowboy and Dawn Masterson were quoted as saying Laura was currently serving time in prison and was scheduled to be released around August 15th. However, investigations by Press Enterprise reporters soon turned up the fact that this particular sentence was being served under the name of Jennifer Lyn Darling, with an AKA of Laura Utley. Confused and perplexed and needing to rectify the mix-up before they could print it, reporters started badgering the California Department of Corrections [CDC].

Authorities there were bemused to hear that Andy's mother, Laura Utley, was supposedly imprisoned at the California Institute for Women in Frontera, but according to prison records, there was no Laura Utley in custody, nor had there ever been. Dawn had told newspaper reporters that Laura was just twelve days away from finishing up her one year and

Deadly Thirst

four month sentence on drug charges. Strange, that was the same term and release date for Jennifer Lynn Darling. Confused, reporters from The Press Enterprise immediately launched their own background search on Laura Utley. They soon uncovered a bizarre identity twist that no one at the state or local level seemed willing, or able, to explain. Even the FBI couldn't give a satisfactory explanation.

The information officer at the CDC insisted they had no Laura Utley in their system and the case everyone was so interested in involved Jennifer Lyn Darling, not Laura Utley. The CDC spokesman said that it was a common trick for arrestees to give a fake name at the time they're booked into jail and fingerprinted. He urged the reporters to inquire at the Hemet Police Department if they needed to straighten out the Darling/Utley mix-up. He finished the conversation abruptly by adding that they had about ten thousand women in prison currently and, since the CDC had processed in excess of one hundred thousand women throughout the years, there was no way they were going to waste time by going back and cross-checking this problem. Besides, he said curtly, it was quite hard to get through the system with an alias. To get through the booking process, court process and imprisonment under an AKA is almost impossible to do, he said.

Still, with everything the reporters could come up with, they could only conclude that Laura Utley was in prison on drug charges, posing as another person. Why would Dawn Masterson and Cowboy say she was in prison if she weren't? Even the release date for Utley matched perfectly with Darling's release. Could it be possible that she'd managed to slip through the prison system under her alias? The CDC would only say "In our system, Utley and Darling are one and the same." Period.

Reporters continued to question the mix-up. How could it be that Utley and Darling were 'one and the same'? There was a real Jennifer Lynn Darling living in Hemet; she was related to Cowboy. And there was definitely a Laura Utley who had lived in Hemet too; she was Cowboy's girlfriend and Andy's mother. So they couldn't have been "one and the same" except on paper. In spite of all those explanations, the CDC held firm.

In spite of the fact that the case documents clearly identified the offender as Darling, reporters seemed certain that it was Laura Utley who was in Frontera until her release date of August 14th. Dawn was quoted as saying that the story could have had a happy ending if Laura had gotten out of prison and gotten into drug rehab. According to the CDC, comments from family members proved absolutely nothing. The reporters didn't let up on the issue though. They continued to sniff out the Utley/Darling alias snafu.

Dawn Masterson was beyond agony. She was employed by the very agency that had made the lethal decisions that she felt had contributed to the murder of her grandson. To say she felt intimidated by The Department of Public Social Services was an understatement. She felt totally censored; it drove her nuts.

The Hemet PD was nonchalant about the Darling/Utley controversy. Finally, they stated that, "No one here will have the time to do the inter-agency research you are asking for." In other words, they were too busy to straighten out the Jennifer Darling/Laura Utley fiasco.

When Andy Setzer's murder became public, outraged citizens virtu-ally stormed county and state officials, besieging them with demands that something be done. How could a foster child end up in the unlicensed home of a convicted criminal? Public reaction was volatile. Associated Press took interest in the story. Television channels 2, 4, 7 and 9 opened their Monday evening broadcast with the news of Andy's torture/murder. Dawn Masterson spoke to channel 2 reporters and her comments were aired on the 6 P.M. news.

When the Press Enterprise reporters began to delve into the criminal history of Laura Utley, Alvin Robinson's criminal history came under scru-tiny as well. Much to their amazement, they discovered that Alvin Robinson had not been fingerprinted at the time of his arrest in October '97. They demanded an explanation from the Riverside County Sheriff's Department. Spokesperson Sergeant Perri Feinstein-Portales gave them one. Standing in front of a statue honoring slain police officers, Portales answered most of the reporters' questions, saying the Riverside County Sheriff's Department processes over 50,000 people every year and mistakes are bound to hap-pen. They'd made a mistake. That's all there was to it.

Although the county court had sent the state the information about Robinson's conviction for vandalism, because the information lacked finger-prints, the Department of Justice misfiled the information and never asked Riverside County for the prints, which they didn't have anyway. Apparently, it was the lack of fingerprints that caused the dangerous lapse of informa-tion within CPS to occur. The Riverside Sheriff's Department had made a "mistake" and CPS officials were insisting that, without fingerprints, there had been no way for them to know of Alvin Robinson's criminal convic-tion—although Alvin admitted to it in writing on their application.

The Press Enterprise quickly reported that, by using their computer sys-tem to run a background check on Alvin Robinson, they had easily turned up Alvin's arrest and conviction. They also located the all-important re-straining order that CPS had overlooked. One reporter casually walked into the Perris courthouse and easily obtained the full details of Alvin's arrest and his criminal history. It was unbelievable that state licensing didn't have a computer system equal to the local newspaper. Just as shocking, social workers at CPS's Perris office on North A Street, just a few blocks from the courthouse, didn't bother to investigate Alvin's version of events either.

"That's not our job," said one social worker. So, everyone let it slide. How could this deadly mistake, this glaring oversight, happen? The people of Riverside County wanted an answer and they wanted it right then!

The California State Attorney General had an answer, albeit an unsatis-fying one. He said that unless the state can match up arrests and convictions with fingerprints, his agency can't disclose any information about the crime or the arrestee because they can't guarantee that it's the right person. Therefore, in Robinson's case, the Justice Department couldn't tell the Department of Social Services about his conviction.

Still, when Alvin and Theresa filled out their application to become foster parents, Alvin had admitted his criminal record, *in writing!* Evidently, licensing thought it insignificant and didn't bother to dig deeper on a local level. Since the county knew it was the state's responsibility to find out about such information before they issued a license, the social worker didn't check out Alvin's story either. Had Social Services bothered to pay attention to Alvin's admission and bothered to check county records, they would have easily seen the conviction that should have barred Alvin and Theresa from becoming foster parents. Not only that, they would have also seen that Alvin was currently on probation and they would have seen the restraining order that Theresa filed against Alvin a mere nine months prior! There, on the attached two-page explanation, was all the proof in the world that Alvin and Theresa were a violent and abusive couple. But, surprisingly, background checks for foster parenting do not search for restraining orders that might signal trouble in potential foster homes. If Alvin had been applying to buy a firearm, the restraining order would have been important and would have prevented him from buying a gun. Since he was merely applying to get his hands on a little kid, a restraining order wasn't important.

On the day after Andy's death, in a ridiculous attempt to save face, the state sent Alvin and Theresa a letter turning down their request for a foster home license. Many people in Riverside County found the letter to be a nauseatingly transparent and belated effort on the part of CPS.

Other letters, in the form of E-mails, were flying back and forth between Andy's grandmother, Dawn Masterson, and Mike and Lynn Herman. The Hermans had seen coverage of Andy's murder on the evening news. They felt compelled to send Dawn an E-mail expressing their absolute shock and overwhelming sorrow at the news.

Setting aside all the misunderstandings that may have existed among the three of them during the past few months, Dawn was quick to apologize for having told the Hermans not to contact her anymore. She said she had only been trying to do what she had thought was best for Andy. Dawn admitted that she had taken some tranquilizers to help her deal with what had happened. Her hands were obviously heavy on the keyboard. She spoke of the heartache she endured as she stayed at Andy's side until he succumbed. "Why the f--- didn't they just give him to me? I trusted them," she wrote.

Dawn needed to make some decisions about what to do with Andy's remains. She and Laura had agreed to have Andy cremated so that his ashes could be saved for Laura when she got out of prison. However, in the hours after that E-mail was sent, Miller-Jones Mortuary gave Dawn some enormously comforting news. They told her they would be willing to hold Andy's body intact until his mother could attend his funeral services. There was no need to rush into the decision of cremation based solely on the issue of waiting a few days. So, Dawn arranged for Andy's body to be kept in cold storage until Laura could attend funeral services after her release from prison. She'd made up her mind that when Laura got out of prison she'd have to find her own way in life. Dawn was finally ready to administer some of that "tough love" she'd tried to dish out on so many occasions throughout the years.

Even though Dawn worked for Social Services, she was appalled by the heavy-handed blunders that she felt had contributed to the death of her grandson. She told the Hermans that she'd contacted the Press Enterprise and she'd been to the Board of Supervisors begging them to do something. Inwardly, she feared her job with the Department of Social Services could very well be in jeopardy if she were too outspoken on the matter, but it was impossible for her to remain silent.

"This cannot be kept quiet," she wrote with trembling fingers. "The public needs to know! I will make as much noise as I can." Strangely though, Dawn Masterson's noise was "silenced" shortly thereafter.

In her grief, she may not have realized that thousands of Riverside County residents wholly supported her and sympathized with her. As Andy's murder sent shock waves throughout the county, throngs of furious citizens demanded accountability from CPS. Their combined anger fueled the sparks which ignited one of the worst firestorms that had ever threatened CPS.

Lynn Herman fell to pieces at the news of Andy's death. Mike was barely able to think straight; but in their sorrow they told Dawn they had saved many of Andy's drawings and she was welcome to have them. They'd also saved his favorite Pooh Bear blanket and the Dalmatian pillow that Andy loved to sleep with.

The day after Andy died, Detective Horst and Sergeant Farrar went to the District Attorney's office and met with Randy Tagami, Denuta Tuszynska, John Monterosso and Kevin Ruddy. As a long-standing DA, Kevin Ruddy was very familiar with Cowboy, Andy's drug-addict father. He'd dealt with Cowboy way back in 1987 and remembered him well. In fact, many at the DA's office were familiar with Cowboy. During the meeting it was decided that Andy's life, while he was in the "protective custody" of CPS, would have to be investigated. One of the first things Horst did was schedule an appointment with the social worker that had arranged for Andy to be taken from his preschool and placed with Theresa and Alvin.

Horst was chagrined to discover that the social worker in question had resigned in the wake of "the Andy Setzer fiasco" of June 3rd. As she sat in her Hemet home preparing to answer the detective's questions, she seemed guarded and defensive. She claimed that on June 3rd she had received a call from, what she described as, her "hysterical" supervisor who ordered her to get Andy out of the Herman house *that day*. Horst asked why she had not given Andy to the grandmother. The stoic social worker had no explanation, except to say foster families are "trained to take children" and that was the reason she considered Theresa to be a more sound choice than Dawn. There were policies and procedures that had to be strictly adhered to, she said tersely. Upon hearing this, Horst confronted her with a copy of the state mandates and the Riverside County Child Protective Services manual which states that a relative, if available, should be the placement for the child. She had no explanation. She maintained, indignantly, that she had made the "right" choice. She said that the department was excited about Andy's placement with Theresa because Theresa's *mother* had been a wonderful foster care provider. Furthermore, she stated that all of her employees were professionals and were trained in induction on how to place and "monitor" children in foster care. However, by their own standards, licensed homes needed only to be monitored once a year.

Horst made notes to carefully check out the records at CPS and find out how often Andy was checked on while he was in Theresa's unlicensed home. He had a nagging suspicion that Andy had been literally abandoned into Theresa's care. But he would find out.

There was one more comment the social worker wanted to make before she brought the interview to a screeching halt. She stated that she had done nothing wrong and that her resignation had paid for any mistakes that she "may" have made. In any event, she was not responsible for the death of Andy Setzer. With that, the interview was cut short.

Horst and an investigator from the DA's office spent several days driving around Hemet interviewing one social worker after another. They all gave the impression that placing a child in a "license pending" home, such as Theresa's, was no different than placing a child in a fully licensed home, which was not in line with their own manual of policies and procedures for general licensing requirements. It seemed as though CPS had the flexibility to make amendments to the rules whenever it made the situation easier for them. In the aftermath of Andy's murder, CPS officials went to great lengths to explain that each state is individually responsible for establishing their own guidelines and the process by which children are cared for. In California, each *county* runs their own Child Protective Services independent of each other and a little different than each other.

What especially troubled Horst was, through all the interviews, there seemed to be a foreboding sense that many of the social workers handling Andy's case did not know what the others were doing. At one point, Horst asked the regional manager of the Perris Child Protective Services office why Andy had not been placed with his grandmother. He was flabbergasted to hear her say that she was unaware that Dawn was interested in taking Andy!

Several of Theresa's past employers were also questioned about her attitude and demeanor while she was a caregiver at various retirement homes. Mrs. Wilks' memories of Theresa's performance, while she worked at Walker's Board and Care facility in Canyon Lake, were particularly worrisome. Theresa wasn't a good caregiver, as Mrs. Wilks remembered. She stated that in March [three months prior to Andy's arrival] Theresa had called to say she was in the process of obtaining a foster care license. Mrs. Wilks had asked Theresa why she would want to do something like that and Theresa had told her that "It was good money." She said she was in the process of a lawsuit for workers' comp, so she couldn't actually "work" at that point. Mrs. Wilks wanted to know how investigators had gotten her name and address. When she learned her name had been listed as a reference on Theresa's application for a foster home license, Mrs. Wilks thought that was very odd. No one from the State of California [licensing] had called her about Theresa's qualifications. No one from the county had called either.

* * *

Two days after the jailhouse doors slammed shut on her, Theresa was arraigned. Her bail was set at a staggering three million dollars. A ghoulish picture of her in shackles took up almost half of the front page of the Press Enterprise newspaper. She sat forlornly, encased in a blue jailhouse jumpsuit. The photo spoke louder than a thousand words. Television trucks lined up outside the Robert Presley Hall of Justice. KCBS channel 2 sent reporter Jaie Avila into court to cover the August 4th arraignment of Theresa Barroso. KCAL channel 9 was there too. After the arraignment, reporters clustered around Monterosso as he stepped into the hallway. Pressed for a comment, he said it was horrible. "Andy died because he was thirsty."

Another interesting thing happened on August 4th. An urgent call was placed to the Riverside Sheriff's office. A woman stating her name as Mary Broughton said she'd just received a death threat on the phone and requested the presence of a deputy right away. Deputy Michael McClanahan—the same deputy who'd responded to Alvin and Theresa's Perris vandalism episode in October of 1997—went to Broughton's residence in Canyon Lake. She explained that the caller had been Mike Herman, the former foster parent of the four-year-old boy, Andy Setzer, who had been murdered two days prior in Perris. She said that Mike was extremely upset about Andy's death and felt that Andy shouldn't have been taken away from him. During the call, she said Mike threatened to kill her.

Feeling despondent after her court appearance and unflattering photo spread, Theresa wrote a letter to Alvin.

Dear Alvin, I need to see you. I know that you haven't been around our house, but I need for you to take my property you picked up at the jail to my mom. Like my purse, keys, license, etc. Can you please call my parents? They have been trying to get a hold of you. Can you please put some money on my books? If you can, please ask if I could call you at your mom's house. I need to hear your voice. You said you would be there with me. I need you to talk to my lawyer. My parents have all the information like his number and name etc. Please get a hold of our pastor Steve and Angela. Ask them if I could please call them. I need their prayers. If you can, please send me their phone number. I miss you so much and I love you so much. The times that I could call are early in the morning [6 A.M. to 8 A.M.] Your wife, Theresa Barroso [Robinson] Please write back to me.

Strange that Theresa would ask for Pastor Steve's prayers now. Months earlier as she had sought to tie the knot with Alvin, she'd disregarded the suggestion of religious counseling and she certainly hadn't turned to her pastor for any prayers as she reeled out of control with Andy. However, now that she was behind bars facing murder charges, she felt the sudden necessity for prayer and begged Alvin to call Pastor Steve on her behalf. That was just one of many instances when Theresa showed that her only concerns were for herself.

Theresa also had another problem that was particularly upsetting to her during her first few days in jail. For her own safety, she had been booked into "special housing" at the jail, but she was learning the hard way that some crimes simply don't sit well with other prisoners. Inmates who killed little kids were considered to be nothing more than sewer rats among the cons who'd gained prestige by killing cops or rival gang members. Theresa was about to get a graphic understanding of the fear Andy must have felt when someone stronger and much more powerful began to vent frustrations through violence. Theresa had definitely earned herself a berth in jail that would be no more comfortable than a bed of nails. Her vehemence had allowed her to rule the roost at 216 E. 6th Street, but in the county jail that vehemence would bring her nothing but fear and anguish, the depths of which she could have never fathomed before. Like Andy, who could not escape his abuser, Theresa Barroso would have to suffer in silence and endure it. To say she wasn't well liked in jail would be a gross understatement.

On August 9th exactly one week after Andy had been murdered, Vern Horst, Bob Peebles, John Monterosso and Forensic Technician Janet Whitfort donned blue paper gowns, facial masks, rubber gloves and slippers and assembled inside the autopsy room at the San Bernardino County Coroner's office. Under the pitiless glare of a vivid florescent light lay the cold, naked body of Andy Setzer. His eyes were closed; his tongue protruded from his mouth as if caught in the midst of a final plea for help, or for a sip of water, or for any of the simple things a four-year-old boy might ask for. The endotracheal and orogastric tubes were still inserted down his throat. The autopsy table was slanted slightly downward toward the foot and guttered on all sides. The fluids that spilled from the body during the autopsy drained off through a spout at the foot of the table and into a sink.

Andy had never been able to tell his side of the story with words. Now, his cold, stiffened corpse would speak for him, giving graphic, uncensored testimony as to what had *really* transpired during his last few weeks with

Theresa. Even to a homicide investigator, it was shocking what the dead had to say.

Among the staff, there was suspended emotion, typical of autopsy rooms. Pathologist Frank Sheridan began Andy's autopsy at 10:15 A.M. with an external exam. Aside from the obvious injuries Andy had sustained, Sheridan discovered the inside of Andy's upper lip [the frenulum] had been torn. Horst, Peebles and Monterosso agreed that this injury had probably occurred when Theresa slammed the palm of her hand into Andy's face, sending him toppling backward the first time. There were small abrasions on Andy's cheeks. His chest and abdomen were scattered with bluish bruises, most prominently around the left nipple area. Some bruising of the abdomen was noted—separate from the scrotal bruising that had spread in a deep radius around his genitals. The external genitalia were described as having "extreme bruising and swelling" and, tearing of the skin on the shaft of the penis was noted. The scrotum was swollen to the bursting point and described as "tense." The abrasion on Andy's right inside thigh was measured to be 7cm X 2cm and was classified as either an abrasion or a burn. There was also a large area of bruising on his left hip area. His back was scattered with faint abrasions, as was the right chest area. All of these injuries were photographed with a small ruler held near the site for measurement. Postmortem total body x-rays revealed no obvious fractures or broken bones.

Then it was time for the internal exam. As the scalpel was poised above Andy's chest, the image of the once giggly, mischievous child forced a strong commitment from all in attendance to avenge his early demise. Horst had been to a hundred or more autopsies during his many years in Homicide, but witnessing the dissection of a beautiful four-year-old child was not going to be easy. By comparison, Monterosso had witnessed only a few autopsies and was already feeling queasy. To make matters even worse, Monterosso had a son almost the same age as Andy. Horst's youngest son was only three years older than Andy. Peebles also had young kids.

Together they stood, Horst and Monterosso, side by side, and watched as Sheridan cut into Andy's torso with a deep square incision that began near his shoulders and ended just above his bruised genitals. After a thorough inspection of all the internal organs, it was determined there had been no blunt force injury to any of the organs. Not even the abdominal organs.

Then it was time to open Andy's head. For this, his head was propped up on a crude wooden block. The scalp was sliced ear to ear and peeled down over his face as if it were a rubber mask. Immediately, the cause of his death was revealed. There were two dark red spots on the right side of Andy's head, just under his scalp. They were described as approximately 4cm to 5cm of hemorrhaging in the right temporal area of the scalp, consistent with Andy's head hitting the nightstand, twice.

The top of Andy's skull was sawed in a circular pattern; the skull "cap" pulled off. Within the brain itself, Dr. Sheridan noted capillary congestion

Deadly Thirst

and hemorrhaging. In addition there was approximately 2cm of underlying hemorrhaging in the posterior frontal area, in front of the vertex. The hemorrhage extended over most of the surface of both dorsolateral convexities; totaling about 10-15cc of blood. Even to an untrained eye, the right side of Andy's brain was literally awash in blood.

Andy's eyes were examined next. Sheridan noted moderate hemorrhage of the right optic nerve sheath and milder hemorrhage of the left. Sliced sections of the eyes showed evidence of a small focus of retinal hemorrhage.

As for Andy's genitalia, Dr. Sheridan noted *extensive bruising and multifocal evidence of tissue necrosis throughout. The scrotum is 'massively swollen' and there is a large amount of bloodstained fluid surrounding the testes. The shaft of the penis also shows extensive hemorrhage, some of which appears to be recent and some older. Scrotal hemorrhage extends up to the front of the bladder but the bladder is intact.*

In conclusion, Dr. Sheridan listed his diagnosis as follows:

Acute and chronic physical abuse; blunt head injury.

Multiple blunt force injuries; upper lip, scrotal and groin contusions, contusions in the epigastric area and contusions and abrasions of the chest, abdomen and lower extremities.

Focal incipient bronchopneumonia.

CAUSE OF DEATH: Blunt head injury, hours.

COMMENT: *The subject died as a result of acute blunt force injury to the head, consistent with the history of being propelled against a hard heavy object, such as the nightstand. Autopsy examination also showed evidence of multiple additional recent injuries, including cutaneous injuries, injury to the mouth and an intra-abdominal injury, as well as evidence of previous abuse, specifically evidence of older injuries to the groin and scrotum.*

The autopsy was completed at 1:15 P.M. Just in time for lunch, but everybody had lost their appetite. It had been a long three hours. As soon as he could get a minute of privacy, John Monterosso called home. It made him feel better.

* * *

On August 13th, eleven days after Andy had died, Brian McCormick received two separate Orders For Release, signed by both Tom Setzer and Laura Utley. Andy's body was released later that day and transported to Miller Jones Mortuary in Hemet.

* * *

More than one hundred and fifty people crowded into The Spirit of Joy Community Church in Hemet for Andy's funeral. His father, Thomas "Cowboy" Setzer, and his grandmother, Dawn Masterson, were seated in the front row. Andy's mother, Laura Utley was there too, fresh out of prison. Amazed at the overflowing crowd, which stretched out onto the lawns and surrounding sidewalks, they were comforted by friends and neighbors as well as complete strangers. It was incredible that a little four-year-old boy could draw the whole community together. Maybe Andy's death wouldn't be in vain after all. Maybe it would be a wake-up call for Laura and Cowboy to get clean and start contributing something positive to society. Many people in attendance that day were thinking such thoughts, but mostly they were filled with grief.

Andy hadn't been cremated after all. His tiny, white and gold casket was draped with white roses and positioned in front of the altar. Mementos from mourners were scattered about. Several photos of Andy and a tiny stuffed dog were placed nearby. As the church filled to capacity and the service was about ready to begin, Laura Utley walked forward and placed a stuffed teddy bear on Andy's casket.

Pastor Vicki Rufsvold began the service. Her voice was only a small solace to those in attendance. She began her sermon by saying Andy's death had been so needless. Children are a blessing, she told the sea of faces, and Andy was a sad reminder of how poorly our society sometimes treats its children.

Several people stepped up to the podium and spoke of Andy's giggles, his laughter and his mischievous ways. Then, Laura took the podium. Wearing her recent prison pallor, she looked out among the grief-stricken faces and began to cry. Laura assumed a pious attitude and asked God to take care of her little angel and not to let him hurt again. She said that in heaven Andy would never be thirsty again.

Cowboy brought his guitar to the altar and pulled up a chair next to Andy's casket. A hush fell over the church as his fingers began strumming an Eric Clapton tune, "Tears in Heaven." It was emotional, even for those who knew that Cowboy's and Laura's drug addiction had propelled Andy into foster care in the first place. But, for just one day, everyone put prejudice and judgment aside. At least they tried to. It was time to heal. Still, some thought Cowboy's melodious tribute to his dead son smacked of a theatrical performance and saw it as nothing more than an attempt to draw attention to himself. More than a few people were disgusted that Cowboy had the nerve to sing a song about meeting up with his son in heaven.

Mike and Lynn Herman were not in attendance at Andy's funeral in Hemet, although Dawn Masterson had invited them. Instead, they held a memorial service of their own in a park where Andy used to play. Friends and neighbors of the Hermans gathered in the shade of two enormous trees to commemorate Andy's life. Sitting on coolers, blankets and lawn chairs, mourners listened as several people eulogized the child they had come to know as "Andrew John Herman." At the end of the memorial, two-dozen balloons were released into the air. More than one person said that Andy would have loved seeing the balloons being set free, going to heaven. Through tears one woman commented that Andy had been such a happy little boy.

It was impossible for Mike and Lynn to believe that Andy had been happy in the last two months of his short life. They couldn't bear to think about the pain and suffering he must have endured during his final days.

When the last of the brightly colored balloons had drifted so high into the sky that they could no longer be seen, people packed up their stuff and went home.

From the parking lot of the Spirit of Joy church in Hemet, a long, black hearse pulled out, carrying the casket of Andy Setzer. The ride lasted only a few minutes. The hearse turned right and passed through the gates into the shady, tranquil grounds of the San Jacinto Valley Cemetery. A small, winding road took the procession past row after row of towering one-hundred-year-old headstones, toward the outskirts of the cemetery. There, along the back fence, Andy Setzer was laid to rest.

Donna Goodenough

Alvin Lee Robinson (Riverside Courty Sheriff's Department)

Theresa DeJesus Barroso (Riverside County Sheriff's Department)

Senior Investigator Pete Harding (Photo by Donna Goodenough)

Theresa's attorney Peter Scalisi (Photo by Donna Goodenough)

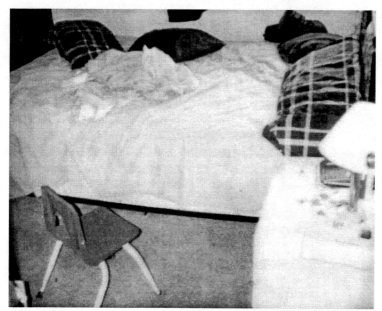

Alvin & Theresa's bedroom as it was on the night of the murder
(Riverside County Sheriff's Department)

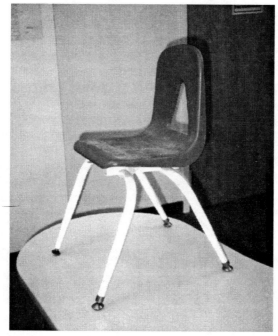

Andy's time-out chair (Photo by Donna Goodenough)

216 E. 6th Street. Kitchen window (left) living room (right)
(Photo by Donna Goodenough)

Alvin's & Theresa's apartment is furthest from the street
(Photo by Donna Goodenough)

Courthouse (left foreground) Robert Presley Hall of Justice (left) District Attorney's Office (right) (Photo by Donna Goodenough)

The Robert Presley Detention Center, more commonly referred to as "jail" (Photo by Donna Goodenough)

Judge Russell Schooling (Photo by Donna Goodenough)

(left) Sergeant Vern Horst (Right) Deputy District Attorney John Monterosso
(Photo by Donna Goodenough)

Donna Goodenough

STATE OF CALIFORNIA - HEALTH AND WELFARE AGENCY

DEPARTMENT OF SOCIAL SERVICES
COMMUNITY CARE LICENSING DIVISION

CRIMINAL RECORD STATEMENT

State law requires that persons associated with licensed facilities be fingerprinted and disclose any criminal convictions. A conviction is any plea of guilty or nolo contendere (no contest) or a verdict of guilty. The fingerprints will be used to obtain a copy of any criminal history you may have.

Have you ever been convicted of a crime? ☐ NO ☒ YES

If you answer YES, attach a signed statement indicating the nature and circumstances of the crime, the date and location in which it occurred.

If you answer NO and you are *wrong*, your answer will be considered as **not true** and held against you. You must disclose convictions, including reckless and drunk driving convictions **even if**:
1. It happened a long time ago;
2. It was only a misdemeanor;
3. You didn't have to go to court (your attorney went for you);
4. You had no jail time or the sentence was only a fine or probation;
5. You received a certificate of rehabilitation;
6. The conviction was later dismissed, set aside or the sentence was suspended.

I declare under penalty of perjury under the laws of the State of California that I have read and understand the information contained in this affidavit and that my responses and any accompanying attachments are true and correct.

FACILITY NAME	FACILITY NUMBER		
BARROSO/ROBINSON FOSTER FAMILY HOME	336402997		
YOUR NAME (PRINT CLEARLY)	YOUR ADDRESS	CITY	ZIP
ALVIN ROBINSON	216 E. 6th St. #B	PERRIS	92570
SOCIAL SECURITY NUMBER	DATE OF BIRTH	DMV LICENSE NUMBER	
563-41-0797	05-11-73	B4001790	
SIGNATURE		DATE	
Alvin L Robinson		2/23/99	

1 Please see Privacy Statement on reverse side.

LIC 508 (10/95)

Alvin's written admission to CPS that he had a criminal record. Apparently, CPS thought it wasn't important enough to investigate.

Deadly Thirst

CRIMINAL RECORD STATEMENT

February 23, 199

I destroyed a stereo that
I owned in an apartment that
we were renting at 114 S. C St, apt A
Perris CA 92570
A neighbor heared the wracket
and called police they thought
the stereo wasn't mine so they
charged me with vandalism.
When I went to court and
presented receipts they said it
wasn't my apartment and
because I did it at the propert
I didn't own (apartment) it
was considered vandalism
even though it was my
own stereo. This was a long
time ago about 2 yrs. on
11/97. I thank you for your
time for reading this,

Sincerely,
2/23/99 ALVIN ROBINSO
2/23/99 Alven Robinson

CONFIDENTIAL
DO NOT RELEASE TO PUBLIC

Alvin's trivial explanation of the circumstances surrounding his arrest.
(written by Theresa)

186

Donna Goodenough

Page one of the restraining order that CPS overlooked. Easily obtainable, documented proof that Alvin and Theresa were a violent, abusive couple prior to applying for a foster home license. It should have barred them from becoming foster parents but CPS didn't bother to check for restraining orders.

Deadly Thirst

PLAINTIFF (Name): THERESA BARROSO	CASE NUMBER:
DEFENDANT (Name): ALVIN ROBINSON	

(THIS IS NOT AN ORDER)

PLAINTIFF(S) REQUEST THE COURT TO MAKE THE ORDERS INDICATED BY THE CHECK MARKS IN THE BOXES BELOW.

9. ☐ PERSONAL CONDUCT ORDERS ☒ To be ordered now and effective until the hearing.
Restrained person must not contact, molest, harass, attack, strike, threaten, sexually assault, batter, telephone, send any messages to, follow, stalk, destroy any personal property, disturb the peace, keep under surveillance, or block movements in public places or thoroughfares.

10. ☒ STAY-AWAY ORDERS ☒ To be ordered now and effective until the hearing
Defendant must stay at least (specify): _100_ yards away from the following persons and places (the addresses of the places are optional and you do not have to reveal them):

   a. Plaintiff ☒ and the other named plaintiffs (names):
      THERESA BARROSO

   b. ☒ Plaintiff's residence (address optional): 216 E. 6th St #B
      PERRIS, CA 92570

   c. ☐ Plaintiff's place of work (address optional):

   d. ☐ Plaintiff's children's school or place of child care (address optional):

   e. ☐ Other (specify):
      (address optional):

11. Will granting of any of the stay-away orders in item 10 interfere with defendant's access to defendant's residence or place of employment? ☐ Yes ☒ No
(If yes, explain):

12. ☒ Plaintiff(s) will suffer great and irreparable harm before this petition can be heard in court unless the court makes those orders requested above effective now and until the hearing. (Specify the harm and why it will occur before the hearing):
When the incident happened he on 11/23/98 he stated to me that he would never leave me alone no matter what happened.

13. ☐ ATTORNEY FEES AND COSTS
Defendant should be ordered to pay plaintiff's attorney fees and costs as follows (specify):

14. ☐ OTHER ORDERS (specify other orders you are requesting):

(Continued on next page)

CH-100 (Rev. January 1, 1998) **PETITION FOR INJUNCTION PROHIBITING HARASSMENT**

Page two of the restraining order.

Donna Goodenough

PLAINTIFF (Name): THERESA BARROSO	CASE NUMBER:
DEFENDANT (Name): ALVIN ROBINSON	

(THIS IS NOT AN ORDER)

Plaintiffs request that copies of orders be given to the following law enforcement agencies:

Law enforcement agency   Address

PERRIS POLICE Department

16. a. ☐ Plaintiff has asked for restraining orders against the defendant before. *(Specify county and case number, if known.)*

b. ☐ Defendant has asked for restraining orders against plaintiff before. *(Specify county and case number, if known.)*

17. Plaintiff requests additional relief as may be proper.

18. ☐ I request that time for service of the Order to Show Cause and accompanying papers be shortened so that they may be served no less than *(specify number):* days before the date set for the hearing. I need to have the order shortening time because of the facts contained in this application. *(Add additional facts if necessary)*:

19. ☒ DESCRIPTION OF CONDUCT
Describe in detail the most recent incidents of abuse. State what happened, the dates, and who did what to whom. Describe any injuries Defendant about 10 minutes to 1 Pm on 11/23/98 called me a "fat bitch". We then got into a verbal argument and he went in the house. He then wouldn't let me in the house when I threatend to leave and call the police he ran up behind me and pushed me int
☒ Continued in Attachment 19.

20. ☐ Plaintiff is not required to pay a fee for filing this petition because plaintiff is seeking order(s) restraining violence or threats of violence. *(Note: If the court finds there has been no violence or threats of violence, then you may be ordered to pay the appropriate fees.)*

21. ☒ Number of pages attached: 2

I declare under penalty of perjury under the laws of the State of California that the foregoing is true and correct.

Date: 11/24/98

THERESA BARROSO
(TYPE OR PRINT NAME)

▶ _(signature)_
(SIGNATURE OF PLAINTIFF)

(TYPE OR PRINT NAME)

▶
(SIGNATURE OF PLAINTIFF)

(TYPE OR PRINT NAME)

▶
(SIGNATURE OF PLAINTIFF)

CH-100 (Rev. January 1, 1998)   PETITION FOR INJUNCTION PROHIBITING HARASSMENT   Page three of three

Page three of the restraining order.

the fence. I tried to leave and he said you're
not going anywhere and pushed me to the ground
As I tried to get up he punched me in the
⬤e and threw me on the hood of the CRX
his car. he held me up there just slapping me
and when he bend over to pick up a wood block
I kicked him in the face as I tried to get off
the car. He then threw the wood block at
me and told me I drove him to do this. I
was just constantly bitching and nagging and
that's why he was doing this. I then told
him to please stop because he was hurting mme.
He then told me I don't know how to fight
he said, "You ain't shit." I told him the cops
are on the way so that he would stop.
He then said please don't send me to jail
you already sent me there before and
I don't want to go back. He then picked
up a pipe and busted the windows on the
⬤r (Acura) and called me "stupid bitch I'm
going to Fuck you up", get in my face again
and I swear I'll put your head through
that windshield. I then replied if your going
to do it, do it one good time because you
are going to jail and I hope you wrought
in hell. He then got down on his knees and
started to cry and begged me please don't
send me to jail, I'll give you your car
back, I'll take all my shit and leave you and
never look back. I told him I didn't care
about the car or him that he should of
thought about everything before he put his
hands on me. He repeatedly repeated to say
he was so sorry, he sweared he would
never do it again, and that he was
wrong, he never should of put his hands
on me. I asked him to please let me leave
because I was running very late to my

Page four of the restraining order.

Donna Goodenough

doctor's appointment to please let me leave I saw the mailman come so I went to check the mail. I went in the house and asked him to please stay outside he then said I'm just going to get my stuff so I said okay He called his parents and said Terry is putting me out please come get me Then he said because she won't let me get my check because I won't go to the doctors appointment with her the I yelled put tell them why I'm kicking you out because you beat my ass. He then said on the phone because she busted out my windows and I said no I didn't you know how he is he did it himself. So then I went back outside and walked out of the fence and got in the truck and started it and put it in drive he then reached in and put it in Park, I put it back in drive and he turned the ignition off. I asked him to please let me leave, he then said all I need to know is Do you love me, I said no now let me go, he said please tell me the truth be very honest Do you love me I said NO! I already told you No, please I said let me go and get out of the window so that I could go He then pulled away and said no matter what I'm not going to leave you, I'm never going to leave you alone, you will always be my woman you're my fat woman and I love every thing about you. If not I wouldn't be with you I then said I hate you and took off. He yelled out that I ran over his foot so I braked and looked back to see if he was okay. I then seen him walk in the fence so I thought he was okay. I left and then I came back at 4:30pm he had already taken his car and his clothes and stuff. When I was going to bed I r the report of what happened 8:30pm so that he will be warned not to come around because I thought He still had the keys.

Page five of the restraining order.

CHAPTER 13

A CATALYST FOR CHANGE
Public outrage demands change in foster care system

Certainly Andy Setzer wasn't the only child to die in foster care. By 1999, there were droves of "Andy's" strung out all across our nation. What made Andy's story so compelling was that suddenly it seemed as if children dying in foster care had become an epidemic. Andy Setzer was only one of many children that had been victimized by a government-funded system that was quickly spinning out of control. Nationwide investigations revealed that it had become commonplace for foster kids to be abused and neglected, to be held "hostage" to bureaucratic blunders and carelessness by the very agency that was supposed to be working in the child's best interest. Outraged citizens felt that the nearly unlimited authority and immunity which CPS so brazenly brandished had turned out to be Andy's worst enemy. Newspapers reported that an estimated fifty percent of all children who died from abuse were already known to CPS. When Andy was murdered, besieged county supervisors were flabbergasted that yet another kid had died while in "protective custody." As more facts about the case emerged, their shock turned into anger.

Supervisor Bob Buster said it was appalling that a home such as Theresa Barroso's could have possibly been approved for foster care. Buster's feelings of outrage mirrored almost everyone who'd heard the horrible details of Andy's death. Buster added that lawmakers were doing everything possible to make sure another child was not thrown to the sharks.

The public was absolutely furious, almost riotous. They'd heard shallow repentance and empty promises from CPS many times before and they were sick of it.

Supervisor Tom Mullen spoke with obvious emotion when he said he wanted to know why that child was placed in *that* particular home. He vowed to demand some answers.

The Board of Supervisors and the citizens of Riverside County weren't the only ones demanding answers from Child Protective Services. Homicide investigators were soon banging at their door.

Horst paid a visit to the Riverside County Department of Public Social Services and seized Andy's thick CPS file as well as manuals, interoffice memos and letters, plus notes taken during caseworkers' conversations with a half dozen of Andy's caretakers. There was also a wealth of information

192

about Andy's biological parents and his grandmother. He learned that the confidentiality laws that cloaked everything in a thick blanket of secrecy were intended to protect the floundering biological parents, not the minor.

At first glance, Andy's CPS file seemed to be littered with mistakes and oversights, which were clearly documented, but later brushed off by CPS as merely an unfortunate set of circumstances. Most importantly, it seemed that Alvin Robinson's written admission of his criminal history had been blatantly ignored, the restraining order was never discovered and Andy's grandmother had been told to "have her ducks in a row" so *she* could get custody of Andy.

According to Child Protective Services' own placement policies, an "outside" non-relative foster home should only be considered if placement with a suitable relative couldn't be found. Dawn Masterson had prepared for and was rightfully expecting to get custody of Andy when he was shunted off to Alvin and Theresa's house instead. CPS had concerns that Dawn's age of forty-nine would be a hindrance to raising a rambunctious youngster like Andy. Did CPS think an obese woman, who weighed in at three hundred pounds, would be better able to chase around after a child as active and mischievous as Andy? Dawn Masterson was slender and in excellent health. She had a positive attitude and was fully prepared to deal with Andy's potty problems. Also, she had already proven her competence by caring for Laura's other young son, Jonathan, with few problems.

Yet, CPS decided Andy would be "better off" with Alvin and Theresa. The deciding factor in his placement with Theresa seemed to have been that CPS considered Theresa's *parents* to be such outstanding foster care providers that Theresa surely must have possessed the same attributes.

They were wrong. Dead wrong.

Andy's murder wasn't the first time a Riverside County child had been killed while in "protective custody." Indeed, it had happened before. It had been a mere five years since the disastrous events of 1994 when eleven Riverside County children had been killed; some allegedly at the hands of their foster parents. Even more horrifying were published reports that several were killed by violent or mentally unstable biological parents that had been known to CPS caseworkers. According to those reports, CPS had not always followed up on complaints of abuse. CPS had been horribly criticized that year and had come under incredible scrutiny for numerous oversights which outside sources believed had contributed to the eleven deaths. Those eleven deaths during the year of 1994 had tarnished the image of what Child Protective Services was all about. Or at least, what it was supposed to be all about.

Published reports also indicated that between 1993 and 1997, the percentage of cases CPS chose to investigate fell from seventy-nine percent to seventy percent. They were simply too over-burdened and too understaffed to deal with each and every case the way it was supposed to be dealt with. The end result was eleven dead kids in one year. In the ensuing uproar,

Deadly Thirst

CPS professed that the department would undergo a tremendous overhaul to make sure things like that didn't happen again. After the 1994 fiasco, CPS was blasted by an outside report which concluded in 1996, that CPS created a dangerous environment for both children and social workers and created a false impression of safety. Newspapers were filled with detailed analyses of the problems and pitfalls faced by overburdened, under-trained social workers. Adding fuel to that fire was the fact that the turn-over rate among stressed-out caseworkers was extremely high, newspapers said. Too many caseworkers within the system were new. Social workers were being paid low salaries, they were buckling under enormously high caseloads and they were cutting corners. Sometimes caseworkers struggled as best they could with more than double the recommended number of kids; thus the stress factor was often overwhelming. Sometimes, well-intended caseworkers were simply unable to meet the state's deadline for quickly checking out abuse reports. And kids died.

To remedy the situation, the county bolstered the staff and increased the salaries for emergency response social workers. But that decision became a double-edged sword for the agency. Social workers who worked with long-term children and families were still left to carry a third more cases than they should. They felt it was unfair to bolster some departments and let other departments continue to be swamped neck-deep in caseloads. Angry long-termers began to protest. Giving bonuses to emergency response workers and ignoring other departments put Social Services in a no-win situation. They were sued for discrimination against employees working with long-term cases. With regard to salary, Riverside County social workers had recently ranked second to last of ten southern California counties. Working for Riverside Social Services was a dismal, depressing, high-stress, low paying job.

In the weeks after the report went public, CPS tried to appease their workers and the citizens of Riverside County, vowing even more reform, promising to swiftly correct the problems within the agency. They blamed most of their problems on a lack of funding. In simple terms, the county didn't have enough money to protect kids the way they were supposed to be protected. The newly hired director of Riverside County's Department of Social Services would spend much of the next three years revamping CPS.

In the months before Andy's death, the director was quoted, perhaps a bit prematurely, as saying he felt the system had been satisfactorily brought up to speed. As far as "the system" was concerned, Andy's murder couldn't have come at a worse time.

Upon learning of Alvin's past criminal conviction—to which he admitted in writing on his foster parent application—and the violent details of the restraining order, the department immediately scrambled to review their records. They vowed to conduct better, more extensive background checks, right away, on the 3,500 existing foster homes. Of those, eleven foster children were removed from homes run by convicted criminals or people facing charges for serious crimes and child abuse. According to newspaper reports, the children who were removed had lived in six homes; only two of the homes were licensed for foster care. In one of the licensed homes, the foster mother had been convicted of abusing her own children. One relative caring for a child had a history of assault with a deadly weapon, as well as drug, burglary and vandalism charges. Still, CPS hid behind their wall of silence and confidentiality and held fast to their position that they had made the "right" and "best" decision for Andy.

A grand jury however, came to an entirely different conclusion. Grand juries are strong instruments for breaking logjams caused by the refusal of people to talk or to hand over evidence. The jury's report surmised that Riverside County's Child Protective Services suffered from a serious deficiency of experienced, trained staff members, rather than from an empty pocketbook. It pinned the blame on the same stale issues of lack of training and lack of accountability among social workers. Most appallingly, the Department of Public Social Services still felt that self-governance was their right. In spite of the highly touted overhaul, many social workers were recent hires and lacked proper training. The grand jury also found that the department lacked uniform procedures.

The Little Hoover Commission, a bipartisan, independent state agency charged with recommending ways to increase the efficiency and effectiveness of state programs, issued a similarly dismal report in 1999. They cited a lack of leadership and a failure to adequately measure or monitor the quality of foster care in California.

A few weeks after Andy's murder, the public was still screaming for some sort of explanation from CPS. Finally, a county paid consultant for the Child Welfare League of America issued a curt statement that shocked everyone who read it in the papers. The spokesman stated that he'd reviewed the case and CPS had made the right decisions. Did those decisions contribute in any way to Andy's murder? No, he said, because by everything presented, Andy had been killed by an individual, not a social worker.

The public was livid. The callous indifference of CPS was nothing short of appalling. CPS had been splattered with blood, but they continued to hold their noses in the air and dole out insulting snippets like that. People were screaming that something be done! Changes had to be made...and they had to be made *now!*

The fact that Andy was dead didn't seem to be something Social Services could be held accountable for, even in light of the county's inept way of doing background checks on prospective foster parents. Ignoring Alvin's easily obtainable criminal history was referred to as "a little blip" that "should" have been more thoroughly checked out. The county considered itself caught in a no-win situation as far as the unfortunate circumstances that befell Andy. If Andy had been abused and had died while in the custody of Mike and Lynn Herman and CPS had failed to remove him from a situation they were "aware of," the county could have been partially respon-

Deadly Thirst

sible for his death. They had "acted in good faith" when they yanked Andy out of his preschool and delivered him into the hands of Theresa. "Acting in good faith" was the magical, often-used phrase that seemed to erase all responsibility and liability of any wrongdoing on the part of Social Services. Acting in good faith. But, of all the foster homes in Riverside County, why in the world had Andy been placed in Theresa's house?

As Andy's caseworkers had put it, it was because Theresa's *parents* had been stellar foster care providers. Andy's placement in Theresa's home had been yet another deadly example of CPS's "good faith" policy. Whenever those words were spoken, it was as if someone had waved a magic wand over the entire situation and made all of the county's liability disappear. Poof! Gone! According to the spokesperson that the county hired, Theresa Barroso was solely responsible for the death of Andy Setzer; the county had no culpability whatsoever.

Another spokesman for the county said that there were cracks in the system, but he didn't think that foster parents with criminal backgrounds were in any way an "epidemic."

Gerry Montrose*, head of the Child Protective Services division of the county's Department of Social Services, told newspaper reporters that he felt the grand jury's report was short on documentation and it ridiculed aspects of the system that are in use, not only in California, but across the nation as well. The public read his statement with contempt. It sounded like an insinuation that because a certain program was in use in other areas of the country it was therefore acceptable if a county-appointed caretaker murdered a foster child. He did acknowledge, however, that his division struggled to serve large caseloads with inadequate resources. The old, familiar empty pocketbook excuse. Again.

It was a fabricated image, he said, that there were a bunch of reckless social workers out there doing whatever they wanted. That was not the case, he insisted. Everything was under the jurisdiction of the courts. Still, many felt that the courts would follow any recommendation given by CPS. After all, they were the "child protectors."

A few months after Andy died, in a widely publicized proclamation, another spokesman for county Child Protective Services stated that they had improved the level of scrutiny and the depth of evaluation of foster parents and they were "satisfied." And, he added, it would be even safer in a year. Officials claimed to have welcomed the opportunity to better their system. And that was about all they had to say for themselves. Case closed. Hiding behind the almighty shield of confidentiality, CPS refused to discuss it any further. To the public, CPS seemed to be talking, chronically, out of both sides of their mouth. In one breath they claimed to have increased scrutiny and the depth of evaluation to a point that they were satisfied, then, in the next breath, they said that in a year it would be even safer. Why were they "satisfied" with a system that, admittedly, wasn't as safe as it could be?

Reporters continued to clamor for more details about how this deadly oversight could have happened. One journalist in particular badgered county CPS and the State Licensing Agency in Sacramento relentlessly for explanations as to how a couple with such a violent, documented history could have possibly been deemed acceptable for foster care. One woman in charge of placement said that in "emergency" situations they have to be able to fall on other alternatives, such as temporary placement with a relative. [Andy's removal from the Herman's house was considered an emergency, so why wasn't he sent to live with his grandmother?] The woman admitted that she knew full well which case the reporter was referring to, but refused to comment on any specific case. When asked if a "pending" status was acceptable, she first said no and then said maybe. The whole process was changing as of November 1st, 2001 she explained. When asked if she would put a child into an unlicensed home, she readily admitted that she would. How about if the applicant had admitted in writing on his application that he'd been convicted of a crime, wouldn't that disqualify him?

Not necessarily, the woman said. They'd run a check, but if the criminal justice system didn't tell them about the conviction, then how was CPS supposed to know? By then, the reporter was tired of beating around the bush and nailed the spokeswoman with direct evidence that CPS *had* known of Alvin's conviction because it had been submitted—in writing—with the application. Her answer was a terse "no comment." After a long silence, she added that it all depended on what the conviction was for and how long ago it had happened. Each case was handled on its own merits. The reporter reminded her that county law enforcement had documented histories of *both* applicants on file, which detailed very violent, abusive behavior. Surely CPS would have wanted to look into something like that, right? Not necessarily. A prudent worker would have, but they may have checked it out and felt that, in spite of it, the placement was ok.

"If licensing had preformed a simple check with the local authorities," the reporter said, "they would have seen that the child was going to be placed into a home where the potential foster parents had been engaged in fights so brutal that the police arrested the father and the mother filed a restraining order against him. Wouldn't that seem to you like a dangerous place to put a child?" The spokeswoman said that she would have done a lot of checking before she placed a child in a home like that. But that alone did not mean that she would rule it out.

"Isn't a restraining order a red flag signaling trouble?" the reporter asked, astounded. Oh yes, the spokeswoman said, unflustered.

"Is CPS colorblind to red flags?" No, the spokeswoman huffed. She would have checked further. Then, under her breath she mumbled that they always say if one thing goes wrong with a case then twenty things would go wrong. But this type of thing only happened about every twenty-five or thirty years, she said. Had she forgotten about the eleven deaths in 1994?

Deadly Thirst

The conversation left the reporter bitter and disgusted. Throughout the next several weeks, newspapers continued to headline recent heartbreaking stories of child abuse and neglect and children dying in foster care.

One such death occurred in a foster home that had aroused the suspicions of social workers on prior occasions. Authorities had been to the home several times to investigate reports of possible child abuse. Indeed, in the two years the home had operated as a supposed safe haven for children, two kids had showed up in emergency rooms with broken bones and a 23-month-old boy was noted to have bruises and scratches. The boy's biological mother claimed to have notified CPS that she'd seen scratches on her son's face and arms when she visited him at the foster home, but no one paid attention to her complaints. Social Services claimed that the foster mother had been investigated three times, but her explanation of injuries checked out. However, the biological parents of children in foster care claimed that complaints and allegations coming from them were hardly given serious consideration. Finally a "hold" was placed on the foster home, meaning no more children could be sent there until the allegations were resolved. However, the very same day the hold was put into force, two other children were sent to the home because social workers were unaware of the hold. Another case of the left hand not knowing what the right hand was doing.

According to a November 2000 in-depth report conducted by Time Magazine, that sort of thing is typical of foster care. And that's exactly what happened in Andy's case.

Further inflaming the situation, one day prior to the hold a social worker had removed one foster child from the same home when the child suffered a broken arm. In spite of all that, no one at CPS saw any red flags. One month later, the 23-month-old boy died of suspicious injuries. The foster mother was charged with his murder. Newspapers reported that CPS claimed in their review that no reports of abuse had been made. CPS officials tried to distance themselves from blame by stating that kids weren't typically removed from homes unless the complaints were validated or confirmed, although it seems safe to assume that Mike and Lynn Herman might have disagreed with that statement. CPS further stated that they were "comfortable" with their decisions and added that it wasn't unusual for a foster home to be targeted with complaints.

In spite of their professed comfort, after the death of the 23-month-old boy, county officials repossessed two other kids that had also been living in the home. As the county explained, these two kids were taken away and placed into the protective custody of yet another foster home.

It wasn't only abusive foster parents that were bringing a bad rap to CPS. Sometimes deaths were a result of children *not* being taken away from abusive, biological parents or mothers who turned a blind eye to heavy-handed boyfriends. Such was the case of seventeen-month-old Allisa Gold* who died one year prior to Andy. The story was shockingly similar

198

to Andy's. According to published reports, Allisa died after allegedly being beaten by her mother's twenty-eight-year-old boyfriend. The reports further stated that Allisa's mother did nothing to stop the beatings, the severest of which landed Allisa in Loma Linda Medical Center on Christmas Eve. She died a month later. Newspapers reported that records obtained from DPSS revealed that it took one hundred and six days and seven hot-line calls for the social worker to finally go and see Allisa for the first time, on Christmas Eve. Investigations revealed that Allisa's case had been closed [due to a lapse of time] on December 22—three days before the fatal beating. Further checks, after the child died, revealed the mother's live-in boyfriend had been convicted, as a minor, of voluntary manslaughter of an eleven-month-old girl left in his care. A more thorough background check might have picked up on that "little blip," but as it did in Andy's case, the system failed.

Thirty days after Allisa died, Social Services proclaimed that they had revised their program to ensure that the problem wouldn't happen again. But it *did* happen again. Social workers were—and still are—simply too overloaded with more reports of child abuse than they can ever hope to handle.

Within a year after Andy's murder—and after CPS had completed its sweeping overhaul—the newspapers were again ablaze with tragic headlines. An eighteen-month-old Riverside County girl died of what authorities claim was a startling case of abuse and neglect at the hands of her biological mother. An autopsy report said she died from blunt impacts to the head, neck and torso. The report noted bruises and scrapes in many places on her small, malnourished body. There were also indications that she had been starved, which was something the girl's biological grandparents had phoned social workers about many times, to no avail.

The Press Enterprise reported that, in CPS's files, caseworkers had validated in recent visits to the home, the little girl and her siblings were "healthy and thriving." Her autopsy report verified otherwise. She had remnants of some sort of adhesive material—possibly duct tape—stuck on her eyes, ears, scalp, chest and legs, which ominously indicated the child may have been bound. The child's mother suffered from long bouts of severe depression and was considered to be mentally unstable. Had CPS actually visited the home or had overburdened caseworkers simply written her off? From behind their comfortable shield of confidentiality, CPS would not discuss it publicly.

Less than a year after Andy Setzer was laid to rest, another Riverside County foster home came under public scrutiny. An eleven-month-old boy was reportedly taken to the hospital with suspicious injuries. An examination revealed the child had recently suffered a skull fracture, numerous abrasions to the chest and a black eye. In addition to those findings, the doctor concluded that the child had gotten a skull fracture on the opposite side approximately three weeks prior. There was also evidence of earlier

Deadly Thirst

bruising and blackened eyes. The child's foster parents were arrested, but that child was lucky; he lived.

In December of 1999—just four months after Andy died—concerned neighbors notified police about a possible child neglect case in Fontana. Officers went into the home and discovered two toddlers soaked in urine and covered with excrement. The home was nothing more than a shack reminiscent of a Tijuana barrio. The children's mother had apparently left them alone for twelve hours while she went to Los Angeles. Further investigations revealed that six other children belonging to this woman had been removed and placed into the custody of San Bernardino County Child Protective Services. The mother and her six previous children were well known to county officials, but CPS does not monitor past clients to see if they may have given birth to more children.

These are by no means the only cases that tarnished the image of CPS in the months surrounding Andy's murder.

The incident in Fontana closed the book on a horrible year during which law enforcement agencies throughout the Inland Empire, which includes Riverside, had uncovered several strange and highly publicized cases of child neglect, abuse and even murder. All of them involved CPS in one way or another. To many it seemed no matter what action CPS took, or what action they failed to take, kids died. Either way, the system failed these kids. CPS was coming under harsh criticism on an almost monthly basis and Andy Setzer's name kept popping up like an unruly jack-in-the-box. County Child Protection officials claimed they'd worked hard to restructure their department and retrain their overburdened, stressed-out, underpaid social workers. However, families simply couldn't be put into a mold where one size fits all. Each case was different and complex. To adequately investigate, each case required time; something socials workers just didn't have. They still don't and they probably never will.

According to their own placement policies, before CPS assigns custody to a non-relative, they should first strive to place a child with a relative. But, a recent independent study in California found that relatives are often the most neglectful. It was estimated that ninety percent of relatives caring for foster kids did not meet current health and safety standards in their homes. Problems ranged from crowding to unsanitary or hazardous conditions. Some children were living in roach infested homes, degraded by plumbing problems and yards filled with stinking, hazardous garbage. In many of these homes, children were sleeping in the same beds or rooms with adults, or in sleeping bags on the floor—as Andy had been doing on the night of his murder.

In some cases, relatives had not been checked for criminal records or their names had not been run through the child abuse registry. Some relatives were allowed to take custody of kids merely by signing an affidavit swearing they had not been convicted of a crime. Alvin Robinson, on his application, *did* admit to his criminal history, but in his sworn, written statement he played it down to such an extent that officials were content to let it slide.

California didn't want to reduce the standards for professional, licensed, non-relative foster care providers, but they also didn't want to require family members to have to endure the lengthy licensing process if they had met basic safety standards and didn't have criminal records. CPS wanted the flexibility to bend the rules here and there, as they did in Andy's case.

The foster care fiasco had been in the headlines for months and the federal government was finally feeling the heat. The foster care uproar became so bad after Andy's death and the deaths that followed his, that the federal government threatened to halt funding if the rules and regulations pertaining to relatives were not brought up to the same standards insisted upon for non-relatives. If federal authorities were to conclude that California didn't hold relative and non-relative foster parents to the same standards, California could loose as much as $300 million in funding.

The county seemed to be in a no-win situation, again. Loosing $300 million would be devastating to them and even more deadly to the kids. Social workers complained the new rules concerning relative and non-relative placement took away all the flexibility they previously had in overlooking such deficiencies as "irrelevant" criminal records.

In the months following Andy's death, Assemblyman Rod Pacheco, a Riverside Republican, was besieged by angry residents and received unanimous support from his colleagues—a 77-0 margin— backing his proposal of AB2623. The bill allowed the Department of Justice, commonly called DOJ, to send complete conviction histories for background checks to all requesting agencies—even if they lacked fingerprints. The citizens of Riverside County felt their long months of letter writing, phoning and E-mailing legislators had finally paid off when AB2623 was signed into law by Governor Gray Davis in September 2000. Had Alvin's conviction been released to the requesting agency, it should have blocked Alvin and Theresa from obtaining custody of Andy. That was, of course, unless the county chose to exercise some of its flexibility and overlook it. On a wider scope, Assembly Bill 2623 should prevent any more kids like Andy from being sent to live with pathetic surrogates who are nothing more than strangers to the foster care system.

According to DOJ, criminal conviction records often don't include the all-important fingerprints of the accused individual. Most often this happens when someone is arrested, cited and released without being incarcerated. Although local law enforcement officials are the ones responsible for making sure each arrestee is fingerprinted, this rule isn't always followed; there are simply too many people coming through the system. And, as the spokeswoman for the Riverside County Sheriff's Department so dryly put it, mistakes are bound to happen.

Because of Andy Setzer's death, AB2623 allows the DOJ to release information that has *not* been verified by matching fingerprints, so long as

Deadly Thirst

DOJ stipulates that fact. After reviewing the facts surrounding the murder of Andy Setzer, lawmakers felt strongly that when foster children are assigned to a new home they deserve more than a perfunctory, superficial check of a dangerously incomplete database.

For many, it seemed to be a light at the end of a very long, dark tunnel. The public was finally seeing some positive results from their months of outrage. Perhaps Andy had not "died in vain" after all, as Cowboy had professed to be so upset about.

Andy's death brought other changes regarding the way background checks are handled. Riverside County beefed up its Sheriff's Department, with ten new positions, to assist the Department of Public Social Services with more thorough investigations into the backgrounds of potential foster parents. Having more deputies involved with background checks will reduce the burden placed on social workers that are assigned the task. Had this system been in effect when Andy was in protective custody he might never have been sent to Alvin and Theresa's home.

In 1995 there were almost a quarter of a million children in the nation's foster-care systems, each child generated federal money for the institution the moment they were taken from their home. By May of 2001 that number had risen to between 550,000 and 560,000 children nationally. In California, the number of children in foster homes has tripled since 1983 and is expected to rise to more than 167,000 by the year 2006. In 1999 it was estimated, in Riverside and San Bernardino Counties alone, there were more than 8,000 kids in foster homes or living with relatives assigned by the courts.

Time Magazine reported that amazingly, even as late as 1999 many state foster-care agencies still worked from hard copy case files. Without modern databases, tracking the fate of foster kids was nothing more than an endless, incomplete and confusing paper chase; a chase that no social worker had time for. Whole files had sometimes been lost. Children had been "lost."

Still to this day there aren't enough administrators to review and follow the overwhelming number of cases or to consider alternatives for kids stuck in bad situations. Oftentimes, police are asked to do welfare checks; CPS simply doesn't have the time or manpower. However, some social workers think the county's chronic use of law enforcement has become a dangerous habit. But, the higher ups claim that using law enforcement is an integral part of child protection and besides, the cops aren't complaining about it. Through it all, there has been little or no accountability for kids that die in foster care. Time magazine referred to it as "child swallowing."

It costs approximately $13,000 a year to care for each foster child; the money usually earmarked for the direct care of kids, in the form of monthly payments to foster parents and salaries for social workers. Still, low salaries and stressful working conditions have hampered a nationwide effort to attract qualified social workers, even though most agencies had reportedly received all the funding they requested to bolster their staffs. The turnover rate for social workers was astronomical in 1999, the year Andy Setzer came to live with Alvin and Theresa. Currently, the turnover rate among social workers continues at an alarming rate, despite all the revamping. In 1999 seventy-four new social workers had been brought on board in Riverside County, which boosted the staff by twenty percent. Too often though, new caseworkers don't have time to familiarize themselves with decisions and recommendations made by their predecessors or other departments.

Although it's the Federal Government that doles out most of the funding for foster care, the welfare of children has traditionally been a state matter and much of that has been delegated further down the chain to each individual county. It has been reported that in California some state-licensed foster agencies had one beleaguered caseworker for every seventy kids! Time magazine reported that some agencies became so desperate to place kids that any home would suffice. Kids, like Andy Setzer, were routinely being sent to the homes of people who were virtual strangers to the system *before* the paperwork had actually been completed, or background checks secured. This trend of "wavering" became standard policy in many overburdened agencies. As the number of kids needing foster care soared out of control, California was one state that began contracting out more and more services to the county level and even to private agencies that had the resources and funding to better deal with the kids. Private agencies usually have about twelve to fifteen kids for every caseworker, in comparison with the county's staggering ratio. Government run agencies still lack the ability to really know what kind of care a child is actually getting in the foster home. Time magazine reported that it was estimated that in the year 2000, as many as 7,500 kids nationwide were being tortured and mistreated in what is technically "government protection." Too often, kids are imprisoned with abuse and neglect, by bureaucratic mix-ups, carelessness and the shortsightedness of an over burdened staff. That's exactly what happened to Andy.

Fact is, there were, and still are, so many different groups and departments within a foster care agency that it is almost impossible for state and county agencies to see the whole picture. One group of caseworkers have the responsibility of taking kids away from their biological parents and another group is responsible for placing them elsewhere and still another group is responsible for overseeing their continuing welfare. No one seems to know what the other caseworkers are doing on any given case and no one sees the whole picture.

This was certainly what happened in Andy's case. When Detective Horst asked the Regional Manager of CPS why Andy had not been sent to live with his grandmother, the woman said she was unaware that Dawn Masterson was interested in taking Andy. And Dawn had asked for custody several times.

Above all, social workers are often under-trained, underpaid, over-burdened and short lived. To add insult to injury, their recommendations on child placement are often second-guessed, ignored and overruled. Corners

Deadly Thirst

are often cut and situations compromised by huge, overwhelming caseloads that are screaming for the individual attention that social workers can't provide. Time reported that in some instances where children were suspected as being abused, caseworkers simply couldn't visit the homes and instead, let a two-minute phone call suffice. Other times, even phone calls went unmade. Across America, there is ample documentation of reported child abuse going unchecked for months, resulting in a closing of the cases without ever investigating the allegations. Again, this is what happened to Andy while he was still living with his biological mother, Laura Utley.

During her term as Health and Human Services Secretary, Donna Shalala promised the most sweeping reform of the foster care system in twenty years. But since the real control of foster care lies at a local level, Shalala's new legislature did little, if anything, to help the situation. In fact, it may have set off a whole new set of problems.

Time Magazine reported that some critics say the reforms in many states actually puts a "bounty" on the kids' heads in the form of financial incentives. In the year Andy died, forty-six thousand kids were legally adopted nation wide, which was a twenty eight percent increase from the year before. The Coalition for Child Protection Reform says that for every kid adopted beyond the number of adoptions the year prior, the federal government pays the states a bonus of $4,000 to be used for the foster care/adoption programs. Placing kids with special needs can fetch a lofty sum of $6,000 but the clincher is, states get to keep the money even if a placement fails as it does in roughly twelve percent of the cases. If they place the same child again, they get to collect all over again. Thus, there seems to be an incentive to place a child with little or no fact-finding about whether the placement is a good one that will last. Reportedly, the pressure is to quickly place the child. This is what happened to Andy Setzer. CPS was in a hurry to find a place to put him.

In California during 1999, kids were falling through the cracks of the child welfare system left and right. After each instance, social workers and agencies promised reform and pledged procedural changes. And then, when the hype faded, it was back to the same old way of doing things. During an August 2002 public hearing, California's Secretary for Health and Human Services, Grantland Johnson, said the foster care system is still "broken" and still needs "fixing." "It's still too bureaucratic and there are still too many disconnections between the state and local agencies and the social worker who is engaging with a child," he said.

Thankfully, Rod Pacheco and the outraged, unrelenting citizens of Riverside County fought hard on behalf of their littlest comrades. Andy Setzer and others like him had not died in vain after all. Laws have been changed. Now, if only Social Services would abide by these laws. The census among those who followed Andy's case is, they probably won't. After all, still to this day, CPS claims they made the "right" and "best" decisions when they placed Andy into Theresa's unlicensed home and they had made the right and best decisions when they turned a blind eye to Alvin's criminal history. They were right to turn a deaf ear to the pleas of Andy's loving grandmother and they were right to snatch him from the Hermans just as his adoption was being finalized. To many it seemed that as long as CPS professes to make their decisions in good faith they will not be held accountable and there has been little if any evidence which proves otherwise.

Moreover, many believe that when CPS chose to look the other way at Alvin's criminal record, they had been negligent to a deadly degree. Many people in Riverside County felt that CPS was as much responsible for the death of Andy as was Theresa. Some even accused the drug addicted, biological parents. Still others feel the guilt belongs equally to all three parties: the biological parents, CPS and the final foster parents.

Angry citizens of Riverside County wanted CPS to pay for what had happened to Andy and all the other "Andy's" that had died under hushed up circumstances. But CPS bows to no one. Not then, not now, and probably not ever. Still to this day, no one responsible for the decisions that put Andy in the custody of killers and into an early grave has been punished in a court of law. Yes, one social worker resigned and some others may have been reprimanded, but no one at CPS was held criminally responsible.

More than a few citizens who were caught up in the angry aftermath of Andy's murder were screaming that the all encompassing power that is Child Protective Services has allowed CPS to become judge *and* jury.

CHAPTER 14

ALVIN ROBINSON'S ARREST
He knew the consequences

In the days following Theresa's arrest, it was decided that all her jailhouse visits were to be tape recorded, especially her visits with Alvin. Investigators from the DA's office felt that Alvin might say something to Theresa that would provide valuable evidence to the prosecution. But Alvin was strictly adhering to his daddy's advice to lay low 'til everything blew over. Visiting Theresa in jail would have surely been the wrong thing to do. Even Alvin's friends were telling him that. So Alvin didn't visit her.

Also, in the days following Theresa's arrest, word had come back to the District Attorney's office and to the investigators working the case that Alvin was, as one investigator put it, just a few bricks short of a load. Alvin's family and his friends were insisting that he was "retarded." This posed a few problems early on, but after Monterosso listened again to Alvin's tape recorded statements to Detective Horst and polygraph examiner Dave Williams, he was certain Alvin was smart enough to have known what was going on and that he could have done something to stop it. He was slow maybe, but no one on the prosecuting side thought for one second that he was actually retarded.

Alvin had been cooperating with police and felt sure that he was not going to be arrested. He was downright cocky. Horst, Monterosso and everyone else involved on the prosecuting side of the case wouldn't rest until they brought Alvin down also, for his part in the murder. But they had to be extremely careful. They needed to get Alvin to admit, in his own words and in a much more solid fashion, that he *had* understood his responsibilities as a foster parent. They needed to hear him say, explicitly, that he *did* know the abuse Andy was suffering could kill him, or at least cause serious injury.

Monterosso needed to enlist the help of another investigator, one who wasn't in on the case yet. Horst was a great detective and an absolutely awesome interrogator, but there was no way that Alvin was going to stretch his neck out on Vern Horst's chopping block again. Monterosso needed someone with crust and a certain kind of no-bullshit tenacity who could get Alvin to relax and tell what he knew. More than two weeks had gone by and he hadn't been arrested. Not even after he flunked the lie detector test. In Alvin's words, he "didn't do nothin'" so he didn't have nothin' to worry about. His father's predictions had apparently come true for Alvin; everything was "blowing over" just as Leroy said it would.

206

Monterosso knew he could be accused of coercing Alvin into a confession or of leading a person with low mental capability into saying things that would later be used against him. Monterosso knew he had to proceed very carefully or his whole case might fall apart. It was a lot like building a house of cards; one wrong move and the whole thing could fall apart.

Senior investigator Pete Harding was assigned to Alvin's portion of the case. The self-described no-bullshit, yard-dog, chomping-at-the-bit-hell-raiser, ass-kicker was more than happy to step in and assist his buddy John in whatever way he could. They'd have to move in slow and easy and plan their attack strategy so that Alvin wouldn't spook. But then, Alvin was "slow" so his arrest would take the work of someone who could convincingly get down on his level.

Pete Harding was all of these things. And more. Harding was an old salt; good at just about everything when it came to police work. He could jive-talk to drug addicts in their own filthy gutter lingo and then turn right around and talk sweet to little kids in a Sesame Street sort of way. He was completely comfortable shifting gears in mid-sentence if he had to. His colleagues valued him for his honesty and his high ethical standards. Pete Harding was also as tough as nails and an absolutely ruthless investigator. For the Robinson portion of the case, there was no better guy than Pete Harding.

Harding and Monterosso were so totally different it was almost comical that they meshed so well together. Their age difference made them almost like father and son, except their appearances were worlds apart. It was obvious that they hadn't emerged from the same womb. Monterosso was a short, dark-haired, brown-eyed, thirty-two-year-old Italian, meticulously groomed and one of the best-dressed men in Riverside County. When Monterosso went on vacation, his idea of relaxation was staying at a plush resort, sipping cocktails from a long slender glass with a little paper umbrella sticking out the top. Rarely did he swear and certainly never around women.

By contrast, Harding was a fifty-two-year-old beer and pretzels, camping and fishing type guy. He was tall and stocky, fair-skinned, blue-eyed and as bald as a buzzard. Harding was more of a casual dresser and wouldn't be caught dead without his cowboy boots. Harding's conversations were heavily slathered with swear words and slang and he liked all kinds of music, as long as it was country music.

Harding's small house in a suburb near Riverside was spotless, reflecting his fastidious personality. Not one item out of place. Pictures of animals and majestic scenes of nature adorned the walls. There was a fireplace and over it was a picture of John Wayne. "The Duke." On the mantle were framed photos of the people and places he loved the most. The décor also reflected Harding's whimsical sense of humor. There was a fish pillow on the couch, which looked and felt like a *real* fish—on both sides. It was a gift someone had given him a few years ago for Christmas. Since Harding loved to fish, a fish pillow seemed appropriate. Everyone one who saw the fish pillow couldn't help but laugh as they fondled it. Then there was the lotion dispenser labeled "bald head cream," that was proudly displayed on a desk near the front door. Comical little touches were so typical of Harding's demeanor. He was a fun guy to have around.

Other touches showed fastidious attention to detail that were somewhat rare for a bachelor. The items in his kitchen cabinets and in his refrigerator were all arranged methodically, in order of height and with all labels facing forward. Towels in both bathrooms and the kitchen were not merely hung on the towel racks; they were perfectly folded and placed "just so." In the driveway was a glistening fifth-wheel Alpenlite travel trailer, which never stayed parked too long. In the backyard was a sparkling swimming pool.

Pete Harding had been around the block many times and, like some of the best cops, had gotten into trouble when he was young. He was led astray at the age of thirteen. His first encounter with the wrong side of the law happened when he and a group of his thirteen-year-old friends were joy riding in a stolen car. The driver could barely see over the dashboard. Things got squirrelly right away and they ended up crashing the car in a riverbed. That time they were all lucky. They ran from the scene and hid from the cops. None were apprehended. Fortified by their luck, they kept sneaking out at night, smoking, getting into fights and stealing cars. "We'd take cars that had the keys in them," he said. "So we didn't think it was stealing. We were just being little assholes." Time and time again, they'd take a car and joyride all over town, usually leaving it wherever it ran out of gas. Sometimes they'd crash. "We didn't mean to wreck 'em; it's just that we didn't know how to drive."

Justice finally prevailed though and he ended up in Riverside Juvenile Hall for two weeks. "Boy, did that suck," he recalled with a laugh. His parents pitched a fit. The County gave him two years probation.

Pete Harding lost his virginity the following year, to a sixteen-year-old girl. His parents had hired her to do some ironing, but as Harding remembered, she got the wrinkles out of a lot more than just the shirts.

After high school, he decided to go to Riverside City College to be a physical education instructor, but that idea soon fizzled. On a whim, he took an "Introduction to Law Enforcement" class. "Two weeks into the class, I knew I'd never do anything else," he said. "The instructor was a kick-ass kind of guy. I really admired him." When Harding applied for the police academy, he was a bit nervous. He wondered if he should reveal that he'd gotten kicked out of school for fighting and that he'd spent some time in juvenile hall. He decided to own up to his checkered past and the powers that be let him into the academy anyway. They knew a person with good cop potential when they saw one and Harding fit the bill perfectly. They couldn't wait to sign him up. "I went from a four unit failure to the Dean's list for the entire academy."

On his twentieth birthday, he was hired as a cadet. He'd hang around dispatch and after his shift he'd ride along with a patrolman all night. "I loved it. I breathed it. I truly believed in it."

Riverside PD hired him when he was twenty-one and he started doing patrol. That was in 1968, a busy year for Harding. His girlfriend and high school sweetheart, Rita, was pregnant. They got married in October and in April his only daughter, Summer, was born.

"Was I a wild cop? You better believe it," he said. "The problem was, I had a perpetual hard-on and I had to share it with the world. A lot of women like cops, so who was I to say no?" The marriage ended after a year and a half but Pete and Rita remained best friends and Summer would always be the light of his life. Rita remarried and she and her second husband continued to live near Pete. Still to this day, the three of them are best friends.

He wouldn't stay single for very long though. Within a year of his divorce, he met Kathy. Soon, they were living together.

He was assigned to the Crime Specific Burglary taskforce and worked that for a year until he started getting antsy. Then he started working the RINET narcotics task force which let him blow off a little more steam than he did working CSB. Nothing could compare to the rush he felt when he was on a roll to a crack house. But it still wasn't exciting enough. Later, a move to "vice" proved to be just the ticket for Harding. "We really kicked ass, back then."

After he and Kathy had been living together for several years, they decided to get married. Like Carmen Horst, Kathy understood Harding's undercover work and the unkempt appearance his job required. She was only concerned with the danger. Still, the work-related stress level was constantly rising and Harding was stressed to the max. He was smoking at least a pack and a half during every eight-hour shift and, off duty, he drank way too much.

In 1980, when he was thirty-three, he was transferred to robbery/ homicide. He hated it. His marriage was faltering along with his health and disposition, so in 1981 he took a transfer up to South Lake Tahoe, thinking the change of scenery would do them both some good. There, he went back to patrol and things settled down for a while. But he hated the snow and found himself becoming extremely short-tempered with just about everything and everyone, especially Kathy. It seemed no matter which direction he turned, he couldn't quite get comfortable with it. Kathy wasn't comfortable either. All that changed when a buddy of his from the Riverside DA's office called him with a job offer. It would be a move that stuck.

He and Kathy moved back to Riverside and decided on an amicable divorce. As their divorce was finalized, he settled into his job at the DA's office doing basic trial preparations. He'd get together with lawyers and go over the files to see what they needed to do to secure convictions. If they needed search warrants or additional arrests, Harding would do whatever

Deadly Thirst

it took. He was good at tying up loose ends. He even worked the Major Narcotics Violator Program for a year, doing trial prep in dope cases.

In 1988 he was assigned to SACA [Sexual Assault/Child Abuse]. It proved to be the best move yet. Although he wasn't real fond of kids, he found that working on the behalf of a child was rewarding and satisfying. It had "internal" benefits unlike any other kind of police work he'd ever done. It was something he could really throw his heart into. Unfortunately, his emotional involvement with the SACA victims ran too deep and he started taking his cases too personally. On the exterior, Harding appeared to be as coarse as sandpaper, but on the inside he was as soft as pudding. His supervisor decided Harding needed a break from SACA and promptly transferred him. For the next three years he worked "backgrounds."

Eventually, he came back to SACA and finished out his career there. When Andy Setzer died, Pete Harding was on the verge of retirement after thirty-two years in law enforcement. He'd been working for the DA's office sixteen years; he'd been with SACA eleven of those years. He was dedicated and undoubtedly the most qualified, well-rounded investigator the Riverside DA's office had. So, when John Monterosso needed a special partner to snag Alvin, Harding was the natural choice.

It was August 12th when Harding joined the Alvin Robinson/Theresa Barroso prosecution team. His assignment was to find out exactly what Alvin had learned during his foster parenting classes and to establish whether Alvin did or did not know he had a responsibility toward Andy. Harding read the transcripts and listened to the taped polygraph session as well as the interview Alvin did with Horst the afternoon Andy died. He interviewed social workers about Alvin's foster parenting classes and did a tremendous amount of prep work before he actually sat down with Alvin. He spoke with firefighters and paramedics and with Alvin's dad, Leroy Robinson.

Alvin may have thought he wasn't a suspect, but Leroy knew better and had already launched a huge "dumb campaign" on Alvin's behalf. According to Harding, during his first conversation with Leroy Robinson, Leroy insisted that Alvin was very dim-witted and as slow as molasses.

"I think Leroy was trying to help Alvin by telling me the way he perceived Alvin to be. Leroy gave the impression that Alvin was 'slow' and that he was so stupid he couldn't put two sentences together," Harding recalled.

But that's not at all the opinion Monterosso had of Alvin and it wasn't long before Harding changed his mind about Alvin too. "At first I almost felt sorry for Alvin. True, he's not a rocket scientist and I sort of thought, 'You big, dumb, stupid son-of-a-bitch.' Once I met him, I formed the opinion that he was trying to portray himself as having an IQ of 2 above plant life to save his fucking ass. But the more you talk to Alvin and you really listen and pay attention to what he says, you realize he can form his own conclusions." In Harding's opinion, Alvin wasn't as dumb as he seemed to be.

210

"He was so slick about how he had all these ladies and Theresa didn't know about it; it was obvious he knew exactly what was up. He knew that screwing around on her was wrong, but if he told anybody he would lose the one who cooked his meals, took care of him and gave him sex." Harding had a much higher opinion of Alvin's dad. "Leroy's a nice man," he said. "I really liked Leroy. He's a hard worker." Leroy had told Harding that Alvin couldn't read the newspaper very well and that Alvin had tried to enter the military but flunked the test on several occasions. Leroy seemed insistent that Alvin was stupid to the bone. Maybe even to the bone *marrow*. It was Harding's job to find out the truth about Alvin's mental capacity. "Leroy asked me what Alvin could be charged with and I said anything from child abuse to first degree murder and that he could get anything from local time to state prison. That really shook Leroy up."

Monterosso knew how to put a case together and he knew, in order to convict Alvin, he'd have to prove—beyond a reasonable doubt—that Alvin *knew* Andy was in danger at the hands of Theresa. He would need to prove that Alvin *knew* and understood that the abuse Andy was being subjected to could cause serious bodily injury or death. Just as important, he would need to convey this information to the jury in a way so they could arrive at no other conclusion: Alvin's failure to protect Andy was tantamount to murder. Under California law, a person aiding and abetting in the commission of a crime is equally guilty of that crime. When Alvin witnessed, on several occasions, Andy's horrific abuse and did nothing to stop it, he was aiding and abetting Theresa in the crime.

California law defines aiding and abetting as follows: *A person aids and abets in the commission or attempted commission of a crime when he or she,*

With knowledge of the unlawful purpose of the perpetrator and

With the intent or purpose of committing or encouraging or facilitating the commission of the crime and,

By act or advice aids, promotes, encourages or instigates the commission of the crime.

In other words, Alvin's failure to protect Andy from Theresa's abuse was legally the same as actually helping her abuse him. Moreover, Monterosso, with Harding's help, would have to prove that Alvin was smart enough to understand that Andy was being tortured in ways that could cause death. They knew Alvin's defense would be his "stupidity," so it was vital that they get Alvin to admit, on videotape, in no uncertain terms that he *did* understand what was going on. They needed to hear Alvin admit that he knew the abuse Andy was being subjected to could kill him. Monterosso knew Alvin was dumb, but he wasn't an idiot. But would the jury believe it?

Monterosso was a dangerous enemy for a felon to have. "Of all the lawyers I've worked with throughout the years," Harding said, "Monterosso is right at the top. I wouldn't want him doggin' me, that's for sure. Horst is a hell of a good investigator too. If I had to pick one person who really threw his whole life into this case, I'd have to pick Horst." When all the people were assembled for battle, there was no way the prosecution could lose. Or so they thought.

Somewhere in the back of Harding's mind, he was worried that the "dumb campaign" might be successful at getting Alvin off. Monterosso was somewhat concerned about it too, although he didn't believe that Alvin was even remotely retarded. Stupid—yes; retarded—no. Harding went over all the evidence and police reports gathered so far with a fine-toothed comb to see if there were instances where Alvin showed some smarts. Indeed, he found several, such as when Alvin didn't hesitate to call 911 to report that Theresa was bashing his car with a fence post. Harding looked again at the transcripts of Alvin's first interview on August 2nd and noted that Alvin was smart enough to know he needed his own copy of the divorce papers. Alvin had clearly stated that just in case Theresa didn't file, then he could do it. Pretty wise words for a "retarded" guy, Harding thought. Going back over the tapes and the transcripts repeatedly, Harding picked up something new each time. He noticed that Alvin was quick with the answers when Horst asked for his address and telephone number. He didn't have any trouble reciting his parents' phone number, including the area code, and their address. He even spelled out the name of their street. He heard Alvin describe how he could call his pager and press fourteen and it would tell him what time a message was left. He talked about how the pager had an access code. Shit, Harding thought, that's a lot of numbers for a retarded person to memorize. Harding swore he must have played and re-played those interview tapes a hundred times and each time another little clue would pop out.

Alvin had told Theresa that it "wasn't right" to wrap Andy in a trash bag on such a hot day. But what really jumped out at Harding was when Alvin admitted that he'd cut his arm putting an engine in his car. Damn, Harding thought, he's pretty smart if he can put an engine in his car. I can't even do that.

Harding spoke at length with Horst, Peebles and Dave Williams, the guy who'd administered the polygraph test to Alvin. Everyone agreed that Alvin had all his marbles; most of them had just rolled to one side of his head, that's all. Most importantly, he seemed willing to talk.

It was finally decided that Jacob Marquist would have to be interviewed at least one more time before they proceeded any further with Alvin. For this, a female CPS worker named Lisa Steinhart* was chosen to sit down with Jacob to see if he could remember anything new about what had happened to Andy during the early morning hours of August 2nd. By then, he'd already been told that Andy died as a result of what had happened to him that night. Jacob had met Steinhart once before and was familiar with her. She had a very slow and gentle way of interacting with children. She was one of Monterosso's favorite CPS representatives.

Jacob was interviewed on October 5th at the District Attorney's office. Monterosso and Harding monitored the first half of the interview together, from a separate room. Steinhart carefully led Jacob into a discussion of all the things he could remember about the time he'd spent in Theresa's home. Jacob referred to Theresa as "Teri" and talked about the favoritism she showed Jessie. He talked about having to go to work with Theresa and how she'd stuck Andy in the lips with a needle to make him eat. He also saw her poke Andy in the arm with a needle and slap him in the face for making noise. Jacob said Andy didn't have potty problems when he first arrived at the home; the problems had started about two weeks later and by then, he was peeing and pooping his pants a lot. Jacob said Andy got cold baths as punishment for potty accidents.

Jacob suffered his fair share of punishments too, while at Theresa's house. She took things away from him, such as his radio, Nintendo, karate lessons, or television privileges. But Andy was punished very differently. "Mean" as Jacob termed it. After Jacob had been at Theresa's home for about a month, he began to loath staying there. He told Steinhart about the hosing-off incident, the choking, and several times when he witnessed Andy being forced to stand on the edge of the bed, the stool, or on his time-out chair.

Then, Jacob was asked to try to remember what happened on the night Andy was taken to the hospital. He said he heard Alvin yelling at Andy. Andy was screaming. There was a loud thump and then he didn't hear Andy anymore. He'd fallen back asleep and the next thing he remembered was Theresa waking him up and saying everybody had to get dressed and go to the hospital. Something was wrong with Andy.

About that time, Steinhart decided to turn the interview over to Harding, who wanted to know more about the yelling that took place that night. Jacob said he'd heard Alvin yelling "Shut up!" and Andy crying as if he were in pain. Next, he heard what he described as a "bang." Then he didn't hear Andy screaming anymore. Harding asked Jacob if the bang he heard that night was a loud bang or one that wasn't so loud. He slammed his hands on the table for comparison. Jacob agreed that the bang he heard the night Andy went to the hospital was a *loud* bang.

Instead of badgering Jacob with too many questions, Harding was careful to lighten the conversation with sports. Jacob was heavily into sports and had just attended a Dodgers' game over the weekend. Jacob said his favorite team was San Francisco. Before Harding could respond, Monterosso entered the room and began talking sports with Jacob. Being from San Francisco, Monterosso couldn't resist a chance to brag about his hometown team. For a few minutes it was friendly sports banter, back and forth about scores, bases and home runs. It was obvious that Jacob felt completely at ease with Harding and Monterosso and viewed them as good people who were trying to help Andy. Talking about sports had loosened Jacob up considerably. Monterosso wanted to know if Jacob could remember anything else that particular night. Jacob said he'd heard Theresa's voice, speaking very softly and he had seen a light coming from under the bedroom door. But then he had fallen back asleep. And that was all he remembered.

The interview with Jacob was tape recorded and videotaped. When Harding and Monterosso studied the tape later, it seemed to implicate Alvin as the one who'd gotten angry and attacked Andy. Jacob clearly said that Theresa had been abusive to Andy, prior, but it had been Alvin who'd yelled at Andy on that particular night and then there was a loud bang and Andy quit crying.

Back in the privacy of his office, Harding went over everything again and considered all the evidence they had against Alvin. The transcripts of Alvin's interviews with Horst and Williams were scrutinized one more time. In the end, it looked like the DA had a solid case against Alvin, but getting a little more evidence could never hurt.

Harding made arrangements to interview Alvin at the DA's office. The meeting was scheduled for October 18th. It was paramount that the interview be tape recorded and videotaped so there could be no accusation of coercion or badgering of Alvin. The prosecution didn't want anyone to be able to say they had taken advantage of Alvin because of his alleged slowness.

Alvin assumed the interview was about Theresa's role in Andy's abuse and murder; and that's exactly what Harding wanted Alvin to think. "When we interview suspects, we elicit what we *want* to hear," Harding said. "I knew what I wanted to hear and I knew what Alvin knew about the abuse. I just needed to get him to say it in clear, specific terms…*on tape*. A lot of times it just takes talking and jiving and bullshitting to get them to say the truth and, Alvin took the bait."

Alvin was more than happy to assist Investigator Harding with the conviction of his estranged wife, but in his eagerness to help tighten the noose around Theresa's neck, he hung himself as well. When Alvin arrived, he didn't seem apprehensive at all. He was more than willing to talk. Right off the bat, he began talking too much. From an adjacent room, Monterosso was monitoring the conversation. He would hang loose until Harding gave him the signal to come in. Harding asked Alvin if he wanted something to eat and Alvin said he was fine except that he had to take his medicine right then. He was diabetic, he explained, but doctors had caught it in time.

Harding tried to loosen Alvin up and put him at ease. He told Alvin that he was free to leave at any time and that he was not under arrest. Alvin said he understood and seemed eager to get on with it.

"So, you're not in custody, you're not going to jail today. Okay? I'm not arresting you or any of that crap." Harding was careful to add the word "today" because, if he didn't, it could be said that Harding had tricked Alvin and gotten him to incriminate himself in an unlawful way. He told Alvin that he just wanted to go over his own understanding as to what actually happened. If Alvin didn't want to talk anymore he could walk out the door, hang a right and leave the building.

For starters, he asked Alvin why he never spoke up on Andy's behalf. Alvin said it was because Theresa was so domineering. "It was Theresa's way or no way," he said, "and if I step into it or whatever it'd be an argument, so I just stay out of it."

"Tell me about the first time you saw her punish him," Harding said. Alvin mentioned that he'd seen Theresa make Andy stand up on the time-out chair and hold his hands straight out. Alvin recollected that the abuse had started about a month after Andy arrived at the home, but Harding wanted specifics. Was that the first time he'd seen Theresa punish Andy?

"Yeah, I mean I seen her push him, kick him, all kinda stuff, but I didn't—"

"Let's kinda go in chronological order if we can, okay?" Harding asked. He noticed that Alvin knew what "chronological order" meant. "I'm gonna take some notes if you don't mind. I'm getting old and I'll forget." He took out some pictures that had been taken inside the apartment the day Andy died. Casually, he picked through them while Alvin continued to talk. He selected a few to use during the interview and set them aside, face up, on the table.

Alvin said he didn't intercede because Theresa was in total control. "She was like, 'Don't worry about it' and she had copped an attitude so I just..." But Harding wanted to know *where* Theresa had kicked Andy. "She kicked him in the nuts," Alvin said in an indignant tone of voice. "I pulled his pants down and his testicles had swelled up."

According to Alvin, when he threatened to call the police, Theresa countered by saying she was going to sic the Mexican mafia on him. She'd told Alvin that some of her family was in the Mexican mafia and Alvin believed her.

Alvin was taking the interview in a direction that Harding didn't want to go. Harding pulled the reigns on Alvin and asked him to go back and describe the details of the kicking episode. Alvin filled in the blanks fairly well. "I seen him go down off the chair and hit the floor. He was standing on that little chair and she was sitting on the bed." Alvin said he'd wanted to call someone, maybe one of his friends and tell them to call the police or something. "See," explained Alvin, "my best friend, his name is Chas, I call him and talk to him about everything, you know. Me and him we just on that level, you know."

"Did you ever call Chas about this stuff?" Harding asked.

"No." Alvin said. "But, I always go over to his house and he be like, 'Man, what's bugging you?' or 'Something's on your mind,' you know?"

"But you never told him? Did you ever tell anybody about this stuff?" Harding asked. Alvin shook his head no. "Nobody? Not even your mom or your dad?" Still, Alvin shook his head no. "...other girlfriends?"

"Naw" Alvin said, adding that he had a whole bunch of girlfriends on the sly and Theresa suspected as much. Harding took note of the "girlfriends" comment and decided to let Alvin screw himself with his own dick.

215

He asked Alvin to describe Andy's testicles and Alvin said they looked exactly like they'd been described in the newspaper; swollen like grapefruit.

Alvin shook his head in disbelief. His tone of voice reflected that he thought the whole abuse thing was horrible, just horrible. Or at least he thought it was horrible now that Andy was dead and Theresa was in jail for murder. Harding was scribbling as fast as he could; he asked Alvin if the note-taking bothered him.

"Naw," he said. "I have a problem reading. I mean, I can read certain things, like, I have a pager that prints out." He retrieved his Motorola pager from a clip on his belt and showed it to Harding. There on the screen was a message. Harding read it.

"Hey, that's pretty neat," Harding said. "I should get me one of those."

"Yeah, it helps me out a lot."

"Okay," Harding said, getting back on track. "Let me ask you this, when she kicked him in the nuts, do you know what that could do to a child?"

"Yeah. I know what that can do to a child," Alvin said.

"What do you think it could do?"

"Probably kill him."

The comment almost made Harding stand up and cheer. Alvin had just slipped the noose around his own neck, but Harding didn't let on. He asked Alvin about other incidences of abuse that he'd witnessed.

"Well, uh, I seen her put him on the bed and she would push him off," Alvin said. He reached over and pointed to a photo of the bedroom. The photo showed Horst kneeling on the time-out chair and Alvin was re-enacting the fatal kick. "You can see in the picture how high the bed is."

"Um hm," Harding said. Keep talking buddy.

"And I was like, 'You don't be doin' that,' 'cause, you know, my mom's a nurse. And I would ask my mom things."

"What did you ask her?"

"I asked her, um, I said uh, Jessie had fallen on something and his testicles swoll up. And I asked how to get those down, you know, and she told me to put an ice pack on it. So I told Theresa to put an ice pack on it."

Harding took careful notes of the crafty way Alvin had substituted Jessie's name for Andy's. He purposely led his mother to think that Jessie was the one with swollen testicles and that the injury had happened when Jessie innocently fell against something at the apartment. Harding also noted that Alvin hadn't cared enough to put the ice pack on Andy himself; he'd merely told Theresa to do it. But Harding knew the swelling in Andy's testicles had returned, after the ice pack was removed and nothing further had been done for him.

Alvin went on to say that he and Theresa were having problems in their marriage and that he would take off and stay gone for days at a stretch. "I'd go out and I would stay out," he said. "I wouldn't come home for three or four days because I couldn't deal with her attitude toward me and the kids."

Harding went back to the time Alvin had seen Theresa push Andy off the bed. Alvin said Andy had landed hard, on his butt. "What do you think would have happened if he had landed on his neck?"

"He woulda been outta here," Alvin said. He was sure about it. It was one more comment that Harding would take careful note of. Alvin had already stated that he knew kicking Andy in the testicles "could kill him" and that if he'd landed on his neck he'd have been "outta here." Those were exactly the types of statements Harding was looking for. The noose was getting a little tighter. Now if he could just get a few more comments like that.

Alvin chuckled as he recalled other instances of abuse. "Some of those times was like, when Jacob was in school," Alvin said. "I seen her kick him, more than one time, in the same place." She'd kicked Andy in the testicles, but when Alvin called her on it, she denied it. "So I says, 'No, I seen where you kicked him at.' And I kept telling her 'You can't do this,' but she's like, 'Whatever I do, I do.'" Alvin said that Theresa had kicked Andy because he'd wet his pants. Now he was shaking his head in disbelief at the way Theresa had mistreated Andy. Now that everything had "blown over," he felt confident enough to confide, man to man, that getting kicked in the nuts would hurt. "Hell, if you kicked me in my nuts, I'm gonna pee and shit on myself too!" For a second time, Harding asked if he thought kicking a child in his testicles could cause serious injury and, for a second time, Alvin said it could do much worse; *it could kill!*

Alvin was on a roll now and Harding didn't want to stop the momentum. Alvin went on to say that he had pulled Andy's pants down and actually showed Theresa the swelling. It was at this point that Alvin started to cry like a baby. "It bothers me right now," he blubbered, "I mean, it just bothers me. The only guys I can talk to about this is you guys and my mom." Harding acted sympathetic. He gave Alvin time to collect his emotions and continue his story. "Um, now that I been able to sit down and think about other things, well, one time he went to the bathroom on his self and she, um, she made him eat his poop."

"Do you know what can happen to somebody that eats poop?" Harding asked. "Do you know what can happen by ingesting or by swallowing that stuff?"

"Yeah, I do know," Alvin said. "It can tear up your intestines. Make you damn sick too. Yeah, real sick." Harding wondered aloud if eating poop could kill a person and asked Alvin if he'd ever talked to his mother about that. No, he hadn't. Harding wanted Alvin to move along and tell him about some of the other abuse he'd witnessed. He asked Alvin if there was anything that differentiated one instance from another. That was a big word to throw at a "retarded" person, someone who was as slow as Alvin was. But Alvin understood. "Yeah, I understand what you're saying," Alvin

Deadly Thirst

replied. Then, he went on to describe how Theresa had made Andy lie on his tummy on the stool with his arms and legs stretched straight out. It was the punishment Andy got because he hadn't eaten his dinner. Harding played dumb.

"Let me ask you something. With all this shit she did, do you think she tortured that little kid?"

"Yeah I think so," Alvin said, but added that when it happened, he just wasn't thinking.

"Explain it to me," Harding coaxed, "in your own words, why you think he was tortured. Tell me." He wondered if Alvin understood what the word "torture" meant.

"Reason I think he was tortured because simple fact that, uh, you put me on the bed, you push me off, I fall off and I hurt my butt. Or you know, make me eat poop…that's uncalled for. She kicked him in the balls!" His voice was faltering now; he was getting emotional again. "Man! Lord have mercy!" Alvin was repulsed at the memories. Harding asked if Alvin could remember other times when Theresa abused Andy and Alvin readily said yes. "And he uh, pooped his self and uh, her mom says 'I can handle that. I'll take care of that.' So she took him in the back room and gave him a cold shower."

"Her mother did?" Harding asked incredulously. Alvin nodded in scornful agreement. He remembered seeing Theresa giving Andy cold showers after that and how he'd told her it "wasn't right" to do that to a little kid. Harding asked Alvin what he thought could happen from giving a kid a cold shower.

"He was only a baby," Alvin said. "He could have gone into shock. And I says to her, 'You're a nurse. You should know this.'" Again, Harding played stupid. He acted as if he didn't know what "going into shock" meant and asked Alvin if he knew what happens when a person goes into shock. "It cuts the oxygen off in your brain, you know. Anything can happen, hey, you can become a fruit, a vegetable…"

Harding asked if he thought going into shock could kill a person. Alvin said yes. The longer they talked, the smarter Alvin got. But Alvin assumed they were only talking about Theresa. Harding knew otherwise, but played dumb. He asked if Alvin could read and Alvin said that on a scale of one to ten he was about a four. Apparently, he'd been told that many times. Harding offered Alvin his business card and asked Alvin if he could read the phone number.

"Yeah, I mean, I can read that, but—"

"Okay, that's the important part. As long as you can read my phone number in case you ever need to call me." Alvin agreed that he could read the phone number. This was vital, because it proved that Alvin could read phone numbers and he knew how to dial for help.

After a moment of reflection, Alvin began to recall the incident that happened at Theresa's place of employment, the event that would become known as the "trash bag incident." Alvin told Harding he didn't think it was right to put Andy in a plastic bag on such a hot day, but there was no arguing with Theresa.

Alvin also remembered how Theresa had "yanked on Andy's dick" and caused it to bleed. Theresa had paged him that evening and asked him to come home. He'd gone into Andy's room to have a look at the damages, but didn't take any action on Andy's behalf.

With all the talking, Alvin was getting thirsty, so he asked for some water. He stated that since Theresa's incarceration, he'd been "taking care of business" and he needed to find out how to get Theresa's name taken off a piece of property they owned. He said he needed a notarized letter. Harding, wanting to get off the subject, said it would be best to talk to a lawyer about stuff like that; he was just a cop and didn't know anything about legal shit. But Alvin was still carrying on about getting Theresa's name off that piece of property. Out of nowhere, Alvin started telling Pete Harding the succession of inheritance on that piece of property, should he die. "If I die, it goes to my son. If he dies, it goes to his son and so on…"

A little later, Alvin told how he used to "pick fights" with Theresa so he could have an excuse to leave and go out with his buddies. Then, right in front of Harding, Alvin took out a small medical kit he used to test his blood sugar level. Harding noted that it was somewhat complicated, but Alvin explained it all. Harding asked Alvin how much the test kit had cost.

"A thousand bucks," Alvin replied. A few minutes later, he took the reading and announced that his blood sugar level was okay. Because of his diabetes, he needed to sleep with water near his bedside. He often got thirsty in the middle of the night. Getting thirsty in the middle of the night was perfectly understandable, Harding said. Alvin seemed to think so too.

Harding carefully led Alvin up to the night when Andy was attacked for the last time. Alvin was articulate about describing the bedroom for Harding and, without so much as a trace of emotion in his voice, he went through the events that led up to the fatal attack. It sounded like Alvin was recalling a movie he'd seen, not the actual murder of a four-year-old child.

"I guess Andy was thirsty. He got into my water," Alvin said. And then, he started telling how everything from that point on happened really fast. Theresa was awakened by the gulping sounds Andy made as he drank from the jug of water. She became furious and slapped the jug out of Andy's hands, causing him to cry. Water spilled all over the floor and the cap was lost. The more Andy cried, the more upset Theresa became. She screamed, "I thought I told you to shut the fuck up!" She told Andy to get his time-out chair and, when Andy complied, she told him to stand on the chair. According to Alvin, Theresa "shoved him with her foot" and he fell backwards off his chair, striking his head on the nightstand. "It was just like a nightmare," Alvin said.

Andy started screaming even louder and Theresa made him get back on his chair and told him once more to shut the fuck up. Andy continued

Deadly Thirst

to wail at the top of his lungs, so Theresa kicked him off the chair a second time. Again, Andy hit his head against the nightstand. But this time, Andy didn't get up.

"He just started shaking real bad," Alvin said in a flat voice, totally void of emotion.

Harding changed the subject and asked Alvin to tell him about the foster parenting classes he'd attended and what he'd learned. Alvin easily switched from one subject to the other.

"Uh, basically uh, you know, you had a responsibility that you're not going to beat 'em or do this or do that to 'em. You know, you can't yell at 'em verbally." Harding noticed that Alvin had just used the word "responsibility" and he seemed to know what it meant.

"Did you yell at Andy the night he died?"

"No, I didn't," Alvin said.

"Are you sure? Think about it."

"I'm *positive.*"

"In the parenting classes, did they teach you what to do if you saw these things happening? If there was a problem? Did they tell you who to call?"

"I didn't handle that situation, you know what I'm saying?"

"You can dial a phone though, right?"

"Yeah, I can dial a phone but I, I, if you gave me the lady's number and name and all that and put the phone in front of me, I could call but I didn't know her name."

"Okay," Harding said, "but you know what the numbers 911 are for, right?" Harding had seen the police reports dating back to when Alvin and Theresa were first dating. He didn't allude to the fact that he knew Alvin had called 911 on two separate occasions when he was fighting with Theresa.

"Yeah," Alvin said. "I know those numbers. That'll get me the police department or the hospital." Harding decided it was time to turn the heat up a little.

"Did they teach you to wipe shit in their face if they shit?" Harding asked.

"No," Alvin said, laughing.

"Did they tell you to kick 'em in the balls if…"

"No…"

Harding went down the list of admissions again, just to get it clearly verified on videotape.

"Okay, you said, if you kick a kid in the balls it could kill him?"

"Right," Alvin said.

"Give 'em a cold shower and they might go into shock?"

"Right," Alvin said.

"Or cause brain damage or maybe kill 'em…"

"Right," Alvin said.

"You shouldn't beat the kid or yell at them, right?"

"Right."

"Did you yell at Andy that night?"

"I don't remember yelling at him. He was saying, 'No, I don't want to stand on the chair.' And he was whining. Andy would whine a lot and stuff. But he was a good kid," Alvin said.

"Alvin, you told me that you saw her do all these things to Andy. Now, I want you to tell me, and I want you to convince me, man to man, why in the hell didn't you call someone?"

"I don't know," he said with a shrug, "I guess I was just scared. I didn't want nothing to happen to *me*." He tried to tell Harding that he was scared to death of Theresa's family ties with the Mexican mafia. Alvin kept on insisting that he was too scared of Theresa to confront her. He insisted he never rocked Theresa's boat. Not ever. As Alvin droned on, Harding remembered Alvin's own admission that he was screwing around behind Theresa's back. Apparently, he wasn't afraid the mafia would come after him for *that*. Alvin had bragged about how "clever" he'd been with his extra marital hook-ups. Harding kept his thoughts to himself.

The conversation was interrupted by a knock on the door, then Monterosso walked in, acting as though he hadn't heard any of the conversation. He took a place at the table and encouraged the two men to continue.

"If you had told somebody,' Harding began, "do you think that little boy would be alive today?"

"Yes."

"And you knew everything that had happened, the kicking him in the balls...you said 'Yeah that might kill him.' Putting him in a cold shower, you said, 'Yeah it can cause him to go into shock, probably could cause brain damage, might even kill him.' Feeding him shit, you said 'Yeah, it could probably fuck up his intestines and that stuff.' All these things are gonna kill that little boy and you didn't do anything. Why? Any good reason?"

"I was just scared," Alvin said. Just scared.

"Of what? There's nothing to be fucking afraid of—"

But Alvin didn't agree. He began whining and complaining about how "slow" he was and how his mom and dad had always taken care of him. Now Theresa was taking care of him and he was just so dependent on her. He didn't want to get into any trouble. Once more, the image of Alvin cleverly screwing around behind Theresa's back came into the forefront of Harding's mind.

Monterosso spoke up and asked Alvin if he could remember how many times he'd witnessed Theresa kick Andy. "Was it just one time or was it a period of like, four or five different times?" Alvin admitted that he had seen Theresa kick Andy on ten separate occasions. Monterosso's style was non-confrontational and seemingly sympathetic. He reminded Alvin that all he had to do was tell his parents about the abuse, or pick up the phone and call the social worker or even 911. Three little numbers. Alvin began to ex-

Deadly Thirst

plain that he didn't read very well, but agreed that he probably could have spoken to someone in his family about it. Probably his mom.

"But you can read those numbers, 911, can't you?" Monterosso asked.

"I can read those numbers. You're right." Besides, Alvin insisted that he thought the abuse would stop if he left the house. After all, Theresa had always told Alvin that everything was all his fault. *He* was the reason she was so upset and ill-tempered. "It's always me. It's all my fault." Alvin clearly thought *he* was the victim.

"Did you ever warn her that you were going to tell somebody about this?" Monterosso asked. Yeah, Alvin said. "Then, you *knew*, that as a foster parent you were responsible for those kids."

"Right," Alvin said.

"You knew you had an obligation…"

"Right."

"And did they tell you that as a foster parent that it's like he's you own kid? You'd be responsible for that child. Is that right?"

"Right." Alvin said. "But sometimes I don't understand everything."

"Yeah, but what was your understanding about what it was to be a foster parent? What was your understanding about your *obligation* toward Jacob and Andy?"

"Well, to take care of 'em, you know."

Monterosso made a mental note of the fact that Alvin knew what "obligation" meant and then went over the long list of admissions once more. He wanted to leave no stone unturned. He mentioned all the abusive acts that Alvin had witnessed. Kicking him in the balls on numerous occasions, the bleeding penis, putting the poop in his mouth. All of these things Alvin had witnessed and still he had done nothing to stop the abuse. He never called anyone. Not even his mom. Alvin kept insisting that he was "afraid" of Theresa.

"But you said you pushed her when she put the poop in his mouth. You weren't afraid of her then? When you pushed her?" Monterosso asked. Alvin said that he was just so angry and that it happened so fast he didn't have time to think. Still, Monterosso insisted, because Alvin had seen Theresa abuse Andy so many times, surely he knew what she was about to do to Andy as he stood on his time-out chair, screaming at the top of his lungs. Alvin reluctantly agreed that, yeah, he probably knew what was gonna happen. "So," Monterosso asked, "whose idea was it to take Andy outside and put him in the dirt?"

"It was all her idea. And I went along with it." Alvin explained that, at first, he'd tried to cover up the truth, but Detective Horst had persuaded him to get real with the facts. "The detective told me that uh, it's my ass, you know."

Monterosso asked Alvin if he'd felt like he could have gotten in trouble by covering it up and Alvin readily agreed. Monterosso and Harding shot each other knowing glances.

"When you and Theresa were talking to Detective Horst at the hospital, you weren't going to interrupt Theresa and say 'No, this is what *really* happened.' You weren't gonna do that, right?" Monterosso asked.

"No," Alvin said.

"Why not?"

"'Cause I was just scared," Alvin said with a shrug.

"You just kinda wanted to go along with it?"

"Yeah, you know."

"You figured that was the easiest, safest way for you to get out of it, right?" There was no comment from Alvin on that question. Instead, he changed the subject. He wanted to know about what was going on with Theresa. He hadn't gone to visit her in jail because his friends and his dad had advised him to "just leave well enough alone."

It was time to cut to the chase. Monterosso informed Alvin that Jacob had recently given another interview that had shed new light on the night Andy was fatally attacked. Jacob had said that on that night, he'd heard *Alvin* yelling at Andy. Alvin said he didn't remember doing that.

"What were some of the other problems you were having with Theresa that made you leave the house?" Monterosso asked. Alvin said she'd suspected he was screwing around on her and admitted that he had been. He bragged about having "more than one" girlfriend. Theresa had confronted him with it several times, but he'd always denied it. He'd gotten his parents to cover up for him. They didn't like Theresa anyway. Once more, Alvin changed the subject and asked Monterosso about getting that notarized letter. Monterosso played dumb and said he didn't know; it would be best to ask "a lawyer" about stuff like that. Harding agreed and reiterated that he had no idea either how to go about getting a notarized letter.

"I'm just a cop," Harding said, "I don't know shit about the law." A cop and a lawyer; neither knew a damn thing about the law! They could hardly keep a straight face. What a team.

Monterosso and Harding were just about to wrap up the interview when Alvin decided to pound a few more nails into his coffin.

"Uh, that next day after everything had happened, you know, I went over there and got my TV. Only thing that was more important to me is my TV 'cause I paid like $400 for it, you know. We got the 'smart' one, you know. And I bought the bed, the microwave and the oven. I bought a lot of little things over there you know. I just spent $200 for that bed." Monterosso and Harding could hardly believe that Alvin had just said the thing that was most important to him was his $400 "smart" TV!

"But you got the TV out, right?" Monterosso asked.

"Yeah," Alvin said with a sigh of relief, "I got the TV out that first night. Yeah, I got that."

"So, when did you think about getting the TV out of there? Was that after you guys got back from the hospital?"

"No, that was after you guys took her down." Right after Andy died.

Deadly Thirst

"Then you went straight back and got it?"

"Right," Alvin said. "I went straight back."

It was nauseating that, even after learning that Andy had died, Alvin's main concern was his $400 television set. The comment had just solidified Monterosso's and Harding's opinions that, contrary to what Leroy had said, Alvin *was* able to take care of himself. He knew how to quickly rescue his TV, his bed, his microwave and a bunch of other "little things," but he failed to put any effort into rescuing a small defenseless child that had been placed in his care.

Harding and Monterosso decided they'd heard enough. That was, if Alvin was finished digging his own grave. Apparently he wasn't. He got up from the table exuding a big-shot attitude. He offered his pager number just in case they ever needed to get in touch with him. Just dial that number.

"It's 1-8-8-8. You can get me at any time with that." Alvin said. The comment didn't go unnoticed. They could barely believe their ears. One minute Alvin was saying he couldn't dial a phone very well, and the next minute he was shooting off his big mouth, offering his four-digit pager number. Harding was very satisfied with the results of the interview. So was Monterosso. They were practically glowing.

But the glow would quickly fade. Monterosso knew it was going to be tough to prove Alvin's level of stupidity or more importantly, his level of knowledge and understanding. He knew Alvin's attorney would undoubtedly hire a psychologist to testify that Alvin was mentally handicapped. The task ahead would be to prove to a jury *the degree* of understanding that Alvin had about Andy's abuse and to convince the jury that Alvin knew the probable consequences of that abuse. It wasn't going to be easy and Monterosso didn't allow himself any grand illusions of victory, yet. He knew better.

Years later, Harding would look back on the day of the interview with Alvin and feel immense satisfaction. "He wanted to show us that *she* did everything. But, in doing so, he showed us that *he* could have saved that kid's life and that he *knew* he had an obligation to protect Andy. Instead, he let Andy die. Once Alvin was re-interviewed, I was sure he was in deep shit. And rightly so. He wasn't stupid. Slow maybe...but shrewd."

The District Attorney now had probable cause to arrest Alvin and quickly proceeded with the necessary paperwork. Three days after he interviewed Alvin, Harding called Leroy Robinson and asked him to surrender Alvin. Bring him on down to the DA's office and everything could be handled right there, he said. Leroy was devastated, but reluctantly agreed to the arrangement. Shortly before 11 A.M. on October 22, 1999, Leroy Robinson brought his son into the District Attorney's building on Main Street. There, in Harding's office on the second floor, Alvin Robinson was arrested for the murder of Andrew Setzer.

Donna Goodenough

Bolstering the old saying, "what goes around comes around," as Alvin was booked into jail he was issued one last memento of his brief marriage to Theresa Barroso. Alvin Robinson was now inmate # 9936541.

PART 6
JUSTICE

CHAPTER 15

TRIAL STRATEGIES
The "dumb" defense

Alvin's arrest was splashed across the front page of the "Local" section of the Press Enterprise newspaper. His preliminary hearing was set to take place in Judge Becky Dugan's court on October 26th. The hearing lasted about one minute. Judge Dugan rescheduled it for November 19th to allow Alvin's public defender, Frank Scott, time to review prosecution documents.

Just as Monterosso had predicted, Alvin's defense was going to be his "slowness." In the aftermath of Alvin's admissions during his two pre-arrest interviews, it seemed like a poor defense, full of holes. But Monterosso knew better than to count his chickens before they hatched; he knew better than to even look toward the hen house.

Leroy had launched a huge "dumb campaign" on Alvin's behalf. Several of Alvin's friends, both male and female, came to the hearings to bolster the opinion that Alvin was dumber than a box of rocks. One young woman approached reporters in the hallway saying she'd known Alvin for several years and was very close friends with him. She didn't know nothin' 'bout Theresa, but she knew Alvin very well. "He's my buddy," she said. "I love him to death, but he's so dumb." Her long-winded description of Alvin's stupidity was laced with the word "dumb." Shaking her head as she got up to leave, she turned toward the reporters one last time and summed it up. "I love Alvin, but he be dumb. Dumb, dumb, dumb."

Leroy and Susie Robinson were hard-working people, thrust into a violent world to which they were not at all accustomed. To say they found being in the spotlight an unwelcome intrusion would be an understatement. Leroy and Susie were torn up about what was happening to their son. They visited Alvin in jail every opportunity they got. This whole situation threatened to be the ruination of their sanity, what little they had left of it anyway. The worrying was making Leroy's hair fall out. It depressed him even more to look around the jailhouse waiting area and see the sour faces of people who'd waited for hours to talk to friends, loved ones or younguns who'd been locked up. What a huge injustice it was to keep his boy behind

226

bars, locked up like a caged rat. It angered him, almost more than he could bear, that Alvin was locked up in a cage with a bunch of tattooed, toothless hooligans. It pissed him off to have to stand in a long, serpentine line and wait all damn day just to speak with Alvin for a few lousy minutes. It's doubtful, in Leroy's state of despair, that he thought about the sad faces that had gathered around Andy Setzer's hospital bed as he lay dying. Or, for that matter, the anguished mourners who had waited in line to file past Andy's tiny casket as it was perched on the alter of the Spirit of Joy Church. Had he given a moment's thought about anything other than his own pitiful situation, Leroy would have realized that he was actually very lucky: he could visit and speak with his son. Those who wished to visit with Andy could only gaze at his tombstone and speak to the wind.

As soon as Monterosso learned the strengths and weaknesses of the case, he set about working out how he was going to argue those strengths and rebut the defense's attack on the weaknesses. He had already started on his opening remarks and his summation and he continued to expand and modify them throughout the pre-trial hearings. He used the months to develop winning arguments and articulations. Alvin's attorney was, no doubt, doing the same. It was something all lawyers did.

Because Alvin's and Theresa's defenses were so totally different, Scott strove for separate trials, but Monterosso dug his heels in to make sure that didn't happen. Both defendants were clearly in this together, just as Theresa had said.

In the November 19th hearing, Monterosso gave a lengthy speech as to why there should only be one trial. Basically, it boiled down to money. "There is a legislative preference for a joint trial of multiple offenses," he said. "All that is required is that the charges be either of the same class of crimes or connected in their commission. Judicial economy dictates that courts should consolidate cases when the statutory requirements are met. A unitary trial requires a single courtroom, one judge and only one group of jurors need to serve. The expenditures for time and jury voir dire in trial is greatly reduced over that of a case that is tried separately." In essence, the public could get two trials for the price of one.

"Furthermore, the public is also served by the reduced delay on the disposition of criminal charges both in trial and throughout the appellate process. Since each defendant is charged with criminal conduct arising from the same set of facts and circumstances, there is no doubt that these two cases are of the same class of crimes and connected together in their commission." He'd made a good point. Judge Dugan agreed. Alvin and Theresa would get two separate juries within the same trial. A two-jury trial was rare. It was a major blow for Alvin's defense. Leroy was fuming about it.

* * *

Meanwhile, out on the streets of Hemet, Cowboy took a break from "turning his life around" and campaigning for foster care reform in order to pull off a violent home invasion robbery just before Thanksgiving.

Everyone knew that his widely publicized remarks about how he was going to quit drugs, turn his life around and lobby for changes within the foster care system were nothing but oral flatulence. Everyone knew Cowboy better than that. Cowboy's idea of avenging Andy's murder was to have Andy's name tattooed on his right wrist and menacingly flaunt new tattoos on the back of each arm that read "white" and "power." So, in keeping with his repugnant behavior, he forced his way into a West Devonshire apartment on November 23 and terrorized the occupant, taking money and a guitar. For several months after that, Cowboy laid low. For the time being, nothing was being done about his involvement.

* * *

Toward the middle of December, a bail reduction hearing for Alvin came and went with little fanfare. Scott wanted Alvin's bail reduced, but that request was flatly denied. Bail remained firmly at $250,000.

Scott tried to get counts one, murder, and two, assault on a child causing death by force that a reasonable person would believe is likely to cause great bodily injury or death, dismissed. In a December 15th hearing, Scott stood before the judge and gave it his best shot.

"My comments really go to counts one and two. I don't believe counts one and two go against Mr. Robinson. I believe those counts require some action on his part; some knowledge on his part; some behavior, some affirmative behavior. There's absolutely none of that," Scott said. "The absence of behavior, that absence of intervention that is testified to goes to count three, felony child endangerment. I think to get to either counts one or two, there has to be some activity or consciousness, some awareness in the mind of Mr. Robinson. Awareness that he was participating in something that was going to be either, as in count one, murder, and in count two, assault on a child causing death by force that a reasonable person would believe is likely to cause great bodily injury or death. The testimony runs opposite. He had no expectation there would be death or injury. He may not have done enough in terms of his requirements of being a foster parent and intervention, but failure under the circumstances we have here does not amount to murder. So, I ask he not be held to answer to those two counts."

Monterosso was quick on his feet to rebut. "The counsel's description of the law is not entirely accurate," he said in his usual suave manner. "There are two basic theories on which we're proceeding. First, simple implied malice, which as the court is aware, is simply any act that is inherently dangerous to life, done with conscious disregard of the danger of the factor. Alvin knew the danger. The act resulted in death to someone. That's implied malice. Murder. Alvin is not an innocent bystander observing; he's a person charged with an affirmative duty to protect this child. His failure to act *is* the act, which leads ultimately to the death of Andy. Through the statements he gave to investigator Pete Harding, he observed horrendous abuse on this child. Not simple slaps or spanks on the buttocks, but horrendous, violent abuse that, in his own mind, was such that it could lead

Donna Goodenough

to Andy's death. He knew the dangers of not acting and disregarded his duty as a foster parent and allowed the acts to continue up until the point where Andy is knocked off the chair and killed. He's even in the position to intervene and stop it at that point when the water is knocked out of Andy's hands. But he doesn't do it because he's consciously aware of the risks. He consciously disregards those risks of non-action. He has an affirmative duty to act as a parent."

It made good sense. Monterosso prevailed: counts one and two would stick.

* * *

It was inevitable that Andy's biological parents, Laura Utley and Thomas "Cowboy" Setzer, would sue the county for negligence. Although the two had shown little interest in the welfare of their son while he was alive, they took great interest in the big bucks his death could net them.

Laura's past was still being vigorously pursued by investigative reporters from the Press Enterprise. By then, it was well known that I had also taken an interest in the Setzer case and I was as eager as anyone else to solve the Darling/Utley mystery. I had obtained a four-page fax from the California Department of Corrections detailing the prison history of Jennifer Lynn Darling. Like many others before me, I was trying to unravel the tangled mess of CDC records and court documents that linked Jennifer Lyn Darling and Laura Utley as "one and the same." Indeed, the CDC had used that very phrase to squelch the reporters that were pestering the hell out of every agency that had ever had the misfortune of crossing paths with either Laura Utley or Jennifer Lyn Darling. I had even contacted the Public Information Officer at the Riverside County Sheriff's office and asked her to explain it. Surely fingerprints could straighten all this out, right? Not necessarily. The spokeswoman said fingerprints are monitored by the Department of Justice, not the Sheriff's Department. It's the responsibility of the DOJ to get back to local authorities if a fingerprint comes up under another name and the DOJ had never contacted Riverside Sheriff's Department about an alias problem for Darling or Utley. In any event, authorities don't "change" a person's file. They merely add that name to the list of AKA's.

It was all very confusing for me; stuff like that was out of my realm. The spokeswoman said the Press Enterprise reporters had already driven her over the edge with inquiries and she didn't have time to research it again. Besides, it wasn't her job. The best she could do was send me a copy of the mug shot. She suggested I call DPSS and ask them. "Yeah right," I mumbled after I hung up the phone. Days later, when the Jennifer Lyn Darling mug shot arrived in the mail, I laughed when I saw the picture. It was Utley.

On December 22, 1999, Cowboy, now feeling the heat from the home invasion robbery, and Laura Utley filed a lawsuit for the wrongful death of their beloved son, Andy. For them, it was a no-lose roll of the dice. It mattered not one iota that Cowboy's and Laura's own negligence had propelled Andy into foster care in the first place; and it mattered not one bit that,

Deadly Thirst

throughout Andy's short life, they had put little effort into regaining custody of him. They clearly had shown themselves to be more interested in drugs than in the general safety of their son. None of that mattered. The facts were pure and simple. Andy had been in the protective custody of CPS when he was murdered. The Department of Public Social Services had made a "small oversight" when they'd placed Andy with Theresa. His murder had been a result of that small oversight. So, the County was stuck between a rock and a hard place. They were going to have to cough up some money, without admitting any wrongdoing, of course.

After Laura and Cowboy filed their suit, Cowboy's luck ran out. He was arrested in late February for the home invasion robbery. But Cowboy had a shrewd attorney, paid for with taxpayer dollars, of course. Under the guidance of his attorney, Cowboy pleaded guilty to the invasion/robbery charges right after his arrest and—more importantly—*before* the final agreement in the wrongful death suit was signed. His attorney was quick to make a public statement that the swift guilty plea had no bearing whatsoever on the prospect that Cowboy might be getting a monetary settlement from Andy's death. The attorney said he didn't want any speculation that the criminal case was being settled to help resolve the civil, wrongful death, case. "Tommy," as his attorney was prone to call Cowboy, was just an innocent father who'd lost a child. It was all so unfortunate for poor "Tommy." He'd just lost his child and now this. How sad.

The County, and the citizens within, thought differently. Many felt that Cowboy and Laura hadn't lost their child—they'd thrown him away like garbage. However, the County decided the best thing to do was to pay off Laura and Cowboy in a very hushed settlement. In a four-to-one vote, the County Supervisors reluctantly voted, without admitting any wrongdoing, to award Andy's drug-addict parents $890 apiece every month for the next ten years.

It was a tough decision, even for those voting in favor of the pay-off. County Supervisors choked at the mere thought of giving one taxpayer cent to either of them. If Andy's parents had shown any parenting instincts, Andy might not ever have been put into protective custody. But the County only had one other option—going to trial—and they knew the cost of fighting it in court would cost the County a lot more. Possibly millions. And the County knew it would lose. The $250,000 award was but a drop in the bucket, a mere pittance, compared to what Cowboy and Laura would almost certainly get if the case went to trial. It was only logical to believe that Cowboy and Laura would most likely use the money to continue their drug use, but the County's hands were tied. They had to settle now, for a quarter of a million dollars, or risk paying out even bigger money if the case went to trial.

Cowboy was in the county jail when the settlement was officially signed on March 9, 2000. By signing, he and Laura agreed that the money would be cut off if either of them were convicted of, or pled guilty to, a misdemeanor or felony, commencing with the date of signature. Many were certain that

230

Cowboy's earlier guilty plea had been rushed to beat the date of signature, although his lawyer denied it. While everyone signed on the dotted line, the County was desperately hoping the settlement would bring a quiet closure to the fiasco that had become known as the Andy Setzer case. They tried to keep the lid on the whole settlement thing; but, like water running through a sieve, word quickly leaked out. The public's reaction was predictable.

Phone calls of protest poured in. Trying to calm the storm, Cowboy's civil attorney told the media that Andy's parents just wanted to get this gosh-awful mess behind them. It wasn't about the money at all. They just wanted to get on with their lives. He expressed his heartfelt wish that the residents who were standing in judgment of "Tommy" and Laura—two grieving parents—could meet alone with them and see for themselves how deeply they mourned. After all, they hadn't just lost a child, that child had been tortured to death. Perhaps the attorney confused the word "grieving" with "greedy."

Neither Cowboy's or Laura's attorney commented on the fact that the "grieving parents" had failed to take any constructive action whatsoever to avenge the murder of their son. They only sought the money.

When Mike and Lynn Herman got word of the settlement, it dredged up emotions from the depths of their souls. They'd hoped the matter would go to court so the County would be forced to defend and explain its actions publicly—and under oath. But the County continued to hide behind their safety shield of confidentiality, preferring instead to quietly pay the pittance without admitting any wrongdoing. The payoff was considered by many to be nothing more than hush money, dripping with Andy's blood.

The outcome of the lawsuit had been a given; their civil attorney had never had it so easy. For his efforts on behalf of the two grieving parents, he netted himself a whopping $83,325.00. He got his share of the riches "cash up front," leaving Cowboy and Laura to each struggle along with a paltry $890 per month.

When Cowboy's ex-wife, Donna, heard that he was going to rake in almost nine hundred bucks a month from the pay-off, she went out and got herself an attorney. Cowboy hadn't paid a dime of child support since Neanderthal days and Donna figured she was at least entitled to back child support. The County eventually agreed with her, although Cowboy's attorney fought it bitterly. In the end, every dime of Cowboy's blood money was diverted to back child support payments for his daughters and to repay the County for money that Donna had drawn on during her welfare years. Although this subsequent development was never made public, everyone who learned about it was glad that Donna was getting Cowboy's money. Even the county was glad. At least it was being put to good use and it wasn't being injected into the veins of drug addicts.

However, Laura's blood money continued to be a thorn in the side of just about everyone. County officials were well aware of the fact that Laura masqueraded under several aliases. Even her time spent in prison was not

Deadly Thirst

recorded by the California Department of Corrections [CDC] because she apparently served under the alias of Jennifer Lyn Darling. Keeping track of Laura's slick and sinister comings and goings was something the county professed an interest in, but, like CPS, they simply didn't have time to check on her. They depended on citizens to do the snooping; hopefully, a Columbo-type person would turn her in. No one from the county expressed a belief that Laura could stay out of trouble for long. Her lawyer, on the other hand, was determined to keep the money flowing.

* * *

It was just before Christmas when Theresa got a new attorney. A highly skilled, well respected, private attorney named Peter Scalisi. Since Alvin and Theresa were co-defendants, two lawyers from the same public defender's office couldn't represent them; that would be a conflict of interest. So it came to pass that the court appointed forty-six-year-old Scalisi to represent Theresa.

Scalisi, his dark hair streaked with distinguishing flecks of gray, had his own private criminal defense practice and had no conflict of interest. His soft-spoken, courteous nature would be a good contrast to Theresa's self-professed monstrous personality. If there was anyone who could take some of the venom out of Theresa's bite, it would be Scalisi.

"I hadn't heard a word about Andy's murder prior to my assignment," he said, long after the trial had been adjudicated. "I got the file and, from reading the file, I learned the facts and didn't know anything about it before that. I'd never heard of Theresa Barroso or Alvin Robinson." Of course, he expressed no qualms about representing a woman who stood accused of committing such a barbaric and heinous crime on a defenseless four-year-old child.

"I didn't give it a second thought," Scalisi said.

He graduated from Claremont Men's College in 1976 and went on to study law at Southwestern University in Los Angeles, graduating in 1979. He passed the bar exam right away and started his career as a Riverside Deputy District Attorney in 1980. There, he became a well-rounded courtroom warrior by prosecuting a little bit of everything.

"It's a way for a lot of young lawyers to cut their teeth and learn how to try cases," he said. "So I tried cases for five years for the DA, prosecuting everything: child abuse, child molestation, murder, theft, robberies, burglary, rapes, everything." From there he went to the Orange County Public Defender's office for about three months and then into private practice in 1985 in Los Angeles and Orange County.

Scalisi decided his specialty would be criminal defense. He had a knack for it; he believed in it. His brother was a cop. Scalisi was well-schooled on both sides of the justice system.

"When you become a lawyer, you take an oath to abide by the ethical rules and one of the rules of ethics is that every lawyer has to represent his or her fair share of unpopular clients. Theresa Barroso, charged with the

232

torture/murder of this vulnerable child was very unpopular. Yet, that's part of the job of being a lawyer." Over the course of his career, he'd had many people ask him how he could represent the so-called slime of society. But, when someone is in trouble they want the best defense they can afford and they want every right pursued and every angle covered. "They have a right to that," he said. "We're just protecting the constitution; people's rights."

Over the course of Scalisi's very successful career, he had been involved in several other high-profile cases. One, the Wallace Kaye trial in 1992, landed him a spot on television. The Kaye case concerned a Hollywood talent agent who was accused of demanding and receiving sexual favors to get parts for young female actresses. The case was profiled on "48 Hours."

Besides Theresa's case, he was representing several other defendants who were standing trial for murder. One was a death penalty case. During a trial, his days started at the crack of dawn. By 5:30 A.M. he was out the door, making the commute from his beach home to Riverside, arriving at his office, two blocks from the Hall of Justice, around 6:30.

Always thinking and planning strategies, Scalisi, like other attorneys, kept a note pad and pen at his fingertips round-the-clock. Often, he would wake up in the middle of the night and write down ideas. His wife, Julie, a public defender, understood completely the stress, strain and total commitment her husband's job demanded. They had met at the courthouse.

Scalisi didn't have his feathers ruffled one bit by working opposite Monterosso, though he knew Monterosso held a firm grip on the public's heartstrings. "Most people are sympathetic with the DA. Most people's sympathies tend to lie with the plaintiff in a criminal case. I was a DA and I know exactly how it works," he said. "My perspective may be a little better than most people's." Besides, Scalisi liked Monterosso; and Monterosso liked Scalisi. Being pitted against each other was just part of their jobs. Nothing personal.

At that point in time, no one suspected that Alvin's defense was about to take a new, intensely fortified turn. It was a turn that would result in a complete and amazing transformation in Theresa's partner in crime.

When the beginning of the new millennium came and went without the annihilation of mankind, everyone breathed a sigh of relief. The wide spread computer glitch that had been forecast never materialized. It was in those first few weeks of 2000 that Alvin got a few rays of sunshine cast in his direction. Those rays of hope came with the appointment of a new public defender. His name was Stuart Sachs.

As soon as Sachs familiarized himself with the facts of the case, he was deeply compelled to base his defense on one theory. In essence, Alvin had such a diminished mental capacity that he simply did not understand that he could have—and should have—protected Andy; nor did he understand that the abuse Andy was enduring might kill him. It was the same theory that Scott had unsuccessfully tried to whip some life into. Everyone expected Sachs would try this approach too. But it was the intensity of Sachs' fight that caught everyone off guard. The differentiating factor this time around was that Sachs truly believed Alvin's retardation rendered him virtually defenseless against the brutal onslaughts of Theresa Barroso. Alvin was a pitiful, gentle giant. She had mistreated him so many times; he was afraid of her. He was afraid to rock the boat. This notion was a fire that burned deep in the soul of Stu Sachs, not just some fancy rhetoric dreamed up as a gimmicky defense tactic.

It was a common and standard practice for a defense attorney to profess belief in his or her client's innocence; but *this* was something else entirely. This was something few professionals at the Hall of Justice had ever seen before. Sachs not only believed with all his heart in Alvin's extremely diminished mental capacity, he was absolutely certain of it. He'd seen the school records from Alabama. From then on, Sachs took Alvin under his wing, so to speak, and honestly considered Alvin to be a unique and special individual. The more he listened to Alvin, the more he developed a deepening respect. It seemed as though Sachs had a fatherly attitude toward Alvin, caring about him in ways that went beyond that which was expected of him as an attorney.

If there was anything working in Alvin's favor since August 2nd, it was Stu Sachs. While Scalisi was busy striving to bring Theresa up from the gutter, Sachs strove to expose Alvin's ignorance and vulnerability, which had always kept him on the bottom rung of society and under Theresa's brutal control. While Scalisi would try to present Theresa's good points to a jury, Sachs would strive to prove that Alvin was nothing more than a helpless retarded man, a lost sheep. An empty shell of what a man his age was supposed to be. A confused, dominated man of twenty-six who was trapped and held hostage by a mental deficiency equal to that of a pitiful third grader.

Some scoffed it off as just another defense tactic. While other attorneys had used the same tired defense, none had ever done it with such an authentic emotional investment as Sachs employed right from the very beginning. Some argued that it was merely a charade that all attorneys used when they were in the presence of a jury. It was nothing more than a show, they scoffed, a front. If that were true, then Sachs kept up his "front" twenty-four hours a day, in spite of the fact that it would be at least eight months before he'd get to act in front of a jury. So why all the theatrics so soon? The answer was simple: Sachs believed in Alvin's innocence. In the months to follow, there would be no one who could rightfully accuse Sachs of lacking concern and sympathy for Alvin. What Sachs felt for Alvin was genuine and it haunted him night and day. The "implied malice" thing and the "aider and abettor" issue had really been eating at him.

* * *

Meanwhile, back in Hemet, on April 12th, a couple identifying themselves as Clinton Darling and Jennifer Lyn Darling [AKA Laura Utley] were arrested in Hemet. The charges were serious: possessing a sawed-off shotgun and being in possession of methamphetamines. Jennifer [AKA Laura Utley] was also charged with possession of paraphernalia used to inject and smoke a controlled substance. The county immediately investigated this arrest to try to determine if it was Laura or Jennifer who'd been arrested. If it were indeed Laura, then she had violated her wrongful death agreement and her blood money would be cut off.

Frustrated, the county reluctantly decided that it had *not* been Laura Utley who had committed the offense. Although Laura was taken into custody several weeks later, after Jennifer Darling failed to appear in court, she argued in defense of her true name and stated it was not her case. That was exactly what she'd done back in February of 1998. Laura Utley was released. Jennifer Darling was sentenced to a one-year, live-in drug treatment program at Crossroads.

* * *

In May, Sachs spoke during a hearing in Department 33, at which time he brought several issues before the judge. It wasn't *what* Sachs argued; it was the *way* he argued. Attorneys need not get theatrical until there's a jury, but Sachs took such a vehement stand that everyone in the courtroom, from shackled convicts to spectators to other attorneys, grew absolutely silent to hear him. Was this an attorney simply out to see that his client's rights were honored? Hardly. It was anything but.

After a lengthy statement regarding the circumstances of the case and others similar to it, Sachs continued, "In the case at bar, there was no intentional act that was proven to have been committed by the defendant from which Andy's death resulted. There was no evidence to support the notion that Alvin Robinson did an act to Andy where it could be inferred that he knew this non-existent act could endanger Andy's life and thus acted with conscious disregard for life. That is simply not the law." His voice reflected absolute conviction. Sachs was not merely going through the motions. He was clearly upset.

"One can't bootstrap inaction into an implied malice theory. Alvin Robinson is clearly not a principal in any felony child abuse scenario whereby implied malice has been shown. The prosecutor is clearly wrong in his argument that knowing there may be danger equals doing some affirmative act. Inaction can't be bootstrapped into implied malice. All life-threatening acts were done solely by Theresa Barroso without any assistance from Alvin Robinson. The defendant's inaction can't be translated into somehow subjectively appreciating a risk to Andy and acting, or in this case not acting, in conscious disregard of Andy's life. Alvin's only other liability is the natural and probable consequences doctrine which is also without evidentiary support.

"The prosecutor has classified Alvin as an aider and abettor. Alvin can no way be viewed as a principal when he never laid a finger on or did anything to harm Andy. While his conduct may not be praiseworthy, his mere failure to prevent a crime doesn't rise to the level of an aider and abettor."

Deadly Thirst

Monterosso, as usual, was fully ready to return fire. He went back over the admissions made by Alvin during the October 18th interview with Senior Investigator Harding at the DA's office. One by one, he named and repeated the instances in which Alvin admitted—in his own words—that he *did* know Andy was being subjected to abuse so horrific it could kill him. It was beginning to sound like old news.

The law says that direct evidence is evidence which, if true, proves a fact in issue without the necessity of drawing any inference. Direct evidence can only be given by the testimony of a witness who purports to have actual knowledge of that fact. The most common type of direct evidence is eyewitness testimony. In the circumstances surrounding Andy's death, Alvin was an eyewitness to a long list of abuses Andy had suffered. And he definitely was an eyewitness to the final assault. Alvin's admissions during the October 18th interview were highly incriminating and Monterosso was determined to let Alvin bury himself with his own tongue.

"The Defendant contends that there was no evidence whatsoever to show that he committed any action whatsoever to aid and abet Theresa in her assault on Andy. This is absolutely false," Monterosso said. Unlike Sachs—who sometimes raised his voice, slammed his file folders down on the counsel table, or allowed his facial expressions to get the better of him, Monterosso was always suave, polite, soft-spoken and well-paced during pre-trial motions. "The evidence produced at the preliminary hearing showed that, immediately prior to Theresa striking Andy off the chair causing him to die, Alvin was heard by Jacob to have been yelling at Andy, which caused Andy to scream as if he was in great pain. The defendant's yelling and Andy's screaming only stopped after Jacob heard a loud bang coming from the room next door, where this commotion was occurring. This yelling was Alvin's instigating or encouraging Theresa to abuse Andy.

"The Court must not look at the defendant's subjective state of mind, but must look at it from an objective standpoint based upon the totality of the circumstances known to the defendant at that time.

"Defendant Robinson contends that he cannot be held to answer as an aider and abettor based solely on omissions. An aider and abettor *can* be liable under the natural and probable consequences doctrine based solely on inaction when there is a legal duty to act. Since Alvin had a legal duty to act, his omissions encouraged and facilitated further abuse by Theresa, which ultimately led to the reasonably foreseeable additional crime of murder."

As for the implied malice theory, Monterosso had this to say: "Malice is implied when a defendant does an act with a high probability that it will result in death and does it with a base anti-social motive and with a wanton disregard for human life. Alvin was well aware of those risks as evidenced by his discussions with Investigator Harding. Alvin deliberately chose to ignore these risks when he yelled at Andy, causing Theresa to strike Andy and kill him. Also, the defendant is liable under an implied malice theory based upon his omissions to protect Andy from the abuse of Theresa Barroso. It is clear in California that a person who has a legal duty to protect another may be criminally liable for failing to exercise those duties."

At the end of the hearing, when Sachs learned that Monterosso had the winning argument, his expression turned sour. He ran his fingers through his curly gray hair, gathered up his file folders in a huff and stormed out of the courtroom. This would become his trademark exit.

Once in the corridor, Sachs shunned reporters with a swat of his hand and pounded the elevator button. Shoving his hand deep into his pocket, he stared straight ahead at the elevator doors until they opened. Angrily boarding, he punched the first floor button and glared at the carpet as the elevator delivered him downward. He walked briskly out of the building, down a flight of stairs and across the street. As he crossed the street and disappeared into the Public Defender's office, his head was still down and his trademark scowl was still on his face. Some reporters questioned what Sachs was always so pissed off about. Was he always this grouchy?

Other attorneys gave no consideration whatsoever to Sachs' display of "heartfelt emotion" during pre-trial hearings, but then, Alvin was not going to be judged by attorneys. Alvin would be judged by ordinary citizens who might forget about the evidence and allow their decisions to be influenced by Sachs' anguished, heart-felt pleas. That possibility was very real indeed. After all, jurors are ordinary people who know very little about the behind-the-scenes jousting of attorneys.

"He's a really class guy," said Scalisi. "He's a good person. He's well-liked and well-regarded." Those who knew Sachs privately knew him to be a kindhearted, understanding and gentle soul. People who lived in his neighborhood often saw him jogging, regimented in his solitary exercise routine. Others often witnessed him casually strolling through the shady, tree-lined streets, lost in thought. Solitude seemed to agree with Sachs. It was during these moments of solitude that Alvin's plight became more than just case number RIF087208.

The ensuing weeks were full of arguing over Alvin. By contrast, there seemed to be very little disagreement as to the charges Theresa faced.

Meanwhile, a jailhouse letter had surfaced that drew the attention of investigators. It seemed Alvin had made friends with another inmate, a homosexual, that jail deputies referred to as "a pain in the ass." According to the inmate, Alvin had asked him to write a letter expressing his innocence so Alvin could say it was from Theresa. The man had feminine handwriting and perhaps Alvin thought the letter could pass as authentic. If what the inmate was saying had any truth to it, Alvin was trying to fabricate a defense by saying Theresa wrote it.

Apparently, after the inmate wrote the letter, he somehow got it back from Alvin and told a jail deputy that he wanted to turn the letter over to authorities. The inmate arranged to leave the letter on the bars of tank 12c1 where the deputy could pass by and pick it up surreptitiously. The pick-up took place and the letter floated right into the hands of Monterosso.

In part, the letter read: *...I know you're innocent and you don't have nothing to do with this, but I'm so scared and I just don't want you to be alone. I want you to know that you're still my man. Please don't hate me for all this. Love, 'You Know Who.'*

Under the law of "discovery," Monterosso had to permit the defense to examine and/or copy virtually all of the evidence he'd gathered, but the defense didn't have to reciprocate. The rationale for requiring discovery from the prosecution is the defendant's constitutional right to a fair trial. The courts have ruled that the prosecution can't be allowed to trip up the defendant with a surprise tactic of introducing evidence at the trial which the defense has no prior knowledge of and no reasonable opportunity to prepare a response to. The reason the defense doesn't have to turn over its evidence is because the defendant might then be furnishing evidence that the prosecution could use against him. Such a "forced disclosure" would violate the Fifth Amendment to the U.S. Constitution.

* * *

It is definitely not the job of the district attorney to schedule appointments with a defendant's family who feel they have been wronged. But Monterosso was not your average district attorney. Leroy was not taking Alvin's arrest well. In fact, his son's dilemma had wreaked such havoc on Leroy that he'd become a nervous wreck. He'd aged ten years since the end of October, when he was forced to surrender Alvin to authorities. He asked for a meeting with Monterosso and Monterosso was nice enough to grant him one. It was a chance for Leroy to vent some of his frustrations and air his opinions. Monterosso was patient with Leroy, letting him get whatever was bothering him off his chest. He understood that Leroy was being eaten alive with worry. Monterosso was a compassionate man, understanding. Harding would later say of the meeting between Monterosso and Leroy that it was typical of Monterosso to do stuff like that.

"He doesn't have to do any of that shit," Harding said, "but he does, because he's a nice guy."

* * *

Every defendant has a right to a speedy trial; the prosecution must race against time to collect all the facts it needs. As with any case, there would be mistakes made in this one. One such mistake was that the DA's office waited too long to get a copy of the 911 call Alvin made on August 2nd.

Jeaneen Gardner, the Custodian of Records for the Riverside County Fire Department informed the DA's office that tapes are routinely destroyed after six months. Monterosso's only other hope was to contact the dispatchers who were involved in the call and see if they remembered anything. Four CDF dispatchers were interviewed: Captain Steve Gallegos, Sean Morse, Jeremy Gerlock and Rebecca Couch.

Dispatchers get thousands of calls like the one that came in concerning Andy Setzer; so, after several months, their memories had faded. About all they could remember was that the call was from a male who stated there was a kid outside having a hard time breathing and the call came in during the early morning hours. Nothing out of the ordinary. In Monterosso's opinion, the tape wasn't remarkable in any way and probably wasn't much of a loss. Still, it would have been good to have had it.

* * *

Sachs knew that Alvin had been professionally evaluated and diagnosed as retarded when he was in elementary school. Still, Sachs thought it wise to have Alvin re-evaluated by a clinical & forensic psychologist named Michael Kania. Sachs asked Kania to focus on Alvin's mental status, his level of intellectual functioning and his recollection of the events that led to the present charges. Having a professional testify that Alvin was actually retarded might help his case. Monterosso expected it, but was livid about it nonetheless. Monterosso thought Alvin's supposed retardation was nothing but fabricated crap.

Sachs felt differently. He knew the evils in our society aren't nearly so often caused by bad men as they are by good men who remain silent when an opinion should be spoken. Even the legendary Dr. Martin Luther King spoke of "the appalling silence of the good people." To Sachs, Alvin was a good man, a gentle giant, who kept his mouth shut when he should have spoken out. Sachs was of the firm belief that Alvin had been rigorously dominated, abused and intimidated by Theresa. Monterosso didn't buy the dominated and intimidated theory at all. Neither did Scalisi.

In May of 2000, before he ever met with Alvin, Kania reviewed what he referred to as "voluminous records" pertaining to the case. These records included a summary of Alvin's psychological evaluations from when he was in elementary school and some of the police reports that involved him. Finally, after Kania felt he'd boned up enough on Alvin's background information, he scheduled an evaluation at what is commonly referred to as the "old" jail which stood midway between the Hall of Justice and the Robert Presley Detention Center. This evaluation was conducted in three sessions, May 2nd, September 26th and September 29th of 2000.

Kania asked Alvin about his family history, educational history, vocational & military history, prior arrests and substance use. Alvin said that in school he was merely passed on from grade to grade and eventually graduated in spite of his learning disability. He also asked Alvin about his health and whether or not he'd ever had any psychological treatment. Kania determined, after talking with Alvin for quite some time, that Alvin's thought processes were essentially logical and coherent yet suggestive of limited intellectual functioning. Alvin said his dad never "whooped" him but that his mom did all the "whooping." According to Alvin, Theresa had been the first person he had felt comfortable enough with to confess his slowness and his illiteracy and Theresa had responded kindly, saying she still loved him. Alvin told Kania that he was often awakened at night by voices and that sometimes the voice was Theresa's. Kania judged that Alvin was able to accurately perceive events occurring around him.

Kania went on to state that Alvin felt "sad" at times, since he'd been incarcerated, and that he sometimes cried at night. He longed to be home with his mother and father. Alvin talked about the dissimilarities between two credit cards he had received in the mail. Once while he was living with his folks, a card had come in the mail and Susie had sat Alvin down to discuss how a credit card worked, adding that when the bill came, she'd help Alvin pay it. Theresa, on the other hand, simply never allowed Alvin to have a credit card, calling him stupid, dumb and irresponsible. Kania stated in his report, that "Alvin is an immature man, but his cognitive functioning is basically intact and his attention, concentration and comprehension is good."

During Kania's long sessions with Alvin, there were instances in which Alvin admitted to violent behavior and then contradicted himself. He admitted that he'd gotten so drunk he got into fights. The next day he'd had what he called "black-outs" and was not able to remember anything that had happened the day before. Immediately after he told Kania of these drunken fights, Alvin denied any history of assaultive behavior.

Kania's report was sprinkled with clues as to why Alvin's self esteem was shredded. For example, instead of Susie telling Alvin he deserved someone better than Theresa, Susie had told him he was an "idiot" for allowing Theresa to use him. Alvin spoke several times of being sad and depressed and of missing his mother, but nowhere in Kania's report did Alvin express any remorse about what had happened to Andy. His sadness and depression seemed only to be the result of the fact that he was incarcerated. He missed his momma, in spite of the fact that Alvin twice mentioned how Susie had told him he was an "idiot." When he had complained to his parents that Theresa was calling him names, Leroy and Susie had told him to come on home.

Alvin also confided to Kania that Theresa had kicked him between the legs on several occasions. When he had been kicked, he left. Alvin insisted that Theresa had warned him repeatedly that when it came to the foster kids, he was not to interfere or intervene in any way. Alvin said he did intervene though, on more than one occasion and it resulted in Theresa's rage being turned against *him*. So, his way of dealing with that was to leave. The reason Alvin didn't intervene on behalf of Andy was because Theresa would become violent toward *him* if he did. In other words, Alvin was looking out for number one, although Kania certainly didn't word it that way. Kania called Alvin's habitual evacuation of the premises "reflective of his limited problem-solving abilities and simplistic moral development" and reported that Alvin didn't understand he had any responsibility to give the boys similar protection from Theresa's wrath.

In closing, Kania said he'd tested Alvin with the revised form of the Wechsler Adult Intelligence Scale and that Alvin was "solidly within the area of mild mental retardation." Alvin was suffering from a situational depression, the result of his present legal status. Furthermore, it appeared that

Donna Goodenough

Alvin did not understand that he had a responsibility to actively intervene in an abusive situation.

Monterosso thought Kania's opinions of Alvin were ridiculous. Of course Alvin knew how to intervene and defend; he'd called 911 just a few months prior to report Theresa's aggression against his automobile. He knew how to call for help. Kania's report irked Monterosso to the bone.

Sachs fought hard to have Kania's findings brought out at the trial, but Monterosso fought back even harder. The diminished capacity defense had long been abolished in California. Sachs should have known better. In a March 23rd motion to exclude Kania's testimony, Monterosso stood before the judge and passionately cited laws that forbid such testimony.

"It appears from the text of Dr. Kania's report that the defendant is attempting to introduce evidence of his inability or lack of capacity to form a specific mental state that is an element of the charged offense. Evidence of this kind is completely inadmissible based upon the decades-old rules established in Penal Code sections 25, 28 and 29," Monterosso said.

Although Kania did review transcripts of Alvin's interviews with police, he failed to list exactly which reports and transcripts he reviewed. Monterosso also noted that Kania had not seen the videotapes or listened to the audiotapes of Alvin's interviews. The tapes, both audio and video, were the most damaging pieces of evidence working against both defendants.

"An expert is also not permitted to opine or present evidence that the defendant did or did not have the capacity to form a specific mental state necessary for the charged offense. Dr. Kania's report does just that. By concluding that the defendant's low intelligence contributed to his inability to understand his responsibility to protect the children, Dr. Kania is opining just what the Penal Code and the Supreme Court says he cannot."

Monterosso was especially upset with Kania's conclusion that Alvin "did not understand that he had a responsibility to protect these children." Monterosso was adamant that that conclusion was completely inadmissible.

"Dr. Kania's opinion that the defendant is currently suffering from situational depression and anxiety is completely irrelevant to the issues before the jury and should be excluded. These only relate to the defendant's current emotional state as he sits in jail awaiting his trial." Who wouldn't be depressed, sitting in a stinking jail cell? "There is only one question that must be resolved by the jury," Monterosso continued, "did the defendant understand his responsibilities to protect his foster children?"

Once more, the judge decided in Monterosso's favor, but not entirely. Some of Kania's findings could be presented to the jury. Sachs was glad he'd gotten at least part of what he wanted. But he still stomped out of the courtroom with a scowl on his face.

* * *

October rolled around and trial readiness conferences were happening left and right. Monterosso wanted to delay because two of his main play-

Deadly Thirst

ers were unavailable. Horst, now a sergeant, was in France working on a Riverside County Homicide and would be out of the country until the end of October. Dr. Schaffner was unavailable until November 5th.

* * *

As another year began ticking away, preparations were made to start voir dire. The juror's questionnaire made it obvious that the case somehow involved child abuse.

Have you ever been a victim of physical child abuse?

Have you ever known a victim of physical child abuse?

Have you ever witnessed an act of physical child abuse or misconduct toward a child?

Have you ever reported an act of physical child abuse or misconduct toward a child?

Have you ever been accused of child abuse or any misconduct toward a child?

Have you ever been investigated by police or any government agency for any reason?

Have you ever been accused of any crime?

Have you ever been involved in any child abuse investigation?

Do you know anyone who has been falsely accused of child abuse or misconduct toward a child?

Do you know anyone who has been falsely accused of any crime?

Have you been involved in any therapy for victims or perpetrators of child abuse?

Are you familiar with the facts of this case from any media reports or other sources?

To some, it seemed odd that there were no questions about experiences with people who were mentally handicapped. Wasn't it important for the prosecution to weed out people who might be sympathetic toward Alvin?

Monterosso's position was that Alvin was not retarded. Period. And he didn't believe Alvin was deficient to such an extent that he was not guilty of criminal wrongdoing. Asking questions about retardation and people's experience with it might add credence to the suggestion that Alvin *was* mentally retarded and Monterosso didn't want to do that. He felt that asking such questions would be a tacit admission that Alvin was retarded. Both Monterosso and Scalisi maintained that Alvin was faking his retardation, or at least exaggerating his mental deficiencies. It was perfectly fine with Monterosso if some of the jurors had experience with people who were mentally handicapped; he felt those jurors would see through Alvin's charade in a heartbeat. And furthermore, they would probably be mightily offended in the process.

Monterosso didn't specifically go out of his way to avoid questions on the subject of retardation, but he wanted to focus on a different aspect of that defense. He wasn't worried about the sympathy factor because, between Andy and Alvin, the sympathy was not going to go to Alvin. "There was no way a juror would feel sorrier for Alvin than for Andy," he said long after the trial had ended.

Monterosso's main concern was to get jurors who would be skeptical of psychological testimony, such as Kania was expected to give. It had been Sachs' main concern to secure jurors who thought favorably of psychological testing; therefore, he spent a great deal of time questioning potential jurors about their experience with psychologists and the like. During voir dire, Monterosso merely followed up on Sachs' questions by seeking jurors that had some sort of skepticism about psychologists. His reasoning was to let them educate the other jurors by acknowledging their opinion that most psychological evaluations were nothing more than educated guesses. In Monterosso's opinion, Kania's testimony wasn't going to be anything but a bunch of crap and he sought to get jurors who felt the same way.

Above all, Monterosso was determined to develop this theory, and stick to it come hell or high water. Instead of reacting to everything the defense threw at him, he'd make the other side react to *his* theories.

As springtime approached, a jury was finally selected.

* * *

Twenty-one months and thirteen days after Andy Setzer was brutalized and killed, the trial for Alvin and Theresa was finally scheduled to begin. It was Tuesday, May 15th, 2001. With the passage of time, Andy's murder had long been forgotten by most folks and replaced with other shocking events.

When Andy's murder occurred during that scorching August more than one and a half years prior, the cold-blooded viciousness of it had stunned the people of Riverside County. Andy's murder had been bannered as a catalyst that would change the system. Sadly however, in the twenty-one months since his death, and in spite of new laws, few changes had been made in the way county and state foster care systems conducted their business of protecting children. The public found it impossible to get the county to admit they had done anything wrong. The cries for reform had subsided and people had found new causes to rally for. The whole thing had blown over. It was exactly why Leroy had told Alvin to "lay low and wait" and it was exactly what CPS had hoped for. Everything had blown over; the vast majority of people had forgotten about little Andy Setzer.

Driving the 91 Freeway into downtown Riverside was a frustrating process during weekday mornings and late afternoons. All lanes of the freeway in both directions were choked with bumper-to-bumper traffic, often grinding to a standstill for long periods of time. Modern housing tracts, malls, and office buildings dominated the western part of Riverside. As eastbound drivers inched along, the scenery began to change in a noticeable and welcomed way. Approaching the 14th Street exit, the strip malls and housing tracks gave way to boulder-strewn hillsides. A little further on, the rounded green roof of the Robert Presley Hall of Justice appeared in the distance. Also coming into view were some of Riverside's original architecture and landscapes from the early 1900's. Their vine-covered façades easily distinguished many of these original structures in the historical downtown area from those that were erected during the building boom of the 60's. Even in 2001, downtown Riverside still had an old charm that drew visitors from far and wide. It was home to the world famous Mission Inn where President Ronald Regan married his sweetheart, Nancy Davis, in 1952.

Exiting the freeway and heading north on 14th street, a fairly pleasant and short drive took commuters to the courthouse in just a few minutes. Many of the area's one-way streets were lined with stately palms and one-hundred-year-old ficus trees, their huge roots buckling the sidewalks. Two-hour parking meters stood guard over every available parking space within a three-block radius of the courthouse and long lines of vehicles formed at every entrance to the five-story parking structure. Over the treetops, the modern architecture of the Robert Presley Detention Center loomed on the horizon, its rooftop cluttered with antennas and satellite dishes.

In Riverside, there are few names as well known as that of Robert Presley. After graduating from the FBI National Academy, Presley served twenty-four years with the Riverside County Sheriff's Department. Presley also served twenty years in the State Senate, from 1974 to 1994. On January 4, 1999, seven months before Andy's murder, Governor Gray Davis appointed Robert Presley Secretary of the Youth and Adult Correctional Agency. At the time of Alvin and Theresa's trial in May of 2001, Presley still served as secretary. Nearly a dozen buildings in the Riverside County area are proudly named after Robert Presley.

In spite of who the buildings were named after, the Robert Presley Detention Center, the Hall of Justice, and the law buildings that surrounded them were considered by many to be ugly, offensive structures that ruined the charm and clashed with the style of the older buildings that still remained.

Sandwiched between the six-story Hall of Justice and a hideous, concrete, five-level parking structure was a lovely little vine-covered building known as Simon's Undertaking Chapel. Built during the citrus boom in 1923, the Simon's Chapel had several small rooms with massive ceiling timbers and wooden arched doors. Heavy wrought iron chandeliers hung from the ceilings. Mexican fireplaces in the viewing and consolation rooms soothed mourners with a sense of warmth and serenity. For almost fifty years, Simon's Undertaking Chapel had flourished as one of the most desirable places for a funeral. Beautiful, hand-made stained-glass windows, hand-carved pews and a fifty-foot wall mural of Christ the Good Shepard adorned the chapel.

Between the years of 1968 and 1973, the county purchased several parcels of land, including the land on which the Simon's building stood. They planned to demolish the Simon's building to make way for a new court parking lot. As zero hour approached and the wrecking ball hung over the little chapel, concerned citizens banded together to save what they considered to be one of the most precious parts of Riverside's history. A ruthless destruction of many grand old buildings had already taken place at an alarming pace and the Historical Society was determined to save what little there was left of Riverside's history. The wrecking ball never got a chance to swing.

So it came to pass that there remained a mixture of old and new. The county, having already bought the Simon's property, could not do with it as they had originally planned, so they found another use for it. In the early 1970's, it became the Riverside County Coroner's office. As for the building itself, few things changed outwardly; vines still covered much of its brickwork. Only one small sign on the rear entrance declared that it had become the county morgue.

Such a small building was ample in the early 1970's when Riverside's population was a mere fraction of what it had become at the beginning of the new millennium. By the mid-90's however, things had gone from bad to worse at the coroner's office. Not only had the population swelled by then, but, new and deadly airborne diseases were common inside the grim quarters of a morgue. In addition to a severe lack of space, the Simon's building lacked adequate ventilation to insure the safety of its workers. The whole area around the Coroner's office was often engulfed in the noxious and putrid odors of death that hung in the air. Something had to give…and soon.

By the time the trial finally got underway, the coroner had just finished moving into new and spacious digs located in the city of Perris. Ironically, the new office was just a few blocks from the place where Andy Setzer spent his last days.

Entering the majestic Robert Presley Hall of Justice, everyone was required to pass through metal detectors and, if the buzzer sounded, submit to a body search. Once cleared for entry, the first thing that court-goers saw was a shiny marble floor flanked left and right by massive staircases. Straight ahead loomed a huge, forty-foot wall mural depicting the signing of the Declaration of Independence. Below it was an immense oval reception area usually manned by a deputy in uniform.

Jury members, witnesses, police, lawyers and spectators all took the same four elevators to the upper floors. Except for the police and lawyers, all took their places on wooden benches in the hallways and waited, sometimes all day, until the court clerk called them inside.

Alvin's and Theresa's trial was scheduled for department 61 on the sixth floor. Judge Russell Schooling would preside. In the hallway, jurors were easily distinguished by their badges which were tagged with either a red or a blue dot. It had been Monterosso's idea that red dots be used for Alvin's jury and blue dots for Theresa's. The word 'red' starts with 'R' and so did the name Robinson, blue starts with 'B' and so did the name Barroso. It would be easier to remember, he reasoned. Judge Schooling agreed. And so it came to pass that roughly two dozen people milling about in the hallway outside Department 61 were identified by their dots. They would be referred to as "the red jury" and "the blue jury."

Because of the additional jury, the number of spectator seats dwindled to a mere eighteen. Crowding was not a problem on the first day of trial, or on any other day. That first day, less than five spectators showed up, two of whom were Alvin's ever-present parents. Not a day would go by that Leroy was not present, at least for part of the day.

On that first day of trial, in the back row sat a small, frail-looking woman with shoulder length gray hair. She was wearing a long black sweater dress and wire-rimmed glasses. This was Andy's grandmother, Dawn Masterson. It would be her only appearance throughout the entire trial. The spectator's section would remain woefully empty, except for Alvin's parents, a couple of reporters and me.

Because lawyers don't want the jury to see their clients in jailhouse garb, or shackles and chains, prisoners are transported from the jail to the Hall of Justice by way of an underground tunnel and shuttled upward on a private, high-security elevator. Upon arriving on their assigned floor, they're quarantined in a holding cell. Every inch of the way video cameras are watching. When their time arrives, they enter the courtroom through a side door that has access to the holding cell. This door is just a few feet from the counsel table and the spectators. Prisoners are carefully guarded even though they are heavily shackled—hands and feet—and their restraints aren't taken off until they are actually seated beside their attorneys.

As the last of the clanging chains were put out of sight, Deputy Wally Sanderson gave the courtroom clerk the go-ahead to call in the juries. It was almost mid-morning when Evangelina Reyes, better known as "Angie," opened the double doors and stepped into the hallway. Jurors were told to form two lines according to dot color. Quietly, those with blue dots were ushered in to their seats inside the small courtroom. Then, those with red dots filed in. Since the trial required two separate juries, half of the spectator seats were removed and jury seats were put in their place. These additional seats were standard, uncomfortable auditorium chairs, placed on a raised platform. It would be a long day for those jurors seated on the platform. That first day, Theresa's jury would get to sit in what would jokingly be referred to as "the good seats," the permanent, luxurious jury seats to the judge's left side, nearest the witness stand.

The two defendants were already seated next to their attorneys at the counsel table in the center of the courtroom. Alvin wore dark slacks, a white shirt and tie and a navy blue pullover sweater. He looked relaxed, well groomed and handsome with just a touch of appealing boyishness about him. Sachs wore his usual unsmiling face and his favorite suit—the one with the leather elbow patches. Sachs was not a showy guy; his style of dress proved that beyond a reasonable doubt.

Theresa's massive girth was draped in what could only be described as a frumpy flower print muumuu that fell just below her knees. Her long black hair was parted on the side and hung in a limp mass across her broad shoulders. Her eyes were outlined with heavy, black eyeliner which added to her already hardened look. Inside her pocket she clutched a small Bible which she had permission to bring into court with her every day.

When the clerk opened the double doors and told the jurors to line up, everyone at the counsel table stood to face the jurors as they filed in. Theresa did her best to look confident and to look each juror in the face as they filed past. It was a tough assignment. Alvin looked slightly nervous.

A few minutes after everyone had settled in, Deputy Sanderson called, "All rise, Court is now in session." Judge Russell Schooling took the bench. Theresa Barroso and Alvin Robinson were now officially on trial for the murder of four-year-old Andrew Setzer.

Schooling had officially retired, but had been brought back for a short, two-month assignment—four and a half years ago. Schooling, a big bespectacled man with gray hair, moustache and goatee, looked a lot like Kentucky Fried Chicken's Colonel Sanders. Several of the spectators noted the similarity. Focused and very slow in speech, Schooling was renowned for his infinite patience, compassion and fairness. Alvin and Theresa were fortunate to have him presiding over their trial.

Judge Schooling instructed both juries for almost an hour on their duties and some of the hardships they would encounter as a result of the trial. They were reminded that what comes from the mouth of an attorney is not fact, no matter how cleverly worded it is. With a smile, he also promised to let the two juries alternate each day between the good seats and the not-so-good seats. Just as the show was about to get underway, it was noon and time to break for lunch.

By 1:30, everyone had again assembled in the hallway and the blue jury was ushered back into the courtroom for opening statements. The red jury was ordered to wait in the hall. Monterosso, dressed for success, stood before the sea of blue dots and started by thanking the jurors for their time. He was dramatic and charismatic in his mannerisms and spoke without referring to any written notes. Poised with one hand on the balustrade, he began telling jurors a capsulized version of the events that led to the death of four-year-old Andy Setzer.

"Andy died because he was thirsty," Monterosso began. "What this trial boils down to is that the person who was responsible for taking care of Andy opted, instead, to violently kill him."

He explained that Andy had had a problem; he frequently wet his pants and he couldn't always control his bowels. Andy had been in Theresa's home for a few weeks when he started wetting his pants and Theresa couldn't deal with his potty training problems, Monterosso said. During that time, Alvin was living at the residence off and on. At the time of Andy's death, Theresa and Alvin were on the verge of a divorce.

Monterosso told the blue jury that Theresa had stuck Andy with needles, forced him to eat hot chili peppers and had given him cold showers.

After a long pause, he went on to describe how Theresa had kicked Andy in his genitals about two weeks prior to his death because he kept wetting his pants. As the jurors' eyes darted over toward the defendant, Monterosso spoke of Andy's forced "death march" to Stater Bros. market during the last full day of his life. It had been over one hundred degrees outside and Andy's scrotum had been horribly sore and swollen to the size of a grapefruit. Understandably in tremendous pain, he had been crying about it.

"But what," he asked, "did his foster mother, Theresa Barroso, do? She made him carry a gallon of milk in one hand and a big bucket of ice cream in the other. Little Andy limped along, struggling all the way home in pain." Then, at some time around 3:00 A.M., Theresa had been awakened by the sounds of Andy gulping water from a bottle she kept next to their bed.

As he described the deadly fit of rage that followed, Monterosso whirled around, jabbed his finger at Barroso and looked her up and down with a scathing glare. The jury was captivated by the handsome, young DA who paced the floor in front of them. He knew how to grab their attention; they could barely take their eyes off him. He took time to look into the eyes of each and every juror. Through it all, Theresa remained stoical, husk-like.

Monterosso went on to describe how Theresa had knocked the bottle of water out of Andy's hands and made him stand up on his time-out chair. Then, she hit him in the face and knocked him backward off his chair, his head striking the nightstand. Andy started screaming. She ordered him to shut up. When he couldn't quiet himself, she made him get back on the chair. Once more she knocked him off the chair. He hit his head on the nightstand again. Only this time, it knocked him out cold.

"In their attempt to cover up their unspeakable act, she told Alvin to call 911 while she took Andy outside and rolled him in the dirt like she was breading a veal cutlet. When help finally arrived," he said, pointing once again toward the defendant, "there were no tears from Theresa Barroso."

"You're about to see and hear a tape of her admission to this crime," he warned. "And you'll hear—in her own words—how she describes herself as a *monster*." With that final, chilling word, he brought his opening statement to a dramatic conclusion. The juror's eyes followed him as he headed back to his seat and then their eyes focused a few seats down the counsel table, on Theresa.

Because Theresa's attorney, Pete Scalisi, opted to withhold his opening statement until a later time in the trial, Theresa's jury was dismissed and replaced by the red jury. Alvin's jury. Again, Monterosso stood before them and offered much the same story in the same riveting and dynamic way, except that Alvin was his target this time around. He told the jurors how Alvin idly lay by and allowed—even encouraged—the beating of a child that was in his custody. "Andy died because he was thirsty," Monterosso said again. He told how Alvin, as a prospective foster parent, was required to enroll in, and indeed *did* attend, parenting classes that taught the defendant how to care for children and how to report abuse. Still, in spite of all that Alvin witnessed, he did nothing to stop the abuse and torture of little Andy. Alvin knew about Andy's swollen scrotum, but chose to keep their "dirty little secret." Monterosso told the jurors that Alvin saw Theresa take Andy's feces and smear it around on the little boy's face and in his mouth, yet Alvin failed to defend Andy.

Pausing for a moment to let the weight of his words sink in, Monterosso went on to tell how Alvin had come home one night to find Andy with a bloody wash cloth wrapped around his penis. The foreskin had been torn when Theresa viciously yanked on it.

But did Alvin try to get help? No, Monterosso said, his voice rising. He opted to keep their dirty little secret and made no effort to get Andy the medical help he needed. Monterosso's rage was genuine; he spoke directly in the faces of the jurors seated in the front row and made eye contact with every one of them, sometimes stepping right in front of them to do so. Toward the end of his opening statements, he told jurors they would be hearing two tapes in which Alvin candidly talked about what he saw, what he knew, and why he didn't do anything about it.

"Alvin claims the reason he never did anything about it was because he was 'scared'." Monterosso labeled Alvin's failure to act a "callous indifference" to Andy's suffering and ended his opening statement with a solemn, "thank you." Many of the jurors let out an audible sigh of disgusted relief as Monterosso turned around and headed toward his chair at the counsel table.

Then it was Sachs' turn. Unlike the immaculately groomed Monterosso who wore shiny, polished shoes, a fine tailored suit and silk tie, Sachs presented his opening statements looking as if he'd just crawled out of bed. His gray hair still sported a flattened whorl where he'd slept on it. His old brown loafers were scuffed, his jacket with the leather elbow patches was shoddy and wrinkled. It was obviously his favorite sport coat; he'd worn it to most of the pre-trial hearings. The jacket with the leather elbow patches would become a familiar sight to everyone in the courtroom. Some days his hair looked less unruly than others, as though he'd spent a few seconds running a comb through it, or, perhaps his fingers. Sachs didn't wear a watch and would frequently turn around and squint at the clock above the door in the back of the courtroom.

Monterosso had paced back and forth directly in front of the jury during his opening statements and had spoken passionately without referring to notes. Sachs chose to plant himself behind a wooden podium and repeatedly referred to a yellow legal pad filled with handwritten scribbles. He would often pause for extended periods of time to flip through page after page of notes. The two attorneys' approaches were as different as night and day and, the jurors reacted accordingly.

Looking tired and drawn, but genuinely convinced of his client's innocence, Sachs asked jurors to "go inside the mind of Alvin Robinson." He painted a sad picture of a pitiful man with an I.Q. of merely 66—equivalent to that of a third or forth grader, an eight or ten-year-old child.

When he wasn't looking down at his notes, Sachs seemed to look beyond the jurors, focusing his gaze on the wall behind them. Often he stared at the floor and seemed to be speaking to no one in particular. He completely overlooked Alvin's jury. He seemed content to let his eyes shift from one wall to another.

Alvin was diagnosed as mildly mentally retarded, Sachs informed the jury. Even his parents didn't know about Alvin's marriage plans with Theresa and were absolutely shocked to find out that Alvin had taken in foster children.

Alvin was horribly dominated by Theresa, Sachs lamented, with just a slight whine to his voice. As a result, Alvin spent a lot of time away from her and the children. He acknowledged that Alvin and Theresa weren't getting along at the time of Andy's death, but the only way Alvin knew how to deal with Theresa's dominant and argumentative nature was simply to leave. Early on, it became apparent that Sachs was going to portray Alvin as the victim.

"Alvin can't read or write. Alvin couldn't possibly have understood his parental obligations because he couldn't even take care of himself." Poor Alvin. He lacked coping skills. Above all, Sachs assured the red jury, Alvin did not have the mental state the law requires for murder. With that, he collected his notes, collapsed into his seat and popped a throat lozenge into his mouth.

The blue jury was then summoned back into the courtroom and the first witness was called to the stand.

Firefighter Justin Scribner strode into the courtroom wearing his uniform. Raising his right hand, he did solemnly swear to tell the whole truth and nothing but the truth. Scribner gave a brief summary of his career, indicating he had been a firefighter for seven years. On the night of August 2, 1999, he was stationed in Perris and received a "person down" call at approximately 3:00 A.M. He recalled that it took his crew four or five minutes to arrive on the scene. There, they saw a heavy-set woman standing at the curb holding a small child in her arms. He recalled the woman as being rather vacant and unemotional. Scribner said that she had walked up to the driver's door of the fire engine and handed Andy over to Manny Reyes. She wasn't crying or asking questions.

Scribner remembered that firefighters and EMT's had only been on the scene for a few minutes and it wasn't until they were in route to the hospital that Andy's swollen genitals were noticed.

With Scribner's first reference to Andy's swollen scrotum, Monterosso put a close-up 8 X 10 color photograph of Andy's genitals on the overhead projector. The jurors' faces first registered shock, and disbelief, then sadness. Some grimaced. All were visibly shaken by the sight. It was the first and most devastating photograph shown. Even Scribner fought his emo-

250

tions while he acknowledged that the photograph did accurately depict what he had seen that night.

Next up was Matthew Brandt, who testified that he had been a firefighter/paramedic for ten years. Brandt's striking resemblance to Jerry Mathers, of the old "Leave It To Beaver" show, had won him the nickname of "Beaver." The guys at the station mostly just called him "Beav" for short.

On August 2, 1999, he worked for AMR [American Medical Response]. Like Scribner, Brandt testified that, in his opinion, the woman didn't appear to be very upset and didn't seem to be very worried about the severity of the situation. Brandt had been the one who had assisted with Andy's breathing, both at the scene and on the way to the hospital. It was the first time in his career that he'd ever seen a scrotum so severely swollen and, he was quick to add he hadn't seen anything like it since.

By the time they were halfway to the hospital, he admitted, they had already decided it wasn't an ordinary case. He recalled how detached Theresa seemed as she sat in the waiting room of the hospital. Brandt remembered the sheriff arriving about twenty to thirty minutes after AMR got there and testified that he stayed at Menifee Hospital for several hours.

The third witness was Sergeant Douglas McGrew. At the time of the incident, he had been a deputy with the Perris Police Department and had arrived at Menifee Valley Hospital about 4:10 A.M. The first thing he noticed about the child was the grotesquely swollen testicles and, soon afterwards, he notified his supervisor.

He recalled the manner in which he questioned the woman and her husband as they sat in the waiting area. The woman stated that the boy had a habit of getting out at night. It was his opinion that something was very peculiar about the whole situation. The man was just sitting there while the woman did all the talking. McGrew described Alvin as passive and Theresa as being very matter of fact about the whole thing. Neither parent said they were aware of any scrotal swelling or discoloration. It bothered him that neither parent expressed any concern for the child.

In a rather emotional moment, McGrew shifted uncomfortably in his seat and stated that he had stayed with Andy for almost three hours, until Andy was airlifted to Loma Linda about 7:45 A.M.

McGrew was dismissed after almost half an hour on the stand and the trial's first day was brought to a close. The judge admonished jurors not to look at the newspapers because the first day of trial was bound to make headlines. Nor were they to discuss anything associated with the trial amongst themselves or with anyone else. He smiled and bade everyone a safe ride home and said he'd see them again in the morning.

The next morning at approximately 9:30 A.M., both juries were called to line up in the hallway according to dot color. They were asked which jury sat in the good seats the day prior. Each jury pointed toward the other and everyone laughed. It was a lighthearted moment, at least until court got underway. Jurors were friendly and seemed to be a nice mixture of differ-

Deadly Thirst

ent types of people. Many read books to pass the time spent waiting in the hallway. One young woman studied non-stop during every break in the trial. Even during lunch break, she could be seen in front of the courthouse hunched over her schoolbooks, earnestly studying and taking notes.

Theresa was wearing the same frumpy dress she'd worn the first day of trial and appeared to be much more relaxed. Alvin was also wearing yesterday's clothing.

The first witness was Dr. Marlowe Schaffner. With the exception of the medical examiner who preformed the actual autopsy on Andy, perhaps no other witness would leave the jurors with a more vivid insight into how badly Andy had suffered during his last two weeks of life.

Schaffner testified that he had been an emergency room doctor for the past thirty-one years and really knew his profession. Schaffner testified that he had treated too many cases to count, "…And I can count pretty well." He had graduated from Loma Linda University and had been a medical missionary in central Africa for sixteen years. When he returned from Africa, he became the associate professor of emergency medicine at Loma Linda University Medical Center where Andy had died. He was certified in pediatrics and neonatal care.

Schaffner continued his testimony by saying, in a stern voice, that the event was "indelibly etched in my mind and will be for the rest of my life." With a sigh, he recounted that he and his staff had had only a few minutes to prepare for Andy's arrival. The paramedics onboard AMR had phoned ahead and briefed him on Andy's critical condition. He knew Andy was already on cardiac life support and intubation. He recalled that Andy was not able to breath on his own at any time during his emergency care.

Carefully referring to his notes, Schaffner described how the little boy appeared to be unclean and had multiple bruises on his back and buttocks. He then explained, directly to the jurors, how a bruise forms and what color stages it goes through as it ages. This is one way doctors can tell approximately when the injury occurred, he said. Andy had many bruises all over his body; some were old, perhaps as old as a week. But, the most noticeable thing was what he called "the massive swelling in the scrotal area."

"Normally," he said, "the scrotum of a four-year-old is quite small." He described Andy's scrotum as having undergone "major swelling" and had turned black and blue.

"In addition to this," he said, "there was an abrasion on the inner thigh of Andy's right leg which had aroused my concern." In all the thirty-one years of his medical experience in emergency rooms, he had never seen scrotal swelling and discoloration like that. Schaffner wasn't quite as unemotional as one might expect. His voice was tinged with animosity as he went on to describe other things he noticed that morning in the emergency room of Menifee Valley Hospital.

Schaffner agreed that part of his job was to notify the sheriff if he suspected child abuse. It had taken him only a couple of minutes to decide that this was indeed a horrific case of child abuse. The initial exam had made it clear to him that these injuries were not the result of a fall.

Monterosso put another photo on the overhead projector. It showed Andy lying on the yellow backboard. Positioned on his left side, several bruises were evident on his back and buttocks. Several jurors clearly had difficulty looking at that photo. During Monterosso's questioning of Schaffner, four autopsy photos were shown.

Next, Sachs stepped up to the podium to take his best shot at the emergency room doctor. Sachs' voice was sometimes barely audible as he asked several questions that elicited simple answers from the doctor. Sachs pointed out the emergency room records which indicated that *both* foster parents were present at the hospital at 4:20 A.M. Schaffner countered by reminding Sachs that not all the notes were his.

That was about it for doctor Schaffner. He had succeeded in giving the jury a vivid and sad view of what he had seen behind the closed doors of the emergency room during the early morning hours of August 2, 1999. Schaffner stepped down and exited the courtroom.

Sergeant Vern Horst took the witness stand as the day's second witness. Dressed in his green sheriff's uniform, he began to explain that on August 2nd he had been a homicide investigator with the Riverside County Sheriff's Department for about six years. He'd served fifteen years as a peace officer and was currently a sergeant working in Riverside. Horst stated that in his career he'd been the lead investigator in more than fifty cases and the secondary investigator in more than one hundred and fifty.

By then, the jury had the feeling that Horst had seen quite a bit of violence and murder during his career. As he continued, the jury saw the recollection of that particular morning was very upsetting to him. By the time he got to Menifee Hospital, Horst said his superior had already told him Andy was not expected to survive. At the hospital, McGrew had given Horst a quick summary of Andy's condition and the circumstances surrounding the incident.

"Then," Horst said with a sigh, "I went in and saw Andy." The way he said "Andy" sounded as if he were talking about one of his own kids. He slumped back in his chair and pondered which words to use to describe what he had seen. With obvious anxiety about having to dredge it all up again and unlock a part of his memory he preferred to keep locked away forever, Horst began to describe, at Monterosso's prompting, exactly what he had seen at Menifee. "The emergency room personnel were working frantically on that kid," he said, shaking his head. The whole scene was vividly coming back to him: the sights, the commotion around Andy's hospital bed, the hospital smell and especially the clicking and wheezing sound of the respirator. He remembered seeing Andy's swollen, blackened testicles and the fecal matter between Andy's legs.

While on the witness stand, it is not permissible to say how one may or may not feel about a particular situation. The court only wants to hear the

Deadly Thirst

facts. In the case of Horst's testimony, his body language spoke louder than a foghorn. He didn't need to say that the sight of Andy's battered body had a devastating effect on him, even though some might have thought him to be "hardened" after so many years on the force. There was just something about the suffering of a small, defenseless child that grabbed the sympathy of anyone with the slightest trace of kindness in their heart. It was becoming obvious to the jury that Theresa had no sympathy for Andy. Horst's most potent testimony was the words he did not say.

Horst testified that after he had spoken to Schaffner and seen Andy, he walked into the waiting room and spoke to both foster parents and eleven-year-old Jacob Marquist. Although he did identify himself as being with the Sheriff's department, Horst testified that he wasn't wearing a uniform at the time. He was dressed in regular street attire and talked to the foster parents in a rather informal, non-accusatory way, which was the way he preferred to interview his subjects.

During his testimony, Horst had no trouble locking his eyes onto Theresa as he relayed incriminating information to the jury. Often his jaw muscles tensed and his lips pressed together tightly as certain things came to mind. He said that Theresa claimed Andy had been perfectly fine until she found him outside in the dirt that morning. During his initial interview with Theresa, her answers had been stiff and monotone and her emotional state seemed very calm—abnormally calm. He stated that officials from CPS came quickly to the hospital to claim Jacob. Horst instructed CPS to take Jacob to the Perris station and have him wait there.

Monterosso prompted Horst to tell the jury what went on after he followed the foster parents back to their duplex-style apartment.

Horst said he'd interviewed each one separately, but it was a small apartment and it was possible that Alvin had overheard what Theresa had said, which may have allowed them to concoct a story together. Theresa claimed that Andy was a sleepwalker and she denied ever hurting the youngster. Horst especially remembered that Theresa never cried or expressed concern for Andy during either interview. After almost thirty minutes, the home interview had yielded few good answers and he had asked the couple to come down to the station.

At the station, Horst first interviewed Jacob Marquist, who was an enormous help to him. The eleven-year-old had witnessed several instances where Theresa had abused Andy. Jacob had seen Andy's swollen genitals and he told how Andy was forced to carry two heavy items on the walk home from Stater Bros. market the day before. Jacob had tried to help Andy, but Theresa wouldn't let him because she was punishing Andy for crying.

"He told me that Andy cried the whole way," Horst said with sadness in his voice, "and that he was having a hard time walking." He testified that Jacob was a smart, well-mannered and very articulate boy. He'd believed what Jacob had told him. After he had concluded his talk with Jacob, he had called Theresa into the small interrogation room and interviewed her for almost forty minutes.

At this time, Monterosso asked Judge Schooling for permission to play the tape of that interview. Deputy Wally Sanderson handed out thick transcripts to each juror. At the counsel table, both Alvin and Theresa had been given a copy of the transcripts, but Alvin's remained closed on the table in front of him. He couldn't read.

After a few minutes, tape 11-A was inserted into the VCR and began playing on seven TV sets situated around the courtroom. The jury seated in the good seats watched on a large television hanging from the ceiling in front of them; the other jury watched a set to their right. Horst stayed in the witness chair and watched on a small set in front of him. At the counsel table, Theresa began to tap her foot nervously as the tape started to play.

Seeing it again brought a frown to Horst's face. He didn't mask his revulsion as his eyes shot repeatedly back and forth from the TV to Theresa. At the counsel table, there were three small televisions, one for Alvin and Sachs, one for the prosecution, and one for Theresa and Scalisi. Theresa's face was about fifteen inches away from the TV in front of her. With a blank face she watched as the tape began. The volume was turned up and jurors also read the transcripts as Theresa's chirpy voice resounded throughout the courtroom. The spectators watched one of the televisions sitting on the counsel table.

"Anything I can do to help, you know," Theresa began in a sing-song voice. She elaborated quite a bit about how she loved children. She chuckled frequently during the interview, but never asked questions about how Andy was doing and she was not at all indignant that she was being questioned as though she were some kind of criminal. Looking at her, it appeared that everything was fine. She claimed that CPS only allotted about eighty-five dollars for a clothing allowance. "But they didn't send anything that first month, so basically, like, we were a month in the hole." Some of the jurors glanced up periodically at the TV as they turned pages and then refocused their attention on the transcripts. Everyone watched as Theresa [on tape] laughed and bounced around in her chair as she spoke to the detective in a lively, animated style, knowing all the while that little Andy was in serious peril because of what she had done to him.

At one point, midway through the tape, Horst informed Theresa that Jacob had already told him about seeing Andy's swollen genitals during the hosing-off incident. Several jurors looked up at the TV to see Theresa's reaction. All they saw was a face totally lacking in emotion. Horst prodded her a little. "Jacob said it was all purple and big."

Theresa said she had always noticed that Andy had a big pee-pee. But no, she hadn't noticed that it was purple.

"No," Theresa said, "no, I didn't notice anything like that." But, on second thought, she did recall that Andy had complained that his tummy hurt

Deadly Thirst

last night when she held him up to the sink to wash his hands. The tape was filled with chuckling and tales of potty accidents.

Finally, Horst asked Theresa if she had ever punched Andy in the stomach or anywhere else, even in play. "Not even joking around or anything?"

"Oh no, no, no," Theresa said in a soft, child-like voice.

He asked her if she'd be willing to take a polygraph. Instead of becoming indignant or asking Horst to let her get back to the hospital, Theresa shrugged and said, "Sure." Horst ended the interview by offering to get Theresa something to eat and drink. "Are you okay with that?" Theresa indicated she would like something to eat and soon after, the tape was over.

Horst was still on the witness stand, looking thoroughly repulsed by what he'd just seen. His eyes went from the TV screen straight to Theresa, who was whispering something into Scalisi's ear. Within a few seconds, he was glaring at her.

Monterosso began setting up the next tape and explained to the jury that the second taped interview was made after Andy had died at Loma Linda. Horst told the jury that he knew Andy had expired toward the beginning of the interview, but Theresa did not know it.

Unlike the first tape, that was originally intended to be used as evidence in a possible child abuse case, the second videotape—the one of the polygraph test—was destined to become compelling evidence in a murder trial. It was recorded at the San Bernardino Police Department, not far from the coroner's office where Andy's body would end up. If there were only one piece of evidence that could flatten Theresa's case like road kill, it was the highly incriminating polygraph tape. Transcripts were again handed out to jurors. As the tape began, jurors saw Theresa sitting, in a somewhat slouched position, looking befuddled, with a female polygraph examiner standing behind her, rubbing Theresa's shoulders in sympathy. There was no laughter from Theresa this time around; her face was stark white with terror.

The tape started with Theresa crying and Horst assuring her that Detective Cardwell (still rubbing Theresa's shoulders) had spoken very highly of her. Theresa was so emotional she could only nod a "yes" or "no" to questions. Her face was puffy; obviously, she was terrified. Horst told her to be thinking of Andy during this interview and not of herself. "What does he deserve? He was just a little boy…" Horst gestured with his hands quite a bit throughout the interview, sometimes reaching out to touch Theresa on the arm.

Theresa wanted Alvin to be present during this interview and Horst had a problem with that. "Well, I gotta tell you," he began, "your husband has told me what happened. OK? But I need to hear it from you." Horst was going for the jugular now and Theresa knew it. She had already been forthcoming with Kathleen Cardwell and Cardwell had relayed the information to Horst. "It's time for you to stand up for what you have done." Horst was incensed that Theresa's only thoughts were still about her own welfare.

"Will I be taken to jail?" she sniffed. Her first clue that things had turned against her came a few seconds later when Horst started reading Theresa her Miranda rights. Afterwards, he began leading her down the trail of her confession. Jurors were riveted to the transcripts, only glancing up at the TV occasionally.

"It all started about a week ago," she lamented. "I was just frustrated one day and really stressed out and I kicked him in his weenie." Horst pressed her for a better term to describe Andy's anatomy.

"What do you call that? genitals? His penis?"

"Yes," she said, obviously too embarrassed to say the word "penis." Then, she admitted that she had kicked him on another occasion, while Andy was in the bathroom, a few days prior. Horst asked her why she'd kicked him. "He had pee-peed on himself again…then I just snapped and, like, I just kicked him." Horst asked her to demonstrate how hard she had kicked Andy. They both stood up and Horst held out his hand and told Theresa to kick it just like she had kicked Andy. All of the jurors glanced up just in time to see it on TV. *Thump!*

"Wow. That hard? That's a pretty good kick," Horst said, rubbing his hand. The jurors' eyes went from the TV screen to Theresa, who sat at the counsel table in front of her own TV. She was clearly uneasy as she watched herself on tape. Several jurors glanced toward the witness stand at Horst; his face mirrored repugnance, his jaw was clinched. Even the jurors in the back row could see the muscles standing out on the side of his neck. He was angry all over again, no doubt about it.

"Then I noticed his wee-wee got swollen and red, so we put ice on it."

On the tape, Horst showed her a photo of Andy's swollen scrotum and questioned her about the large abrasion on the inside of his thigh. Several jurors looked up at the TV in time to see that Theresa had no trouble whatsoever looking at the photo of Andy, which showed the youngster splayed out on a hospital gurney. The large red abrasion Horst was pointing to was clearly visible and right next to Andy's hugely swollen and purple testicles. Certainly an innocent person who had been unaware of the injuries would have erupted into a barrage of comments and questions. But she didn't. Theresa was sphinx-like as she looked at the photo. She showed about as much emotion as if the photo had depicted a complete stranger, happy and smiling.

She couldn't imagine how that red abrasion on Andy's leg had happened, she said. In spite of her having just promised to tell what really happened, she began denying kicking Andy more than one time on each occasion. But Horst reminded her that Alvin had already told him what happened and Alvin had said Theresa kicked Andy repeatedly in the groin, several times. Horst wasn't going to let go of the issue.

"So how many times was it?" Realizing she'd been betrayed by her own husband, Theresa reluctantly began to come clean. Tears came to her eyes briefly while she seemed to be weighing her options. Finally, she spoke.

"Probably five times," she said wiping tears from her face. The tears came and went quickly; it took only a few seconds for her to regain her composure and continue talking in the flat monotone that chilled Horst to the bone. She said this particular incident actually happened about a week and a half ago. The men in the jury looked especially sympathetic with Andy, knowing how painful a kick to the groin can be. Then Horst guided her on to explain the incident that had happened on Saturday, when Andy had pooped his pants at her workplace and she'd hosed him off in the yard after they got home.

"Does he wipe the feces on his face or do you?" Horst wanted to know. Again, she said Andy wiped his own feces on his face. A little later, she went into her bedroom and found Andy standing on top of her bed, peeing.

"And I just, kinda like, snapped again. And I grabbed his wee-wee and I guess I grabbed him and squeezed him too hard..." The jury looked up at their monitor to see Horst sticking out his finger. He asked Theresa to pretend it was Andy's penis. He wanted her to show him how she'd grabbed it. Some of the jurors watched, open-mouthed, as she reached out and yanked on Horst's whole hand pulling it toward her. Theresa said that when she saw blood dripping from Andy's penis, she'd become alarmed at what she'd done. She'd called Alvin and asked him to come over. The jurors watched as Theresa spoke some of her most incriminating words so far: "Why am I becoming such a monster?" she cried. A "monster"...*that* word stuck with the jury. Monterosso was pleased at the obvious impact it had on them. Horst too paid close attention to how the jury reacted when Theresa described herself as a "monster."

She said that during the night they'd been awakened by the sounds of Andy gulping water from a jug they kept beside their bed. On the tape, her emotions were turned back on like a water faucet, releasing tears in short bursts. "And I just snapped," she sobbed. "And by this time he was, like, screaming, you know. And so I told him, 'Didn't I tell you to be quiet?'" Still, Andy continued to wail. "Didn't I tell you?" With that, she demonstrated how she'd slammed the palm of her hand into Andy's face and had sent Andy flying backward off his time-out chair. "And then he hit the nightstand and he started screaming even more. So I told him 'Get back on your chair and be quiet'. But he was still crying. So I did it again, but this time..." her voice trailed off. Little Andy had been knocked backward off his chair a second time.

Quickly, she gained the upper hand on her emotions and began to speak in monotone again. "And then we turned on the light and that's when we seen, he was, like, out of it. And so my husband goes, 'Let's call 911,' but then we started freaking out, like, what are we gonna do? So my husband goes, 'We'll just tell them that we found him outside.'"

"Who says that?" Horst asked.

"Alvin." From his seat at the far end of the counsel table, next to Sachs, Alvin began adamantly shaking his head "no" in stern disagreement with what Theresa had said on the tape. Next, the tape showed Theresa demonstrating how she had actually taken the unconscious child outside and rolled him in the dirt.

In the courtroom, Horst sat on the witness stand, watching the tape and silently reliving every minute of it. Periodically, his eyes darted over to the counsel table where Theresa was slouched, watching the tape with her attorney. Horst's contempt for Theresa was palpable; the whole courtroom vibrated with hostility. On the tape, Horst excused himself for a minute and said he'd be right back. Instead of asking if Andy was going to be all right, Theresa was only interested in seeing Alvin.

"Can I see Alvin now?" she whined.

"No," Horst said.

When he reentered the room a few minutes later, Horst wanted her to show him exactly how much force she'd used when she knocked Andy off his chair the second time. The jurors glanced up at the TV monitor just in time to see the hit. The sound of an abrupt slap filled the courtroom and jurors flinched when they heard it. The jury was clearly horrified at what they were seeing. As the tape drew to a close, Horst had one last question for Theresa.

"Why didn't you just give him back?" As if on cue, Theresa's emotions flared up again.

"I tried," she said, suddenly sobbing. Horst is seen on the tape as being fed up and finished. He'd gleaned enough information from the interview. He rose from his seat with a sigh and headed for the door, saying he was going to talk to Alvin for a minute. As if it were inconsequential, Theresa meekly inquired, finally, how Andy was doing. "How is Andy?"

"Andy has died," Horst said and walked out the door. As the tape came to an end, Theresa was alone in the interrogation room, squalling.

Everyone in the courtroom let out an audible sigh when the tape ended. Theresa, seated beside her attorney, was finally showing some emotion: she was crying. Scalisi put his arm around her.

Soon after the tape ended, Monterosso ended his questioning and Scalisi rose from his chair. It was a tough act for Scalisi to follow, but he chose to deflect the attention away from Theresa. He asked Horst if Alvin had any trouble understanding the questions during his interview.

"His answers fit," Horst testified.

"I have no further questions, your honor," Scalisi said. Horst was dismissed, but, instead of leaving the courtroom or taking a seat in the spectator's section, he took a seat between Monterosso and Scalisi at the counsel table. That would be the seat from which Horst would watch the rest of the trial. He was an impressive sight, in his uniform and all. Scalisi didn't like it one bit that Monterosso was going to use Horst as a visual re-

Deadly Thirst

minder of the power of law enforcement. But there was nothing he could do about it.

It already seemed like the end of a long day by then, but it was only lunchtime. Outside, the sun was shining, temps were in the high eighties. In the distance, bells from the Mission Inn chimed the noon hour. The magnolia and jacaranda trees were in a froth of bloom, their white and purple blossoms filling the air in the courtyard with the heavenly fragrance of springtime. Sidewalks were awash in delicate pedals that swirled around the feet of people passing by. The smells of fresh coffee brewing and hot-dogs sizzling on the grill emanated from a vendors cart nearby. On this particular day, you could actually see the mountains.

Many of the jurors chose to sit in the courtyard between the Robert Presley Hall of Justice and the old courthouse, which had been built at the turn of the century. The few lanky palm trees here and there provided little shade. Nonetheless, every concrete bench that had even the slightest speck of shade was occupied by as many people as could fit on it.

As the lunch break drew to a close, those jurors that had taken the op-portunity to step outside were thankful they had done so. It was the only breath of fresh air they were to get. Things were only going to get worse, once court resumed after lunch. Even so, the jury would hear only a ghastly portion of all that had really happened to Andy Setzer.

Proceedings resumed at 1:45 as Dr. Frank Sheridan was sworn in. He was immediately prompted by Monterosso to tell the jury about his career. In his thick Irish accent, Dr. Sheridan said he was a forensic pathologist; in fact, he'd been the chief pathologist of San Bernardino County since 1988. Sipping frequently from a glass of water, he told of receiving his medical degree in 1971 from the University of Dublin, Ireland. In his long career, Sheridan had testified many times. He was an excellent witness. He turned and spoke directly to the jury, not to Monterosso. He kept his answers simple enough for them to understand and took the time to explain, in laymen's terms, the way things worked during an autopsy. His testimony would prove to be emotionally difficult to listen to, but very simply worded, providing a vivid picture of what he had seen.

He said he had specialized in brain injuries and that he'd done more than three thousand autopsies, several hundred of those on children. He stressed that he specialized in autopsying children with head injuries and had testified in hundreds of cases in several counties. Filling his empty wa-ter glass from a pitcher nearby, he took a long drink of water and began to tell jurors exactly what is done during an autopsy.

The first thing the pathologist does is X-ray, he said, and then there's an external exam, followed of course by an internal exam. The last part of an autopsy, Sheridan explained, is the microscopic exam that may take place several days or weeks after the autopsy has been completed. When the results are in, the pathologist can learn more about when the injuries occurred.

Even though Dr. Sheridan agreed that Andy's groin injuries were gruesome and his genitals were "extremely swollen," those injuries were not life threatening. In other words, the groin injuries weren't what killed Andy. But they were certainly the most conspicuous, he added. Andy's scrotum was dissected and slices of it were examined under a microscope. The examination showed the injuries were at least a few days old and that there were at least two ages of injuries, meaning Andy had suffered abuse on prior occasions.

"In pathology," he explained to the jurors, "we look for signs that the body has had time to react, such as redness or swelling." As Monterosso slid the 8 X 10 color photo of Andy's genitals onto the overhead projector, Sheridan said he wasn't sure if he'd ever seen that kind of swelling before.

Monterosso pointed to the back injuries and bruises, which Sheridan said were caused by multiple blows. He testified that he had immediately noticed three different kinds of injuries on the child. Andy's left ankle had a fresh cut on it; his scrotum was extremely swollen and discolored and he had bruises on his shoulders, abdomen, back and buttocks.

Monterosso replaced the groin photo with an autopsy photo of Andy's face. His mouth, pulled open by two hands encased in thick blue gloves, was full of blood, his tongue protruding. Between the front teeth and upper lip, there was a noticeable tear. Such a tear, Sheridan said, was typical in smothering victims, or when pressure was applied to a child's mouth to shut him up. Monterosso asked if someone hitting Andy in his face could have also caused a tear like that. Sheridan replied that indeed it could.

At first, Sheridan had noticed no external head injuries, but when an ear-to-ear incision was made in Andy's scalp and the scalp was peeled away, he saw two internal bruises. One was in the right temple area and the other was close to the top of Andy's head, most likely caused by two separate impacts. Then, he told the jurors that he sawed off the top of the skull and removed it like a cap. Andy had a sub-dural hemorrhage, which is a major injury. The brain was extremely swollen; it had been subjected to horrific force. He also noted hemorrhaging around the optic nerve and told the jurors that Andy's brain injuries were similar to that of "shaken baby syndrome." Andy's injuries were equivalent to falling from a two or three story building and landing on his head. Several jurors glared at Theresa, who was whispering demurely to her attorney. A direct blow caused the internal head injury, the doctor said.

Sheridan concluded his comments about the brain injury by saying that without immediate medical intervention, death could have occurred within minutes. Dr. Sheridan had been very thorough in his explanations and, because he had laid it all out in simple terms, the jury had understood everything.

Sachs had a few questions he wanted to ask the pathologist. "About those scalp injuries," Sachs asked, "They weren't visible with the naked eye, is that correct?"

"Correct."

"Were the groin injuries consistent with punching or kicking?"

"Yes, they were."

"And the penis…was the tip of Andy's penis torn by a pinch type movement?"

"Quite possibly."

"No further questions, your honor."

Scalisi now stood before Sheridan, who was busy pouring another glass of water for himself. The doctor had taken a lot of time explaining everything in meticulous detail for the jury and his throat had become dry. Occasionally, his voice cracked as he spoke, but still he continued in a very methodical and patient manner, sipping water all the while.

Sachs had left the photo of Andy's swollen genitals on the overhead monitor. Scalisi quickly removed it, slapping it face down on the counsel table. Of all the questions Scalisi could have asked the person who performed the autopsy on Andy, his main question was to establish that the head injuries were caused by two separate blows.

"Correct?" the attorney asked.

"Correct," the doctor answered.

"Nothing further, your honor." With a smug look on his face Scalisi sat down.

The doctor was thanked for his testimony and was excused from the witness stand. The jury and everyone else in the courtroom were exhausted. It had been a grueling, gut-wrenching day full of taped murder confessions, graphic testimony from the coroner and gory autopsy photos. Now, the jurors had to deal with rush hour traffic.

May 17th was day number three. When the court assistant stepped into the hallway, she asked that only the red jurors line up. Those were Alvin's people. Horst was standing at the counsel table next to Monterosso as the jury filed in and took their places in the good seats. If only one jury was in the room, they were always treated to the good seats.

For the second time, Horst was called to the witness stand. Fortunately, he worked on the first floor of the Hall of Justice and was glad to be Monterosso's trump card, his ace in the hole. He was seated next to Monterosso at the counsel table almost the entire time. His presence was invaluable and Monterosso knew it. Monterosso asked Horst if, when he interviewed Alvin, had he told Alvin anything that Jacob or Theresa may have said about him? No, Horst said, he didn't tell Alvin anything. He wanted Alvin to cut his own path.

Monterosso asked for permission to play an audiotape of the interview between Horst and Alvin on the morning of August 2, 1999, when Andy was still clinging to life. Again, transcripts were passed around to the jurors. Tape # 26A was put into the cassette player and soon the familiar voice of Horst could be heard in the courtroom.

Within the first few minutes, Alvin asked how Andy was doing and Horst assured him that the little guy "was pluggin' right along." Alvin sounded upbeat and confident as he answered questions about his employment, but his tone of voice changed when questions arose about his relationship with Theresa. He started complaining about the divorce papers not being copied for him. He said he had to make copies of all of them so he could have his own set in case she didn't file.

"Then I can file them myself," Alvin said in a defiant tone of voice. Monterosso desperately hoped that the jury was paying close attention to what Alvin was saying. As the tape droned on, Alvin had no trouble remembering how long he'd been married or how his pager worked. He even said he'd cut his arm putting a new engine in his car, one of Alvin's most damaging comments. Monterosso hoped the jury would realize that it was cognitive thinking—from a guy who was supposedly retarded. Horst's eyes darted toward the jury, perhaps trying to see if the important comment had registered with them. On the tape, Horst sounded relaxed and seemed to go along with the flow and let Alvin bushwhack his own path. Alvin had no trouble remembering that Andy arrived at their house on June 3rd. He also told about taking the kids up to the mountains. Soon, Alvin was telling the detective how his friend Chas had invited him to go to a nudie bar called Temptations. However, Alvin ended up not going because he was tired from a whole week spent carousing with his buddies. Alvin told Horst about Andy's trip to Theresa's workplace on Saturday and how he had taken the boys to a nearby auto parts store.

"It's an accessory shop," he clarified. Alvin got around to the time when Theresa wrapped Andy in a plastic bag after he soiled his pants at the weight clinic. Alvin said he didn't approve of her doing that. "I told her it ain't right to do that," he said. But he didn't actually see her hose Andy off afterward in the yard. He claimed that the only reason he went over to the apartment on Sunday night was because she had paged him and asked him to come over. He assumed they were going to have sex. "I thought she was gonna give me some, you know." From his seat at the counsel table, sitting next to Sachs, Alvin began to chuckle. The two men leaned toward each other and shared a whispered comment. Both snickered. On the tape, Horst clarified the statement by calling it a sexual encounter. "Yeah, right," Alvin laughed.

"So did you have sex?" Horst asked.

"Well, we didn't, it was just basically..."

Horst wanted specific information that was not forthcoming from Alvin and finally said to him, "I feel like I'm having to pull information out of you." Horst told Alvin he didn't want to have to extract anything from him. Alvin understood what "extract" meant and agreed with Horst. He spoke of baby-sitting the kids while Theresa was at work. And then, with Horst pressuring him to come clean with the facts, the jury listened as Alvin began crying and agonizing about the possibility of going to jail. From that point on, it was downhill for Alvin. Incriminating information flowed from his mouth like vomit. He recounted many instances when he'd seen Theresa abuse Andy and admitted that he had done nothing about it. Yes, he knew it was wrong and dangerous but he didn't intercede. Why not? Because he was scared. As the tape neared its end, Alvin described the events that led to Andy's hospitalization and his death. A photo was put on the overhead projector. It showed Horst kneeling on Andy's time-out chair and Alvin demonstrating how Theresa had pushed Andy off the chair with her foot. That was obviously what Alvin had referred to as the "kick."

The jury reassembled the transcripts, passed them toward the end of each row and back to Deputy Sanderson. Then, all eyes were on Horst.

There was only one more thing Monterosso wanted Horst to clarify for the jurors.

"Alvin told you Theresa had leaned over him to kick Andy off the chair, correct?"

"Correct."

"Did Alvin make any effort to stop Theresa from attacking Andy?" Horst shot Alvin a piercing glare and replied that Alvin had made no effort to stop her.

Those words painted a grim picture of child abuse and, as luck would have it, the picture was left hanging in the jurors' minds as they left the courtroom for lunch break.

Those who'd chosen to sit in the courtyard in front of the Hall of Justice may have noticed Monterosso crossing the street in front of his office building. Walking with him were a young boy and a woman.

Testimony resumed at 1:45. This time, both juries were led into the courtroom and thirteen-year-old Jacob Marquist was called to the stand as the second witness of the day.

Jacob was dressed in a plaid short-sleeved shirt and jeans, his blond hair neatly combed. His slender build was dwarfed even more by the enormity of the judge's bench and the witness stand. Jacob was relaxed, having been well prepared by Monterosso about the way it would be when he gave his testimony. Jacob was self-assured and precise. The jury was clearly impressed with him early on.

He testified that he was thirteen now, in the seventh grade and was living in a group home. When Monterosso asked Jacob if he saw Theresa Barroso in the courtroom, he said yes and pointed his finger in her direction. His face mirrored slight animosity. Jacob told the court how he'd witnessed Theresa hosing Andy off in the yard with the garden hose and how she'd whipped him with it. No, he hadn't actually seen the hose come into contact with Andy's body because Theresa and Andy were around the corner of the apartment. But there were only two people back there, he said, and he'd seen Theresa flailing the hose and he'd heard Andy screaming. Jacob testified that he'd walked around to where Andy was lying in the mud and he'd seen Andy's private parts, which he described as being swollen and black. Theresa was squirting Andy and hollering at him to shut up.

Jacob testified that both Alvin and Theresa made Andy eat hot peppers. Monterosso questioned Jacob about what he'd heard in the time just before Theresa rushed into his bedroom and told him to hurry up and get dressed because Andy had to go to the hospital.

He'd heard *Alvin* yelling at Andy to be quiet. He was sure about that. Andy cried a lot, Jacob added. Then, he'd heard a "bang" on the wall and then, no more crying.

Next, it was Sachs turn to question Jacob. Cross-examination takes on more importance than direct questioning, because jurors seem to listen to it more closely. They know that, unlike direct examination, there haven't been any test drives in the lawyer's office. They also find it more interesting due to the adversarial nature of it. Since Jacob was so young, some of the jurors looked apprehensive. Would he be able to hold his own, to hold up under the intense questioning of hard-hitting defense attorneys like Sachs and Scalisi? Monterosso had done his best to prepare Jacob for his time on the witness stand, but it was all up to Jacob now.

Sachs asked Jacob to tell the jury about the day he and Andy had accompanied Theresa to her place of employment. When, exactly did that happen? As Jacob began to answer, it was clear to everyone in attendance that Jacob had gotten Saturday, the day Andy soiled his pants at Theresa's workplace, confused with Sunday, the day of the death march to Stater Bros. market. Sachs knew that the passage of time had fogged Jacob's memory and he questioned him for several minutes about it. He allowed him to restate exactly when they had gone to Theresa's workplace. Still, Jacob testified that the day he and Andy had gone to Theresa's workplace was Sunday, when in fact, it had happened on Saturday. The fact that Jacob had gotten the days confused did not adversely affect his testimony. Two years had elapsed and to a thirteen-year-old boy, a Saturday or Sunday that had occurred almost two years prior are pretty much the same. It wasn't like he had marked the events on his calendar. It wasn't critical, so Sachs didn't push it. The jury seemed to understand Jacob's confusion. Sachs finally ended his questioning and returned to the counsel table next to Alvin.

The third and final witness of the day was retired Senior Investigator for the DA's office, Pete Harding. It was fast approaching 5:00 P.M. and, due to the late hour, Harding wasn't on the stand very long. He did manage, however, to relate how Jacob had told him he'd seen Theresa poke Andy in the lips with a hypodermic needle because he wouldn't eat his French toast strips.

As Judge Schooling brought the day's proceedings to an end, he once more warned the jurors not to look at the newspapers. They were bound to be full of information about the trial and the judge didn't want anyone tainted.

Deadly Thirst

He need not have worried. The newspaper's coverage of the trial was, at best, sketchy and lackluster. Articles usually amounted to only one or two brief tidbits about what had taken place inside the courtroom. Much of every article concerning the case was a rehash of how Andy Setzer, 4, was knocked off his chair for getting a drink of water and how Theresa Barroso, 23, and Alvin Robinson, 26, were being charged with his murder. If the public was thirsty for details, they sure weren't going to get many from the newspaper.

Only a few people made the effort to attend the trial. The gaggle of people who once clamored for information about the Setzer case, were gone. It seemed that Andy Setzer was merely a faded memory to most people. Everyone was getting on with their lives. The majority of spectator seats would remain hauntingly vacant throughout the trial. With the exception of day one, Andy's grandmother, Dawn Masterson, could not bring herself to attend. The testimony and photographs were simply too much for her to deal with. Andy's biological parents weren't there either. Cowboy was in prison again, so he had a good excuse; but where was Laura?

Neither Mike nor Lynn Herman attended. With the exception of a brief appearance by Mike midway through the trial, neither wanted to hear what Alvin and Theresa had done with the vibrant blonde-haired boy they'd loved so deeply and tried to adopt. Aside from the Press Enterprise reporter, who managed to attend for at least an hour most days, and me, only Alvin's parents were faithful—especially his dad. Leroy obviously anguished over the predicament of his son. It was difficult to witness the emotional agony Alvin's parents were enduring.

On Monday morning, May 21, at 10:40, only the red jury was seated when Harding once more took the stand. Monterosso began asking him about his interview with Alvin in the DA's office on October 18th of 1999, a few days prior to his arrest. Deputy Sanderson, his arms stacked high with transcripts, walked toward the jury members who were seated in the "good" seats. Once more, several jurors fished out their reading glasses as they prepared to follow along with another tape-recorded interview. Harding explained that, at that point in time, Alvin was not yet under arrest; however, he was arrested a few days later.

It was a long interview, an hour and forty minutes. Harding followed along through the transcript, only occasionally glancing up at either the jury or Alvin. As usual, Alvin's copy of the transcript stayed closed on the table in front of him. Sachs read along & scribbled notes while Alvin stared off into space. Often, during the tape, Theresa leaned toward Scalisi and whispered something in his ear. Scalisi's head usually nodded affirmatively.

On tape, Alvin recalled several instances of abuse he'd witnessed, abuse that was simply "uncalled for." Harding, Monterosso, and Horst kept their fingers crossed hoping the jury was paying close attention to the little clues Alvin was giving, that pointed to the fact that he wasn't as retarded as Sachs was trying to make them believe. It made for a very tense situation.

There was absolutely no way to gauge the juror's thoughts or assumptions. If any of the jurors were to let their mind wander for even a moment, they might miss crucial evidence that verified Alvin understood the abusive and dangerous situation that Andy had been in.

The jurors seemed to be listening closely as Alvin admitted pulling Andy's pants down and seeing his testicles swollen "like grapefruit." Then, they heard Alvin describe how he'd seen Theresa make Andy eat his own poop. He admitted knowing that eating poop could make a person "damn sick." He admitted that he was well aware that kicking a kid in his balls could kill him.

There was no getting around the fact that Harding cussed a lot. In the taped conversation, the two men talked in blunt terms. The words "fuck" and "shit" were tossed around and used without apologies. They talked about getting kicked in the "balls." It was man to man. No bullshit. From time to time, Harding threw a sheepish glance toward the jurors, but luckily no one seemed offended by Harding's street talk.

Alvin said he'd seen Theresa make Andy stand on the edge of the bed and then push him off backwards. Andy had landed, hard, on his butt and had cried about it. Harding asked Alvin what he thought would have happened if Andy had landed on his neck.

"He'd have been outta here."

Harding wondered if the jury noticed that Alvin, though he was supposedly retarded, seemed to completely understand the meaning of big words such as, "chronological," "ascertain," "differentiate," "condescending" and "obligation." So far, their faces weren't giving anything away. Seemingly insignificant comments on the tapes were so crucially important that Monterosso was constantly on edge about it.

They listened as Alvin expressed an urgent need to obtain a notarized letter so he could get Theresa's name off a piece of property they owned. A few jurors grinned when they heard Harding say, "I'm just a cop and I don't know shit about the law." In the courtroom, Harding broke into a wide grin when he heard himself say that on the tape.

Then there was the discussion of the cold showers. Alvin said giving a kid a cold shower could make him go into shock. He admitted that he thought Andy had been tortured. He recalled how Theresa had paged him and pleaded with him to come to the apartment the night she'd yanked on Andy's penis.

As the jury flipped through page after page of transcribed words, Alvin sat beside Sachs, staring into space and playing with paper clips, as if he had no concern whatsoever about all that was happening. On tape, he adamantly denied ever yelling at Andy or punishing him. During the majority of the tape, Alvin's courtroom behavior was baffling. He appeared not to even be listening, but when they got to the part where Alvin admitted he had no idea why he'd married Theresa, he laughed out loud and shook his head. Perhaps he was paying attention after all.

It was a long tape, but, they were nearing the point where Alvin was about to utter some of his most self-incriminating comments so far. On tape, Monterosso was heard joining the interview. Together with Harding, the two men asked Alvin why in the world he didn't tell anyone about the abuse Andy was suffering and why he didn't call for help. Alvin said he was just scared.

"If you had told somebody," Harding asked, "do you think that little boy would be alive today?"

"Uh-huh." [Affirmative].

"And you knew everything that happened, everything that you saw her do...the kicking him in the balls, you said, 'Yeah, that might kill him.' Putting him in a cold shower, you said, 'Yeah, it can cause shock, probably could cause brain damage, might even kill him.' You know, feeding him shit. You *know* it. You said, 'Yeah, it could fuck up your intestines and that stuff.' All these things are gonna kill that little boy. And you didn't do anything. Why? Any good reason?"

"I was just scared."

"Of what? There's nothing to be fucking afraid of."

On tape, Monterosso drilled Alvin as to whether or not he could dial a phone. Could he dial 911? Did he know what would happen if he dialed 911? During this part of the tape, Alvin appeared to suddenly realize that perhaps he'd said too much. He began to falter and stammer.

"Yeah, I can dial a phone," he said, "but I...I...if, if you gave me the lady's number and name and all that and put the phone in front of me I...I could call; but I don't know her name."

Harding and Monterosso chipped away at Alvin's supposed stupidity. They drilled him on everything he'd learned in foster parenting class. Then, they got Alvin to admit, one more time, that he did understand the abuse Andy was being subjected to could kill him.

"Yeah," Alvin said.

Alvin admitted that he knew what his responsibilities were as a foster parent and he knew he had an obligation to take care of Jacob and Andy. On tape, both Harding and Monterosso were hammering Alvin now, getting him to admit that he did know what was going on. It came across perfectly clear, on tape, that Alvin did not realize he was incriminating himself. He thought he was merely helping convict Theresa. He continually made reference to how horrible the whole thing was. He did not seem to realize he had just slipped the noose around his own neck.

Monterosso and Harding made a hell of a tag team. Toward the end of the tape, Monterosso went for the jugular with his questioning. He asked Alvin if he had been scared about what would happen to him if he had told anyone about Andy's abuse. Alvin admitted that he knew he could get in trouble for trying to cover it up. He also admitted that he screwed around on Theresa and that he "was clever with it."

As the most incriminating part of the tape rolled around, Monterosso swept his eyes across the jury. He was looking for anything that might say whether or not they'd figured out that Alvin's intelligence wasn't quite as low as Sachs wanted them to believe. There was absolutely nothing registering on any of the faces. He desperately wanted to stop the tape and say, "All right now, I want everyone to pay extra attention to what Alvin is about to say." But he couldn't do that. He could only hope they were still listening. It didn't appear that they were. They were tired and it was getting late in the day. Several jurors were fidgety and kept ogling the clock. It was obvious that several of them were anxious to adjourn early enough to beat the traffic. He wanted to snap his fingers, or pound on the counsel table to wake them up. Still, the tape droned on.

"The next day after everything happened," Alvin said, "I went over there and uh, and got—the only thing that was more important to me is my TV 'cause I paid like $400 for it, you know. And I went over there and I picked up my TV. Well, you know, I bought the bed, I bought the microwave and I bought the oven. I bought a lot of little things over there, you know. So I says, I'm gonna get me a U-Haul and I'm gonna come back over here and gonna do this and do that." Alvin was anxious to collect all the stuff that was rightfully his. He seemed to be angry when he recalled seeing all his stuff at the apartment and he had no way to get it out. He didn't want to leave any of his stuff behind. Monterosso asked if the truck was to be used to get all of his stuff out of the apartment and Alvin said yes. Alvin made no mention of feeling sad as he walked among the things Andy had left behind.

Nothing was registering on any of the bored faces in the sea of red dots. Monterosso sat in agony throughout the entire tape.

Alvin lamented that Theresa's parents had changed the locks and he was incensed that he couldn't get his microwave, his $200 bed, and his "smart" TV.

"So," Alvin said, "my dad says just to wait 'til everything blows over. And then we'll take the cops and we'll go get your stuff." But, Alvin added, that he never did go back because things weren't blowing over quite like he and Leroy had hoped they would.

"But you got the TV out?" Monterosso asked.

"That first—night, yeah. I got that." Alvin seemed relieved that he'd moved quickly enough to rescue his TV. Had the jury caught that cold-hearted statement about how, *as Andy was in route to the morgue*, Alvin's main concern was to rush back home to rescue his TV? There wasn't a hint of anything registering on the jurors' faces.

At last, the tape ended. Monterosso felt somewhat defeated, but there was nothing he could do about it now. They had to have been listening very closely to hear all of Alvin's self-incrimination. If their minds had wandered for even an instant, they might have missed something crucial. The transcripts were handed to the end of each row and collected by Deputy

Sanderson. At one hundred and eleven pages, multiplied by fourteen jurors, Sanderson had quite a load of paper to carry.

Harding was still on the witness stand. Monterosso asked him if he'd made a deal with Alvin and, perhaps, told Alvin that he would get immunity if he testified against Theresa. Harding said no; he didn't even recall telling Alvin he was a suspect. He never told Alvin that he had nothing to worry about as long as he cooperated with investigators. He'd made no promises whatsoever to Alvin. Then, Harding was dismissed. It was none too soon as far as he was concerned. He had his motor home packed and ready to head up to Bishop for the annual Mule Days celebration. Court was recessed until 9:30 Thursday morning.

The first witness of the day was Joanne McHugh* a social worker for Riverside County for the past thirty-two years. She spoke in a friendly, open manner and frequently turned to face the jury when she gave her answers. Currently, she was an instructor, training prospective foster parents. Along with two other employees, she had been training for five years. She explained that it was mandatory for prospective foster parents to take eight classes, each class lasting three hours. Those classes, in the order they were taught, were: [1] Rights and responsibilities, [2] Separation and loss, [3] Discipline, [4] Teamwork, [5] Child abuse cycle, [6] Behavior modification, [7] Child development, [8] Self-esteem. McHugh testified she had checked the sign-in sheets and the computer database for class attendance to verify she had been Alvin's and Theresa's trainer in several of the classes they took. Alvin and Theresa had attended the orientation on December 8th and they had received a booklet with licensing rules and regulations. While there was a written booklet about these rules and regulations, it was also taught verbally in class. The subject of discipline was discussed *very* thoroughly. Monterosso broached the subject of corporal punishment and McHugh agreed that CPS had very stringent rules as to what was considered corporal punishment.

"If a two-year-old reaches for the hot stove," she said, "and you smack his hand, that is corporal punishment." The classes were always taught orally to make sure everyone understood what they could and couldn't do, as far as discipline was concerned. They discussed the "mandated reporter" issue as she explained that one of the duties of a foster parent is to report even *suspected* child abuse. Furthermore, parents are told who to call and they are given an emergency phone number to call.

In her class, McHugh taught that abuse was a cycle, going from generation to generation, and they talked about breaking that cycle. Alternatives to punishment were discussed. The subject of bedwetting was thoroughly discussed in class three [discipline] and parents were taught how to avoid getting upset when toilet training problems arose.

In class number eight [self-esteem] parents were taught praise and encouragement. Alvin attended all of the classes, except the third class about discipline; but that didn't necessarily merit concern because discipline was taught in other classes. Therefore, there was no way a parent could not have learned about discipline. Looking at her notes, she concluded that Theresa had missed two classes, but had attended the enriched team classes which dealt with kids who had been through multiple placements. Those enriched classes taught parents to deal with special needs kids like Andy.

On cross examination, Scalisi asked McHugh if teachers made sure that parents understood the lessons.

Yes, of course.

Next, Sachs had something he wanted an answer to. According to sign-in sheets, Alvin took a June 5th class and Andy arrived at the home on June 3rd. So, technically speaking, Alvin had not completed all of the required classes by the time Andy and Jacob arrived at the home. Right? With a smile, McHugh conceded that was correct.

McHugh testified that instructors take a head count of attendees so they will know how many attended. She admitted that no written test was given to ensure that the parents had understood everything they'd been taught.

About those enriched classes, Sachs said, shouldn't a person be more qualified after taking those classes?

Yes, they should.

For the remainder of her time on the stand, McHugh's questioning and testimony was like a volley ball game. So many questions bounced back and forth about which parent had missed which class that jurors simply lost track. Through it all, McHugh smiled.

McHugh was the last witness for the prosecution. It was now the defense's turn to call witnesses. Sachs got the first opportunity and called Alvin's most avid admirer, his mother.

Jurors were aghast at Susie Robinson's body language. She plodded up to the stand toting her own unique brand of motherhood. As she slogged past the jury box, her shoulders drooped forward, her face hung in a frown and her arms dangled limply at her sides. The thin soles of her shoes slapped the floor with each step; the sound echoing throughout the courtroom.

Dressed super-casually in dirty tennis shoes, stretch pants and a garish colored top, Susie appeared to have about as much concern for her appearance as did Alvin's patches-wearing public defender. She seemed embarrassed to be there. Her body language spoke volumes while her mouth spoke jive-talk peppered with improper grammar. She acted as if the whole trial was a waste of her time.

One ploy though, was getting a lot of attention from those seated in the spectators' section. Leroy and Susie had chosen this day to bring their adult daughter, who suffered from Down's syndrome, to court. She had no idea what the whole shebang was about and she couldn't have cared less. Several spectators grumbled that she shouldn't have been there. She played and giggled and drooled and kicked the back of the chair in front of her while Susie was testifying. Her raspy breathing made it hard for those seated near her to hear the proceedings. Several people got up and moved as far away from the woman as possible, but the courtroom was small and there were only eighteen chairs to choose from with the Robinson woman smack dab in the center. One spectator turned around to glare at Leroy but Leroy's eyes were glued on Susie.

It would certainly stand to reason that a mother would try to aid her son's defense, but Susie did Alvin no good whatsoever. With one exception perhaps. It became abundantly clear that she and Alvin were cut from the same cloth. There was no doubt which parent had left their genetic imprint on Alvin. It was obvious and unmistakable; Alvin was his mother's son.

It was also obvious that the jury was giving Susie their complete attention. Their expressions ranged from suppressed amusement to outright shock at times. Susie plopped down in the witness chair and gave off a sigh that sounded like *hurry up, let's get this over with*. Her tone of voice literally dripped with boredom.

Susie was asked to describe Alvin's intellectual ability. She stated with a shrug that when Alvin was a kid in Alabama, he was always in TMR class in school. After some prompting, she clarified that TMR stood for Trainable Mentally Retarded. The family had moved to California in 1991. Yes, she said, Alvin graduated from high school, but he couldn't read or write very well. He could write his name and address and, that was about all. He was twenty-eight-years-old and he'd lived at home till he was twenty-four or twenty-five. Then he'd gone off to live with Theresa in 1998. Yes, he had a driver's license, but he'd flunked the written test several times and he'd finally had to take an oral test.

Susie's facial expressions smacked of irritation and boredom. She testified that Alvin had been totally dependant on her and Leroy 'til he moved in with Theresa. Alvin had still come back home at least two or three times a month, so when they got married in February of 1999, her and Leroy had been absolutely shocked. As for the foster children, well, her and Leroy had no idea he was even considering becoming a foster parent. The first she'd heard of it was when Alvin showed up one day at her house with two little kids. Even after he got the kids, he'd still come home, just like before.

Yeah, she said, her and Leroy knew Alvin had some marital problems with Theresa. It was 'cause Theresa was so bossy.

"It was done her way or not at all," Susie said. And the reason they'd never called CPS was because her and Leroy never figured it'd go through. Yeah, she was a licensed nurse, and yeah, Alvin did ask her what to do about swollen testicles. She'd advised him to put ice on it, she testified, but she had no idea that it was Andy who was suffering from "swollen nuts," as Alvin had worded it.

When her testimony came around to the events of the last week in July, Susie said that Alvin had been back home with her and Leroy about a week or longer at that time. She admitted that she sometimes filled out Alvin's employment applications for him and tried to discourage him from going back to Theresa.

Sachs had nothing further.

Monterosso asked Susie to tell the jury exactly how Alvin had asked her about what to do for swollen testicles.

"He said, 'What would you do for someone who had swollen nuts?'" With a shrug, she added that since she'd become a nurse, he'd asked her 'bout a lot of stuff. Susie claimed that her and Leroy never used corporal punishment on Alvin, but added that he did get spankings. This comment brought a snicker from several people. Obviously, Susie didn't understand the definition of corporal punishment.

Scalisi began questioning Susie by asking her if she remembered seeing a Dissolution of Marriage form on July 30th. Susie said she saw the form, but she didn't know nothin' about Theresa's plans to file for divorce. Upon further questioning, she said she had no idea Theresa had filed a restraining order against Alvin in October of 1997. Susie didn't know nothin' 'bout no divorce, or no restraining order or about any domestic violence stuff. She didn't go gettin' into Alvin's business.

Scalisi wanted to know if Alvin could write a letter. Susie mumbled that he probably could; whereupon, Scalisi showed her a letter that was supposedly written by Alvin. Susie took one glance at it and said that it wasn't Alvin's writing. Did she know whether or not Alvin had written to Theresa since she'd been incarcerated? With another one of her shrugs, Susie answered quite simply, "I don't know what he do on a daily basis."

Scalisi asked her where she had been when she heard the news of Andy's death. She'd been at home; Alvin had called to tell her. As his mother spoke, Alvin made a dramatic show of snatching tissues from a nearby box and dabbing at his eyes. Susie never looked at Alvin.

Then, Sachs rose from his seat for a second round of questioning aimed at Alvin's most valuable witness. What did she think when she learned Alvin and Theresa were getting a divorce? Susie said she was thrilled to death. Sachs asked if Alvin could take care of himself and Susie said, "No." With great fanfare, Alvin snatched another tissue from the box and then another. Susie was dismissed. Her exit was just as mournful as her entrance. The jurors' eyes followed her in a stare of disbelief as she trudged toward the door. She stopped long enough in front of Leroy to claim her purse and her daughter. Together, and much to every spectator's immense relief, the three of them left. Leroy returned, alone, a few minutes later.

The second witness of the day was Alvin's long-time buddy, Richard Crane, a young African-American man who'd known Alvin for more than ten years, almost his entire adult life. Alvin started bawling almost as soon as Richard sat down in the witness chair.

At Sachs' prompting, Richard gave a quick run down of Alvin's work experience and described him as being "slow." Richard testified that Alvin's jobs had been mostly physical and didn't require a lot of mental skills. At

Deadly Thirst

those low paying, menial jobs, Alvin did average work and he required supervision.

Most startling was the fact that even though Richard and Alvin were extremely close friends, Richard had not known about Alvin's plans of marriage until the day before the wedding. He said that almost as soon as they got married, it was apparent that they were having problems and it looked as if Theresa had control over Alvin.

Once more, Alvin yanked a tissue from the box and practically waved it in the air like a white flag of surrender, finally bringing it to his eyes and dabbing. Each time a tissue was snatched from the box, it made a distracting sound which never failed to catch the attention of at least one of the jurors.

Monterosso stood up to address the witness. He got Richard to say that he wasn't aware of the fact that Alvin had taken in two foster children. He hadn't even known about Andy until after Andy died. Monterosso asked Richard if he considered himself to be best friends with Alvin. Richard nodded as he said "yes." Bingo! Monterosso had just shown the jury that Alvin had enough intelligence to withhold upsetting or damaging information from friends and family when he knew they would disagree with him. It was yet another example that showed Alvin's ability to plot, scheme, withhold information and to cover up. Just like the "swollen nuts" question he'd so cleverly phrased to his mom, it showed that Alvin knew the difference between right and wrong. Monterosso had no further questions.

Scalisi did. During grueling cross-examination, he tried to establish violence by Alvin toward Theresa, but Richard denied any knowledge of it. Alvin wasn't that type of guy. Scalisi had nothing further. Richard was excused, but not before Alvin conspicuously snatched and waved another tissue…and then another.

Sachs called the Reverend John Davenport to the stand. He was to be Sachs' shining star—along with Alvin's mother, of course. What finer witness could one have than a man of God? As questioning began, Leroy anxiously perched on the edge of his third-row seat and draped his arms over the empty seat in front of him. He gazed up at the Reverend with pride at having a preacher-man stand in defense of Alvin.

Leroy and the Reverend had no way of knowing how much the Reverend's testimony would irritate Monterosso. But for then, Monterosso just had to sit quietly and let Sachs do his thing.

Sachs gently prompted the Reverend Davenport to describe what he knew about Alvin. In a very soothing and serene voice, coupled with a tranquil expression of confidence, the Reverend floated through the history of his friendship with Alvin. He said much the same things about Alvin's slowness as Richard Crane had said. Reverend Davenport had been a Pentecostal preacher for six years; he'd known Alvin for about seven years. They'd gotten close when Alvin worked in Perris, at Star Crest Products, a warehouse that shipped mail-order novelty items. Alvin had held one of the easiest

274

positions available, that of a stock clerk, but he couldn't do it. So, they made him a "runner" but he couldn't do that job either. Eventually, Alvin quit Star Crest, but he and the Reverend remained friends. The Reverend was also on close terms with Leroy and Susie.

Reverend Davenport admitted that Alvin had asked him to perform the marriage ceremony two days prior to the wedding, but he had declined. He had tried to get Alvin and Theresa to take some counseling first, but Theresa wouldn't have it. And she was the boss. Yes, he said, he knew about Alvin's marital problems. He'd even gone so far as advising Alvin to leave Theresa in the summer of 1999. But Alvin was easily persuaded by Theresa. In spite of the fact that Alvin and the Reverend were close friends, Reverend Davenport was not told about the foster children—not until *after* Andy died. Like everyone else, he was shocked when he learned of the circumstances.

Sachs had nothing further.

Finally it was Monterosso's turn to take a bite out of Reverend Davenport. His first question was a set-up that the Reverend didn't see coming. He asked if Alvin was an honest person. Smiling like a Cheshire Cat, the Reverend purred yes. That seemed to pull the pin on Monterosso's grenade.

In a loud voice, Monterosso demanded to know if having someone else fill out Alvin's employment applications for him didn't show dishonesty? While the Reverend stammered around for an explanation, Monterosso paced the floor. "Well?" Monterosso bellowed impatiently, his hands on his hips. From the spectator seats, Leroy's smug face had slackened and turned sour; his hands balled up into tight, white-knuckled fists.

Finally, having sworn to tell the truth, the Reverend relented that yes, he supposed it did show dishonesty. It was clearly something the Reverend didn't want to say. Upon further grilling, Monterosso got Reverend Davenport to admit that Alvin had told him Theresa had "kicked the boy in the balls." Reverend Davenport tried to clarify that when he'd heard that statement, he hadn't known Alvin and Theresa were foster parents, so he didn't know who "the boy" was. The comment left Monterosso seething.

"Does it matter *who* got kicked in the balls?" But Reverend Davenport tried to explain the kicking statement had been made about a month or so before Andy died. "So what!" Monterosso yelled, "as a man of God, isn't it your duty to be concerned about others?"

Yes, the Reverend mumbled, but he didn't think the kicking was serious. Alvin's attitude didn't convey concern, he said. That statement threw Monterosso into a further fit of yelling. He shouted at the Reverend, who by then had sunken down into his seat, that if *he* had been the one who'd been kicked in the balls, wouldn't he think that was serious?

Well yes, the Reverend blushed, but—

Monterosso cut him off. "Do you deal with abused kids in your ministry?"

Yes, Reverend Davenport said, and then added that if he'd known of any pattern of consistency, he would have called the authorities. Monterosso was gritting his teeth.

"Does there have to be a 'consistent pattern' before you'd notify authorities?" The Reverend's shoulders began to droop when he realized he was in a no-win situation. Monterosso had made a fumbling idiot out of him. Reverend Davenport had done no good whatsoever for Alvin's case, although his intentions had been honorable. He looked foolish, beaten and ashamed. Leroy looked like he was boxing with invisible demons; his fists twitched in tight little punching movements; his head bobbed and swayed to and fro as comments flew back and forth between the Reverend and Monterosso.

"Wasn't Alvin only concerned about his own problems?" Monterosso asked.

The Reverend sidestepped with a defeated sigh. "What mattered to me was that he get out of the relationship." Monterosso had humiliated Reverend Davenport and in the process infuriated Leroy. As the Reverend was dismissed and slunk from the courtroom, Leroy got up and went with him. Outside in the hallway, the Reverend headed for the nearest wooden bench and dropped upon it like the rock of ages. The ordeal was over, thank God. Minutes later, when jurors filed from the courtroom, they saw the Reverend Davenport sitting there with his head in his hands. Next to him sat Leroy, his mouth going a mile a minute.

Tuesday morning, May 29th. Day nine of the trial. The first witness was another friend of Alvin's, Chas White. With the massacred remains of Reverend Davenport still dripping down the walls of the courtroom, Sachs led Chas through a brief background on his relationship with Alvin. Chas testified that he and Alvin had been friends for fifteen years; they had met when they were neighbors and they'd attended the same high school together. Alvin had been in SDC at Valley View High School in Moreno Valley. SDC stood for Special Day Classes for the mentally slow, Chas explained.

Chas admitted that he'd often filled out Alvin's employment applications for him because Alvin didn't understand where to put certain information. Alvin used a cue card his mom had made for him; but, since he couldn't read, he didn't know where to put pertinent information like his social security number and so on. Some of Alvin's jobs required a test and Chas cautiously admitted that he had sometimes taken the test for Alvin. Chas said he always had to drive Alvin to his first day on the job because Alvin couldn't read the street signs.

During Sachs' questioning, he attempted to get Chas to verify Alvin's mental disabilities, but was stopped by constant objections from Monterosso. Judge Schooling cautioned the jury that the opinions of a witness were not fact.

Chas testified that he'd worked with Alvin at Air Force Village West and, in spite of their long friendship, he'd only found out about Alvin's wedding on the very day of the wedding. Furthermore, he'd never met Theresa before Alvin married her. Even after the marriage, he had only seen Theresa four times and each time she was definitely the one in control. Sachs asked Chas to describe the relationship between Alvin and Theresa.

"He's quiet; she's calling the shots," Chas said.

Several times during Chas' testimony, Alvin made yet another noisy display of snatching tissues from the box. In exaggerated movements, he'd pull one tissue out, wave it high into the air, and then yank another from the box. Theresa hadn't yet reached for the tissues and continued to sit like a slab of granite next to Scalisi.

Chas testified that he'd had no idea Alvin was even considering becoming a foster parent. After he got the kids, Alvin acted like a big brother to them. Chas had seen Theresa yell at Andy, but not Alvin. He'd also seen her grab Andy in a rough manner. Alvin avoided conflict, Chas said, he would just leave whenever an argument erupted. Sometimes Alvin slept in his car in front of Chas' house. Chas admitted that Alvin wasn't real keen on dealing with Andy's potty problems.

"He asked me to go with Andy to the bathroom and wipe his butt," Chas said. As Alvin dabbed his eyes with a wad of tissues, Sachs said he had nothing further.

Finally, Monterosso got his chance to question Chas about Alvin's slowness. Chas reluctantly admitted that Alvin knew better than to let the kids run into the street.

He also knew that he had to put Andy in a car seat. Right?

Well, yes but--

"Then Alvin *did* have parental instinct about protecting a child, didn't he?"

Chas admitted that Alvin did, but...

"I have nothing further your honor."

Scalisi asked Chas if he was concerned about Alvin's drinking. Chas said yes, that sometimes he'd drive Alvin's truck home when Alvin was too drunk to drive. Finally, Chas was dismissed and managed a weak smile to Alvin as he snailed past the counsel table and out of the courtroom. Alvin lunged for another tissue.

Alvin was called to the witness stand as the day's second witness. When Alvin was asked to raise his right hand and swear to tell the truth, he didn't seem to have trouble figuring out which hand was the one he was supposed to raise. There would be many such giveaways on Alvin's part, but whether or not the jury noticed any of them would remain a mystery until the bitter end.

Alvin spoke in such a low mumble it was almost inaudible. Judge Schooling instructed Alvin to sit closer to the microphone, speak up and turn more toward the jury. Right off the bat, Sachs had Alvin tell the jury about his intellectual abilities, or rather, the lack thereof.

Deadly Thirst

"I have a learning disability," Alvin said. He testified that he'd taken special education classes at Valley View High School and that he'd graduated in 1992, some nine years prior. Alvin couldn't remember ever having been evaluated by a mental health expert. Throughout his testimony, Alvin would express an inability to remember many things. Contrary to that, other times he expressed confidence in his ability to remember certain things that had happened long ago. "I can copy some things down," he said of his writing abilities, but added that he couldn't read a newspaper. He tried to write a letter once, "...but the words was all misspelled."

Sachs led Alvin through his years of employment and Alvin testified to having had several jobs, mostly clean-up work. He spoke of his reasons for quitting Star Crest, Air Force Village West and Green River. Even though he'd tried to hide his illiteracy, his co-workers always had found out and ridiculed him for it. Alvin said he'd quit because people were teasing him. "I couldn't deal with it, so I just left." He said he never went alone to fill out a job application because about all he could do was sign his name. On the overhead monitor, Sachs put a copy of the sign-in sheet from one of the foster parenting classes. He asked Alvin if he recognized the document. Alvin said no; he couldn't read anything.

Sachs was laying the groundwork against Monterosso's expected claim that Alvin could read and write because he'd filled out the sign-in sheet for foster parenting class. Theresa's handwriting was unmistakable, round and large. Alvin's handwriting was stunted. It was obvious Alvin was the one who'd signed them both in for that particular class. Sachs asked Alvin if he was the one who'd put a "3" in the proper column. Yeah, Alvin said, he'd put the three there, but only because everyone else had put a "3" in that column. "FFH" was in all the other columns, so he wrote "FFH" too, although he didn't know what it meant. He didn't know what he was signing. Sachs asked Alvin if he could recognize Theresa's handwriting and Alvin said yes.

Alvin looked tired and forlorn, his eyes puffy. He used the same poor grammar his mother had used while she was on the stand. Periodically, he snatched a tissue from the box on the railing and dabbed at his eyes in spite of the fact that they appeared to be as dry as the Sahara. Still, he spoke so softly several of the jurors leaned forward and squinted in their efforts to hear him. Yeah, he said, he'd gotten a CPR certificate in class, but he didn't know what it was for. Yeah, he recalled telling investigators [two years prior] that he knew CPR, but he didn't know why he'd lied about it. He "didn't have no idea" what CPR was, let alone how to do it.

Sachs led Alvin through the incident that happened in 1997, when he'd kicked the stereo and the police were called. Yeah, he 'membered one time when the cops was called, but he couldn't 'member nothin' else. Then Alvin blurted out that he did not break the stereo; but he had agreed to take the rap for it because he'd wanted so desperately to get out of jail and go home.

Donna Goodenough

His recall of an incident that happened in 1998 was somewhat better. In that incident, a car window had been broken and Alvin testified with confidence that Theresa had broken it. He admitted to going to nightclubs with his buddies. Even after he married Theresa, he had kept up that behavior. Even after his marriage, he'd often spent the night with his parents. With emotion pulling down the corners of his mouth, he snatched another hanky from the box and dabbed at his eyes.

"She'd just throw me out," he whimpered. He had depended on Theresa to take care of him because he couldn't take care of himself. He had decided to marry her "cause she wanted to. I wanted to make her happy." Alvin said he didn't know what a restraining order was, but confessed that he continued living with Theresa even after the restraining order was filed. No one had explained it to him. He testified that he got back together with Theresa because she'd promised him sex. Theresa was domineering and she would take his whole paycheck, stickin' him with only fifteen or twenty bucks a week. The recall of that particular problem caused Alvin to hang his head with shame.

Sachs prompted Alvin to discuss his reasons for becoming a foster parent, asking him if he knew all that was involved in caring for a child. Alvin answered the question by insisting that he couldn't even take care of himself. "I told her I didn't want to do it, but she start fussin' with me, so I say, 'Okay whatever you want.' I was scared of her because of the way she do me."

Alvin testified that he never told his folks about his foster parenting plans. He hadn't attended all of the required classes; he was sure he'd missed some, although he couldn't remember which ones he'd missed. He stated that he had never studied for the foster parenting classes and he hadn't paid attention in class. Sometimes he had just signed in and then left, because he hadn't understood what was going on. Sometimes he'd hung out in the bathroom, or gone to see Chas. And besides, he said, Theresa took care of everything. Alvin testified he "had no idea of what being a foster parent meant. I didn't know what I was supposed to do." Theresa had told him that she would be taking care of the kids. He hadn't even known who his social worker was. "Theresa take care of all that." No, he never disciplined the kids, "That was Theresa's thing," he said. Alvin adamantly denied that he had ever spanked Andy and said he'd lied to the police about whipping Andy with a belt. He claimed that Theresa forced him to lie about it "'cause she told me to lie."

Alvin told the jury that he was never at home when social services paid a visit because Theresa had told him it didn't concern him. She wanted him to be gone when the social worker came by.

In spite of the fact that Alvin had trouble remembering many things that happened around the time of Andy's death, he was absolutely certain that he'd seen Theresa kick Andy in his crotch twice. "I says, 'Why you kick him?' and she say, 'Mind your own business.'" On the witness stand, he denied having seen Andy's swollen scrotum and then immediately blurted "It wasn't as swollen as it was in the picture, but it was swollen." Goof-ups like that were a problem for Sachs, who was doing his best to steer Alvin on a good course and curb his wildly flapping tongue. Once Alvin opened his mouth and stuck his foot into it, there was nothing Sachs could do to erase what had been said. However, that was okay because Sachs was striving to show the jury just how stupid and dominated Alvin was. So, if Alvin stepped on his own credibility it would only reinforce the theory of his ignorance. Or so Sachs hoped.

Alvin claimed he wasn't intrusive in the relationship he had with Theresa. "I mind my own business," he said. Yeah, he'd seen Andy's bleeding penis, but he couldn't remember when he'd seen it.

There was something else that Sachs wanted Alvin to clarify in his own words. About the icepack advice he'd gotten from his mom: who's idea had it been to call Susie? Alvin said it had been Theresa's idea. "Theresa tell me, 'Don't say nothin'.'" So, they'd fixed up an icepack and told Andy to "hold it on his pee-pee." In spite of the fact that he'd earlier testified he hadn't seen Andy's swollen scrotum, Alvin now said that the swelling had gone down with the application of the ice. Would the jurors see how contradictory Alvin's testimony was? Would it matter? It was almost lunchtime and the jurors were beginning to get distracted by hunger and the need to use the restroom. Some were avid clock-watchers. All wore blank faces.

Alvin admitted that he had witnessed Theresa making Andy eat his own poop. He said he'd tried to intervene, but Theresa had told him to mind his own business. "Anytime anything happen, she tell me to mind my own business. I told him to spit it out, then I left." Alvin didn't like having to recall the abuse, but what really broke Alvin up was when he recounted how Theresa had taken his money. "She took my whole paycheck, man." With that, the floodgates burst. His hand reached over to the tissue box and once more the old familiar sounds of tissues being pulled from the box, one after another, resonated throughout the courtroom. He began to wail. "She tell me that the reason she be doing all that was because it be all my fault. So I left."

Alvin said he hadn't thought Theresa was committing a crime when she abused Andy. He had thought the abuse would simply stop if he left. He was adamant in saying he didn't think what had happened to Andy was his [Alvin's] fault. He testified that he had never seen Andy pee or poop on himself. When Andy had "pooped his self" at Theresa's workplace, Alvin said he knew what Andy had done "'cause I smelled it."

Alvin admitted it was true that they'd talked about divorce and yes, he'd signed some divorce papers; but in the next breath he said he hadn't understood what he was signing.

On the last evening of Andy's life, a Sunday, Alvin testified that he came home around 9:30 P.M. after Jacob had already gone to sleep. Andy was in a sleeping bag at the foot of their bed which wasn't unusual. Alvin said that

Andy was being kept away from Jacob because Theresa didn't want Jacob to see Andy's swollen testicles. As a photo of the bedroom was put on the overhead projector, Alvin recounted how he'd been awakened by Theresa's yelling at Andy for drinking water.

"I just remember her leaning over me and knocking the water out of his hand." Then she had told Andy to get on his chair. "He was crying," Alvin said, "then she pushed him in his stomach area with her foot. He hit his head on the nightstand and he didn't get back up." Sachs put another photo on the projector of Alvin demonstrating how Theresa had kicked Andy. Once more Alvin began to cry. "It happened so fast," he blubbered, reaching for more tissues. He was absolutely certain that he'd never yelled at Andy that night. "I'm positive," he said. He'd never raised his voice at Andy and he hadn't been upset that Andy was drinking water. But Theresa had been *very* upset about it. Still, he hadn't done anything to stop her from kicking or pushing Andy. He hadn't given a thought to his responsibilities as a foster parent. He said Theresa had told him to call 911 and say they'd found Andy outside. "I can't think of nothin' that fast." Theresa had admonished him not to say anything to paramedics or firemen or anyone else. Don't say nothin' to nobody. Finally, Alvin admitted that he'd changed his story and had confessed to police "'cause they told me nothin' would happen to me."

At that point in testimony, court adjourned for the noon lunch break. After the jurors left, Alvin's hands, stuffed full of dry tissues, were cuffed by Deputy Sanderson and, he was led away.

Once court proceedings got underway again in the afternoon, the first question Sachs chose to ask Alvin was why hadn't he left Theresa?

Sachs wasn't merely an attorney going through the motions with his client; it was undoubtedly more than that. It was real, tangible sincerity. You could see Sachs' genuine compassion for Alvin. He seemed to forget that there was a room full of very important people hanging on Alvin's every word. At times, it was as if the two of them, Alvin and Sachs, were talking confidentially about what really happened. It wasn't a show. At least not on Sachs' part.

Alvin's testimony was disjointed, often contradictory. He'd say one thing then turn right around and say the opposite. Sachs would offer a weak smile as if he understood and sympathized with Alvin's two-sided testimony. Some at the counsel table scoffed at Sachs' inability to control his client, but Sachs knew Alvin's fate wasn't in the hands of anyone at the counsel table. Alvin's jury was made up of people unfamiliar with law and courtroom tactics. They weren't privy to any behind-the-scenes arguing that had gone on in months past. They were ordinary citizens who were quite capable of being emotionally swayed and Sachs knew it. Let Alvin trip over his own tongue; what was said was said. In the aftermath of Alvin's verbal assaults upon himself, Sachs would look at Alvin with a combination of fondness and great pity for his shortcomings. As Alvin gave Sachs sour lemons, Sachs made sweet lemonade out of them. And very convincingly. From the looks of things, the jurors were not angry or appalled at anything Alvin was saying. Many of them were wearing the telltale signs of sympathy on their faces. For the prosecution, it wasn't a good sign.

After a few moments of studying his notes, Sachs took up where he had left off. Why hadn't Alvin left Theresa?

"I thought I loved her," Alvin said.

About that October 18th interview with investigator Harding, Sachs asked, had Harding promised Alvin anything? Yeah, Alvin said, he'd been promised that he wouldn't be charged if he testified against Theresa.

Horst was obviously angered by Alvin's declaration of promised immunity, but he managed to keep his facial expressions blank. His message, however, was loud and clear. His face had reddened with anger. He leaned toward Monterosso and the two men conferred with their heads together.

Alvin said he'd never been told that anything he said could be used against him. And for all the jury knew, that was the truth. Nowhere on any of the tapes had anyone read Alvin his Miranda rights, but he hadn't been under arrest during those tapes, nor was his arrest imminent. Harding had specifically told Alvin that he was free to go at any time during the questioning and that he wasn't under arrest at that time. The arrest had come days later.

Long after the trial was over, Harding would have plenty to say about Alvin's claim that he'd been tricked into self-incrimination. "If you're not going to interview the crook after you arrest him, you don't have to advise him of his rights," Harding said. "If you want to interview him and he's *not* in custody, you have to make it very clear that he is not in custody, does *not* have to talk to you and is free to leave at any time." And that's exactly what Harding and Horst had done with Alvin. "If you do that and the idiot is stupid enough to admit to whatever, you can still arrest him on the spot and it will stand up in court."

In his initial interview with Horst and again during the polygraph with Williams, Alvin had clearly been anxious to rat on Theresa and to help investigators in convicting her. Although Alvin didn't realize it, he was equally guilty and should have laid low as Leroy had advised him to do. As a result, Alvin had snared himself in the trap he was trying to set for Theresa. Still, some of the jurors may not have known the law regarding when Miranda rights are supposed to be read and they may very well have thought that Alvin had, indeed, been bamboozled.

The seed of doubt had been planted—and watered. And the jury would be instructed that, when in doubt, they had to decide in favor of the defendant. If anyone on the jury was confused about when a person's Miranda rights are supposed to be read—if at all—it could come back to haunt the prosecution. After all, when Alvin did the initial interview with Horst and later did the polygraph with Williams, his Miranda rights were never read to him on tape and he was not under the guidance of a lawyer. He was on his own and that was all the jury saw. Sachs had brought up a good point.

Williams merely got Alvin to sign a form stating that he understood that he did not have to take the polygraph and that he understood, as far as the polygraph was concerned, there was no promise of immunity. In fact, Williams had made it easy for Alvin to understand what he was signing by rephrasing it to simpler language.

Williams had said, "no one ever said to you that no matter what you said that they were not going to prosecute you." Alvin agreed that no one had told him that. But still, as ignorant as Alvin was, he could have easily been confused and only understood it as an assurance that no matter what he said he wouldn't be prosecuted for it.

Horst and Monterosso leaned toward each other and whispered a few words back and forth, then drew apart, silent. For the time being, they'd have to sit there with their mouths shut. The promised immunity issue was such a problem that Monterosso would have to recall one or two of his witnesses to straighten it out.

One item at a time, Sachs methodically chipped away at everything Alvin had admitted to on the tapes. He knew, quite feasibly, the jury could decide Alvin's fate based on the testimony that rang loudest in their ears and tugged the hardest on their emotions. Yes, there was a dead child, but here was this poor, confused man—trapped by a mental deficiency, suffering from an inability to reason and to know right from wrong. Perhaps some of the jurors had mentally challenged children of their own. Who knew? Perhaps their work involved caring for the mentally challenged. Questions pertaining to the jurors' experience with people who were mentally handicapped were completely lacking in the voir dire questionnaire. Until then, it had never seemed necessary to ask. In Monterosso's opinion, it had been ludicrous to think that any of the jurors would fall for the theory that Alvin was even mildly retarded.

As Alvin continued his testimony, he said he didn't know that giving Andy cold showers could send him into shock. At the time Andy lived with him, he didn't know he had a responsibility to protect him and even now he didn't understand why he was being charged with Andy's death. After all, he hadn't done nothin' to Andy; Theresa done it all.

Finally, Sachs said he had nothing further and slumped into his seat, wearing a look of great emotional distress. He looked up at Alvin on the witness stand and smiled a sad, fatherly grin. Then Sachs shook his head and seemed to glower at the supposed injustice of having a man such as Alvin try to speak on his own behalf.

Monterosso rose from his chair with his usual self-assuredness. Right away, he blasted Alvin about his self-centered sexual expectations the night Theresa paged him to come home. Alvin had rushed to the apartment with a mouth-watering anticipation of sex, right? Alvin began to stammer as Monterosso continued to pelt him with rapid-fire questions. After he'd ar-

Deadly Thirst

rived at the apartment, he'd found out that Theresa hadn't called him for sex. "She told you that she'd grabbed Andy's penis and had pulled on it, causing it to bleed, isn't that right?" Alvin agreed and admitted that he had seen the bleeding, but they had chosen not to seek medical attention for Andy. Monterosso asked Alvin if administering to Andy's needs was the reason he'd returned to the apartment. Alvin said he'd come back because Theresa had asked him to come. Then, Monterosso switched gears.

"What is abuse?" he asked with his hands on his hips.

"It's doing something bad to him," Alvin said, clearly intimidated by Monterosso's aggressive style of questioning. Alvin insisted he didn't know it was dangerous or wrong to kick a small boy in the testicles. Alvin never thought he'd get in trouble for Andy's injuries, especially his death.

Monterosso refreshed Alvin's memory about the taped interview he had done with Horst the afternoon Andy died. Reading from the transcript of that interview, Monterosso made it clear that in the moments prior to his confession about what had really happened, Alvin repeatedly asked if he'd go to jail. Because he knew that he'd done wrong. Monterosso demanded an explanation. Did Alvin *now* remember asking over and over if he would go to jail?

"Well yeah," Alvin stammered, "but—"

"Well, did you have a revelation from heaven or something that helped you remember?"

"I didn't know Andy was getting injured."

"On the tape," Monterosso hollered, thumping the transcript, "didn't you say you'd pulled down Andy's pants and seen his injuries?" Yeah, Alvin admitted, he'd seen Andy's injuries, but then he left, figuring that if he left, Theresa would get Andy to the doctor. The jurors watched as Alvin's hand reached for the tissues again.

"Every time Theresa do something to one of the kids, I'd leave," Alvin said in a quivering voice.

Monterosso reminded Alvin that he'd testified he would leave whenever Theresa did something to *him*. So, which was it? The jury was wide-awake now.

Alvin stammered that he left because of what was happening to "the baby" and was quick to add that his memory wasn't that good. But, Monterosso had an excellent memory and, just in case anyone on the jury had forgotten, Monterosso read a quote from the August 2nd Horst interview transcript. Alvin had said that he'd left "'cause I knew if I didn't, they were gong to fall on me," meaning the charges. Taking it one step further, Monterosso flipped to the part of the interview of October 18th where Investigator Harding had asked Alvin "Why in the hell didn't you call someone?" To which Alvin replied, "I don't know. I don't want nothin' to happen to me." Monterosso turned toward the jurors and repeated the words again, slowly, letting the comment hang in the air like a foul odor.

284

Monterosso walked over to a cabinet on the far side of the courtroom and grabbed a little blue chair: exhibit #1. Holding it high above his head as he walked back to the center of the courtroom, he practically taunted Alvin with it.

"So," Monterosso snarled, "you didn't think swollen balls were serious enough to call 911, but you called 911 twice when your car was being damaged?" The heads of the jurors were going back and forth from left to right as if they were watching a tennis match. With every answer from Alvin, they looked toward Monterosso for his comment. Then back to Alvin. The jury was riveted—totally focused.

Cautiously eyeballing the chair, Alvin timidly said that he'd thought auto damage was more important than getting kicked in the balls. He hadn't known getting kicked in the balls was bad until Sachs told him so. "Mr. Sachs told me it was bad."

Monterosso was fuming mad; Horst was even madder. Both men were quaking. The air was electric with tension. Monterosso sat the chair on the floor in front of Alvin, who was clearly unnerved by the sight of it, and switched his questioning. Pointing to the chair, Monterosso wanted to talk about what happened immediately after Andy had been kicked off the chair. What was Alvin's first reaction when he'd seen that Andy was unconscious.?

"My first instinct was to run," Alvin said. Monterosso waved him off, but Alvin kept talking. "I can't help myself, how could I help him?" He'd wanted to run, but Theresa wouldn't let him. "Theresa wouldn't let me run. Theresa say for me to be a man now and call 911. And I says 'You call; you're the one that fucked up.'" Alvin further stated that his thoughts of flight were only for Andy's welfare. "I thought if I left, Theresa would give Andy the help he needed." Monterosso commented about Alvin's ability to dial 911 on that particular night, so, why hadn't he called before things got so out of control? Alvin was quick to downplay it by saying Theresa had been standing right next to him when he'd dialed.

Throughout Monterosso's cross-examination, Alvin seemed to selectively revert to statements of, "I don't know" or "I don't understand."

Monterosso seared Alvin with questions about his marital problems. Things were bad, weren't they? Yeah, Alvin admitted. Monterosso chided him saying the marital problems were serious enough for him to complain to his friends and his parents about them, but Andy's problems weren't important enough to mention to anyone. Right? Alvin was practically cowering behind the wooden railing that surrounded the witness stand. He often spoke into his lap.

Once more, Judge Schooling had to remind Alvin to speak up and turn toward the jury. Alvin testified again that he always did what Theresa told him to do. But Monterosso mocked him and showed the jury how Alvin chose to obey Theresa sometimes; but, in spite of his insistence that he was scared to death of her, he often ignored her orders and did as he pleased.

Deadly Thirst

Monterosso reminded Alvin that he had boasted he'd been clever with hiding his sexual infidelities. An angry Alvin glowered down at Monterosso, but it was too late. Monterosso had nothing further.

Scalisi had a few questions for Alvin. He put a handwritten letter on the overhead projector and asked Alvin if he recognized it. Alvin said the handwriting wasn't his and he couldn't read any of it. Scalisi was trying to ascertain whether or not the letter had come from Alvin. Judge Schooling interjected at this point and clarified for the jury that Alvin could be the author of the letter even if he hadn't actually written it himself. It didn't matter; Alvin didn't remember or recognize the letter. Scalisi performed some crafty handwriting analysis in front of the jury by comparing the letter with other signatures and written documents. Through it all, Alvin insisted he couldn't read or write so, Scalisi switched gears.

"Now," he said, "about that restraining order Theresa filed while you were living with her at the 6th Street apartment…"

Alvin claimed he didn't know nothin' 'bout no restraining order, but Scalisi didn't let up. Scalisi wanted to know if Alvin had cut the phone lines which had led to him being arrested for vandalism. Alvin couldn't remember. With further prodding, Alvin admitted that he was arrested, yeah, and taken to jail. And yeah, he pled guilty to vandalism. But he couldn't remember nothin' else. "She's a smart one," Alvin said, wagging his finger at Theresa. "She know how to do stuff." Alvin denied ever damaging any property in a fit of rage, or otherwise. But Scalisi had photographic evidence which proved the opposite. Another photo was angrily slapped onto the overhead projector. It showed a close-up of the bedroom door at 216 East 6th Street, the bedroom where Andy was fatally injured. Scalisi zoomed in on the doorknob area and pointed to it with a pen. The door showed obvious damage, but Alvin said he didn't know nothin' 'bout that. Nor did he know about any marks on the bedroom wall that were made when he allegedly threw an alarm clock at Theresa.

Scalisi asked Alvin how Theresa had injured her knee and Alvin said she'd hurt herself "fighting with some girl." Scalisi was trying to establish Alvin's propensity for violence, especially when he was drunk or mad. But Alvin denied it all. His memory seemed sharp. He did admit that he had a problem with drinking too much alcohol, but immediately contradicted himself and said he didn't have a drinking problem.

The pager was another thing Scalisi brought up. It had a printed message. Could Alvin read his pager messages? Yeah, but—

Scalisi jumped to another subject. On the night Andy was attacked for the last time, who was sleeping closest to Andy's time-out chair? Alvin said he was, but insisted that he'd never hurt Andy.

"I never done nothin' to that boy! I couldn't have reached that chair."

"Oh," Scalisi scoffed, "so you couldn't reach it huh? You were closest to it, but your claim is that Theresa reached over you and kicked Andy off the chair? Is that right?"

Quick on his feet, Scalisi barked another question. Jacob had testified that he heard *Alvin* yelling at Andy the night of the attack, not Theresa. Alvin admitted, under constant pressure from Scalisi, that it was possible that Jacob could have heard him yelling at Andy to shut up. Alvin was slouching again, hunkered down in his chair. Once more, Judge Schooling told Alvin to speak up and turn toward the jury.

Scalisi kept the heat on. He reminded Alvin that he'd already testified that he'd done nothing wrong and yet his first instinct was to run. Why?

"Every time she'd do somethin' to Andy, I'd leave."

Not long after that, Scalisi said he had nothing further and took his seat beside Theresa. She immediately began whispering in his ear.

Sachs had a few things he wanted Alvin to explain. He asked Alvin why he'd left the house the first time he'd seen Andy get kicked in the groin. Alvin said he'd left because he hadn't known what else to do.

Sachs asked Alvin if he and Theresa were still married and Alvin said he didn't know. Sachs paused, looking as though he needed a moment to collect his thoughts. He seemed to be pondering Alvin's last answer. How sad it was that Alvin didn't even know whether or not he was married. There was a long silence in the courtroom. The truth was, at the time of the trial, they were still married. Theresa would eventually file, from jail, a Dissolution of Marriage Without Children form on August 10, 2001. The papers would be returned to Theresa on October 23, classified as "un-served."

Sachs asked Alvin to describe how he felt about Andy. Alvin shrugged and said he "felt like Andy was a cousin or somethin'." Alvin didn't remember Andy having a toilet-training problem, but he did remember the exact position of the time-out chair on that fateful, deadly night. He testified that he did not know what "obligation" meant.

Body language was doing a lot of testifying in Department 61 during the trial of Alvin and Theresa. Horst was beside himself with anger and Sachs was not behaving like a typical lawyer. Sachs behaved like someone who knew, for a fact, that Alvin truly did not understand what the heck was going on. Sachs seemed frustrated, almost to the point of tears. He was not merely defending Alvin, he appeared to be genuinely concerned for a very unfortunate, gentle giant.

Time was dragging, not just for Alvin, but for the jurors as well. By then the trial was going into its eleventh day, much longer than anyone had expected. Judge Schooling was concerned about the hardship it was placing on some of the jurors and was careful to compliment them on the excellent job they were doing. He said he doubted that he'd ever seen a more attentive group of jurors.

Court was adjourned until 9:30 the following morning. The jurors filed out. Alvin was handcuffed and stumbled from the witness stand clutching a large wad of tissues.

At 9:45 A.M. Alvin returned to the witness stand. Still dressed in the same clothes he'd worn the previous day and the day before that, Alvin looked rested, but bewildered. Sachs looked absolutely frazzled. He looked like he'd slept in his jacket with the leather elbow patches.

Schooling began the day's proceedings with a polite greeting and thanks to the juries. Monterosso also took a moment to thank the jurors before he proceeded with the questioning. Alvin seemed to start the day in a clear state of mind, saying he'd never said nothin' that had been recorded on paper by Social Services. He was positive about it. But then, in response to many other questions, he lapsed into a fatigued repetition of "I don't know" or "I don't understand." Monterosso questioned Alvin as to whether or not he had assumed that Theresa would kick Andy. After all, Monterosso reasoned, that was her favorite form of discipline, right? No, Alvin insisted that he hadn't thought nothin', he had just wanted to get back to sleep. Alvin said he'd never wanted to be a foster parent because, "I can't even take care of myself."

"But you do know what it means to be a foster parent?"

"Yeah," he said. But then, on an afterthought, he changed his answer to "No. I don't know what that means."

"Did Andy call you 'Daddy'?"

"Yeah," Alvin said.

"Well then," Monterosso sneered, "you're saying you don't even know what being a daddy means?"

"I wasn't thinkin' at that time," Alvin stammered. Besides, just 'cause Andy had called him Daddy, it didn't make him feel like he had any responsibility toward the kid.

Monterosso was already disgusted and abruptly stopped his questioning. The jury looked perplexed. He seemed to have aborted his questioning in mid-stream.

Scalisi asked Alvin if he'd pled guilty to vandalism in Perris in November of 1997. Alvin admitted that he had. He remembered the circumstances of the arrest very well, although it had happened almost four years prior. Scalisi held up a document where Alvin had initialed each of his rights and written the word "guilty." Alvin denied writing the word "guilty" because, he said, he couldn't spell it. When Scalisi questioned him as to whether or not he'd read the document, Alvin said no, because he couldn't read. However, his often-blank memory was as sharp as a tack on that particular incident; he absolutely did not write the word "guilty." He was absolutely sure of it. Alvin also was crystal clear about his sleeping position on that night, almost two years prior, when Andy was attacked for the last time. Alvin vividly recalled how he'd been sleeping on his back when Theresa leaned over him to knock the jug of water out of Andy's hands. He was absolutely certain that Theresa had used her right arm to reach out and whack the jug. He recalled that the bedroom door had been closed, but insisted that he could not have reached the chair even though he'd been the person sleeping closest to it at the time of the attack. His explanation seemed rehearsed. Right arm, left arm—who would remember such trivial things when they're awakened from a sound sleep?

Scalisi was trying to show the jury that it was Alvin who had administered the fatal blows to Andy. Jacob's testimony, about hearing only Alvin yelling, was compelling evidence that it was actually Alvin, not Theresa, who'd killed Andy. As Scalisi put a photo of the kitchen on the overhead projector, he was sharp to point out that the jug had somehow traveled from the bedroom to the kitchen. How? Alvin had no answer. Scalisi magnified the photo. Pointing with a pen to the gallon jug sitting to the right of the sink, he again asked Alvin, rather sarcastically, how it had gotten there.

"Did it grow legs and walk?" Alvin didn't know; he didn't even remember any water being spilled on the floor. But he did remember that the square, gallon jug in the photo was not the jug in question. He was sure. Scalisi had nothing further.

Sachs rose from his chair as if he were ninety years old. He searched the counsel table for the "rights" document Scalisi had used and slapped it onto the overhead projector again. He asked Alvin if he had known what he was signing.

"No," Alvin said. They'd told him to sign, so he had signed. Sachs slammed his papers on the counsel table and became visibly upset. Anger radiated from his body and the jury seemed to be alarmed. Sachs got Alvin to talk about how Theresa had ordered him to leave the house whenever anyone from Social Services was expected. Sachs then asked Alvin what he thought he was supposed to do with a little kid Andy's age.

Alvin said, "I thought I should play with him."

Sachs had nothing further. He stalked over to his chair and threw himself into it. From his pocket he pulled a peppermint candy, un-wrapped it and popped it into his mouth. His voice was getting pretty raspy.

Monterosso had only one question: if Alvin was so sure the jug on the kitchen counter wasn't the jug in question, what had happened to the jug Andy had been drinking from? Huh?

Alvin said he couldn't remember.

Scalisi asked Alvin if he knew what "released on own recognizance" meant and Alvin said yeah, but he never knew why he had been arrested in 1997, or what the charges were. He also denied knowing what the word "victim" meant. Alvin said he never made any decisions concerning the kids. Scalisi was quick to remind him that his own statements indicated he frequently babysat the kids. He took them to the park, to Mount Lakes Resort, Lake Elsinore, the auto accessory shop, Carl's Jr., and a slew of other places. Scalisi grilled Alvin mercilessly, with hawk-like precision questioning, about his interactions with the children, but Alvin held firm. Contrary to what he'd stated about having taken the boys to Lake Elsinore two days prior to Andy's death, Alvin denied knowing anything about any danger associated with allowing small children to venture too close to the water. He

Deadly Thirst

testified that he didn't know what "danger" meant. Scalisi and Monterosso smirked.

Then, Scalisi asked who had taken care of the kids while Theresa had worked at the weight clinic. Alvin said he had. Perfect! Scalisi had lead Alvin right into his own trap.

"So," Scalisi snarled, pointing his finger at Alvin, "*you'd* be responsible for taking care of the boys, right?"

"I don't understand," Alvin said. However, under Scalisi's relentless questioning, Alvin admitted that he did recall taking care of the boys on at least two occasions, but insisted that he had never made any decisions whatsoever. "I don't make decisions at all."

Scalisi had nothing further. As he headed for his seat beside Theresa, his eyes swept the juror' faces. There was no emotion to be seen there. Poker faces, every one of them. Some were looking at the clock. If the jury had doubted Alvin's testimony, they would have been looking toward Alvin, not at Scalisi. It troubled everyone at the counsel table. Alvin had indeed made a pitiful spectacle of himself.

Alvin was dismissed from the witness stand, but his mental state lingered. As he resumed his seat at the counsel table, Sachs smiled understandingly and patted him on the shoulder. Sachs called Doctor Michael Kania to the stand.

Kania, a clinical forensic psychologist, had been hired by the defense to evaluate Alvin. Monterosso fought tooth and nail to have Kania excluded as a witness, or at least to prohibit his testimony about Alvin's mental capabilities. As the doctor strode to the stand and took the oath, Monterosso and Horst sat side by side, apprehensively staring at him. Scalisi was still busy listening to a barrage of information that was being whispered in his left ear by Theresa. He took notes as fast as his hand would move.

As usual, Sachs chose to glue himself to the wooden podium as he questioned Kania. Flipping through several pages of notes scribbled on a yellow legal pad, he began by asking the doctor to tell the jurors, in simple terms, what he does for a living.

Kania explained in a soothing voice that he was trained in evaluating the mental processes of people and he'd received his bachelor's degree at Cal State Fullerton in California. He was a clinical psychologist at Patton State Hospital and had been licensed since 1980. He explained that a clinical psychologist is trained to understand why people behave as they do. The term "forensic" relates to how psychology and the law interact. It was his job to determine if the person was able to understand.

Monterosso was perched on the edge of his seat waiting to object. More than any other witness expected to testify, it was Kania who Monterosso was most concerned with. Kania spoke in a soft, lilting voice typical of psychologists, which grated on Monterosso's nerves. He recited his long, glowing list of accomplishments and qualifications, smiling and looking directly at the jury while he spoke.

290

Kania testified that he had reviewed the facts of the case and had seen some school records and assessments from Alabama and Moreno Valley. He'd met with Alvin in jail and had gotten a thorough idea of what his life had been like. He had taken extensive notes on Alvin's demeanor, speech and language. He had given Alvin an I.Q. test and had questioned him about the arrest and his role as a foster parent.

About that I.Q. test, Sachs asked, did it seem as if Alvin understood the questions?

Kania said he had to simplify many of the questions for Alvin and often had to repeat the questions several times. "He had a tendency to say he 'didn't know.'" Kania stated that he'd tested Alvin with the Wechsler Adult Intelligence Scale which indicated that Alvin could read at a third grade level. He had scored Alvin, verbally, at 67 and had given him a performance level of 68. Alvin's full scale I.Q was only 66, which meant, he concluded, that Alvin was suffering from mild mental retardation. Kania testified that Alvin suffered from a mental defect. The overall population routinely falls into the 90-100 range and only one percent of the population falls into the range which Alvin was part of. In fact, he said, fewer than one percent of the population falls into the 66 range where Alvin ranked.

"He would be one of the lowest people to understand things," Kania said, throwing Alvin a fatherly glance. Sachs asked what Alvin's overall function was. Kania stated that he functioned at the same level as that of an eight or ten-year-old child. The doctor agreed that Alvin had scored a dismally low score overall. "He's logical at a very basic level," he said. "For example, he doesn't see the whole picture. He doesn't understand details."

Monterosso objected. Sustained.

Alvin had been ridiculed and teased as a young child, Kania said, and had always tried to hide his mental incompleteness. "People like Alvin, understand that they *don't* understand."

Kania kept his eyes on Sachs, the jury, or Alvin. He never looked at the prosecution. It was common, he said, for people like Alvin to have a dependant personality. "He'll back down if someone yells at him," Kania said. His coping skills were shallow too. In fact, his relationship with Theresa was typical of his behavior. He was the submissive one. "He avoids situations of conflict and he demonstrated no parenting skills. He didn't understand his parenting responsibilities—"

Monterosso voiced an objection to that statement. Sustained.

When the doctor continued, he stated that Alvin thought his role was to play games with the children. Monterosso quickly cut in with another objection, stating that Kania wasn't allowed to testify to what Alvin was thinking. Showing slight agitation, Kania revised his statement, enunciating each word in a prissy sort of way. "He has a tendency to be agreeable so as not to let on that he doesn't understand. He doesn't anticipate any kind of consequence. He—"

Deadly Thirst

There was another objection from Monterosso, this one done with a smirk. Again, Judge Schooling sustained it. Kania's eyelids fluttered in exasperation. Sachs too was irritated by Monterosso's constant objections and asked the doctor to rephrase his answer...again.

"He doesn't see the big picture. He was shown three pictures of someone building a house: the foundation, the framing, and the painting and he couldn't put the pictures in order. He doesn't understand that he may have—"

After yet another objection from Monterosso, Judge Schooling decided that it would be a good time to break for lunch. A little early, but the jurors were obviously antsy. Some had been fidgeting and eyeing the clock for the past half hour or so.

Soon after court was called back into session at 1:30, Monterosso began to question Kania. Monterosso's immediate concern was that Alvin was playing stupid for the benefit of the test. He insinuated that it was always easy to fake being stupid and almost impossible to fake being smart. Kania kindly rebuffed Monterosso's accusation. He had constantly questioned the integrity of the evaluation.

"I'm always considering that he's not being honest with me," Kania said and then added that he always tries to get the best effort from his subject. "Most people try their best to be smart," Kania said. Monterosso didn't swallow a drop of it.

"Did it occur to you that Alvin has an incentive to *not* look smart?" Kania sidestepped the question.

"I look for consistency," Kania said smoothly. "I felt he gave his best effort. He was definitely of limited intelligence."

Monterosso got Kania to admit that he had not listened to the taped confessions Alvin had made on the day and evening of Andy's death. Instead, Kania had apparently felt it was sufficient to review the police "summery" of the events. He had also reviewed the Harding tape of October 18th. Apparently, the tapes had no bearing on Kania's opinion of Alvin's intelligence.

"The basis of my opinion stems from my dealings with him, not by viewing the police tape the night Andy died."

Monterosso kept the pressure on. He hammered Kania about Alvin's ability to recall times and events when he had thought he was aiding in the conviction of his wife. However, when he had realized the jail cell doors were about to clang shut on him, he had begun to act ignorant. Monterosso reminded Kania that Alvin had clearly stated he knew it was wrong for Theresa to kick Andy that way. Yet, Kania stood his ground. He didn't think his assessments were wrong or inaccurate. Not in the least. Undeterred, Monterosso kept chipping away at the tactics Alvin had begun using once he realized he was going to stand equally accused of Andy's death.

"I was aware," Kania said in a rather superior tone of voice, "that his drinking problem was more severe than he was letting on to." Apparently,

292

this was supposed to show the jury that Alvin couldn't possibly have pulled the wool over Kania's eyes. From his place at the far end of the counsel table, Alvin was crying again and wiping his tears with the back of his hand. The nearly-empty tissue box was pushed closer to him.

Monterosso brought up the vandalism charge of 1997 and Kania coolly confirmed that he had reviewed that report. Kania said that Alvin had never admitted that he'd yelled at Andy the night of Andy's death, insinuating that Alvin could have been yelling at his wife to shut up and not at Andy.

"But," Monterosso said, "what if he's heard yelling 'shut up' and the only other sounds were of the boy crying?"

"There's no doubt that he has thought process, but it's a matter of knowing the ramifications." Monterosso shook his head and decided to take Kania's evasive answer and run with it.

Monterosso drew the doctor's attention to the written transcripts of the police interview with Alvin just after Andy was admitted to the hospital. He honed in on Alvin's statement about not wanting to go to jail.

"Doesn't that show a knowledge of ramification?!" Monterosso's voice was pitched at an all-time high. He was pacing and thumping the transcripts like a Southern Baptist preacher thumps the Bible.

"I don't think it necessarily shows his knowledge of what happened," Kania said smugly.

"Alvin was looking out for himself," Monterosso said curtly. "Right?" Kania breezed past Monterosso's accusation by saying that he didn't interpret it that way at all. Monterosso tried to get Kania to admit that Alvin was at the *high* end of mild mental retardation, but Kania skirted the question with examples of how Alvin showed "confusion." During the test, Alvin had said "domestic" meant "violence" and "assemble" meant "use your hands."

Next, Scalisi came forward with a few things he wanted to clear up. He grilled Kania about the fact that Alvin's I.Q. rating could classify him on the borderline of higher intellectual functioning. Then, he started snapping off questions so fast Kania barely had time to answer. Alvin could decide what kind of gas to buy for his car, couldn't he? He never put diesel fuel in his car, did he? He knew to put the child in the car seat, right? He knew he needed to use a seat belt for himself and Jacob, right? He knew how to set the alarm clock and how to tell time, right? He could take two rambunctious kids to a lakeshore and supervise them and then go to a fast food drive-through, read the posted menu, order food for everyone and pay for it, right? Right? He knew the rules of the road, didn't he? Huh? He frequently babysat the kids while Theresa was at work, didn't he? Huh? He played football in high school, right? Did you ask him if he understood the rules of the game? Huh? Huh? Huh?

Kania leaned back in his chair and waited for Scalisi to stop barking questions long enough for him to get an explanation in edgewise.

"No," Kania finally said tersely, slightly miffed, "I didn't ask him that." Scalisi had made many good points. Then, Kania was led down the path

Deadly Thirst

to discuss Alvin's version of why Theresa wanted them to become foster parents. Alvin had said that Theresa wanted to do it for the money, so she wouldn't have to go to work. Surely then, Scalisi said, that shows thought process, doesn't it? Not necessarily.

Kania testified that Alvin had confided he'd had a lot to drink on Sunday, the day prior to Andy's fatal attack.

"So," Scalisi prompted, "tell the jury what Alvin's demeanor was like when he was drunk."

Kania haltingly replied that Alvin admitted that he got into fights when he drank. That statement led Scalisi to explore Alvin's penchant for violence which had several members of the jury looking very absorbed in thought. Perhaps Scalisi had finally pulled up the shade, so to speak, on the docile giant that Sachs was trying to portray. After Scalisi finished questioning Kania, Alvin stood exposed as possibly being the one who had attacked Andy during the early morning hours of August 2, 1999. After all, Jacob had testified that he had heard *Alvin* screaming "shut up," not Theresa. Scalisi did serious damage to Alvin at Kania's hands. It was probably his best work so far. As Scalisi triumphantly took his seat, the jury focused on Alvin, who sat playing with a piece of paper, staring off into outer space. A couple of crumpled tissues lay on the desk in front of him.

Sachs was not put off by Scalisi's blistering revelation about Alvin's alcohol-fueled violence.

"Did Alvin tell you that the word "terminate" meant "you're fired"? And did he then tell you he knew that one?" Sachs asked. Kania agreed.

"Alvin didn't anticipate what might happen as a result of…"

"Objection," Monterosso said with another smirk and stated for the umpteenth time that the witness wasn't allowed to state whether or not the defendant had the capacity to form any such conclusions. The judge agreed. Monterosso leaned back in his chair, tapping a pen against his lips.

Annoyed, Sachs stood stroking his chin for a few minutes while he re-phrased the question. Kania reworded his answer accordingly.

"I never got the *impression* that he felt responsibility."

Sachs had nothing further and Kania was dismissed.

It was time for Scalisi to give his opening statement, which he had with-held during the first day of trial. It's a tactic lawyers often use if they feel that presenting their theory at the beginning of all the fireworks will cause it to lose some of its clout. He wanted his views about who really had in-jured Andy that night to be fresh in the jurors' minds when his client took the stand. It was obvious that Theresa was gearing up to be on the witness stand soon.

After a 3:00 P.M. break, Scalisi took his place in front of the juries. He reminded them not to form any conclusions or opinions about what had happened until after they'd heard from Theresa. He began his opening statements by saying that Alvin had abused Theresa and she had finally had enough of him. On the weekend before Andy died, she'd made up her mind to go through with the divorce and she'd told Alvin about it. She'd told him of her plans to move out and that her plans did not include him. Theresa's plans had clearly infuriated Alvin. Pointing an accusing finger at Alvin, Scalisi said *that* was what made Alvin fly into a rage "and do what *he* did to Andy."

It was exactly what everyone had expected: Theresa planned to blame it all on Alvin. As everyone anticipated her imminent testimony, an audible rumble swept through the five or six spectators when Scalisi called Deputy Michael McClanahan to the witness stand. Everyone would just have to wait a little longer to hear what Theresa had to say for herself.

Word had spread that Theresa's time on the witness stand was at hand and a photographer from the Press Enterprise newspaper hovered around, waiting to snap a photo for the following day's front page. Of course, Alvin's parents were there to hear her testimony, as well as a reporter from Associated Press and a law student. A dozen seats remained empty.

Scalisi asked McClanahan to tell the jury what his occupation had been back in October of '97. McClanahan had been a sheriff's deputy in Perris at that time and remembered very well the 1997 incident in which Alvin was arrested for vandalism. Theresa had been the reporting victim and Alvin had been the suspect. McClanahan had considered the problem to be a domestic issue.

Then it was Monterosso's turn. He asked McClanahan if each defendant's statement had been contradictory of the other's. McClanahan said yes, they had been extremely contradictory. Alvin had said that Theresa was the one who had done all the damage and vice versa.

Sachs came to the podium and broached the subject from a different angle. He was anxious to clarify what had happened the day *after* the vandalism incident. McClanahan said that Theresa had changed her story and said that the phone cord had been broken during a scuffle between the two of them and that Alvin hadn't cut it. She didn't wish to press charges against him after all. It had all been nothing more than a silly little spat.

McClanahan was dismissed shortly thereafter. His total time on the stand had been about ten minutes. Everyone in the spectators' section seemed sure that Theresa would testify next. The photographer readied his camera. Once again, they were disappointed.

Social worker Fernando Melendez was called into the courtroom. Walking with a pronounced limp, Melendez made his way past the jurors to the witness stand and took the oath. He testified that he'd been a social worker for Riverside County for nine years and it was his job to assess potential foster parents. He did this by one pre-announced visit to the home. During this single visit he not only evaluated the prospective foster parents, he also evaluated the home. It was for this visit that Alvin finally had permission from Theresa to be present in his own home. And with good reason: both parents must be interviewed. Melendez admitted that, although the

Deadly Thirst

actual interview happened on April 22nd of 1999, his report was dated June 15th; twelve days *after* Jacob and Andy arrived at the home.

Melendez was a horrible example of a social worker. Or perhaps he was an excellent example. He gave the impression of being inept and bumbling, which to many was exactly the way CPS had conducted the background checks on Alvin and Theresa. His testimony left a sour taste in almost everyone's mouth. One spectator would later comment that Melendez had about as much warmth and charm as a tax auditor.

Although he hadn't brought any of his notes or case documents with him to court, he said he had interviewed both parents for two hours in their kitchen. He specifically remembered asking Alvin questions about the task of being a foster parent. Monterosso was incensed that Melendez had the gall to show up in court without any notes or documents, but Melendez didn't seem concerned about making a good impression.

Monterosso asked how many interviews Melendez conducted in an average month. About fifteen and yes, the subject of discipline is discussed with both parents. According to Melendez, Theresa had understood the "no corporal punishment" rule and Alvin had specifically said that his idea of discipline was to "teach the child a better way." Alvin had also stated that sometimes "yelling at children could be more abusive than hitting."

Monterosso was careful to elicit the fact that both parents had been nodding in agreement throughout Melendez's interview and Alvin had not taken a passive position. Alvin had told Melendez that he took care of his Down's syndrome sister and that he protected her.

According to Melendez's description of his duties as a social worker, he had assessed the marriage to be stable. Theresa had commented to him that Alvin was very considerate of her, was a hard worker, and a nice man.

Melendez went on to say that Alvin returned Theresa's praise with a glowing compliment of his own, saying that she was a strong woman and she treated him nicely. Alvin had assured him that their minor conflicts had been resolved and the decisions that were made in the household were made jointly.

Monterosso questioned Melendez about Alvin's written admission of his arrest for the 1997 vandalism charge. Melendez answered that Alvin had acted like it was no big deal. Alvin had told him they'd been wrestling when the stereo had gotten knocked over and broken and that the apartment manager had called the police.

"Did you follow up on that claim, or check it out in any way?"

"No," he said with a shrug.

Then, Sachs took his usual position behind the wooden podium and asked Melendez why, as a social worker he had cleared the couple in spite of their acknowledged criminal history? Melendez's answer sent a shock wave through the juries. He'd made the good assessment of Alvin and Theresa's home because he was familiar with Theresa's parents. He felt her mom and dad were good foster parents.

At that instant, a profound silence fell over the entire courtroom as Melendez sat smug-faced on the witness stand. Several jurors wore a look of absolute shock. Melendez admitted that the children had been placed in the home on June 3rd—twelve days *before* his report was submitted. Yes, he said, the kids had been placed in the home with full knowledge that Alvin and Theresa were not yet licensed and they had not completed the required training and that Alvin had a criminal conviction.

Most of the jurors still had their mouths hanging open in disbelief; several jurors who'd been methodically rocking in their chairs, abruptly stopped. Sachs had done an outstanding job of showing the jurors that Melendez's work ethics left a lot to be desired. Upon further questioning, Sachs got Melendez to admit that yes, he realized that a full two months had elapsed between the interview and the sign-off, but he gave the familiar excuse that the staff was over-burdened. Then, Sachs asked him if he knew about the restraining order. No, he had not known about the restraining order; Theresa hadn't told him about it and it wasn't his job to check on stuff like that. "The state does that," he mumbled. He had, however, checked for prior convictions and had found none. Melendez quoted Alvin as saying about himself that he'd "make a good authoritive figure."

Then, it was Scalisi's turn. He put a document on the overhead projector. It was the budget information sheet Alvin and Theresa had filled out, stating their meager finances at the time. Melendez said he had felt the pair could survive without assistance. He said the fact that Theresa worked in a board and care facility for the elderly made her a good choice for foster parenting. Obviously, Melendez hadn't bothered to ask Theresa's supervisors or the abused residents at Walker's Board and Care their opinion of her. It's a wonder Monterosso hadn't called a few of the residents to testify about the way Theresa had treated them.

There was one other thing that Alvin had managed to wedge into the interview the day Melendez had assessed their home: Alvin had told Melendez that he didn't drink. Scalisi had nothing further.

Sachs took the podium again and read a section from Melendez's written assessment: he'd written that he felt Alvin "seemed to be mentally prepared to have foster kids." Melendez said that, at the time, it had seemed that way. But then, he'd been too overburdened to see the whole picture. In any event, he'd felt Alvin was appropriate.

When Melendez was dismissed, he slunk down off the stand and limped out of the courtroom like a wounded dog. The eyes of every juror followed him all the way out the door.

It seemed almost certain that Theresa would be the next witness, but it was already four o'clock. The possibility that Theresa wouldn't make an appearance weighed heavily on the newspaper photographer who'd been hanging around all day, waiting to snap a picture of her on the stand. He'd just have to wait a little longer.

Deadly Thirst

Horst was recalled and got up from his chair at the counsel table. Dressed in his sheriff's uniform, he strode to the stand and was reminded that he was still under oath. Horst testified that he'd interviewed Jacob Marquist on the morning of Andy's death and it had been tape-recorded. Jacob had confirmed the trip to Lake Elsinore and said that Andy had asked Alvin for water several times during that outing. It had been a very hot day. Jacob said that Alvin had given Andy some water, but Andy became thirsty again and kept asking for another drink. Finally, Alvin scolded Andy for asking. Sachs wanted Horst to clarify that Jacob had said Alvin finally scolded Andy because he "kept on nagging for water," not that he'd merely asked once or twice. Sachs had nothing further.

Monterosso rose from his seat and placed a photo of the kitchen on the overhead projector. He zoomed in on the half-full gallon jug which was sitting on the kitchen sink. Horst was asked if he had seen a jug of water in the bedroom when he had accompanied Alvin and Theresa back to the apartment. No, he had not. It had been in the kitchen. Horst was also asked whether or not Alvin had been promised any sort of immunity. Horst said no. Then, Horst was dismissed and returned to his seat beside Monterosso at the counsel table.

There was a buzz of whispering between Theresa and Scalisi. Theresa was poised with her hands on the armrests of her chair. She had arisen half out of her seat when she was cautioned by Scalisi to stay seated for a minute more. All eyes were trained upon her. There seemed to be some disagreement among counsel whether Theresa should take the stand so late in the day. Scalisi wanted to adjourn early; he felt the jurors were tired, worn out. They wouldn't be able to concentrate and Scalisi wanted Theresa fresh for her appearance. The newspaper photographer readied his camera once more.

The juries were sent from the room. There was much discussion that the trial had already lasted longer than planned. Judge Schooling reminded Scalisi that jurors had received permission to be excused from their jobs for only a certain amount of time and that time was about to run out. Schooling thought it prudent to get maximum use out of each court day and ordered Theresa's testimony to begin.

"Court will adjourn at the regular 5:00 P.M. time," Schooling said. The juries were ushered back in.

At 4:18 on May 30th, Theresa was called to the witness stand. She got out of her chair as gracefully as she could and waddled past the juries, smiling and nodding hellos. Stepping up to the witness stand, she cheerfully raised her right hand and swore, in a tiny voice, to tell the truth. She hovered over the witness chair and descended upon it like a laying hen, wiggling back and forth until she was comfortably distributed. With a big smile, she answered Scalisi's questions in a peppy, chirpy voice and directed all of her answers straight to the jury. It was as if she were auditioning for a role in a movie.

Donna Goodenough

It was an amazing transformation. Whispers echoed throughout the spectators' section. Theresa looked better than anyone could have anticipated. More than a few of the spectators actually had their mouths hanging open as they watched and listened. During the past year and a half, I had been observing her closely at her pre-trial hearings. To me, she had seemed about as animated as a petrified tree stump, as cheerful as a salted snail. Now, I was flabbergasted at how good she looked and how she preformed right on cue. Obviously well-rehearsed, the smile did wonders for her face. Under the spotlight now, her hair was Breck-shiny and it was apparent that she had been carefully made up for this very important day. She sat erect; chin up, smiling, smiling, smiling. She made eye contact with every single juror. Her jurors were in the good seats for this occasion. They needed to be closest to her so as not to miss anything she might say.

Unlike her husband, who shied away from the jury and mumbled his answers into his lap, Theresa leaned forward and spoke directly into the microphone as she cocked her head to the left and looked at the jury. She smiled. She seemed upbeat. And she smiled. Quite surprisingly, she appeared confident and calm. Scalisi stood before her with his hands raised as if he were about to conduct an orchestra.

Scalisi began to prompt Theresa to give a personalized tour of her wonderful, pre-Alvin life. With a smile, she presented a solid and admirable picture of her education, saying that she'd been attending Riverside Community College at night and taking care of her relatives' kids during the day. When Scalisi moved the questioning along and finally mentioned the name of Alvin, Theresa's brow puckered and the smile faded from her face. With a heavy, painful sigh, she answered in an agonized tone that Alvin had wanted her to quit school; so, reluctantly she had. She spoke of tending her half-brother, Jessie, off and on at that time. In September of 1997, she had moved into the C Street apartment. The first episode of violence had erupted there, one month later. When Scalisi asked her what had happened, she sighed and said Alvin had pulled a knife on her and said he was going to kill her. He ended up going to jail.

The constant, over-exaggerated sighing was maddening to Monterosso and Horst, and probably Sachs too. Horst glared at Theresa, contempt dripping from his face. Once more, his body language was literally screaming.

From her position on the witness stand however, Theresa never let her eyes stray anywhere near Horst. She kept her focus strictly on Scalisi and her jury and nothing else. One of the spectators would later say that a bomb could have exploded right in the middle of the courtroom and she wouldn't have looked at it.

So, Scalisi asked, what happened after Alvin went to jail? Well, she sighed, the next day Alvin's dad had called her and accused her of ruining Alvin's life. An audible snort of disgust could be heard coming from the back row where Leroy was sitting with Susie.

It seemed to be too painful for her to recall. She looked up at the ceiling as if praying for the strength to continue. She shook her head sadly as she let her gaze fall into her lap. Biting her lip with emotion, she looked back up at her attorney. The abuse she'd suffered at the hands of the man she loved was almost too dreadful to speak of. She continued her testimony by saying that Alvin had called her from jail, apologizing and begging her not to press charges. He'd said the booze had made him do it.

"He drank every time we went out," she lamented. "He got drunk just about every day." Furthermore, she said, Alvin became mean and mad when he drank. The reason she'd called the police the next day to recant her statement was because she believed he would change and besides, by that time, she had already fallen in love with him. "Very much so," she said with an affirmative nod and a sweet smile.

Throughout the trial, Alvin had mostly appeared bored; but, when Theresa was on the stand he was alert and hung on every word she said. His head shook constantly in an open display of disagreement.

All too soon, it was time for court to adjourn. Theresa had been on the stand for only half an hour and she'd done remarkably well. Horst was utterly galled at the mere sight of her. The photographer was, perhaps, the only one who left the courtroom satisfied that day.

Before the juries parted, they were admonished not to look at the newspapers that would undoubtedly be splattered with a photo and an article about the case. Judge Schooling apologized for repeating the warning every day, but explained that he was required to do so. He said he felt confident the jurors in this case knew better and he thanked them for their patience. Judge Schooling was a good man, a compassionate man. He was very concerned that the trial was already threatening to extend into overtime.

After the juries left, Theresa's smile vanished, as did her perkiness. Once more, her eyes took on a cold, reptilian stare. Deputy Sanderson opened the drawer behind his desk and took out a heavy, clanging set of manacles and dutifully approached her. Once tethered, she was led away, like a circus walrus, through a side door. While Sachs watched, Sanderson retrieved a second set of manacles for Alvin and he too was led out of the courtroom. After a few comments between the lawyers and the judge, everyone left.

The next morning, the Press Enterprise ran a large photo of Theresa on the witness stand. The consensus was that she looked pretty good. It was a far cry from her last photo, almost two years ago, when she bore a striking resemblance to the Michelin Man.

Theresa didn't look anywhere near as coiffed and reassured for her second day on the stand as she had for her first. As the jurors filed in, her mouth stretched into a broad smile as if she were greeting old friends. She mouthed "hi" to a few and looked each juror directly in the face. To the handful of spectators, the way she turned the charm on and off was about as subtle as a blow from an ax. Until she had been called to the witness stand, she had sat, day after day, like a statue carved from stone. Never, not once, prior to her time on the witness stand, had Theresa cracked a smile. But on this day—her day—she looked almost giddy. The smile she wore on her face did little, if anything, to mask her corrosive personality. She knew she was in for the fight of her life and Scalisi had prepared her very well. It was part of his job. It seemed obvious that Horst found it nauseating to watch someone with so little concern for a child's life fight so intensely to save her own.

As her second day of testimony resumed, Theresa continued to be coddled gently by Scalisi. He wanted to take some of the sting out of questions he was certain the other sides would ask. He wanted to give Theresa the chance to explain things in a positive light. She spoke at length about the admirable qualities of her life, such as her schooling and her honorable work with handicapped and disabled people. And, of course, she spoke of the many elderly patients she'd had the pleasure of working with throughout the past few years. She'd worked with victims of Alzheimer's and loved the work. Helping people who were at a disadvantage and were unable to help themselves gave her great joy.

Scalisi eased Theresa into her testimony about the relationship she had with Alvin. She said that she was paying for almost everything in her marriage. Alvin had convinced her to sell her Pontiac; he'd told her it had one foot in the grave. But, after she'd sold it, she realized that Alvin just wanted her to be dependant on him. She told the jurors about the time Alvin had left Jessie and her stranded at the auto parts store. As Theresa recounted the problems she'd had with Alvin, Alvin sat at the counsel table adamantly shaking his head no.

She described the fight that had erupted later on. She told of Alvin smacking her and busting out the windows in his Chevy S-10, sending glass flying. He'd broken out the windshield and the passenger window of his own truck. Jessie was in the back, filled with terror and throwing up. Theresa sighed at every opportunity as though she couldn't bear to recall it aloud. Yet, her voice never cracked, never broke as if she were truly upset.

Theresa spoke of her engagement and how she'd said no the first time Alvin had asked her to marry him. She testified that Alvin would pick fights with her and that they incessantly argued about money. She recalled another event when Alvin had thrown Jessie and her out of the car in the rain. That was the catalyst that caused her to break her lease on the 6th Street apartment and move back in with her parents briefly. Momentarily she let her sorrowful gaze plummet into her lap. It was always a power struggle, she said, peeking up at her jury. Alvin wanted to be the boss. He had a Motorola pager with a print out that did all kinds of stuff like sports, weather, and time. Alvin didn't have any trouble reading his messages. She claimed that he had sent her a two-page letter while she was in jail and she insisted that he could read and write. Not very well, but he could do it. She'd seen him write many times. She spoke of a courtroom incident that had occurred many months back, during a pre-trial hearing at which Theresa and Alvin were inadvertently seated near each other. Although detainees are not permitted to speak to each other, Alvin had leaned toward Theresa and told her she was an ugly bitch and that she'd better cover up for what he'd done to Andy.

Next, Theresa described a leg injury that occurred as a result of an argument she'd had with Alvin. Although it had happened long ago, she testified that she still wore a leg bandage from that injury. Yes, he'd been drinking that night, as always. "He'd go on binges," she sighed. He liked to call her a fat bitch and he became abusive, physically. In spite of all that, she still loved him and they started talking about making a baby together in early 1999. She'd never observed him displaying any reluctance about having kids. He liked kids and so did she.

In late 1998, she'd asked for a restraining order and filled out the paperwork right there at the courthouse. She agreed that she'd written two full pages of problems she'd had with Alvin. The two pages focused on a particularly violent fight they'd had about Alvin not wanting to drive Theresa to her doctor's appointment. At the time she had still been on crutches from her knee injury and it had been hard for her to drive. Her forehead wrinkled as she groped for the mildest words to describe what happened next. He'd pushed her down and thrown a block of wood at her, she said. Then he'd gone on another one of his window-bashing tirades and busted out the windows in a car they owned. Theresa began to swivel back and forth in her chair as she told the jurors of Alvin's abuse, her voice heavily laden with sighs. She said she'd never actually filed the restraining order because she had believed he would change. Even after all he'd done, she still loved him.

Scalisi gently questioned Theresa about the traumatic events that led up to her deciding to file for divorce. As she began to recall them, she looked forlornly toward the jury. With a slight whine in her voice, she agonized at having to reveal the dark side of the man she'd married.

She began by saying Alvin had been gone about a week when she'd made the decision. She'd been stuck without a car and forced to ride the bus. She was stressed. She had had to take the children to work with her. Alvin had been very angry when she'd handed him the divorce papers and he hadn't wanted to sign. They had argued. They'd gone home after work and had continued arguing after the kids were in bed. He'd been mad because she was going to move to a nicer area of Perris where things would be better for her and the boys.

Scalisi carefully eased Theresa into an explanation of what had happened in the days just prior to Andy's "hospitalization." Scalisi was careful not to say the words "murder" or "fatal attack." "Hospitalization" was a much less graphic, less hazardous word. Well, she sighed, Alvin had been drinking. It was Saturday and she'd worked half a day. Alvin ended up sleeping on the couch until 2:00 A.M. and then he went home. She next had seen him on Sunday and he'd been drunk again. He began to argue about the divorce and ended up staying at the apartment until after she'd put the boys to bed. Andy had fallen asleep on her bed and she'd transferred him to a sleeping bag at the foot of her bed. Alvin had been especially mad that night because Andy kept crying and he was already mad about the divorce. He got mean when he was drunk and he was certainly drunk that night. Theresa mentioned a few episodes of past abuse and how Alvin had broken the bedroom door on two occasions. The first time, she'd run into the bedroom to escape his wrath, locking the door behind her. Moments later he'd bashed through it. Scalisi showed a photo on the overhead projector of the damaged door. Zooming in on the doorknob, he pointed out several areas of splintered wood and what appeared to be nails. In a very gentle and sympathetic tone, he asked if this was the damage that her abusive husband had done to their bedroom door. Yes, she said, thoroughly ashamed. The next occasion of violence was after he'd gotten drunk and she, appalled at his drunkenness, wanted to sleep by herself; so she locked him out of the bedroom. Whereupon, Alvin busted down the door.

Scalisi put the kitchen photo on the overhead projector and asked her to look at it. With a pen, he pointed to a plastic gallon jug of water on the kitchen sink and zoomed in on it. Was this the bottle Andy had been drinking from the night Alvin hit him? Theresa said yes. She said Alvin had taken the jug into the kitchen after the paramedics had left with Andy. Scalisi wanted Theresa to start from the beginning and tell the jurors what happened.

As she recalled, they'd gone to bed around midnight on the night of Andy's "hospitalization." She always slept by the window and Alvin slept next to the nightstand. The next thing she remembered was being awakened by the sounds of Andy gulping water. "I remember him standing there with the water jug," she said. "Alvin yelled, 'I told you not to drink any water!' in a really harsh tone of voice." Then, Alvin had gotten up, turned on the light, and came back to bed. Theresa admitted that she had told Andy to get his time-out chair, but only because she was protecting Andy from Alvin's rage. "I didn't want my husband to do anything to Andy so I had him get his chair." Yes, she'd told Andy to stand on the chair, but it was Alvin who had done all the yelling. He'd told Andy to shut up several times. "He's screaming 'Shut up!'" She said the bedroom door had been open. She'd known Andy was in deep trouble and tried to quiet the child. She demonstrated how she'd put her finger to her lips and gently whispered for Andy to "shhhhh." "Alvin slapped him with his right hand and the baby fell over. He slapped Andy in the face." As Horst sat there listening to Theresa blame everything on Alvin, a brick-red flush crawled up the back of his neck.

Andy had fallen backward and hit his head on the nightstand. "Once he hit the dresser he quit crying," she said with a shrug. The whole sordid event was revealed without a trace of emotion. Her frequent sighs were

Deadly Thirst

ringing hollow by then and had been for the last two hours or so. There were several jurors who openly displayed a look of disbelief and disdain for Theresa, perhaps without realizing it. Horst was beside himself; her testimony had infuriated him. His face was a constant, heartfelt scowl of contempt, flushed red with anger. Her monotonous, emotionless voice was the thing that irritated him the most.

Continuing with her story, Theresa said she had immediately jumped out of bed and picked Andy up. "My husband goes, 'What's wrong with him?' and he was shaking Andy by the shoulders. My husband's like, 'Quit faking it, get up...' and so I told him to call 911."

And then what?

"He said 'No. We're gonna get in trouble.'" Theresa said she'd tried to leave the room to call 911 for help, but Alvin wouldn't let her. Finally, Alvin had called 911 a couple of minutes after he had knocked Andy unconscious. It'd been all Alvin's idea to tell dispatchers that they had found their "foster baby" outside. She said Alvin was scared of going to jail. He'd pushed her outside and "Told me to put dirt on him so we could say we found him outside." Afraid, she'd done as she was told. It was all Alvin's idea. She'd thought that, if she didn't go along with Alvin's hastily thrown-together plan, he wouldn't call 911.

"I was just thinking about getting help for Andy," she said. As they'd gone toward the street to await paramedics, Alvin had glared at her, relaying a silent threat. Alvin was afraid she would tell the police what really had happened.

When they'd arrived at the waiting area at Menifee Valley Hospital, Jacob had been sent into the adjacent area to get candy from a vending machine. During his absence, Alvin had ordered her not to say anything. Jacob had been surrendered to CPS officials before they left Menifee. Then, Horst had asked to accompany them back to their apartment for further questioning. Theresa said that Horst had driven his own car while she and Alvin had driven together in their car. On the ride home Alvin had gone hog-wild, grabbing at her and warning her that, sooner of later, he'd be out of jail...

After Horst had looked around the apartment briefly and questioned them together, he had asked them both to come down to the Perris PD for another round of questions. Then, Horst had left the apartment and headed to the Perris station, which was right down the street. In the few minutes they were alone after Horst's departure, Theresa said that Alvin had warned her again. "He said 'Because of my record, they'll never believe me and, if worse comes to worse, you'll have to say you did it because they'll believe you.'"

Scalisi asked Theresa if she recalled the things she'd said on the tape that had been played in court at the beginning of the trial. Yes, she remembered. Why had she lied and confessed to a crime she hadn't committed? Theresa lowered her gaze to her lap, swallowed hard and bit her lip. "I had to protect him." Yes, she'd lied to the cops, but she'd done it to protect her man and cover up for him. Yes, Alvin's life was steeped in sin, but she loved him in spite of it all. Throughout her testimony Theresa remained dry-eyed, her voice steady and flat. The hollowness of her voice was the thing that rang loudest in the jurors' ears.

Reading the faces of the jurors was easy, ridiculously so. The body language of several spoke volumes. Some sat with a look of scorn on their faces; others folded their arms across their chest in an unconscious defensive posture. Monterosso and Horst, even Sachs could easily guess what Theresa's verdict would be.

Scalisi ever-so-gently asked Theresa if she'd seen Andy's swollen scrotum. He didn't dare put the gut-wrenching color photo on the overhead projector; he didn't want to inflame the jury. Since juries were usually sympathetic to the victim, he wanted to put as much distance between Andy's testicles and Theresa's testimony as he could. Finally, in a whisper, Theresa said yes, she'd seen Andy's injuries.

Scalisi began to ask Theresa about a letter that Alvin had written to her. That remark caused a furious uproar from Sachs which startled Judge Schooling and several of the jurors. Testimony came to a screeching halt. Theresa sat swiveling back and forth in her chair while Judge Schooling called for a sidebar. Sachs, Scalisi, and Monterosso clustered before the bench and tried to hash out what to do about the letter problem. Court reporter Karen Heggi's fingers were flying over the stenograph machine. Sachs appeared to be ready to either burst into tears or to walk off the job right then and there. He was sincerely offended that Scalisi had said that Alvin had written a letter when, in fact, Sachs was vehemently maintaining that Alvin couldn't write.

"He can't write!" Sachs hissed. He was so distraught that Judge Schooling immediately ordered the jurors from the room. Something was awfully wrong. Even after the jurors left, Sachs continued to be outrageously insulted and adamant about Alvin's illiteracy, insisting that he couldn't write. In the absence of the jury, Sachs could have calmly discussed his opposition and been equally convincing. There was no need for all the hoopla and fireworks when the jury was nowhere around. But, because he continued to rant and rave, his face contorted in fury, the judge felt compelled to order handwriting samples from both Theresa and Alvin.

With that, Sachs became even more furious, insisting again that Alvin couldn't write. How was he going to comply with an order to give a sample of his handwriting if he couldn't write? Judge Schooling sat on the bench, truly torn between the concerns of Sachs and the suggestions of Monterosso and Scalisi. Sachs was insisting his client could not comply. Period! Scalisi insisted that Theresa said Alvin *could* and *did* write a letter. Monterosso felt they should compare samples already in evidence with the new ones. The handwriting expert would need a variety of samples, not just the new ones, in order to get a solid analysis.

Schooling held his head in his hands and thought long and hard about what he should do. In his usual slow, methodical way of speaking, Schooling began again to tell both defense attorneys to get new handwriting samples from their clients. He wanted each defendant to write six signatures plus six samples of each other's names printed in block letters. He also ordered the word "remember" to be written, not printed. The samples would then be turned over to a handwriting expert for analysis.

Sachs appeared to be on the verge of a nervous breakdown. He kept insisting that Alvin couldn't comply because he couldn't write. Monterosso and Scalisi kept beseeching the judge to see it their way.

Monterosso felt that there were many samples of each defendant's handwriting—both printed and written— already in existence, that should be included in the comparison. Why make judgments based entirely on new samples since Alvin might try to change his writing? Scalisi tended to agree. They should get new samples and combine them with previous samples already in evidence. Schooling listened patiently to each argument. Once more, the judge told Sachs to get the samples so they could be compared with those already in evidence.

Defeated and angry, Sachs stomped over to the counsel table. He tried to explain to Alvin that he had to write his signature six times, then print Theresa's name six times, then he had to write the word "remember". Alvin looked up at Sachs and asked how to spell the words. The foster parent application and the letter Alvin had supposedly written to Theresa while she was in jail were lying on the counsel table. In exasperation, Sachs grabbed the letter and put it in front of Alvin who was having a hard time figuring out which hand to hold the pen in. He didn't know what he was supposed to try to write or where he needed to write it. Sachs hunched over him, trying to explain. He shoved the letter under Alvin's nose so he could copy what he was supposed to write. Monterosso and Scalisi simultaneously exploded like the Fourth of July. They both hollered in unison, "Don't show him!" The atmosphere inside the courtroom had all the tension of an imminent barroom brawl.

Once again, Sachs began to complain bitterly that Alvin couldn't comply because he couldn't write. Judge Schooling stepped in immediately and demanded Sachs not to show the document to Alvin. With a rare tinge of irritation in his voice, Judge Schooling ordered, "Just tell him what to write and where to write it and let him do it on his own. He'll just have to do the best he can." Sachs furiously slapped the letter face down in front of Scalisi who snatched it away and shoved it to the far side of the table.

To the couple of spectators, Sachs' behavior was convincing, but at that point it was totally unnecessary. The jurors were long gone, so why was he still carrying on? The only conclusion was that Sachs was not simply trying to defend a client. It seemed to be much more than that. It was as if Sachs knew, for a fact, that Alvin was so mentally incompetent that he couldn't spell his wife's name.

With a smile, Theresa quickly scribbled her samples and handed them to Scalisi in a matter of seconds. Alvin, on the other hand, still had not put pen to paper after ten minutes. It was twenty minutes before the juries were allowed back in. As the jurors passed by on the way to their seats, they saw Sachs standing next to Alvin; his face tight with anger. The judge, still slightly irritated, thought it was a good time to call for an early lunch. Everyone needed a breather. He apologized for having to say it again. "Please do not discus this case among your selves or with anyone else. Court will resume at 1:30."

After the juries had filed out and the double doors clanked shut behind them, Deputy Sanderson opened a drawer and pulled out a set of heavy shackles and chains. Theresa was shackled as she stood next to the witness stand. Then, she was led to the prisoner's holding area just beyond a side door. Sachs shoved both hands into his pockets and hung his head while Sanderson shackled Alvin and led him away. As the door slammed shut on Alvin, Sachs gathered up his tattered file folders and headed for the door, squinting up at the clock as he passed under it. Of the three attorneys, Sachs was the only one who didn't use a rolling briefcase. Instead, he simply carried his enormous armload of well-worn files. In the hallway, Sachs shunned a reporter's question with a stiff swat of his hand.

A little fresh air did everyone good. It was springtime. The heavenly scent of magnolia blossoms drifted in delicate waves, mingling with the lusty aroma of jacaranda. A quick cup of coffee and a hot dog from the vending cart served as lunch for many who were on the run.

When court resumed at 1:30, a box of tissues had been strategically placed on the railing between Theresa and her jury. If she should need to wipe a tear away, the jury would surely notice her reaching for the tissue. However, it was wasted effort. Theresa had not yet shed one tear and it didn't look like she was going to.

About Andy's swollen scrotum, Scalisi gently asked, do you know anything about how those injuries happened? No, Theresa said, she had no idea. But she did see Alvin kick Andy about a week and a half prior to his death. She'd heard Alvin yelling at Andy saying, "I'm gonna kick you in your nuts!" And then he had kicked him. She'd seen it happen. She'd been standing in the hallway and Alvin and Andy were in the bathroom. Andy was crying because he had peed on himself.

With that, Scalisi finished prepping Theresa for the imminent attack headed her way. He threw her a smile of encouragement and took his seat.

Monterosso gave Theresa a menacing glare as he rose out of his chair. Pacing the floor, he asked if she remembered the mandatory reporting that is required of all foster parents. Yes, she did. He asked if she'd given Andy hot chili peppers. Theresa admitted that she had.

"It was either me giving him one or my husband giving him ten."

Deadly Thirst

"Oh, so you were doing Andy a favor?" Monterosso sneered. Theresa thought so. Her voice was repugnant to Horst. Although he'd tried to prepare himself to hear her blame it all on Alvin, he was obviously appalled by Theresa's false testimony. Monterosso put the coroner's photo of Andy's swollen scrotum back onto the overhead projector and left it there. Theresa never looked at it. Monterosso asked about the cold showers. Theresa said that Alvin had given Andy the cold showers, not her. Her's were lukewarm, she said. "I knew if I didn't give Andy a lukewarm shower, my husband would give him a cold one."

Monterosso asked her if she'd told her parents about her knee injury and Theresa, wondering what her knee injury had to do with anything, said yes. "But you never told them about Andy's injuries, right?" Theresa merely shrugged. She said that when Alvin had first kicked Andy, she'd tried to take Andy to the doctor, but Alvin wouldn't let Andy get out of the car. When Andy had complained that his leg was hurting, Theresa had tried again to take Andy to a doctor but "My husband told me not to." She said she'd relented because she was trying to protect Alvin. Monterosso brought up the ugly issue of the impending divorce that had loomed over the last days of Andy's life.

"So, then you decide to lie and spend the rest of your life in prison for a man you wanted to divorce?"

"Yes," she said. Monterosso walked over to Horst and grabbed his shoulder.

"Do you recognize this man right here?" he yelled. Horst leaned forward in his seat and glared at Theresa. His eyes sliced into her like razor blades. He held a pen in his hand and was tapping it on the table, waiting for her to respond. Theresa glanced ever so swiftly at Horst and, with a slight smirk, coolly acknowledged that she knew who he was. Finally, she said that Alvin had forced her to say that she had done the injuries to Andy's genital area.

"...His...his...wee-wee," she stammered. As Monterosso stood there with his hands on his hips, looking incredulously at Theresa, the noise of Horst's pen tapping on the table continued to echo throughout the courtroom. Horst was gritting his teeth, his jaw clenched tight enough to make the veins in his neck pop out.

Theresa's upper lip began to glisten with sweat. She admitted that she'd said on tape that she had intentionally kicked Andy, but now she was telling the truth. All of those past statements were lies. Horst smacked his pen down on the table and slumped back in his chair. He began tapping his foot. Tapping, tapping, tapping until his whole leg bounced.

When Monterosso sarcastically commented that Theresa had seemed "happy" as she talked with female detective Kathleen Cardwell during the beginning of the polygraph, Scalisi flew out of his chair with an astonishingly vigorous objection. A sidebar was called. As the three attorneys huddled at the bench, Horst continued to stare straight at Theresa, clicking his pen on and off.

Theresa was no longer making eye contact with her jury and she certainly didn't look at Horst. Sweat trickled down the side of her face, but she quickly whisked it away with a flick of her hand. After the sidebar, Monterosso moved on to a different subject. He began throwing out questions at random.

"Why did you put dirt on Andy?" Theresa said she had to, because if she didn't her husband would have left him to die. She'd wanted to jump into the car and rush to the hospital right after the paramedics had taken Andy, but her husband wouldn't let her do that either.

"What happened to the divorce papers?" Monterosso asked. She didn't know.

"Why did you confess to kicking Andy in the groin five times?"

No, that was all a misunderstanding. Pointing to—but not looking at Horst—Theresa said, "*He* said my husband had told him I'd kicked the baby five times." Horst drew a deep breath and blew it out. Monterosso asked permission to play a short clip of the polygraph videotape where Theresa admitted she'd kicked Andy five times in the genitals. The judge called a short break while Monterosso advanced the tape to the part where Theresa kicked Horst's hand in a demonstration of how she'd kicked Andy. When the jurors returned, a short portion of the tape was played, but Theresa barely glanced at the television monitor.

Monterosso stood facing Theresa with his hands on his hips. "Well?"

"I was showing him what *my husband* had done."

Horst was livid. Theresa's jurors weren't buying it either. It was plainly evident they didn't believe what they were hearing. Their eyes darted back and forth from Theresa to Horst. Monterosso got her to admit that she'd called Alvin on Saturday night and told him she'd pulled on Andy's penis causing it to bleed. But, she testified, she hadn't hurt Andy on purpose, she'd merely been trying to look at Andy's genitals.

"I just touched his…his…his…his…*thing.*" Penis was an unspeakable word for Theresa. She denied that she had gotten angry when Andy soiled his pants. She worked with Alzheimer's patients and they did that all the time. She was used to it. And no, she hadn't been embarrassed when Andy soiled his pants at her workplace and stunk up the whole office. Yes, she'd put a trash bag around Andy's waist for the ride home, but only because her husband wouldn't let him in the car dirtied the way he was. As for the walk to Stater Bros. market on the day prior to Andy's hospitalization, Theresa admitted that Andy had been walking funny.

"Well," Monterosso growled, "did you have to ask him why?" She didn't answer that question, instead she said that on the way home she'd made Andy carry the bread and *that's* what he'd been crying about.

"He's complaining about his nuts hurting, right?"

"No, he's saying it's heavy."

Deadly Thirst

"So you gave him more stuff to carry, right?"

"Yeah." She claimed she was only trying to "teach Andy a lesson." And sometimes she "scared him with needles to make him eat."

"So now you're in jail for something you didn't do, right?"

"Right. I was putting it all on me to protect my husband."

Monterosso asked Theresa if she still considered herself a monster. No, no, that was another misunderstanding. "*My husband* said I'm a monster."

"He's four years old and he can't have a drink of water when he's thirsty?"

"No."

"*You* made him get on that chair, right?"

"No, *my husband* did."

"And *you* knocked him off, right?"

"No, *my husband* did."

Monterosso waved her off and plopped into his chair.

Next, it was Sachs' turn to question Theresa. As Monterosso had done, Sachs chose to mix up his questions. Monterosso had purposely left the photo of Andy's swollen scrotum on the overhead projector the entire time he'd questioned Theresa. Sachs reached over and straightened it a little. By that time, the groin photo had been in everyone's face for about thirty minutes, but Theresa never looked at it.

Sachs wanted to know what the attraction was between Alvin and Theresa. Theresa said he made her feel pretty. No, she'd never lured him back home with the promise of sex. Horst was leaning back in his chair, rocking as he listened to Theresa.

"*You* were the dominant person in this relationship, right?" Sachs asked. Theresa denied it. She also denied that she used her family's good standing in foster parenting as an influence to get her own foster kids. She said she was a Christian and she'd wanted to get married so they wouldn't be living in sin anymore.

"Didn't you promise him sex to get him back?"

"Mr. Sachs, I don't have the body to tempt anyone with sex."

From the back of the spectators' section, Leroy grunted his agreement. Sachs cocked a half-smile and let her comment hang in the atmosphere for a while. He paused and flipped through several pages of scribbled notes before he continued. From his habitual position behind the wooden podium, he asked her if Alvin had to call an 800 number so someone could read his messages to him.

"No," she said, "I've seen him read the messages other people sent him."

"Did you write that letter to yourself?"

"No," she said.

"What was it about Alvin that made you think he'd make a good parent?"

"I liked the way he played with kids."

Sachs asked Theresa why Alvin would break out the windows in his own truck. Theresa said the Chevy S-10 actually belonged to her at that time.

"You controlled him, right?"

"No sir. I was in love with him."

"At the time of the restraining order you wanted absolutely nothing to do with Alvin, isn't that right?"

"Yes, *at that time*."

Sachs asked her why they had still pursued becoming foster parents when they knew their relationship was unstable. Why had they proceeded?

"But Mr. Sachs…"

"Just answer the question!" A look of alarm swept across the jurors' faces. Judge Schooling did a double-take.

"Our relationship was at two extremes," she tried to reason. Things got better for a while, between them, after they started going to church and all. But then, she said, her husband started abusing her again right before the kids arrived. "When he'd start trippin' I'd get scared. But then we'd make up and my love took over."

"But you didn't tell your social worker about Alvin trippin', right?" Right. "Didn't Alvin try to avoid confrontation?"

"No," Theresa said, "actually it was the other way around."

Going back to the Stater Bros. incident, Sachs insinuated that Theresa knew Andy was struggling because his testicles hurt.

"It was from the *previous* injury," she said, "when *my husband* kicked him."

Jumping from one subject to another, Sachs accused Theresa of pulling hard on Andy's penis.

"I was just looking at it. I was just…just…holding it," she said, extending a cupped hand. Sachs commented that the coroner had testified Andy's injuries were recent. Sachs reminded Theresa she had testified that Alvin had been gone during the week prior to Andy's death. Theresa acknowledged her prior testimony.

"Those injuries were caused when *you* were alone with Andy, right?"

"No."

"Who woke up first when Andy drank the water?"

"I believe it was my husband," Theresa said. Once more she recounted how Andy was knocked off his chair, blaming everything on Alvin. She insisted it was Alvin's idea to put dirt on Andy.

"So the man you're trying to divorce is making all the critical decisions now, right?" Right.

Sachs was practically tearing the pages off his yellow notepad each time he flipped another page over. He was so angry he stammered; little specks of saliva flew from his lips. His mind was racing and his mouth couldn't keep up. His voice had sunken to a strained, nearly inaudible grumble. He

Deadly Thirst

brought up the subject of the polygraph and how Theresa had told Horst that she had "snapped" in the seconds that preceded the two separate attacks on Andy. Did she recall saying that she'd "snapped"?

"That's what happened with *my husband,"* she said. *Alvin* had been the one who'd snapped. She testified that everything she'd told detectives on the day of Andy's hospitalization was a lie. She'd said it just to protect her husband. This clearly increased Horst's anger. He was tapping his foot again and clicking his pen off and on. Leaning forward in his chair, he glared at Theresa until he could stand the sight of her no more. He took off his glasses and clanked them down on the counsel table. Rubbing his eyes slowly as if he had a headache, he reached for his pen and began clicking it on and off again. Finally, Sachs said he had nothing further. He returned to his seat beside Alvin and searched his pockets for another throat lozenge. He was beginning to feel the onset of a sore throat.

Monterosso questioned Theresa relentlessly about the divorce and their relationship at the end. Theresa held her ground and insisted she loved her husband right to the bitter end.

"Your love for him didn't change after you saw him kill Andy?" No, she said, it didn't.

By the time Theresa's testimony drew to a close, she'd been on the stand two full days. She had shown no emotion at any time and not once had she appeared close to tears for any reason. There was no doubt in anyone's mind that Theresa had torpedoed her own boat. But Alvin Robinson's fate was a mystery.

Susie Robinson was recalled to the stand. Again, the jurors watched in comical amazement as she reenacted her first trip to the witness stand. Seeming to be just as bored as the first time, she plopped down on the still-warm chair and heaved a sigh of annoyance.

Sachs asked her if Alvin had ever taken care of his Down's syndrome sister. Susie said Alvin was of very little assistance with her. She'd only let Alvin baby-sit for an hour or so at a time, because the girl had seizures and Susie wasn't sure if Alvin knew what to do for her. Furthermore, Susie flatly denied ever having driven to pick up Theresa after Alvin supposedly kicked her and Jessie out in a rainstorm.

"I have never driven with that woman," she said, scowling. And she certainly wasn't aware of any restraining order against Alvin. When asked if she approved of the relationship Alvin had with Theresa, Susie shot Theresa an icy glare. She certainly did *not* approve, she snipped. As for Theresa's knee injury, Susie said she'd heard that it was caused by Theresa's weight, not Alvin's abuse.

Among the handful of spectators, opinions varied on Susie's behavior and Sachs' reason for calling her to the witness stand—not once, but twice. Some of the people in attendance viewed her as a poor witness; others thought she mirrored her son so well that putting her on the stand, instead of Leroy, was a smart move on the part of Sachs. After all, Alvin was mildly retarded and there was no doubt whatsoever that his sister suffered from Down's syndrome. Bringing her into court for show-and-tell spoke volumes in favor of Alvin's retardation. Looking at Susie on the stand, her actions, her mannerisms and her speech patterns all reflected Alvin. The vocabulary of Susie and Alvin was identical; their speech littered with poor grammar. The way Susie slogged past the jury was exactly the way Alvin had slogged past them. They were cut from the same cloth, no doubt about it.

Leroy, on the other hand, held his head high, had a rapid and a concise speech pattern, albeit brimming with jive-talk. He walked with a brisk, determined stride, whereas Susie tended to amble and mumble. Some felt Leroy could have benefited Alvin much more than Susie. Since Leroy was so passionately defensive and loyal, it was a mystery why Sachs hadn't called him to testify. Others reasoned that maybe Susie's traits, attitude, and mannerisms were precisely why Sachs had called her to the stand. Could it be that perhaps he wanted the jury to see that Alvin's mental deficiencies were real, possibly inherited and handed down from one generation to another?

Susie definitely provided food for thought. Sachs was smart to call on Susie to visibly support Alvin's retardation. Sachs was a self-admitted nuts and bolts kind of guy.

Several spectators felt that Dr. Kania's testimony had had a self-serving ring to it and certainly not all of the jurors had believed everything he'd said. After all, Monterosso had made a good point when he'd asked if Alvin might have been trying to appear dumber than he really was.

However, some things just can't be faked and Susie Robinson definitely rang true. Susie was the last witness to take the stand. No one had taken the stand in defense of Theresa. Testimony in the case of Alvin Robinson and Theresa Barroso was finished.

Jurors were asked to wait in the hall. As they filed out, Alvin's jury had a vivid picture of Alvin's pitiful mother burning in their memories. Trying to read their faces was like trying to read a blank sheet of paper. What were they thinking? Did they have sympathy for Alvin or did they feel anger toward him? More importantly, did any of the jurors have mentally handicapped relatives? Did they have friends who had retarded or slow children? Were they sympathetic toward people of lesser intelligence? Had any of them ever been evaluated by a clinical psychologist? Was there a psychologist in any of their families? All of these things could influence the jury. It was an extremely tense time for everyone.

The consensus among spectators was that Theresa would get a guilty verdict. Easy. But Alvin's jury gave no hint as to which way they were leaning. According to Judge Schooling's admonition to them earlier, if they were in doubt, they'd have to vote in *favor* of the defendant. "Doubt" was all Alvin needed to keep him out of prison. I certainly was afraid that Sachs had been successful at planting that one solitary seed of doubt in one juror's mind. All Sachs needed was one sympathetic juror. Who was that one juror who could identify with Alvin?

Deadly Thirst

A couple of the spectators were fairly certain that Sachs had gotten exactly what he wanted. Alvin was a sorry, pitiful excuse for a man and it was doubtful that he'd be found guilty of murder. In fact, some were saying "No way in hell."

Sachs watched as Deputy Sanderson shackled Alvin and Theresa and led them out through the side door. With both defendants and both juries out of the courtroom, there was no need for Sachs to keep the scowl on his face. But there it stayed. He'd been feeling under the weather for the past few days and seemed to be nursing the onset of flu. While Scalisi laughed and smiled as he talked about the impending birth of his baby, Monterosso talked about baseball scores and his daughter's upcoming dance recital which he'd probably have to miss. Deep in thought, Sachs sat alone at his end of the counsel table, pouring over his notes. He had no time for small talk. Once in a while he'd get up and go fish a piece of peppermint candy from Deputy Sanderson's candy drawer or turn around to squint at the clock over the door. Other than that, he stayed locked in deep thought, not looking at anyone. It had definitely been a trial of feelings and emotions. And doubt. His voice was getting weaker and raspier by the minute and, although he said he felt fine, he didn't look well. He was worn completely down, both physically and mentally. He looked like he hadn't had a good night's sleep in six months.

There were a few things that had to be ironed out before the two juries were sent into the deliberation rooms. It's up to each attorney to submit to the judge the law they believe applies to their client and the reason they believe a particular jury instruction should or should not be given. Each side can state their position on the record to preserve their objections for appeal. Most attorneys start thinking about their proposed jury instructions the day they take the case. Monterosso, Sachs and Scalisi—all fine lawyers—were no exception.

Scalisi got the ball rolling. As for the first-degree murder charge against Theresa, Scalisi thought that involuntary manslaughter would be more appropriate. As for the torture charge, Scalisi felt that slapping Andy off the chair didn't amount to torture and Andy's murder certainly wasn't premeditated. Monterosso disagreed and said that Theresa did intend to inflict torture when she slapped Andy off his chair.

"She was trying to persuade Andy to do something when she knocked him off the chair. She wanted him to stop crying, stop drinking. And that's what torture is all about," Monterosso said. "Torture is the intent to inflict extreme pain." He did, however, agree with Scalisi that the murder had not been premeditated.

Stu Sachs wasn't in favor of Alvin's jury even considering his role as second-degree murder. He thought assault was more fitting. Furthermore, the charges of felony child endangerment should be reduced to mere child abuse.

Back and forth they volleyed and argued. Judge Schooling listened, sometimes holding his head in his hands. He wanted fairness and agonized over every argument that was put before him. He sat submerged in deep thought, carefully weighing each comment from all three attorneys. It would have been almost impossible to find a more fair and compassionate judge than Russell Schooling. As the afternoon dwindled and each attorney was still fervently arguing about what he did and did not want the jury to consider, Judge Schooling grew weary. He took off his glasses and rubbed his eyes.

"These are some of the most convoluted instructions I've ever encountered," he moaned, scratching his head.

The trial had lasted a lot longer than anyone had imagined and, while everyone was unanimous in feeling that Theresa's jury would convict in record time, no one knew what in the heck was going to happen to Alvin. It was entirely possible that his jury might deliberate for days and then come back with a "not guilty" verdict.

The jurors were brought back in just before 5:00 P.M. only to be told to return at 9:30 A.M. the following day, Wednesday, June 6th. As they headed out the door, grumbles were heard about having been turned loose just in time to fight the rush hour traffic.

Theresa dressed appropriately for her last day in front of her jury: she wore black. Her hair was pulled back in a ponytail and she wore no make up. She was back to her old self. It was baffling why Scalisi hadn't seen to it that Theresa was made up and well groomed for the entire trial, not merely for her first and shortest day on the stand. Alvin and his jury would be called in after Theresa's jury had heard closing arguments. As usual, Horst was present at the counsel table with only one chair separating him from Theresa. Before he turned his face toward the jury, he gave Theresa a chilling glare that reflected, quite vividly, his absolute disdain for her.

Wearing a dark suit, a crisp white shirt and silk tie, Monterosso stood directly in front of the jury. He was impeccably well-groomed; his shoes were shined, every hair was in place. Monterosso was the epitome of what every fine lawyer should look like—and, undoubtedly, what a lot of them wished they could be.

Monterosso apologized that the trial had taken longer than expected, but added that four-year-old Andy was worth their time. He reminded the jurors of the taped confessions that they had heard for themselves. He asked them to remember Theresa's demeanor when she had confessed the wretched, heartbreaking details of the fatal attack in a completely emotionless way. He reminded them that they had actually watched Theresa confess to repeatedly kicking Andy in the testicles and of rolling him in the dirt as a way of covering up her dastardly deed. Whirling around, he stabbed his finger at Theresa, raking her body with a contemptuous glare that would leave even the most composed person flushed with embarrassment. Turning back

Deadly Thirst

to the jurors, he reminded them that Theresa had shown no regret or emotion as she had sat on the witness stand spewing lies.

"Even now," he said, pointing once more at Theresa, "she's a person with no conscience or regret." He told them about a marathon he'd recently participated in and spoke of how hard it had been to keep pushing himself to the limits of endurance. Sometimes it's hard to reach the finish line, he told them, but once you cross over it, all the pain and agony is worth it. He urged the jury to cross that finish line and, though it would certainly be unpleasant, to return with a conviction. The trial had been difficult on everyone involved. Everyone was tired, worn down and depressed by what they had heard and seen. But it was almost over now...just a few more steps...

Monterosso's final job on behalf of Andy Setzer would be to wrap up all the major facts of the case and present them in a blockbuster package that would erase all doubt about Theresa's murderous rampage and her absolute guilt. He would need to tie in all the trivial details also—little comments, actions and admissions that, all put together, would prove beyond a reasonable doubt that Theresa Barroso was guilty of murder.

Then, Monterosso began using a very effective tool for digging the grave of Theresa Barroso. From his end of the counsel table, he retrieved a remote control device. Pointing it toward the television that hung in front of the good seats, he clicked his way through a concise and brilliantly crafted summation of all the evidence that clearly proved Theresa was Andy's killer. Slowly and precisely, he went through each and every piece of incriminating evidence the jury would need in order to convict. Once more he clicked and the word "murder" appeared on the screen. Under "murder" the definition was displayed. Then, finally, the facts of the case that proved Theresa was guilty of murder. The visuals were extremely effective in combination with Monterosso's brilliant presentation. Next, the meaning of "assault on a child under eight resulting in death" was clicked onto the screen. The graphics had been skillfully designed: the definitions were in the left column and the facts that proved Theresa's guilt were on the right for easy comparison. Monterosso went down the list, reminding the jurors of how everything fit together. With further use of his remote control, he explained the meaning of "malice aforethought" and "torture." As the jurors intently studied the visuals, he began to talk about the grim torture that little Andy had endured.

"Torture is the intentional infliction of pain or suffering," he said and reminded them that Theresa had kicked Andy on numerous occasions and had knocked him off his chair *twice* that final night. His death was no accident. "The first knock wasn't good enough, so she knocked him off the chair again." Monterosso stood silent and let that thought sink in for a few seconds. Then, he pointed the remote toward the TV again and clicked. The term "causing great bodily injury" appeared on the screen. Monterosso reminded the jurors why Theresa was guilty of causing great bodily injury

316

to Andy and that his injuries appropriately fit the term inasmuch as Andy's testicles had swelled to grapefruit size and were as purple as a ripe plum. Moreover, he said clicking the remote again, to find Theresa guilty of "assault on a child under eight resulting in death" there needed to be no intent whatsoever on the part of Theresa to actually kill Andy.

Without a doubt, Monterosso's use of the television and the remote clicker was his most powerful weapon. Time and time again, on the left of the screen he'd shown the jury what they needed to convict Theresa and on the right side he'd shown them the facts that had been proven in court.

"Put the two together," he told them. "Don't sign the lesser degrees." With that, Monterosso was finished.

Scalisi stepped forward and immediately came off as trying to buddy-up to the jurors. Smiling, he said he had only one opportunity to explain his side of the story. Scalisi was well dressed in a dark blue suit, a powder blue shirt and a striped tie. His shoes were shined; his salt and pepper hair was neatly combed. He looked handsome, confident and rested.

"The most important thing about our system is the presumption of innocence. Reasonable doubt was heavily talked about." He asked the jurors to do some soul-searching. "Will your decision stand the test of time? Ask yourself, will I be at peace with my decision?" He spoke without referring to any notes and paced slowly, back and forth, in front of the jury. He was careful to stare into the eyes of each juror. "It's hard to envision a more terrible thing than the murder of a child. But there were *two* adults in that room the night Andy died," he said. "Do you know *for sure* that Alvin didn't do it? Do you believe anything he said? Does his story add up?" In Scalisi's opinion it made a heck of a lot more sense that Alvin had slapped Andy and knocked him into the nightstand. After all, Alvin had been closest to Andy at the time of the attack. He reminded the jurors that they should be skeptical since Alvin had first claimed that Theresa had "pushed" Andy off the chair and then later he claimed it had been a "kick."

"And what about Jacob? He hears *Alvin's* voice; an angry, mean, hostile voice saying 'shut up' and then he hears a bang...a thump. Are you going to convict Theresa without thinking about Jacob's testimony? One of them is lying...either Alvin is lying...or Jacob is lying. Jacob has nothing to loose or gain, Alvin has everything to loose." Scalisi reminded the jurors that Alvin had scolded Andy at the lake for pestering him for water. He ridiculed Alvin's retardation and called it ridiculous. "He can read. He can understand a lot of complicated stuff." Scalisi reminded them that Alvin had been drinking the day Andy died. "Alvin's a mean person and you know he's a mean drunk. He wants to be married on *his* terms, always running home to his parents and going out to bars." Scalisi reminded the jurors that they had heard for themselves how Alvin had repeatedly agonized about going to jail and that his first instinct was to run. "Now who," he said with dripping sarcasm, "is more likely to have injured that little boy?" He told jurors to rise above the feelings they got when they looked at the photos of

Deadly Thirst

Andy's injuries. He cautioned them not to be overwhelmed by the emotions those pictures evoked. Scalisi seemed to skirt around the fact that a child had been murdered. Instead, he spent most of his time badmouthing Alvin and portraying Theresa as the helpless, longsuffering victim of a mean and hateful husband.

He painted a sad picture of Theresa's life and told the jury that no one could ever know what it was like to walk in her shoes. She was so in love. Scalisi insisted that involuntary manslaughter was about all they could possibly convict her on. "You know Alvin's lying," he said. "I don't want to beat that dead horse anymore." He picked up transcripts of Alvin's taped interrogations and counted off six times that Alvin had lamented about the possibility of going to jail. "The only thing on his mind is going to jail." Of course, he failed to mention that Theresa had reacted the same way.

During Scalisi's closing comments, Sachs, sickly and totally frayed, had taken a seat in the spectator's section and was ever so softly groaning his disapproval of the things Scalisi had said. Some of the spectators felt that the trouble with Scalisi's closing argument had been that he'd spent way too much time shifting blame instead of discussing evidence that pointed to his client's innocence. Monterosso's closing arguments had taken forty-five minutes; Scalisi spent an hour. The more Scalisi blamed Alvin, the deeper Sachs sunk into his chair. By the time Scalisi stopped talking, Sachs looked like someone had clobbered him over the head with a baseball bat. He was definitely hurting and genuinely upset. And by then, he was seriously ill; he should have been home in bed. Whatever illness had been hounding him all week, it had finally struck—with a vengeance.

Finally, Monterosso had one last chance to sway the jurors. He accused Scalisi of using war tactics. "This case is about Theresa's word...verses Theresa's word." Waving the videotape above his head, he reminded the jurors that they had heard for themselves, Theresa's confession...in her own words. He again referred to Theresa's total lack of remorse. "I think all of us were more upset by what happened to Andy than she was," he said, pointing his finger at Theresa. From her end of the counsel table she still sat, as stone-faced as Mount Rushmore.

He asked the jurors to take a good, long look at Theresa. From her seat next to Scalisi, Theresa began to tap her foot as the jurors stared at her. Once more, Monterosso gave her that brutal up-and-down glare he was so famous for and threw in a smirk for good measure. Anyone on the receiving end of a look such as that would feel belittled and humiliated and despised. It was enough to knock the wind out of a pirate's sail. Monterosso's soft brown eyes had turned hard, almost black with anger and disparagement. As the jury sized her up, Monterosso kept pointing at her and with heavy sarcasm he asked the jury, "Does Theresa looked like someone who could be easily intimidated? No," he smirked, "*she* was clearly the intimidator in this case. He began to talk about watching something with his kids on the Discovery Channel, something about a scorpion and a rat. While the mother

318

Donna Goodenough

rat was away, a scorpion had tried to sneak into her den and devour the newborns. Monterosso paused for a second or two, smiling, and then said he wondered how they got the camera down into that tiny little hole in the ground. Several of the jurors smiled. They liked Monterosso; it was easy to see.

Anyway, he said, the mother rat fought the scorpion and had successfully chased him out of her den. Mother rat had done what she had to do to protect her babies. She had risked her own life to save her babies. That's the true nature of the mothering instinct. Even rats had it. He went on to compare Theresa to a common rat. Then, he turned and stabbed his finger in her direction again. "Theresa Barroso doesn't even have the mothering instincts of a rat." It was a brutal comparison. But it fit. Then, it was up to the jury to decide.

Schooling instructed the jurors carefully. In his usual slow, deliberate and intensely methodical way of speaking, Judge Schooling thanked Theresa's jury for their time in this very important matter.

"You have two duties to perform," he began. "First, you must determine what facts have been proven from the evidence received in the trial and not from any other source. Second, you must apply the law that I state to you, to the facts, as you determine them, and in this way arrive at your verdict and any finding you are instructed to include in your verdict.

"You must not be influenced by pity for or prejudice against a defendant. Statements made by the attorneys during the trial are not evidence. Do not assume to be true any insinuation suggested by a question asked a witness." It was extremely important that the jurors fully understood the definition of words such as *willfully* and *knowingly*.

"The word willfully, when applied to the intent with which an act is done or omitted means with a purpose or willingness to commit the act or to make the omission in question. The word *willfully* does not require any intent to violate the law, or to injure another, or to acquire any advantage. The word *knowingly* means with knowledge of the existence of the facts in question. Knowledge of the unlawfulness of any act or omission is not required.

"If circumstantial evidence as to any particular count permits two reasonable interpretations, one of which points to the defendant's guilt and the other to innocence, you must adopt that interpretation that points to the defendant's innocence. If you find that before this trial the defendant made a willfully false or deliberately misleading statement concerning the crimes for which she is now being tried, you may consider that statement as a circumstance tending to prove a consciousness of guilt. Evidence that at some other time a witness made statements that are inconsistent or consistent with her testimony in this trial, may be considered by you not only for the purpose of testing the credibility of the witness, but also as evidence of the truth of the facts as stated by the witness on that former occasion." It was clearly an invitation to remember and consider Theresa's taped confessions.

"A witness, who is willfully false in one material part of her testimony, is to be distrusted in others," Schooling said. "You may reject the whole testimony of a witness who willfully has testified falsely." That pretty much squashed Theresa right then and there.

"Motive is not an element of the crime charged and need not be shown. A confession is a statement made by a defendant in which she has acknowledged her guilt of the crimes for which she is on trial.

"A defendant in a criminal action is presumed to be innocent until the contrary is proven, and in case of a reasonable doubt whether her guilt is satisfactorily shown, she is entitled to a verdict of not guilty. Persons who are involved in committing or attempting to commit a crime are referred to as principals in that crime. Each principal, regardless of the extent or manner of participation is equally guilty.

"A person, having care or custody of a child, is under a legal duty to not willfully cause or permit the person or health of that child to be injured, or to willfully place the child in a situation where the child's person or health may be endangered."

Theresa's jury was patient and they listened carefully to what the judge said. No one fidgeted. All eyes and ears were trained on Judge Schooling as he described the definitions of child beating, assault on a child under eight resulting in death, felony child abuse [neglect and endangerment included] torture and battery. Thanks to Monterosso, the jury already knew those definitions. Judge Schooling expressly instructed jurors that if they found Theresa guilty of the crime of murder, but had a reasonable doubt as to whether it was first degree or second, they were to find her guilty of the lesser. In closing, he instructed them how to go about requesting a review of evidence, such as the videotapes, actual trial transcripts or the photographs and told them that all twelve jurors must be in agreement. He smiled, thanked them and wished them well. Angie Reyes opened a door at the rear of the courtroom through which they were ushered into the deliberation room. Immediately, one juror asked to see the videotaped confession again. As their request was being satisfied, Alvin's jury was being seated to hear closing statements.

Monterosso began. "Alvin's knowledge is the issue here," he said. Then, as he had done with Theresa's jurors, he used the remote control to show the correlation between the law and the facts of the case. Click by click he showed them exactly why Alvin was guilty of murder. The words "malice aforethought" were shown on the left of the screen and under it, a concise definition. On the right were all the things Alvin had done that proved him guilty of malice aforethought. Monterosso went over the meaning of "implied malice" and explained to the jury why it fit...perfectly.

"There was a conscious disregard for human life," he said, "and a definite knowledge of the danger. Alvin is here because he [using his fingers to emphasize quote marks] 'didn't do anything.' He consciously disregarded Andy's welfare." He reminded the jurors of the taped interview between Alvin and Investigator Harding days prior to Alvin's arrest. One by one, he went through the list of Alvin's responsibilities as a foster parent and, each time he repeated Alvin's affirmation that he had understood his responsibilities, but hadn't done anything because he [again using his fingers to emphasize quote marks] 'didn't want to go to jail.' Monterosso reminded the jurors of Alvin's words and how Alvin had admitted to Harding that he'd understood the dangers. With any luck, by the time Monterosso finished with the visuals, the jurors would be absolutely certain that Alvin's hands were not merely stained with Andy's blood; they dripped scarlet.

Finally, with one last click of the remote he showed the jury a list of all the times Alvin had failed to protect Andy from Theresa's abuse.

"These were all the duties that were *not* performed by Alvin," he said, "and that constitutes murder. What Alvin actually perceived is not important; only what a reasonably prudent person would have perceived." Then, standing directly in front of the jury, with the television over his left shoulder, Monterosso had one closing comment for the jurors to think about as they deliberated. "The only person who had the opportunity to save Andy was Alvin. Instead he only chose to save himself." With that he was finished.

Judge Schooling politely mentioned that it had gotten a little bit late for lunchtime. Everyone was kindly admonished not to begin their deliberations until they were told to do so, and then they were dismissed for lunch. Monterosso had given Alvin's jury quite a bit to chew on and digest.

From the last row in the spectator's section, Leroy and Susie wearily hauled themselves out of their chairs and headed for the hallway. At no time during the trial—or at any of the pre trial hearings for that matter—had Leroy or Susie spoken to the press.

After lunch, when Alvin's jury had reassembled in the good seats, it had already neared 2:00 P.M. Sachs was looking and sounding even more horrible than he did before the lunch break. He had definitely come down with something vile, although in spite of the way he sounded he still insisted that he felt well enough to finish up. His voice was all but gone and he looked seriously ill.

No one could accuse Sachs of over-dressing for the occasion. But then, Sachs had never come off as a fancy, superficial guy, but rather someone who was more concerned about what was in a person's heart. He was down to earth and simple. Wearing scuffed, casual loafers and his favorite, worn out sports jacket with the elbow patches, Sachs looked like he'd been tumbled at a laundromat. He was obviously distressed that his voice had chosen this, of all times, to give up the ghost. His voice was nothing more than an inaudible croak.

Unfortunately, Sachs had several things working against him that day. For one, it had been unusually hot and stuffy in the courtroom after lunch

Deadly Thirst

and several of the jurors were fanning themselves and yawning. They were tired. So was Sachs. Looking feverish, he gathered up his yellow, legal note-pads from the counsel table and made his way toward the jury. Instead of standing directly in front of the jury, as Scalisi and Monterosso had done, Sachs chose to plant himself behind the wooden podium, again. He didn't even pull the podium a few feet across the carpet so as to be right in front of the jury when he spoke. He left the podium exactly where it had been, off to the side, and allowed it to become a barrier between himself and Alvin's jurors.

After a few coughs, he began to read from page after page of handwritten notes. Frequently he stopped and distracting gaps of silence hung in the air as he flipped back and forth through his notes, clearing his throat again and again. He went to the counsel table and poured himself a glass of water, hoping it would help his voice. It didn't.

He continued to croak and crackle through his monotone speech with hardly any eye contact with the jurors. He stared at the floor, he stared at the wall in back of the jury, he stared at the balustrade, he stared at the chalkboard in back of the witness stand and most of all he stared at his notes. He spoke to the air, not the jurors. He asked the jury not to convict Alvin because of his association with Theresa. Yes, Alvin had made some mistakes, he croaked, but his state of mind was the critical issue in this case. Some jurors in the back row had to strain to hear what was being said, although Sachs was talking as loud as he could. He used a cruel approach to the rational judgment of Jacob Marquist. He said that Jacob had been eleven years old when the murder happened and he hadn't done anything to protect Andy either and Jacob had been of a higher intelligence than Alvin.

"How do we know Alvin wasn't yelling at Theresa to shut up on the night of Andy's death?" As his vocal cords grew weaker, Sachs said that Alvin's biggest mistake had been made when he turned his life over from his mother, to Theresa. From the back of the courtroom, Leroy shouted "Amen!" Schooling shot him a glance, but said nothing.

"Alvin was just a big brother to Andy. Alvin had no idea of the position the county was putting him in by allowing him to have those children." As Sachs droned on and on, several of the jurors began getting sleepy-eyed. Soon, two were dozing. It had been an unfortunate combination of after-lunch-sleepiness, a stuffy courtroom and, outright boredom. There was no passion or variation in Sachs' raspy voice; just drone. Moreover, it was the same old speech they'd heard several times already. The jurors looked distracted and utterly tired. It's doubtful that Sachs even noticed, because he hadn't looked at the jurors. Even Judge Schooling had trouble staying alert. It seemed to be all Sachs could do just to remain on his feet and talk. It didn't look like he was going to make it.

Finally, Monterosso took a microphone from the counsel table and positioned it on the podium in front of Sachs. Sachs nodded his appreciation as he swallowed a few sips of water. Thankfully, the microphone gave

Sachs' voice a much-needed boost. The sleepy jurors woke up, but it was too late. He resumed, going back over things the jurors had already heard too many times. He spent too much time blaming CPS and reminding the jurors of how stupid Alvin was. "He can't put things in order or anticipate the consequences."

Alvin, at the far end of the counsel table, stared into space as if he were completely unaware of all that had been happening around him. He doodled. He picked his cuticles. He hooked and un-hooked paper clips.

In an almost inaudible whisper, Sachs finished. "I ask you to vote not guilty on all counts." With that, Sachs gathered up his notes, turned and walked to his place beside Alvin. He collapsed into his seat, blew his nose and popped another throat lozenge into his mouth.

It had gotten crucially late in the afternoon when Monterosso began his impassioned rebuttal. The tapes, he told the jurors, had been the most credible evidence that Alvin had known full well what was going on and yet, he had done nothing to stop it because he'd known he could get in trouble for it.

Out came the remote, and with it, his most efficient means of putting Alvin behind bars. One by one he listed the things that Alvin had witnessed; the kicking, the bleeding penis, the pushing, the acts of torture Andy endured on the chair and the time Theresa had made Andy eat his own excrement. All of those instances were neatly listed in the left column. Each instance was countered, on the right, with a devastating, incriminating quote from Alvin himself.

"So," Monterosso snarled as he jabbed his finger at Alvin, "he says he didn't know who to call when Andy was being abused. But he sure knew who to call when he wanted to go to the nudie bars and when Theresa was 'running his money.'" That statement had gotten a smile from several jurors. Monterosso reminded them that Alvin had moved quickly to rescue his television set—even arranging to rent a U-Haul—but he hadn't lifted a finger to help little Andy. "He knew how to get his TV out of that house but he claims he didn't know how to get Andy out." Then, in a face-to-face stare with front row jurors he was visibly angry; his hands clinched into fists at his sides. Monterosso's final statement was not a plea to convict; it was an *order*. "Don't tell me Alvin didn't know there was a scorpion in that den."

Alvin's jury was allowed a brief recess before they were seated in front of Judge Schooling to receive their own unique set of instructions. All over again, Judge Schooling began his hour-long monologue. He read from page after page of instructions, turning each page face down after he had finished reading it. Most of it had been memorized, but his eyes skimmed along the words anyway. Most of Alvin's instructions were the same as Theresa's, but because of Alvin's diminished mental capacity, the "intent" and "mental state" issues were included.

He instructed the jury that Dr. Kania's testimony could be considered only for the limited purpose of showing the information upon which Kania

Deadly Thirst

had based his opinion. Schooling quickly added that Kania's testimony was not to be considered as evidence of the truth.

"Whether a consequence is 'natural and probable' is an objective test based not on what the *defendant* actually intended but on what a person of reasonable and ordinary prudence would have thought likely to occur." This sentence made Sachs shudder.

Also in Alvin's instructions, Schooling defined "criminal negligence," "aforethought" and "malice." Sachs sighed and stared at the papers scattered in front of him as Judge Schooling explained each term carefully.

"Malice may be either expressed or implied. Malice is expressed when there is manifested an unlawful intention to kill a human being. Malice is implied when: #1 the killing resulted from an intentional act, #2 The natural consequences of the act are dangerous to human life, #3 The act was deliberately performed with knowledge of the danger to, and with conscious disregard for, human life. When it is shown that a killing resulted from the intentional doing of an act with express or implied malice, no other mental state need be shown to establish the mental state of malice aforethought, which does not necessarily require any ill will or hatred of the person killed.

"If a person causes another's death by doing an act or engaging in conduct in a criminally negligent manner, without realizing the risk involved, he is guilty of involuntary manslaughter. If, on the other hand, the person realized the risk and acted in total disregard of the danger to life involved, malice is implied and the crime is murder."

Sachs agonized over that particular instruction because if the jurors had paid attention during the playing of Alvin's taped interview with Investigator Harding, they would have heard Alvin admitting, over and over, in no uncertain terms, that he *did* understand the abuse Andy was being subjected to could kill him. Sachs was obviously deep in thought, as if perhaps wondering if there might have been something else he could have done to better illustrate Alvin's retardation. He'd done his best; in fact he'd done more than what was typically expected of him. He'd just have to wait it out like everyone else. Sachs considered the extent of his own emotional involvement with Alvin and he could scarcely imagine the agony that Alvin's parents were enduring as the jurors were sent off to deliberate. He felt deeply sorry for Alvin and his parents. Never in his career had feelings of this nature so engulfed him and haunted him. He was so distraught, he didn't want to turn and look at Leroy and Susie. He knew they were both crying, and he couldn't bear to see it.

In the hallway, I sat with newspaper reporters and waited. We'd brought books, magazines and laptops to occupy the time, but no one could concentrate enough to do anything constructive. Absolutely no one had given a second thought to Theresa's verdict; she'd be found guilty in a heartbeat. But Alvin…his situation was pitiful and the outcome was totally unpredictable. Still, few thought Alvin would be convicted.

Before anyone had a chance to get bored, the elevator doors opened and out came Monterosso, Horst and Scalisi. Theresa's verdict was in! The jury had taken less than two hours!

The handful of faithful spectators returned to the courtroom. There at the counsel table stood Horst, Monterosso, Theresa and Scalisi. For several minutes everyone was silent and then Judge Schooling came to the bench. After everyone had been accounted for, Angie Reyes brought the jurors into the courtroom through a back door. The judge asked the jury if they had reached a verdict and the foreperson agreed that they had. Theresa was told to stand up, face the jury, and receive her verdict. As the verdict was handed to Angie Reyes, Horst clasped his hands in front of him, bowed his head and earnestly began praying. From where I sat, I had a side-profile of his face; I could see his lips moving.

...We find the defendant Theresa DeJesus Barroso guilty of penal code 187 and fix the degree as murder in the first degree...

...Guilty of penal code 273ab; Assault on a Child Under eight Resulting in Death...

...Guilty of penal code 206; torture...

Guilty on all three counts. When the verdict was read, Horst took off his glasses, buried his face in his hands and sobbed. Several jurors smiled and nodded as they watched Monterosso drape his arm around Horst's shoulder and give him a friendly hug. At the far end of the table, Theresa still stood; her face mirrored a soul totally devoid of remorse or conscience. Theresa did not shed one tear. But Horst was completely undone by the verdict. Several of the jurors looked as if they were on the verge of tears.

As soon as he could regain his composure, Horst wiped his cheeks dry with his hands, put his glasses back on and turned to look at Theresa. And the tears came again. By now, several female jurors were weeping along with him, dabbing their eyes with tissues they'd brought with them from the deliberation room. I was crying too. It was very emotional to see a cop cry like that. I turned to look at Leroy and Susie; they were both stoical, no doubt fearing Alvin's imminent verdict.

After Theresa's jurors had been dismissed for the last time, Theresa was shackled and led out a side door. Most of the people inside Department 61 that afternoon were jubilant that Theresa had been found guilty; but almost everyone had expected it. Rushing into the hallway, the newspaper reporters whipped out cell phones to call in the news. I hurried to the pay phones near the elevators to call my best friend and asked her to spread the word. After the flurry of calls had been made, we returned to the hard wooden benches in the hallway to await Alvin's verdict. After about ten minutes, Horst and Monterosso stepped from the courtroom wearing broad smiles. They were immediately hounded with questions from newspaper reporters.

Then, it was back to waiting. Prepared to spend days in the hallway, the couple of reporters and I settled in for the long haul. It was June 11th.

Deadly Thirst

Timothy McVeigh had been put to death that very morning and the newspapers that were scattered about the hallway benches were full of detailed accounts of his last hours. Ironically, it was also just one day prior to the five-year anniversary of the O.J. Simpson murders. Those two landmarks in time were much discussed in the hallway as the number of spectators dwindled to four. No one knew where Leroy and Susie had gone to await the verdict in seclusion. They certainly weren't in the hallway. And where had Andy's grandmother been? Everyone thought for sure she would have been there for the verdicts, but she wasn't. The noise she had vowed to make had been permanently silenced long ago. Neither were the Herman's or any of Andy's other caretakers on hand to witness Theresa's verdict. Perhaps the silencing mechanisms that had effectively snuffed out Dawn Masterson had also snuffed out the Herman's fire. To my knowledge, even Theresa's parents had not attended the trial, but I'd heard it was because they had received death threats.

Perhaps they chose not to show up for other reasons. Horst later said that Theresa's parents had been devastated when Theresa was arrested for Andy's murder and they had been disgusted with the allegations of abuse. Perhaps also, they could have been fearful that Theresa's bad reputation with CPS might be accredited to their record. After all, CPS had been quick to accredit Theresa with the glowing attributes of her parents, so what was to stop CPS from assuming Theresa's parents weren't just like her? Personally, I agonized for Theresa's parents and I agonized for Leroy and Susie. There were many innocent people who had paid a heavy price for what Theresa had done.

There had been only three constant faces in the spectator section, Leroy, Susie and I. The newspaper reporters weren't constant because oftentimes they had only sat in on an hour or so of testimony, and sometimes no reporters had been there. But I had always been there; all day, every day. The trial had required a lot of time and commitment from everyone.

After less than two hours, those weary souls in the hallway were shocked to see Horst and Monterosso walking briskly toward them.

"Alvin's verdict is in," Monterosso said as he breezed past and entered the courtroom. Seconds later, another elevator door opened and a haggard-looking Sachs emerged. Behind him were Leroy and Susie. All three were wearing a look of doom and walked as if their legs were made of Jell-o.

When the spectators had finally been ushered into the courtroom, Leroy and Susie sat in the very back row. Two armed deputies were positioned strategically between Alvin's parents and Monterosso; one was standing right next to Leroy and the other was stationed at the bar, close to Monterosso. Once more, Angie Reyes brought the jurors in through the back door of the courtroom and, after a few minutes Judge Schooling came to the bench. Looking almost as worn out as Sachs, Judge Schooling asked the jurors if they'd reached a verdict.

"Yes, your honor, we have."

Alvin was told to stand and face the jury. Sachs had to tap him on the arm and tell him to stand up. The deputy nearest Leroy and Susie turned and looked directly at them as the verdict was read. The deputy nearest Monterosso also faced toward Leroy and Susie.

...We find the defendant Alvin Lee Robinson guilty of section 187 of the penal code, murder, and fix the degree as murder in the second degree...

Everything seemed to come to a surreal standstill as the words sunk in. From the back of the courtroom, Leroy had started to moan. The rest of the words seemed to come in distorted, jumbled pieces and reverberated around and around the courtroom...

...Guilty of assault on a child causing death...

Then, a louder, more agonized moan came from the back of the courtroom along with the anguished cries of Alvin's mother. Leroy had come unglued. The deputy that was stationed nearest Leroy was poised to wrestle him to the ground if need be. Emotions run high at verdict time and Leroy's extreme dislike for Monterosso had been evident for quite some time. The deputy who had stationed himself at the bar near Monterosso grew alarmed at Leroy's outburst.

Leroy pointed his finger at Monterosso and yelled, "I want to have a word with that one!" When Leroy stepped into the isle and tried to approach Monterosso, the deputies immediately blocked his path and ordered him—in no uncertain terms—to sit down!

Monterosso turned around and smirked at Leroy.

Alvin was perplexed; what was all the fuss about? Sachs leaned toward him and explained that they'd found him guilty and he'd probably have to spend the rest of his life in prison. Alvin's first response was to look toward his parents for help. Leroy could bear it no more and fled the courtroom, his face pale with shock. Susie followed him, bawling out loud the whole way.

As Judge Schooling brought the trial to an end and thanked the jurors, Leroy was angrily pacing in the hallway. Monterosso would have no choice but to come out and face him, and when he did, Leroy was determined to have his say. The spectators eventually came out and as I passed Leroy in the hall, I heard him say, "I'm gonna get that DA if it's the last thing I do!"

Deputies were fast to get all over Leroy, telling him to settle down and go on home. Sachs emerged from the courtroom shortly thereafter and found Leroy pacing and smoldering under the threatening glare of the two armed deputies. Instead of thanking Sachs for all his efforts on behalf of Alvin, Leroy hollered more jive talk, ranting that there ain't no way a black man can get justice in our society. Leroy had obviously forgotten all about the injustice that had sent little Andy to an early grave. And Andy was white.

Sachs had done his very best for Alvin and had gone above and beyond his duties as Alvin's public defender. It was obvious that Leroy's comments hurt Sachs' feelings; you could see it in his face. The verdict had been an

Deadly Thirst

emotional wallop for him too. It seemed almost shameful that Leroy hadn't expressed some sort of thanks to Sachs. Deputies stood close by and kept Leroy under surveillance until he left the premises. It was about an hour later when the jurors emerged from another door at the far end of the hallway, accompanied by Horst. Sachs was again in the hall around this time, looking pale and grief-stricken. The Press Enterprise reporter and I were the only ones who had waited it out, hoping to get comments from some of the jurors or the jury forewoman. We weren't disappointed. The forewoman readily commented that Alvin had cared more about his $400 television than he had for Andy. Furthermore, Alvin's jury had not believed Sachs' claim that Alvin had been mentally incapable of protecting Andy. Apparently, they *had* been paying close attention to the tapes after all. "It was repulsive," she said. "Alvin and Theresa sounded like two five-year olds bickering." The jurors had all been on the same wavelength, she said, in reference to deliberations. They hadn't needed to view the tapes again; they'd felt certain that Alvin could have called 911 for help. After all, he hadn't hesitated to do so when his car had been battered.

The forewoman railed the foster care system too, saying the whole situation with CPS was "beyond horrible." She said there had been total apathy in the system. Andy's situation could have easily been prevented, she said. Sachs was beaten down; his almost heroic efforts had been defeated. Still, he was totally committed and his face was clearly slack-jawed with sorrow. The Press Enterprise reporter and I stood shoulder to shoulder and asked him for a comment. Sachs looked only at the newspaper reporter and ignored me completely, not ever making eye contact with me. He said that Alvin hadn't even understood that he'd been found guilty. "I had to explain it to him." He shook his head in disbelief and stared hard at the floor. He turned and walked to the elevator. Slowly and decisively he pressed the button and waited, his eyes cast downward and his shoulders hunched heavy with burden. As the elevator swallowed him up and the doors closed, Sachs was leaning in the corner, alone; his eyes still as downcast as the corners of his mouth.

It was past 6:00 P.M. when Horst, me and several of the remaining jurors crowded into the elevator and headed down. Horst was going to accompany everyone to the parking structure...just in case. Leroy had been pretty hot.

On the way down I told Horst what I'd heard Leroy say about "getting that DA" and although Horst hadn't voiced his concerns to me at that time, he forwarded the information to Monterosso who in turn told Investigator Terry Fisher about it. Fisher contacted me a few days later by phone and got a complete statement as to what I had witnessed. Threats against the District Attorney [or anyone else at the courthouse] were a very serious thing. A deadly ambush was entirely possible.

I had been watching Susie and Leroy carefully over the past several months. I told Fisher that I didn't believe Leroy would cause any problems

328

Donna Goodenough

because he'd always shown such an astonishing depth of self-control. Leroy had never spoken to anyone, I said, except Alvin's attorney—and then it had always been in hushed whispers. Fisher understood the agony Leroy was experiencing and felt sorry for him in that respect. Emotions always flair at verdict time. Still, I had to confide that I sensed something else had been going on between Leroy and Monterosso. Leroy seemed to hold Monterosso personally responsible for Alvin's predicament, I said. As if Monterosso had some sort of personal grudge against Alvin or something.

CHAPTER 16

SENTENCING
No remorse

Theresa Barroso was sentenced on September 7th, four days before the terrorist attack on the World Trade Center. There were several familiar faces in the hallway that particular morning. Of course the Press Enterprise had a reporter there to cover the sentencing, and of course I was there too. But what had been most surprising was that one of Theresa's jurors had come back. He'd been so affected by the atrocities that Theresa had committed against little Andy and her complete lack of emotion or remorse, that he'd been compelled to come back and hear her being sentenced for what she had done. He wanted to see if she'd cry.

Just as Angie Reyes opened the double doors and motioned everyone inside, Monterosso emerged from the elevator. The juror—a young man—had been sitting with me on a hallway bench. We'd been talking about my plans to write this book. Monterosso extended his hand to both of us and thanked us for coming, especially the juror. Then, we went inside.

Theresa was seated alone, in one of the good seats and, she was crying. She was clutching a piece of paper and it was suspected that she might have written a few words of apology that she would read to the court and perhaps to any of Andy's family members or custodians that showed up. But, other than Monterosso, no one had shown up on Andy's behalf, at least, not until Sergeant Horst walked in.

Horst took a seat off by himself, on the far side of the spectator section, where the additional jury seats had been located during the trial. The platform had been removed by then and the spectator section had been put back to its original arrangement. Horst looked sad and gave a feeble wave to the juror and me as we sat huddled together on the opposite side of the courtroom.

No one would ever know what had been written on the paper Theresa held in her hands, because she remained stone-cold quiet. Instead, her Godmother said something on her behalf.

Her name was Rosie Gonzales* and she was accompanied by a Spanish interpreter. Gonzales was visibly shaking as she stepped up to the bar to say her speech in front of Judge Schooling.

"I just want to tell the family, I want to tell Theresa's family that we are very sorry for what happened. Especially I want to tell the mother of the child that we're praying for her and the child. And I'm not justifying Theresa. She's going to have to suffer the consequences and also she's going to go through punishment." Theresa's chin was quivering and tears streaked down her face as she listened to Gonzales speak.

"But I want to tell you that she's like my daughter. She's a good person. She's always had a good heart. And I assure you that she is the first person who is remorseful. And the mother of the child, I wish her restoration and happiness for the rest of her life."

Certainly Laura and Cowboy had found restoration and happiness when the county awarded them a $250,000 settlement.

Judge Schooling thanked the woman and asked if anyone else would like to say a word. No one cared to say anything else on Theresa's behalf, not even the two heavy-set Hispanic women in the back row who were rumored to be her sisters.

"Perhaps someone from Andy's side would like to say something," Schooling said. His eyes scanned the courtroom, but no one had stepped forward. I found it profoundly sad that no one from Andy's side had shown up, except for Monterosso and Sergeant Horst, and Horst had chosen to remain silent on this occasion. There was a long hush in the courtroom while Judge Schooling and Monterosso looked around for somebody...*anybody* who would like to say a few words on Andy's behalf. I was certainly tempted to march up to the bar and give Theresa a piece of my mind, but I decided I'd better keep quiet. I was too emotional and my mouth had a tendency to slip into overdrive when I least expected it.

It was especially sad that no one who had known Andy was willing to take the opportunity to stand in front of Theresa Barroso and tell her, right to her ugly face, how much sadness she had inflicted on everyone involved. Her hatefulness had caused tremendous grief and irreparable damage to so many lives. Andy's murder had affected thousands of people; the crime was so horrific it had inspired new legislation to prevent it from happening again. And yet, no one was there to admonish Theresa to her face. I literally had to force myself to stay seated and quiet. I wanted to spit on her. Judge Schooling seemed a bit disappointed that no one had chosen to speak on Andy's behalf. He let a long silence elapse as he straightened some papers on the bench and fidgeted with various items, thinking. During that time, no one spoke.

Andy's grandmother, Dawn Masterson, later told the Press Enterprise that she hadn't attended the sentencing because she didn't believe in carrying around resentment. She said she'd become a Christian and she was content to let God do the judging of Theresa Barroso.

Andy's biological mother wasn't there either. She too had flapped her lips to the press about being a Christian and then further stated that she prays everyday that Alvin and Theresa get what they deserve. Hardly something a "Christian" would pray for, but then few really believed that Laura Utley was what she claimed to be. She said the guilt she had experienced at having Andy taken away from her and put into foster care, had passed. So, she was not in attendance the day her son's killer was sentenced. The apathy was disturbing; you could see it in the faces of Schooling, Horst and Monterosso. Finally, Schooling looked toward Monterosso and asked if he had anything to say.

"Yes your Honor. Thank you. I think the memories of this trial will be with us forever, everybody who participated in this. So I don't want to talk about Theresa. What happened to Andy was the most callous and evil conduct that I have ever seen; especially callous and evil because of the person it was committed against. We're not talking about someone who could fight back. We're talking about a four-year-old child, Andy Setzer, the most vulnerable among us. He was vulnerable because he was part of the system. He was given to Theresa for care, to be taken care of. Instead, she murdered him in a brutal, remorseless way. I do say remorseless.

"I appreciate the comments of the lady, but I disagree with one comment she made. There is no remorse from Theresa. She may have made her peace with God but I don't think she's made her peace with this court. For that, I believe she rightfully deserves to forfeit the rest of her life in society."

Then, with a sigh, Monterosso held up a beautiful color photograph of Andy, which had been given to him by Mike and Lynn Herman. It showed Andy wearing goofy sunglasses, smiling and dancing silly alongside a parade. What a vibrant little boy he was. It was hard to believe he was gone.

"Andy was, from what I know from talking to people who knew him and from seeing photographs of him, was a child who would have blessed our society if he were still with us." Giving the photo one last look, he laid it on the counsel table, face up.

"The court is obviously not considering probation in this matter. I don't think she's suitable for that. With regards to consecutive sentencing, I think this case clearly calls out for the maximum possible punishment because this was the maximum amount of evil I think any of us has ever seen. So she deserves the maximum punishment.

"But I do believe count 3, as alleged, was committed at a different time for different conduct, that being the torture that Andy suffered prior to the day of his death. For that I believe she deserves a consecutive life term. With that, I submit."

Scalisi was given the opportunity to say something, but he declined. Monterosso did have one more thing he had forgotten to say.

"Just so the court knows, I talked to the grandmother, Dawn Masterson, just yesterday and she stated to me that she didn't know if she would be here because of the emotions involved. She didn't know if it would be something she could handle. And I don't believe the natural mother intended to come. There is nobody else here to speak for Andy but me," he said. "And of course, Sergeant Horst."

Judge Schooling looked toward the back of the courtroom at Horst who sat alone, looking pitifully sad. His left arm was draped across the back of the empty chair next to him, his right hand reaching across his lap toward the empty chair, palm up. Almost as if he were clinging to a tiny, invisible hand. It seemed as though Andy had been called out of his grave to come and sit next to Sergeant Horst, and hold hands with him for this very important day. Andy's murder may have faded from the minds of the public, but Horst had not forgotten him. How could he? The sight of Andy's battered body was still just as vivid and upsetting to Horst as it had ever been.

"All right," Judge Schooling finally said. It was obviously hard for Schooling to put into words his feelings about Andy's torture/murder. But he would try. In his usual slow, meticulous way of speaking, he wrung his hands and struggled for a place to begin. The courtroom was silent as everyone sat perfectly still, waiting to hear what the judge had to say. Once more he began to fidget with papers and other items spread out in front of him.

"The trial in this matter is one in which I hope we never have to go through again. It took a great deal out of me as it did out of everyone who in any way participated, observed or had any part in the trial. It's a case, which we can only hope and pray the likes of which will never be a part of our lives again.

"It is the opinion of the court that the actions herein are probably one of the more heinous that this court has ever observed. Especially in light of the defenseless nature and condition of the victim and, the position of trust in which this defendant was placed and the total reliance upon her by the child in her custody. Anyone who has ever had any contact with young children is going to be deeply affected by this for a long period of time.

"The court must make comment upon the fact that not only was there no remorse at any point shown, but the attitude and content of this defendant's statements while testifying indicated that she had not a clue as to the enormity of the evil that she had presented upon this poor, defenseless and very beautiful child. Her denials, her fabrications, it appears that she had not a glimmer of recognition of the evil upon which she embarked when she decided to vent her anger upon this child." Schooling fell silent and shook his head in disbelief. He massaged his forehead as if trying to ward off the onset of a headache. Again, he slowly began straightening papers and rearranging various items from one position to another. He was obviously deep in thought, pondering the innocence and vulnerability of not just Andy, but of all children.

Who could describe Theresa Barroso? Antisocial? Psychopath? Both seemed fitting. She was a stoical antisocial fortress. A vicious, remorseless monolith of brutality. Only one percent of females display this personality. The percentage is small but the damage a female antisocial can do is enormous, especially when defenseless children are involved. A true psychopath cannot put herself into another person's shoes; they are completely lacking of vital emotions such as feelings of concern and compassion for others. They easily and completely sever themselves from another person's pain. Theresa Barroso's self-pitying tears had dried as soon as Rosa Gonzales

Deadly Thirst

finished speaking. By the time Judge Schooling began to speak she had reverted back to the empty husk of a human being that had tortured and murdered a defenseless child. For what? Wetting his pants and getting a drink of water? Judge Schooling could have spoken harshly about Theresa, but he didn't. It wasn't his character.

Scalisi looked like he wanted a chance to say something after all. Judge Schooling was accommodating. "Just, your Honor, that we'd ask the court to consider running count 3 concurrent." [At the same time].

Schooling weighed Scalisi's comment for quite some time before he spoke. He stated that Theresa was absolutely ineligible for probation. "The court is indicating a consecutive sentence as to count 3 vis-à-vis a concurrent sentence," Schooling said. In other words, no. Theresa Barroso would serve out one sentence and when that one was finished she would begin to serve the next sentence. She'd be in prison for a long, long time.

"Further, and almost of paramount importance, is the fact that in the opinion of the court the defendant has not shown any remorse, not even at the guilty verdict. So there is nothing further for the court to do but to impose the sentence indicated by law. For violation of Section 187 [murder] the defendant is sentenced to California Department of Corrections for a period of 25 years to life. Count 2, violation of Section 273ab is determined to be 654 with count 1. Count 3, a violation of section 206 will be consecutive with the sentence imposed in count 1." [654 of the Penal Code prohibits a defendant from being sentenced for the same conduct that the DA has chosen to file in separate counts and under different Penal Code sections. For example, stealing a car can be filed as 10851 of the Vehicle Code and as Grand Theft of the Penal Code. If convicted of both, a person can only be sentenced for one.]

In closing, Schooling looked over at Theresa and shook his head. He had truly hoped to see even just a shred of remorse from her, but there was none. Her tears had long since dried by then. Once more, she sat Sphinx-like and dry-eyed. It gave the judge a shiver to look into the face of a ruthless murderer, who felt compassion for no one and remorse only for the circumstances she found herself in. He looked toward the back of the courtroom and saw Sergeant Horst still sitting there in the far corner, dejected, even though Theresa had gotten her deserved punishment. At the counsel table stood Scalisi and Monterosso. It was to them that Judge Schooling made his final comments. With a pained expression he began.

"One of the things I've got to say to you now that sentencing has been completed, is I know that this was a tough case for the court and for the prosecutor who has a child about the same age and for the defense counsel, whose wife is expecting. It makes it doubly difficult for people in that position. And I have ten grandchildren, so I know how vulnerable children are. I want to congratulate each of you for your objectivity and the manner in which you represented your respective sides in a most professional manner."

As everyone filed out of the courtroom, Monterosso, Sergeant Horst and I took a minute in the hallway to look, one more time, at the photograph of Andy Setzer. I asked Monterosso if I might be able to have a copy of the photograph for this book, but he declined. It had been given to him by Mike and Lynn Herman to be used strictly for court purposes. He explained that when Alvin and Theresa become eligible for parole, that photograph of Andy will be shown during the eligibility hearing. Giving it another long look, he put it into an envelope. Silently, I vowed to attend that hearing and have my say in the matter.

By then, it was pretty obvious to everyone that I had developed a crush, so to speak, on both Monterosso and Horst. I was attracted to Monterosso because of his extraordinary good looks and I would freely admit that I idolized both men for their compassion and the way they brought punishment for Andy's killers. I respected both men, more than I could say—and I said quite a bit. Perhaps I had stars in my eyes. But there was something else I felt for Sergeant Horst. By my own admission, I had put him on a pedestal all his own, high above everyone else.

Perhaps I'd been keeping company with the wrong types of men throughout my life, but I had rarely seen a man cry. Certainly, I'd never expected Sergeant Horst to get so emotional at the guilty verdict. No one did. Not even the Sergeant himself, who was probably as surprised as anyone that his emotions had run away on him like that. He'd felt it in his soul. It had been the defining moment. He had become my hero, my knight in shining armor. Ever since the day Theresa's verdict was read, I had been devoted to Sergeant Horst, singing his praises to anyone and everyone who would listen. And even to those who wouldn't. Still to this day, I insist that the adoration I felt for Sergeant Horst stemmed from the fact that he cared enough about Andy Setzer to cry. He was sensitive; something I found very endearing...and rare among the men I'd known in my life. I admired him because he truly cared about a little lost boy and his emotions had manifested in a most touching way.

* * *

Alvin was sentenced on October 12. Much had changed in the United States since the terrorist attacks of September 11th. Courthouse security was super tight; lines at the metal detectors were long and slow. Sachs was still fit to be tied that Alvin had been found guilty of anything. He presented to Judge Schooling a twenty three-page motion, which the judge said was too long to be filed. Sachs apologized but launched into yet another long-winded lecture about how Alvin didn't know any better. Even though Sachs said he wouldn't be repetitious in his statements; he was exactly that, although his demeanor was a little bit more resigned by now. He wanted the jury's verdict, basically, overturned. On and on he droned, and Judge Schooling listened carefully, giving his full attention to each point Sachs made.

When Monterosso got his turn to speak, he took each of the points Sachs had made and, just as he did during the trial, blew each one to smith-

Deadly Thirst

ereens. It was a long speech by both men; Alvin's case was highly unique and in no way fit into tidy confines that could be explained in a brief statement by either man.

Finally, after Monterosso and Sachs were finished, Judge Schooling sat for a minute or two contemplating the facts of the case. He made eye contact with no one and seemed to stare off into oblivion, fidgeting with a stack of papers that were in front of him. He was clearly striving for the most fair and just way to sentence Alvin.

It could never be overstated that Alvin and Theresa were damn lucky they had Judge Russell Schooling presiding over their trial. Some judges roaming the Robert Presley Hall of Justice were infamous for the brutal and swift way they threw down stiff sentences. No one could ever accuse Judge Schooling of jumping the gun or being abrupt in any way with anyone. He was extremely polite and patient with everyone. To Judge Schooling it mattered not one iota if the person he was speaking to was wearing a business suit or shackles; he spoke to them respectfully. Not a soul had anything negative to say about Judge Schooling.

Alvin did indeed evoke at least some sympathy from Schooling and the judge certainly felt sorry for Alvin's parents, who were sitting in the back row of the courtroom agonizing about what was to come. Nonetheless, he refused to overturn the verdict of the jury and said Alvin's yelling at Andy on the fatal night maybe had not facilitated the ultimate death but was a causative factor in the escalation of the cruelty.

"No, Alvin Robinson is not equally culpable with Theresa Barroso. She is indeed the most evil person and the jury so found. She is one of the most vile people that this court has had the unfortunate experience of having encountered. Especially when you look at the before and after pictures of the victim." Judge Schooling could not look at anyone in particular as he spoke, but fixed his eyes on the papers he was shuffling around. Shaking his head in disgust, he said that seeing pictures of what Andy looked like after Theresa Barroso got finished with him was enough to wrench any right-thinking person's heart out. As for Alvin's comments of rebuke toward Theresa for abusing Andy, Judge Schooling called them "half-hearted."

Schooling said he did not think that Sachs had made a good enough case for a new trial. Furthermore, Schooling didn't think the sentence that he was about to hand down would in any way be cruel or unusual punishment for Alvin.

"Just because one person is more evil than another does not mean that the one person who is less evil is entitled to some kind of bonus by the legal system by virtue of giving that person a considerably lesser punishment." He also made it expressly clear for the record that he wanted there to be no doubt whatsoever that he knew he could set aside the verdict. Judge Schooling adamantly refused to do that.

True to his gentle nature, before Judge Schooling sentenced Alvin, he gave anyone who wished to speak on Alvin's behalf a chance to be heard.

Sachs introduced a wisened little old gray-haired black man who sat next to Leroy and Susie. Leroy helped the Reverend Oscar Wilcox* out of his chair and guided the feeble old man to the bar. Apparently, Reverend Davenport was not willing to return to Department 61 again and subject himself to the possibility of being put through John Monterosso's meat grinder one more time. It was a fair assumption that Reverend Davenport probably never wanted to lay eyes on the likes of Monterosso again for as long as either one of them lived. Being publicly massacred once was plenty.

Instead, Leroy had managed to persuade another preacher to say a few words on behalf of Alvin. So, here was this old, feeble gentleman, crippled up with arthritis, standing on wobbly legs fixin' to say somethin' to the judge. With one hand on the bar and the other clutching an intricately carved cane, he began to address the court while Leroy and Susie looked on real nervous-like.

"I been preaching sixty-six years this year. I been knowing this young man ever since he was real young. I've never known him to be violent. Huh-uh. Never. This is strange to me. That's why I'm old. 9-5-17. And I desired to come here today because I wanted to meet you."

The Reverend Wilcox began waving his cane in the air and poking the tip of it at the judge.

"I see a lot of mercy in you," he said, poke, poke, poke. Then, in a sudden shout that startled everyone in the courtroom, most of all Judge Schooling, the Reverend yelled, "I'm a prophet!"

If there was anyone who hadn't been giving the Reverend their undivided attention so far, they certainly gave it to him from that point on. Monterosso turned around with a startled expression on his face and watched, halfway bemused, as the Reverend launched into a long-winded, cane-waving sermon about being merciful.

"There's a lot of mercy. The devil may want to go over it, but there's mercy here. Blessed are the merciful for they shall obtain mercy. I am preaching!" He poked his cane in Monterosso's direction and said, "They tried to stop me. But they don't hire me. When you don't hire me you can't fire me." Swinging the tip of his cane in Schooling's direction, the Reverend continued. "And I thank God to look in your face. Yes, I see mercy there.

"I never knowed him, all I knowed about this child," he said with the tip of his cane wandering toward Alvin, "was work. Got a good father and a good mother."

From her seat beside Leroy, Susie erupted into a flood of tears. Leroy did his best to remain composed; his turn to speak was coming next. He was visibly nervous; his mouth twisted.

"Yes," the Reverend said, poking his cane at Alvin. "Work. He wasn't lazy. He be on the cars and the hood up in there, all that kind of stuff. All that other, I don't know about it. But I just know him and I'm down here in defense. Have mercy today. And God bless you."

Just as Judge Schooling opened his mouth to thank the Reverend for his comments, the Reverend erupted again.

"I see mercy in your face!" he bellowed, poke, poke, poke. Judge Schooling's mouth slapped shut. "I been prophesying ever since I was little. I started preaching when I was little. I stand on the side so the people could see me. I never stopped."

It was some of the best theatrics ever seen inside a courtroom! Monterosso was barely able to keep the grin off his face. I couldn't help but giggle all the way through the mercy monologue. Too bad Sergeant Horst isn't here to see this, I thought, he could use some amusement.

"I raised my boys. My boys are on the armband, my three boys. Got 'em on my arm. Ronnie, Charlie and Robert. Yes. And I'm here in his defense. That's why I'm here. I didn't feel like coming. I got arthritis. I'm old. You know, I gotta stay at home. But my desire was to come here in his defense. I'm asking you, God bless you, for mercy."

Judge Schooling waited until the tip of the Reverend's cane touched down on the floor and Leroy came forward to retrieve the old man. After the Reverend was safely lowered into his chair, Judge Schooling, sensing it was now safe to talk, graciously thanked the Reverend for his efforts.

"I know it was at some considerable effort and inconvenience for you to be here and perhaps, it appears, pain." And then, Leroy was allowed to speak.

For those who had enjoyed the Reverend's sermon, they were about to get an encore in African-American jive-talk, minus the cane. With his jaw set in determination, Leroy strode up to the bar, and Alvin grabbed a tissue from the box.

With one hand shoved deep into the pocket of his pants and one hand gesturing toward the judge, Leroy's first comment was, of course, about Alvin's stupidity.

"My son is slow, ya' Honor. He got into something that it coulda happen to anybody. He married a woman and she take control of everything. His life is shot. It's no good for nothin'. If you give him all this time that you guys keep talking about, you say he was convicted by peers. They was peers all right. People over him, more intelligent than him could look at his level of what was goin' on. This boy just like a kid. He's very slow.

"I'm sure, now that he's had time to think about it, he's been locked up for just about two years, that if he know, he would have did things different. They just told him to get off the premises over there. That's her place. That was her place to be living in. That was her place that she got people from the county to be on." Now Leroy's voice was rising, both hands were on his hips now and his head was just-a-bobbin' in rhythm with his jive-talk rhetoric.

"Everybody in this case," Leroy fumed, jabbing his finger at Monterosso, "from the county people that put those kids there to the District Attorney to the attorneys to me, we all be guilty for letting her take control of my boy's

Donna Goodenough

life! Letting her take control of those kids' life. They wasn't even licensed. They didn't have a license to put children in their house, but they put them in there. They didn't have a license!

"This boy didn't know how to take care of himself. This woman, your Honor, she cause so much grief on me and my family, I can't...I lost my hair! I done lost my hair for worry. This is eating away at me like cancer.

"Your Honor, please don't send my son to prison for nothin'. He ain't did nothin'! He ain't have sense enough to know that this woman take control of his life and was so mean and evil. It's wrote all over her, Judge. It's wrote all over. That have something to do with sending this boy away. They going to suffer just like he goin' to suffer. Your Honor, I been down here day after day after day listening to everything. She went to jail and she called my house. 'Come on down here and help me do this time. Help me do this time. What, *he* gonna do some time for something *she* did?!'"

Leroy needed to calm down and put a little bit of control into his tone of voice. He was shouting. He'd already greatly offended Monterosso by saying that Monterosso was somehow responsible for what Theresa had done.

"Sure, he shoulda tried to do somethin' that stopped it. But he turned around and came home with his head down. What's wrong son? Things ain't goin' right at the house. He didn't have enough sense to tell me. Then you would have put *me* in jail for abusing the baby the way she did!" That statement drew a look of slight indignation from Judge Schooling and got an outright glare from Monterosso.

"I would have gone over there and wrung her neck. Then you would be sentencing me to prison. This boy, he can't hardly get around that corner without walking all over himself. He ain't got no sense, Judge. He's slow. I don't care what you guys do, what you say, he need to be sent to a place where he can get some education. Give him back to me. Give me another chance with him. Let me have him. Let me have him for one year, Judge, and I promise you'll see a different person. You'll see a guy out in society doing somethin' for everybody. Please, Judge, give me my chance." And with that, Leroy slumped into his seat next to Susie, who was weeping uncontrollably.

Of course, Leroy had had twenty-six years to make a better person out of his son and this was the end result of his handiwork. Leroy's parenting skills were as deadly as Alvin's and Schooling wasn't about to consider Leroy's ridiculous request. Furthermore, Leroy wasted his time before the judge by ranting and raving about how Alvin didn't have enough sense to tell anyone about the child abuse. It was glaringly apparent that Leroy had conveniently overlooked the fact that Alvin had enough sense to come home complaining about how Theresa was "running his money." Moreover, Alvin had clearly demonstrated that he had enough sense to call 911 for help when his car was being bashed. Alvin had priorities and Andy hadn't been one of them. Leroy also conveniently omitted referencing the time

339

when Alvin had his mother on the telephone, asking her what she would do for "someone" with swollen nuts. *That* would have been Alvin's best chance ever of telling his parents about the abuse. But did he? No. He had enough sense to look out for numero uno and, in Alvin's own words, Andy was not number one, Alvin was. And if Alvin was in such dire need of some sort of extended education, why didn't Leroy set him up, a long time ago, with a tutor or something? All Leroy did was dump the blame on everyone else. Alvin was stupid because society had slighted him. Neither Leroy nor the Reverend Wilcox had said anything of value during their requests for leniency, which they turned into nothing more than a comical, long-winded, cane-waving, finger-poking, jive-talk blab session.

Schooling said that he could not let this opportunity pass without saying that he wholeheartedly agreed with Leroy when he'd said that the county had been at least, party to blame for what had happened to Andy.

"There is no question about the fact that this county should never have placed those children in the custody of Theresa Barroso. And I'll tell you one other thing. I had a hard time not coming unglued when I heard the probation officer testify that the place was unlicensed and that they had done no background check. I was disgusted by the cavalier attitude county officials took toward placement in this foster home, which wasn't in fact a foster home, it was just a home. When there are so many people who are crying out for children…" He paused to shake his head in disbelief. "And then they place this child with someone like that. It made my blood boil. I can tell you that right now.

"And I agree with you wholeheartedly when you say that this blame must be shouldered by more people than Alvin. And believe you me that the sentencing in this does not in any way, in the opinion of this court, alleviate the responsibility of anyone. We're not talking about the county. We're not talking about Miss Barroso. We're not talking about anybody but Alvin right now. And the people in the county who placed that child there should be thankful forever that they are not before me, because it would not go well for them. So I do not disagree with you. Yes, he is slow; there is adequate evidence that he's slow. But, it is clear that his impairment was not to that great a degree that he had no ability to do anything to prevent this tragedy. And it can be characterized in no other fashion but a huge, huge tragedy."

After a minute or two of silence, Schooling said that if there was nothing further he'd go ahead and sentence Alvin. But Sachs had something he wanted to say and as usual, he wouldn't say it quickly.

"I don't think Alvin Robinson would be a threat to children or anybody else if he was released," Sachs said. He then went on to say the County of Riverside needed to bear the brunt of the blame for what had happened to Andy. He said it seemed safe to assume that Alvin and his family would never be in a position to supervise a child again. "But he would certainly not benefit at all from any type of incarceration. You can see what incarceration will do to Alvin's family." With a sweeping hand gesture toward the farthest row of the spectator section, he gazed with sorrowful eyes at Leroy and Susie. They were crying. Apparently, Sachs had forgotten that the whole purpose of incarceration wasn't meant to be a benefit, it was meant to be punishment, which Alvin deserved.

He said that when one weighs all the facts in this case, those factors outweighed the vulnerability of Andy. To most who heard that comment, it was nothing but a cold hearted, ruthless remark to make. And coming from Sachs, it shocked everyone. It sounded so unlike anything he would say. Andy had been a defenseless four-year-old child that was used as a punching bag by a three hundred pound beast of a woman who was overflowing with rage and hatred. His comment caused a flutter to erupt within the room, but no one interrupted Sachs. He said that Alvin had already spent two years in jail and was well prepared for probation. Sachs seemed to forget that when Andy was murdered, Alvin was already on probation. A child had been murdered while in the protective custody of Alvin Robinson—while he was on probation! It was insanely ludicrous for Sachs to insinuate that Alvin was a good prospect for more probation!

He said that if the court would take all these factors into consideration, that the factors favoring probation greatly outweighed the reasons to deny it. Apparently, Sachs was trying to convince the judge that incarcerating Alvin would upset Leroy and Susie so much, that Alvin should be let off the hook. He strongly urged the judge to give Alvin another chance, to give Alvin's parents another opportunity to supervise him much more closely than they did before.

When Sachs had finished, Judge Schooling commented that he had received from Sachs, and filed one of the longest probation reports the court had ever received, consisting of eighteen pages and about seven addenda pages to it. No one could accuse Sachs of giving a half-hearted attempt at defending Alvin. Sachs went way beyond what he needed to do. And he'd done it with his utmost respect and concern for Alvin.

Then, Judge Schooling asked Monterosso if he had anything he wished to say. Of course, he did. And he turned toward Leroy to say it in no uncertain terms. With anger evident in his voice, he began slowly.

"I do *not* accept *any* responsibility for what happened to Andy. I cannot argue that this county bears some responsibility, but what I have seen throughout this trial is the constant deflection of blame from Alvin Robinson to everybody else in the world. And this is not my fault. This wasn't because of me and I will not be blamed for this."

As he locked eyes with Leroy, Leroy fumed. So did Monterosso. The tension was palpable.

"And we can blame the county for putting Andy there in the first place, but the fact still remains that only one person had the opportunity to save Andy...and that person was Alvin." Monterosso paused for a second to gather his self-control, but then he slapped down his papers and turned

Deadly Thirst

once more toward Leroy. "And it irks me to constantly hear this argument that Alvin can't be blamed because it was Theresa's evil, it was the county's negligence and society in general for putting Andy there. I don't accept that." Giving Leroy that withering up and down glare, which said so much more than words could ever express, Monterosso turned toward the judge, adjusted his tie and continued. He rebuffed Sachs' claim that Alvin had no violence in his past; he had been on probation for a domestic violence-related crime at the time of Andy's murder, for crying out loud!

"I don't recall exactly what the testimony was but it was essentially in a fit of rage that the defendant destroyed numerous items of property in his house. This is a side of Alvin Robinson that many people may not have seen. Another side of Alvin Robinson many people did not see was his anger expressed toward Andy the night Andy wanted a drink of water. On the outside he seems gentle, but there's another side to him that we saw in evidence that isn't consistent with that. And there is a side of him that I am not comfortable with ever seeing again in the presence of a child, ever again.

"And we can say that the Robinson family will never allow him to be around kids again, but I am just not comfortable accepting that. He took in a foster child without even informing them. It's clear that he lives his life independent of his family and would not heed advice necessarily if they gave it to him. And this is what *they* [turning to stab his finger at Susie and Leroy] testified to." Leroy glowered at Monterosso. "Unfortunately, I don't share that same confidence that Alvin will never be in a position again to either personally harm a child or ignore a child in his care who cries for help. On that basis alone I think probation should be denied." He turned and shot Leroy one final up-and-down glare before he angrily took his seat. The two sides were definitely at war. Leroy was hoppin' mad.

But Sachs got the last word in and said that contrary to everything Monterosso had said, there was simply no evidence that Alvin had a violent side to him. He slogged off the notion that Alvin might be a danger to children as merely "speculative." Then, he went on to use the old theory that everybody was trying to "bootstrap" Alvin with stuff he hadn't done.

"He feels bad about it and he will do everything in his power to make sure something like this never even comes close to happening again." Sachs seemed to have completely forgotten that he'd just spent the past year or so trying to convince everyone that Alvin had absolutely *no* power, none whatsoever. He was just a helpless retarded man. The comment wasn't lost on Monterosso and, while the judge was not obligated to let the arguing go back and forth any further, Schooling was considerate and patient. He could clearly see that Monterosso wanted to say something in response. Monterosso reminded the court that Alvin had admitted to Horst that he'd whipped Andy on his butt with a belt. "It's misleading to suggest he never displayed violence against a child when clearly from the defendant's own mouth he *did.*"

Judge Schooling sided with Monterosso. Schooling said he disagreed that Alvin would not necessarily be a danger to others. "To that, the court disagrees with the probation officer's assessment," Schooling said. "There is no showing that the defendant is remorseful. In fact, even though you say he's sorry, he does not show any real remorse in the opinion of the court. The injury he inflicted upon Andy was not only physical, but also emotional, because he abandoned Andy when Andy most needed his support and his protection. Instead of protecting the child, he just walked out the door. He scolded the child for drinking his water…his precious water… in the middle of the night." Schooling shook his head.

Sachs asked if the court would consider a diagnostic treatment center or confinement at an institution where Alvin could learn to read and write. Monterosso was quick to say he didn't see any benefit in that. Schooling agreed with Monterosso.

"He needs to learn to read and write," Schooling said. "And that is certainly something that hopefully will be addressed while he's incarcerated." Looking down at Alvin, Judge Schooling said in a commanding voice, "Stand please, sir."

Sachs thumped Alvin on the shoulder and told him to stand up. Sachs stood right next to Alvin, their shoulders touching. Schooling sentenced Alvin to twenty-five years to life for count two [273ab].

Sachs looked like he might faint.

From the back of the courtroom, Leroy was moaning, "ohhhh…"

"Furthermore, the defendant is sentenced as to count 1 to fifteen years to life, which will be concurrent. In addition, as to count 3 the defendant is sentenced to six years but that will be concurrent with the sentence imposed in counts 1 and 2." So, unlike Theresa, Alvin would get to serve his sentences at the same time. But that factor was completely lost on Leroy. He was too overwhelmed with grief. The sentence pretty much shot Reverend Wilcox's prophesy of mercy all to hell.

Judge Schooling advised Alvin of his appellate rights. They were long and confusing, but when the judge asked Alvin if he understood his rights, Alvin said yes. Alvin was required to pay a restitution fine of $10,000. Then, it was over.

Or so everyone thought. Leroy had stormed out in a burst of fury. When Monterosso gathered up his paperwork and stepped into the hallway, Leroy let him have it. Once again, I witnessed almost everything.

When I walked into the hallway the first thing I heard was Leroy hollering. Leroy was down by the elevators, screeching and shaking his finger in Monterosso's face. Monterosso was just standing there, waiting for the elevator door to open up and swallow him so that he might escape the deafening rage of Alvin's dad. He said nothing; he just let Leroy vent and vent and vent.

Deadly Thirst

"That could be *your* son!" Leroy was saying over and over, shaking his finger right in Monterosso's face. Finally the elevator door opened, Monterosso got in and then it really was over.

* * *

A few days later I got another call from Terry Fisher. I'd halfway been expecting it. Before Fisher had a chance to explain why he was calling, I said, "I know why you're calling. Yes, I saw what happened between Monterosso and Leroy." Fisher listened to my recollection and agreed that something needed to be done about Leroy. Not that I expected Leroy to really do anything to Monterosso, but you just never know. Anger can manifest itself in strange, even deadly ways sometimes. Andy Setzer was proof of that. People go postal all the time and Leroy obviously hated Monterosso and blamed him for his son's twenty-five year sentence. Fisher talked to me a while about his long friendship with Monterosso and said he personally felt that John Monterosso was one of the kindest, most compassionate men he'd ever worked with and a really great guy to boot. Unless of course, you were on the wrong side of the law, which Alvin definitely was. Monterosso had not taken Leroy's reference to his children lightly at all. Certainly one of the most ignorant moves a person can make is to utter even a veiled threat to the District Attorney or his family.

The following day, a group of several huge, burley men in uniform knocked on Leroy's front door in Moreno Valley. They made it exceedingly clear to Leroy that he was to *never* even so much as *think* about talking that way to or about John Monterosso ever again. They asked Leroy if they had made themselves perfectly clear.

Yes, they had.

Good.

* * *

In December of 2001, Monterosso filed a document in which he asked that Theresa Barroso never be granted parole.

"The District Attorney of Riverside County recommends in the strongest of terms that Ms Barroso never be granted parole and never be released into civilized society. The crime she committed against Andy Setzer is a crime in which the most vulnerable of all people, a four-year-old child, was brutally abused, tortured, and ultimately murdered by the person who had been given the unique responsibility to care for, comfort and raise him.

"Andy Setzer lived almost his entire life in foster care. He came to the Barroso/Robinson home in June 1999 and was murdered by his caretaker on August 2, 1999. Instead of getting the nurturing, loving environment needed from a foster family, Andy was treated to repeated kicks in the groin, violence toward his genitalia and ultimately a death sentence for drinking water. No victim could be more vulnerable than Andy. Therefore it is hard to imagine conduct that would be more evil than the conduct perpetrated by Ms Barroso toward Andy. It is not difficult to care for and love a small child. In fact, it is a natural human instinct to care for small children.

344

Ms Barroso consciously disregarded that human instinct on, not one, but several occasions. Ms Barroso would constitute an extreme risk to society if she were allowed to roam free among us. Any person who is capable of doing what Ms Barroso did to young Andy is capable of doing much more evil to other children and other people. Therefore, the District Attorney respectfully requests that Ms Barroso not be granted parole and that she remain incarcerated for the full extent of her life."

CHAPTER 17

AFTERMATH

Some who were familiar with the case of four-year-old Andy Setzer believe his final foster mother, Theresa Barroso, was responsible for his murder. But Theresa is only part of a bigger, much more insidious problem. That problem is the deplorable state of the foster care system.

Some put the blame squarely and totally on the foster care system for letting Andy fall through the cracks of a system that was supposed to protect him. Many people feel that our foster care system is dangerously dysfunctional and in dire need of a massive overhaul and complete restructuring.

Others find fault with the drug-addicted, biological parents who had put Andy at risk from the moment of his conception and sent him on his way down that dead end road of protective custody. Personally, I feel that all of these parties share a responsibility for Andy's death.

Whichever way one chooses to look at it, Andy Setzer faced overwhelming odds. And he lost the battle. In his memory, Assembly Bill 2623 was signed by Governor Gray Davis and passed into law in September of 2000.

After Andy's murder, Jacob Marquist was sent to live in a group home. At trial he appeared to be a well-adjusted, intelligent, respectful young man but statistics reveal that many kids like Jacob may never be able to overcome the effects of the abuse they have witnessed or been subjected to. Perhaps Jacob will be the exception; I certainly hope so. For me, it was impossible to imagine the horror that Jacob must have experienced when he learned that Theresa had murdered Andy. For an eleven year old boy it must have been nightmarish; his trust of adults surely must have been seriously jeopardized. I shudder at the thought of what Andy Setzer's murder has done to Jacob.

Theresa De Jesus Barroso was sent to Central California Women's Facility in Chowchilla, north of Fresno. There, she wears the indelible bulls-eye of child killer although her murder conviction has since been thrown out due to a "technicality."

In the summer of 2003 a three-justice panel of the state's 4th District Court of Appeal in Riverside made the astonishing ruling: the murder conviction of Theresa Barroso had been made in error. Theresa's conviction had been based on the felony murder rule, which stipulates that deaths occurring during certain felonies, such as robbery, burglary and rape, are deemed first-degree murders and torture was not a qualifying felony until January 1, 2000...five months *after* Andy died. It mattered not one iota that

Donna Goodenough

Andy's death was a direct result of the torture that Theresa Barroso inflicted upon him when she kicked him off his chair a second time. Her murder conviction has been wiped from her record. If she had been robbing Andy when he died, the first-degree murder conviction would have stayed.

There is, however, one bit of solace. Theresa's life sentence remains intact because she is still guilty of assault on a child causing death. Rest assured that for every day she's incarcerated, women much more aggressive and vicious than Theresa will be anxious to give her a daily dose of her own bitter medicine; using her as their target for venting pent up frustrations and anger. And like little Andy, she won't be able to escape her tormentors. She'll just have to suffer in silence like Andy did.

To many stunned residents of Riverside County, it seems to be a strange twist of fate that while Theresa has been allowed to shed the title of murderess, Alvin Lee Robinson's murder conviction will stick.

"Each case," Monterosso said, "was looked at completely independent of the other. They had two separate juries and you can't start relating what happened to her to what happened to him. Had I not been greedy when I went for the first-degree murder and simply used the same theory that I used with Alvin, she would have been guilty of second-degree murder. We could technically re-try this case, but it would only result in the changing of one word."

Alvin is serving his time at California State Prison in Centinela, in the mercilessly hot town of Imperial, opposite the border from Mexicali Mexico and south of the dusty Salton Sea. New inmates, especially the ones who are non-aggressive, are anxiously awaited and viewed as fresh meat by other depraved men who are determined to get sexual gratification any way they can. Perhaps Alvin's early training in male/male sexual gratification prepared him for his indoctrination into the brutal, day-to-day activities within the grim confines of prison, but I doubt it.

It should come as no surprise that when I was ending my research for this book in December of 2002, Thomas "Cowboy" Setzer was back in prison, serving a four year term for first-degree burglary. He was busted within days of his last parole.

It's anyone's guess where Laura Utley is currently, or for that matter, *who* she's masquerading as. There is a major loophole in her settlement with the County of Riverside which states her money will continue so long as she is not convicted of a felony or misdemeanor criminal offense within any jurisdiction of the United States. According to the settlement, a plea of guilty is the same as a conviction. However, a plea of 'nolo contender' will not be deemed a conviction. In other words, if Laura should be lucky enough to slip through the criminal justice system under one of her aliases, or she simply pleads no contest to the charges and serves her sentence, her money keeps coming.

According to Kent Livingston, the Senior Liability Claims Adjuster for the County of Riverside, it will take the effort of a determined *citizen*—not the county—to catch Laura in her evasive game of deception. Law enforcement will not voluntarily send information on the arrests, convictions, or current legal status of Laura Utley because they don't have time and it's not their job to interfere with that aspect of her life. Surprisingly, the county doesn't periodically investigate her current legal status either, because they don't have time. Livingston told me that it irks him to think that Laura may be receiving money which might be in violation of her agreement, but there is nothing the county can do about it. At least, not without public help. What is needed, he said, is for a concerned, Columbo-type *citizen* to take an aggressive stance against her. Even if efforts were successful at proving Laura had violated her agreement, it isn't retroactive and it would take months of costly legal battles to prove the allegations and finally stop the payments. It would cost the county much more to stop the payments than to continue paying Laura's pittance, which, in my opinion, is dripping with Andy's blood.

On a brighter note, Mike and Lynn Herman have since been blessed with a child of their own; a daughter.

In early 2003 the Little Hoover Commission released its latest evaluation of California's floundering foster care system and sited the same ailments as in previous years. In the scathing 36-page report titled *Still in Our Hands* the commission says the foster care system is still broken and still needs fixing. The buck stops nowhere, they say. The supposed reforms are inadequate and have failed to put into place the management structure that would allow any of these incremental efforts to be implemented correctly or to hold anyone accountable for their failure or success. The report calls for consistent public attention and asks that the public demand changes that would hold state and local leaders accountable. [The report is available in its entirety on line at: www.lhc.ca.gov or using the search words "Little Hoover Commission."]

Pete Harding has retired and still lives in the small house with the sparkling swimming pool, the fish pillow and the pump dispenser of baldhead cream. He still takes his travel trailer up to Bishop every year for Mule Days and spends as much times as he can enjoying the great outdoors. His collection of suits and ties have pretty much been pushed to the far corner of his closet these days in favor of more comfortable attire. His favorite T-shirt has a picture of the electric chair with a caption that reads, "Regular, or extra crispy?" Above all, Harding still vividly remembers the little boy he belatedly came to know as "Andrew." Harding still swears a lot. "Alvin was dumber than shit, but he knew what was going on and he could have done something to stop it. Therefore, he got what he deserved."

There was never any doubt whatsoever that Stu Sachs was emotionally broad-sided by the guilty verdict and Alvin's harsh sentence. He admitted to suffering some depression after the trial and continues to carry Alvin's burden, still to this day.

"That was the very first time that I've had a client convicted of murder that I was requesting the court to grant probation," Sachs said in retrospect. "I'd never had that situation come up before. I think Alvin is an extremely unique individual. I'd represented him for close to two years and never had an ounce of trouble with him other than his ability to understand sometimes what was going on. I shudder at the prospect of Alvin going to state prison where he's going to come out—if he ever *does* come out—a much worse person than he is today." Sachs said he wonders if the jury would have favored Alvin more if Alvin had made even one phone call to seek help for Andy or to alert authorities about the abuse a little sooner. Seems to me that Sachs should have sorted out that possibility before the trial, not afterwards. Besides, if Alvin had made that one little effort, more than likely there would have been no dead child…and no murder trial for poor Alvin.

In March of 2002 I was invited to visit Theresa's attorney, Peter Scalisi in his first floor office, three blocks from the Hall of Justice. Surrounded by pictures of his family, Scalisi was a bit philosophic about justice.

"Well, it's hard to be objective about that," he said. "The jury said that she was guilty so no matter what I think, justice was served because the jury said she was guilty. I don't know if she's guilty or not. I do know that she has always maintained her innocence. She's never, from the day I met her, and I've probably talked to her and interviewed her and gone over the case with her hundreds of times, never once did she ever waiver in that. Many times you're representing a defendant and you see them at different points in their lives. People are not the same every day. But you get to develop a certain understanding of who they are; you can kind of read the moods and learn a lot about them. So often, a criminal lawyer will meet a client and they'll say 'I'm innocent' but over the course of representing them, you'll see a few kinks in their armor. Little clues come out. Theresa never did that."

But what about the horribly incriminating videotapes?

"I know she said it on tape and it was very damaging. But it doesn't mean that I believe she was innocent, it means that she never wavered from it. She always maintained her innocence. And objectively, I might want to say, 'well that doesn't really make sense' or 'gee, there's a lot of evidence that says you aren't innocent.' But there was one thing. If a client can show you something in the case that is sort of a stumbling block, then that helps." Scalisi said that this case clearly had a stumbling block. "And that was the fact that the other child, Jacob, was 100% certain that he heard *Alvin* yelling at Andy across just a couple of feet of hallway and then he heard the thud. He seemed to be saying that Alvin was the one who was screaming and then hit Andy. In the greater scheme of things that might not amount to much except that Alvin said, clearly, that he did not yell at Andy. One of those two has to be lying. So that fact alone made me believe in Theresa's innocence. It was a big factor in this case, a point that has always bothered me. Still.

Deadly Thirst

"Problem is, if you're a normal human being and you're bombarded with pictures of Andy and the way he was brutalized and you go into that jury room with eleven other people, it's really convenient to overlook a fact like what Jacob was pointing out to get your guilty verdict. I guess the ends justify the means." In spite of his harsh words about the display of Andy's hospital and autopsy pictures in court, Scalisi did confess that the photos had disturbed him terribly. They were something he'd never be able to forget.

Scalisi had total respect for the job Sachs had done for Alvin. "In many ways, Sachs had a more difficult client to represent than I did." It still irked him to think back on how Monterosso had used Horst as a visual reminder of the good half of good and evil. "It's a common technique that all Deputy DA's use to reinforce the full authority of law enforcement behind every case," he said. "But during long trials, the presence of a law enforcement officer can be a real problem for the government. I've noticed some law enforcement offers making faces in reaction to testimony, making inappropriate gestures, whispering things to the deputy DA; things that are often overheard by everyone. I've had many jurors comment to me that they were offended, and that the actions of the law enforcement officers worked to the DA's *dis*advantage."

There was never any personal animosity between Horst and Scalisi or Scalisi and Monterosso. All three hold each other in high esteem in spite of the disagreement about using Horst as a visual. But Scalisi still thinks that most law enforcement officers can't restrain their emotions and bias enough to remain poker-faced during a trial.

"Most seasoned prosecutors," Scalisi said, "have grown out of the need for the presence of a law enforcement officer." Regardless, the law allows for an investigating officer to sit at the counsel table during trial and neither Sachs nor Scalisi could gripe about it because they have no justification to complain. It's common practice.

Seven months after the verdicts rang out in Judge Russell Schooling's courtroom, I went to visit John Monterosso in his sixth story office. It was an honor to be invited into his private domain, to sit face to face with him and listen to his personal take on the whole situation. Framed, on the wall in back of him were his law diploma, his college diploma from USF, his bar certificate and a certificate for participation in the law review. And there were sports pendants.

Proudly Scotch-taped on a filing cabinet to his right were several drawings, in crayon, obviously from one of his kids. One was titled "The Courthouse." It was a fine rendition of a child's version of his father's very important workplace. Monterosso's extremely wide range of tastes in art seemed to mesh well inside the office. He surrounded himself with things that meant the most to him, things that gave him comfort. On top of the filing cabinet was a framed picture of him and his beautiful wife, taken on their wedding day. It was positioned so that he could see it from where he was sitting and everyone else could see it too.

Throughout the trial, it had been Alvin's fate that concerned everyone. We all knew Theresa was doomed, but Alvin could have very easily been found innocent. I asked Monterosso what troubled him most about Alvin's defense. He replied that the sympathy factor [sympathy for Alvin] hadn't bothered him nearly as much as the psychological testimony of Doctor Kania. *That* had been the thing he found especially worrisome.

"Sachs spent a great deal of time questioning potential jurors on their experience with psychologists, etc. My main concern was finding jurors who'd be *skeptical* of psychological testimony." Although Monterosso had a world of respect for Sachs, he hadn't agreed with Sachs' method of defense for Alvin.

"I think Sachs lost focus during the trial," he said. "One of the things I think he made a mistake about was trying to portray Alvin as the victim. Especially when he started getting really indignant in his argument about how Alvin was misled and 'poor Alvin...Theresa took advantage of him... so did the DA...poor Alvin.' Wait a minute, how can you get indignant about Alvin when you've got a dead child? None of the jury bought that 'poor Alvin' stuff. Was Alvin so mentally deficient that he couldn't stop this? No. He chose not to stop it for selfish reason. His defense was misguided. Things could have turned out differently for Alvin if he'd taken the stand and said he'd made a mistake and that he was really sorry. He may have gotten some sympathy, but what he said got him no sympathy at all."

Monterosso felt that both Alvin and Theresa got what they deserved; perhaps Theresa's punishment wasn't severe enough. "Think about how badly Sachs' argument played when he suggested that Alvin's confession was the product of deception by Pete Harding and me." Monterosso had nothing but praise for the job both juries had done.

I asked him why he didn't ask potential jurors if they'd had any experience with people who were mentally handicapped. Perhaps some of the jurors had someone in their family who was mentally impaired. Wasn't this important?

"If you polled one hundred prosecutors, probably fifty of them would've done just what you suggest and maybe more. This wouldn't be wrong, it just goes to show that what most of us do is based on gut reactions." Monterosso didn't want to give any ballast to the idea that Alvin was retarded because Monterosso thought that Alvin was faking it, or at least exaggerating his supposed retardation.

In spite of Monterosso's career becoming even more successful than it had been when Alvin and Theresa were tried and convicted, he still manages to get home to his family by 6:30. He jogs religiously. He says it helps alleviate stress.

"Burn out is a major problem in this job," he told me. "There are a lot of times I feel like the stress is overwhelming. Usually that's when there are

Deadly Thirst

so many things going on at once that I can't keep a grip on it all. Those times pass, however. Everything always seems to work out. Many prosecutors put their heart and soul into their cases and end up burning out. The key is to maintain a balance in one's life. I maintain a life outside of the office, which is just as important." I asked him if he could narrow it down to just one thing that helps him keep his sanity. His answer was easy. "My family diverts me from the ugliness that I see everyday." Of course, he also gives his intense interest in sports a lot of credit for diversion and alleviating stress. When he has time, he plays golf. And he still loves the Giants and the 49ners, which are both San Francisco teams.

In January of 2003, Monterosso happily packed up his office on Main Street in Riverside and transferred to the new, miniscule in comparison, courthouse in Murrieta. He was happy to be leaving the traffic congestion and smog of Riverside behind him.

For years after Andy died, Sergeant Horst continued to carry around the heartache that stemmed from vivid memories of an innocent, beautiful child that the system had sacrificed to the devil.

"In my whole career," he told me, "there have been two cases that stood out the most; that affected me the most. One was Andy. Still to this day, I'm reminded of it in a lot of ways but I really have to work at saying it's behind me. This is something that will consume you and eat you alive. It will destroy you if you allow it to."

Andy Setzer had left his mark on many people and Sergeant Horst probably wore that mark deeper than anyone else. Dawn Masterson, Andy's grandmother, may have thought she'd known all the gory details of Andy's death, but she didn't. Sergeant Horst did. And it had a devastating affect on him.

Still, the words of John Monterosso describe Andy's plight the best. "Andy died because he was thirsty. There was no one to speak for Andy but me. And of course Sergeant Horst."

Author's note

This story will haunt me for the rest of my life.

Sergeant Horst had told me that I would never fully understand what it's like to witness the things a cop witnesses. He said I would probably never understand the necessity of keeping emotions separate from the job. He warned me early on that if I dwelt on the circumstances of the victim in a personal way it would devour me.

"It will drive you crazy," he warned. "Something like this will throw you into despair so deep you won't be able to find your way back to sanity." As I came to know Sergeant Horst, I saw what the Andy Setzer case had done to him. And now, after writing this book, I understand.

ISBN 141200552-3

9 781412 005524